AGONY
AND
ELOQUENCE

AGONY AND ELOQUENCE

John Adams, Thomas Jefferson,
and a World of Revolution

DANIEL L. MALLOCK

SKYHORSE PUBLISHING

Skyhorse Publishing books may be purchased in bulk at special discounts for sales promotion, corporate gifts, fund-raising, or educational purposes. Special editions can also be created to specifications. For details, contact the Special Sales Department, Skyhorse Publishing, 307 West 36th Street, 11th Floor, New York, NY 10018 or info@skyhorsepublishing.com.

Skyhorse® and Skyhorse Publishing® are registered trademarks of Skyhorse Publishing, Inc.®, a Delaware corporation.

Visit our website at www.skyhorsepublishing.com.

10 9 8 7 6 5 4 3 2 1

Library of Congress Cataloging-in-Publication Data is available on file.

Cover design by Jane Sheppard

Print ISBN: 978-1-63450-528-4
Ebook ISBN: 978-1-63450-832-2

Printed in the United States of America

CONTENTS

Introduction

T HOMAS JEFFERSON AND John Adams first met as members of the Continental Congress; both had signed the Declaration of Independence, and later served as diplomatic colleagues at the leading courts of Europe. Their long friendship was marked by profound mutual respect and deep personal affection until a bitter breach separated them during Adams's presidency.

When the French Revolution erupted in 1789, Adams and Jefferson, after a brief shared enthusiasm, found themselves on opposite sides. Jefferson wholeheartedly supported the Revolution—regardless of the horrific crimes that its supporters and leaders committed—while Adams came to despise it and accurately predicted its ultimate collapse. Their stridently differing views about the Revolution in France, American relations with the new French Republic, and regarding fundamental matters of government finally destroyed their friendship. Only the tireless efforts of a mutual friend and fellow signer of the Declaration could repair it after ten years of silence.

As different in their views and personalities as one might expect a Massachusetts Puritan would be from a son of the wealthy landed New World Virginia gentry, Adams and Jefferson were first drawn together by their love of liberty and desires for American independence. They shared an adoration of learning and the attainment of knowledge. Both appreciated the other's great depth and complexity of character. Their friendship was founded upon mutual appreciation and shared personal and public aspirations.

Both men significantly influenced events and national policy. Their political rivalry became the great contest for the future course of the country; in this conflict their professional relationship was the first casualty—their friendship soon suffered the same fate.

This American drama is documented in their extraordinary letters. The Adams-Jefferson correspondence has long been recognized as a landmark achievement in American letters, known as much for the beauty of their language as for its historical importance. Their epistolary discussions included subjects from philosophy to politics, history, literature, science, architecture, and more. They both desired that all of these letters should be published.

In his First Inaugural Address, Jefferson told the American people that without positive associations—friendships—"liberty and even life itself are but dreary things." Jefferson publicly identified friendship as essential to the quality of life and fundamental to the proper enjoyment, and even the function, of "liberty."

These two great men, friends, colleagues, and then rivals came to be seen in their time as the leaders of the opposing American political parties of the late eighteenth century. The political partisanship of that era is perhaps surpassed only by that of our own time.

Jefferson later came to agree with Adams that the eradication of political partisanship was essential to the continuing existence of the Union, and that friendships immune to the destructiveness of absolutism and party prejudice were crucial to the success and longevity of the new democracy. Long after both had left politics they became convinced that partisanship and rigid political views that left little or no room for compromise were active and perpetual threats to the future success and life of the country.

There is great drama here, internal and external enemies, wars and rumors of wars, great social and political upheavals, and then, finally—at the end of tortuous roads—a mutual realization that friendship was more important than either had previously realized.

The French Revolution, and conflicts with England and France, forms the international backdrop of the larger drama of the new American Republic struggling to retain its independence and democratic character in the face of intense internal and external pressures.

It is also the story of events and people in the early years of the United States from Washington's retirement to Adams's and Jefferson's administrations, and on into the long introspective and active years of their retirements.

Every generation has its own times that try the souls of men and women, and each prefers to make its own way unfettered by any debts to the past. The present belongs to the living; in these times that try the souls of our people, there are no bills in arrears-only a gift paid forward by two of the most important men in American history.

We owe no debt to these great men but to learn from the wisdom that they left for us.

1

"The Best Letter That Ever Was Written"

THE BRISK, LATE autumn winds blowing inland from the Atlantic, and the bitter cold air streaming south from Canada, howled through the cracks in every structure in Quincy, Massachusetts. During that particular early morning, most citizens of the town would have been at their breakfast tables near a warm hearth trying to avoid the chill New England winds of approaching winter that, rolling in off Quincy Bay, made their windows rattle and floors and walls cold to the touch as the first meal of the day was served. So it was at "Peace field," the solid and comfortable but not ostentatious home of John Adams, retired second president of the United States.

Mr. John Adams, or "the president," as his grandchildren preferred to address him, was eighty-nine years old in November, 1823, unusually long-lived for a man of that or most any time. Most of his friends, and his beloved wife Abigail, had, by then, preceded him to their rewards. Adams, made of sterner stuff than even he had suspected (and sometimes perhaps likely desired) remained, and waited.

Perhaps one of his grandchildren brought the morning's mail to the elderly statesman that day. All the family assembled around the table would have recognized the now familiar handwriting on the envelope; it was from former President Thomas Jefferson, then Adams's most important correspondent—his greatest and oldest living friend. His eyes failing, Adams likely asked a favored family member to read the letter to him. Sometimes his correspondence was read to him privately but, for this important missive, Adams could not wait; it must be read aloud, now.

John Adams had rekindled his old friendship with Thomas Jefferson late in 1811 at the incessant yet creative urgings of their mutual friend and fellow signer of the Declaration of Independence, Dr. Benjamin Rush of Pennsylvania. Rush, who had died in 1813, was delighted that he had been the instrument to bring his two old friends back to one another after over a decade of silence between them. Now, at breakfast and with his extended family in his old family home, once called Stoney Fields, then Peace field, then "Montezillo" as a humorous homage to his greatest friend's stately and famous home, Monticello, Adams must have felt some trepidation as the envelope from Jefferson was displayed at the table.[1]

The cold autumnal winds blowing in from the Atlantic over the low hills of Quincy, much of it Adams land, beating on the hardy frames of Montezillo located on what is now Adams Street in Quincy, Massachusetts, must have been particularly portentous for the former president. An old error in judgment, harsh bitter opinions and recriminations, and an excess of rhetoric and partisanship over a decade old that Adams had hoped and expected would never see the light of day until after his death, if ever, were about to invade his usually peaceful morning meal. Jefferson had no doubt learned of these things; this, then, must be the subject of the letter that Adams's granddaughter now held in her hand, waiting for the patriarch's nod to open and read it aloud.

Described by one noted biographer as "rude, tactless, and hot-tempered,"[2] John Adams was sometimes injudicious and excessive in his written communications, particularly in his retirement years. Jefferson was also guilty of occasional heated rhetorical indulgences in his correspondences. Like many subjects of mutual interest, this habit of epistolary backbiting and overheated language was an unfortunate indulgence practiced by both men, however much to their own later frustrations and disappointment. Adams's vanity, irascibility, and garrulousness were widely acknowledged by friends and family; Adams himself admitted to these traits (particularly vanity). His colleagues and enemies were also not unaware of them. His brilliant and supportive wife Abigail had always done her best to keep this part of her husband's character in check.

Jefferson was also aware of Adams's lesser qualities. Weighing them against the better parts of Adams's nature, Jefferson had found his old friend's more challenging traits forgivable. In a January 1787 letter to James Madison, Jefferson wrote that Adams "is vain, irritable and a bad calculator of the force and probable effect of the motives which govern men. This is all the ill which can possibly be said of him. He is as disinterested as the Being who made him. He is profound in his views, and accurate in his judgment, except where knowledge of the world is necessary to form a judgment. He is so amiable, that I pronounce you will love him, if ever you become acquainted with him."[3]

Seated at the breakfast table with his family around him, a little hand held an as-yet unopened letter from Thomas Jefferson. With his failing eyesight, Adams perhaps looked around him at his large extended family, gripped the arms of his chair just a little tighter, and thought back over a decade to another family breakfast in which the words of a very different correspondent had been the subject of conversation.

* * *

In their retirement years Adams and Jefferson had both taken extraordinary pains to assure that the historical record would present an accurate representation of them to posterity. Adams's concern for his historical reputation might now be seen as a kind of neurosis, though he was not in any way alone in his concern for how he would be viewed and judged by later generations of Americans. This obsession with posterity prompted many letters, both public and private, from Adams's pen.

In an August 1812 letter to his friend Dr. Benjamin Rush, Adams asked rhetorically, "How is it that I, poor, ignorant I, must stand before posterity as differing from all the great men of the age? Priestley, Price, Franklin, Burke, Fox, Pitt, Mansfield, Camden, Jefferson,

Madison!" Believing his historical reputation already permanently sullied, Adams speculated that he would be "judged the most vain, conceited, impudent, arrogant creature in the world. I tremble when I think of it. I blush. I am ashamed."[4]

Once retired, Adams had engaged in a lengthy and very public defense of his political career by submitting extensive essays and letters to the *Boston Patriot* newspaper from 1809 to 1812. One Adams historian describes these lengthy, often caustic and critical essays as "the final installment in Adams's long effort to exorcise his personal demons, all undertaken in the guise of 'setting the record straight.'"[5] Few readers of the *Boston Patriot*—and there were many in Massachusetts and beyond—were favorably impressed by Adams's essays. Expecting many repercussions and public denunciations, Adams found the reaction to his essays was far more muted than he had supposed. Shortly after the first essay was published, a distant relative wrote to him in an elevated and personally complimentary style expressing interest in his political career, and declaring his support for Adams's *Boston Patriot* efforts. Favorably impressed by this writer's positive reaction to his very public self-defense, Adams began a correspondence with this distant cousin that would later result in unpleasant repercussions and put his most important friendship at risk.

* * *

John Adams and William Cunningham had corresponded intermittently since 1803. Cunningham, a Federalist journalist and lawyer, was a distant relative of Adams.[6] It was not however until Adams's first essay appeared in the *Boston Patriot* that their correspondence became regular. They mutually agreed that their letters were to be kept confidential and never published until after Adams's death, if at all.

In an 1804 letter to Cunningham, written during Jefferson's first term as president, Adams harshly criticized Jefferson and implied that his friendship had been false. Adams also wrote, "I shudder at the calamities, which I fear his conduct is preparing for his country: from a mean thirst of popularity, an inordinate ambition, and a want of sincerity." At the close of this letter, Adams reminded his correspondent that "I write in confidence in your honor as well as your discretion."[7]

Adams used both the *Boston Patriot* and his private correspondence with Cunningham as outlets to defend himself from what he perceived as a pervasive negative view of his character and his political record. Hypersensitive, Adams gave his pen and his anger free reign. He would sometimes hit a positive note, however, as he did in this compliment of Jefferson's political motives. "I have great reason to believe, that Mr. Jefferson came into office with the same spirit that I did—that is, with a sincere desire of conciliating parties, as far as he possibly could, consistently with his principles."[8]

The *Boston Patriot* essays were an important tool for Adams through which he could accuse his enemies with his understanding and interpretation of historical events, and gain a victory by their deafening silence. He explained his purpose to Cunningham in July 1809. "I am in a fair way to give my criticks [sic] and enemies food enough to glut their appetites," Adams wrote. "They spit their venom and hiss like serpents. But no facts are denied, no arguments confuted. I take no notice of their billingsgate. Let it boil and broil. I have had their secret hatred for ten years, for twenty years, for all my life indeed. And I had rather have their open hostility than their secret."[9]

Over time, however, Cunningham became less a flatterer than a critic of Adams, taking particular umbrage at his repeated and often harsh criticisms of Jefferson and Alexander Hamilton.[10] Cunningham's shift from favor to enmity started slowly before finally arriving at a critical mass. His rhetoric struck such a pitch as to finally overshadow Adams's own self-indulgence of his ire at his many targets and cause him to pause, and presciently wonder as to Cunningham's mental stability. The first hint of serious trouble was Cunningham's letter of June 14, 1809, in which he somewhat inappropriately, via hearsay and gossip, introduced the former president's family into the discussion.

"An elderly and respectable clergyman, on his way home from Boston," Cunningham wrote, "called on me last Friday, and continued over night. He informed me without any reserve, that Mr. Whitney, your Minister, represented to him, that your resolution to rescue your reputation from reproach, is regarded by your whole family as an unfortunate determination, but that you are inexorable to their entreaties to desist."[11]

Adams replied on the twenty-second of the same month. Not yet cognizant of the growing schism between them, and still then not fully aware of Cunningham's growing ire, Adams responded to the suggestion that his family disapproved of his public essays in the *Boston Patriot* with kindness and jocular humor. Making matters worse without realizing it, Adams sarcastically described to Cunningham the scene of laughter when he broached the subject at the dinner table.

> I most sincerely thank you for your excellent letter of the fourteenth. It contains an abundance of matter that deserves, and shall have my most serious consideration. But at present I have not time to be serious. I had a delicious laugh with my family. I said nothing till we were all at table at dinner: My wife, my two daughters in law, my niece, Miss Louisa Smith, and my two grand daughters, misses, just entering their teens. My son was at Cambridge. I assumed a very grave countenance, and said I had received information, from fifty miles distance, that I had given offence to my family. I was very sorry to hear it, I wished to know which it was, that I might make my apology or give some satisfaction. Lord! Who? What? Why? what, sir, can you mean? sounded instantly from all quarters.
>
> I learn that my family is grieved at my Letters in the Newspapers, and have intreated me to desist, but that I obstinately go on to their mortification. The whole table was in a roar at this. My Wife had read every line, I believe, but one letter, before it went to the press. She was not alarmed. My two daughters declared they had never said a word . . . Never, sir, was a more groundless report or a more sheer fabrication. Mr. Whitney never could have said any such things.[12]

Adams's hilarity at Cunningham's expense was graciously received.[13] But Adams did not realize until too late that his correspondent's once-strong support for him and his public attacks on others was changing mightily.

Upset by Adams's harsh criticism of Jefferson, and of the tragically deceased Alexander Hamilton, Cunningham's tone changed
from flattery to one of deep, bitter anger. Eventually, Cunningham threatened to publish their correspondence. Horrified at Cunningham's catastrophic shift against him, and alarmed at his harsh,
threatening rhetoric, Adams soon realized the dangerous situation he
himself had created by opening his unedited heart and soul to this
distant relative and one-time friend.

Replying to a flurry of three letters in which Cunningham asserted
that he would breach their agreement of confidentiality and go public
with the letters, Adams wrote on January 16, 1810, "I have received
your three last letters. The correspondence and conversations which
have passed between us have been under the confidential seal of
secrecy and friendship. Any violation of it will be a breach of honour
and of plighted faith. I shall never release you from it . . ."[14]

Believing that Cunningham's argumentative, accusatory, and
alarming tone signaled not only personal and political disagreements
but perhaps a profound mental disturbance or break, Adams continued, "I hope you will consider, before you plunge yourself into an
abyss, which the melancholy and disturbed state of mind you appear
to be in seems to render you at this time incapable of perceiving
before you." Adams signed this letter, "In hopes you will soon be
more calm, I am your well wisher, John Adams."[15]

Despite his threats, William Cunningham kept his original promise to Adams and did not publish their letters. Cunningham's final letter to Adams was sent in January of 1812. Cunningham wrote, "I have
been cruelly and unjustly treated by you—I have, nevertheless, in all
that I have done, been sparing."[16] This concluded their communications; there is no record of Adams having replied. Adams's fears that
his trust in Cunningham had been misplaced would rest for ten years.

Confirming Adams's concerns for his emotional stability, William Cunningham was swallowed by the abyss. Cunningham committed suicide in 1823.[17] His death would not, however, put the matter
of their unfortunate correspondence to rest.

When Cunningham died, the 1824 presidential election campaign was underway. Adams's son, Secretary of State John Quincy

Adams, was running against war hero and populist General Andrew Jackson in a heated political environment in which partisanship was the order of the day. In 1823, the abyss reached out for John Adams through Cunningham's son.

Soon after his father's death, Cunningham's son Ephraim May Cunningham, a partisan Jackson supporter, published the confidential and damning correspondence between his late father and John Adams.

When Thomas Jefferson's expected letter arrived at Montezillo in Quincy, Massachusetts, on that November morning in 1823 as Adams was sitting for breakfast, the Adams-Cunningham correspondence had already by then been widely distributed. Adams fully understood that what he had written to Cunningham could be used to undermine his son's presidential aspirations, as well as do significant damage to his own admittedly limited future (not to mention his historical reputation). More personally significant, as the fiftieth anniversary of the founding of the republic approached, his most important friendship was now at stake—a friendship that pre-dated the republic.

* * *

"A letter from Mr. Jefferson, says I, I know what the substance is before I open it. There is no secrets between between Mr. Jefferson and me [sic], and I cannot read it; therefore you may open and read it," Adams wrote to Jefferson on November 10, 1823. He was describing the scene in his kitchen as Jefferson's letter of October twelfth was received, and opened.[18]

Though his vision had by then become so poor as to make reading difficult, perhaps in having his grandchildren read the letter aloud he was quietly communicating his fear also; he couldn't bear to read the letter himself knowing that it might include Jefferson's ire at his ill-tempered and unfortunate correspondence with Cunningham. There is humility and fear in Adams, and regret; the renewed Adams-Jefferson friendship, which, by 1823, was then eleven years old, had become for Adams his most important correspondence and non-family relationship; he did not want it to die.

"I do not write with the ease which your letter of September 18 supposes," began Jefferson. "Crippled wrists and fingers make writing slow and laborious. But, while writing to you, I lose the sense of these things, in the recollection of antient [sic] times, when youth and health made happiness out of every thing. I forget for a while the hoary winter of age . . . until the friendly hand of death shall rid us of all at once."[19]

The child continued reading aloud, the entire company enraptured by the prose of the sage of Monticello. As Jefferson described his efforts to create the University of Virginia, Adams must have been distracted with suspense, but not for long.

"Putting aside these things however for the present," Jefferson continued, "I write this letter as due to a friendship co-eval with our government, and now attempted to be poisoned."[20] This was the signal to Adams that Jefferson was, at least, aware of the Cunningham letters. "I had for some time observed," continued Jefferson, "dark hints and mysterious innuendos of a correspondence of yours with a friend, to whom you had opened your bosom without reserve, and which was to be made public by that friend, or his representative. And now it is said to be actually published. It has not yet reached us, but extracts have been given, and such as seemed most likely to draw a curtain of separation between you and myself."[21]

Jefferson acknowledged that throughout their lives their friends and supporters had "placed us in a state of apparent opposition, which some might suppose to be personal also." More importantly, there were those who "wished to make it so, by filling our ears with malignant falsehoods, by dressing up hideous phantoms of their own creation, presenting them to you under my name, to me under your's." Jefferson wrote that men "who have seen the false colours under which passion sometimes dresses the actions and motives of others, have seen also these passions subsiding . . . dissipating, like mists before the rising sun."[22]

Embracing this idea that schemers, partisans, and men without honor and compassion could not destroy their friendship, Jefferson concluded this extraordinary letter of forgiveness and affection with assurances and loyalty. "Be assured, my dear Sir, that I am incapable of receiving the slightest impression from the effort now made to plant thorns on the pillow of age, worth, and wisdom, and to sow tares between friends who have been such for near half a century. Beseeching you then," Jefferson continued, "not to suffer your mind to be disquieted by this wicked attempt to poison its peace, and praying you to throw it by, among the things which have never happened, I add sincere assurances of my unabated, and constant attachment, friendship and respect."[23] The response at Montezillo's breakfast table to Jefferson's sincere letter of appreciation, friendship, and forgiveness was electric.

Replying on the tenth of November, Adams wrote that when the reading of the letter "was done, it was followed by an [sic] universal exclamation, The best letter that ever was written, and round it went through the whole table—How generous! how noble! how magnanimous! I said it was just such a letter as I expected, only it was infinitely better expressed. A universal cry that the letter ought to be printed. No, hold, certainly not without Mr. Jefferson's express leave."[24] Adams concluded his grateful letter to Jefferson with, "I salute your fire-side with cordial esteem and affection. J. A. in the 89 year of his age and still too fat to last much longer."[25] Though it was clear to Adams that there could be little time remaining to him he had no fear of death.

Fully aware that he was then at the conclusion of his life and that the final act must be fast approaching, Adams welcomed life's next phase. Jefferson, too, at age eighty, was keenly conscious of his mortality, and felt his increasingly fragile health heavily. Both men notably retained their intellectual vigor to their very last days, with Adams reasonably expecting to precede Jefferson in death. "I am now the oldest of the little Congressional group that remain," Adams wrote Jefferson in 1821. "I may therefore rationally hope to be the first to depart; and as you are the youngest and most energetic in mind and body, you may therefore rationally hope to be the last to take your flight."[26]

2

"An Affection That Can Never Die"

Since the renewal of their long friendship after a decade of silence, the correspondence between the two founders and retired presidents had not gone unnoticed. Their letters from 1812 to 1826 cover an extraordinarily wide range of topics, which was entirely understandable as both men were much more than retired ex-presidents of the United States. The "Sage of Monticello" and the contentious philosopher of Montezillo, once described by Jefferson toward the end of his life as having been a "colossus on the floor" of Congress,[1] together produced not only a "great monument of American literature"[2] through their letters, "but one of the most learned and provocative correspondences—literary, philosophical, political, and scientific—in the history of the American republic."[3] Adams had once mentioned that he would have "no personal Objection to the Publication of it in the national Intelligencer."[4] Two years later, Jefferson informed Adams that "our correspondence has been observed at the post offices . . . Would you believe that a printer has had the effrontery to propose to me the letting him publish it?"[5] Later, Adams suggested that Jefferson's letters alone should be brought before the public. "I hope one day your letters will be all published in volumes; they will not always appear Orthodox, or liberal in politicks; but they will exhibit a Mass of Taste, Sense, Literature and Science, presented in a sweet simplicity and a neat elegance of Stile, which will be read with delight in future ages."[6]

Their letters to each other took on a vast importance for both men. The disparity in the number of letters passing between Quincy and Monticello has been characterized by some historians as evidence that the relationship was more important to Adams than it was for Jefferson. One historian of the Revolution notes, "Of the 158 letters exchanged, Adams wrote 109, more than doubling the pace of the correspondence from Monticello."[7] Page Smith in his two-volume biography of Adams wrote that, "the correspondence between the two men was fitful. Sometimes as much as six months would pass, with three or four letters from Adams, before Jefferson replied. When he did, Adams would invariably dash off an answering letter within a few days."[8] Dumas Malone, in his massive, award-winning biography of Jefferson, wrote that Adams "appears on the whole, and especially at first, to have gained more pleasure from their renewed friendship than his correspondent did. The older, lonelier, and the less occupied of the two, he seems to have had more need of it. It was precious to both of them, however, and well deserves its renown."[9]

Shortly after the renewal of their friendship in 1813, from June 28 to August 14, Adams sent twelve letters to Jefferson before finally receiving a lengthy response in early September. Acknowledging the disparity, Adams wrote humorously and with self-deprecation in the midst of the deluge of letters he sent from Quincy to Monticello, "Never mind it, my dear Sir, if I write four Letters to your one; your one is worth more than my four."[10] This should not be misconstrued as false modesty on Adams's part but rather seen in context as a demonstration among many made by Adams throughout the correspondence with which Adams expressed deep affection and respect for Jefferson. These feelings were entirely reciprocated by Adams's former vice president, and expressions of mutual care, regard, concern, and deep fondness went back and forth from Quincy and Charlottesville with every communication between them. For example, Jefferson's response to Adams's twelve-letter flurry closed with a declaration of affection that he would expound upon repeatedly, ending his letter with, "ever and affectionately your's."[11] These statements of mutual affection are essential signals in gaining further insight into Adams and Jefferson as individuals, and the value that both placed upon this most important and long-lived friendship. Though these signals of mutual affection now seem clear, it had not always been so.

Page Smith, a noted biographer of Adams, believed that "it was revealing of the two men that Adams in his letters to Jefferson signed himself, 'Yours affectionately'; 'With the most cordial esteem, your friend and servant'; 'My dear friend, adieu'; while Jefferson never varied from the correctly formal, 'Dear Sir, your most obedient humble servant.'"[12] However, Smith's assertion that Jefferson "never varied" his letter closings from the formal, somewhat emotionally distant style is not correct. "The warmth and affection of their relationship, to be sure, had been rather more in John and Abigail than in Jefferson," wrote Smith. "As with most charming men, the Virginian held something of himself in reserve. There was in him an ultimate area, a kind of interior arctic region—remote and lonely and cold. It might be said that Jefferson was so gracious, so affable, so easy to know, that few men ever knew him; Adams, on the other hand, awkward and stiff, often repelled people on slight acquaintance, but when he gave his friendship he gave it as he gave everything without reservation or restraint, abandoning his defenses and opening his heart."[13]

Smith mistakenly and somewhat controversially concluded that "it might be said that Adams loved Jefferson, while Jefferson liked Adams."[14] Jefferson's own attestations of his affection for both Abigail and John Adams were often described to them directly in his letters, as will be shown, which further illustrate Smith's error. Jefferson's emotional "reserve" as noted by Smith and many others has long been accepted as a component of Jefferson's character, as have Adams's garrulousness, vanity, and contentiousness. The great value in the relationship between Adams and Jefferson as played out and recorded not by others but by each other through their personal letters is that it illuminates deeper facets of these great men that no biographer or historian can properly summarize in a line, or a "thumbnail sketch." It is simply a mistaken over-simplification to suggest that Adams and Jefferson did not love each other, as respect and affection is inscribed in numerous expressions and turns of phrase in almost every letter that passed between them.

By the time their friendship was renewed many of the sharp edges of partisan bitterness, disappointment, and hurt had been softened by the passage of time, particularly for Adams. Jefferson for his part knew that this was so—his magnanimous response to Adams regarding the publication of the Cunningham letters was sure proof. What in past decades could easily have destroyed their friendship was allowed to dissipate like a wisp of cold November wind against the sturdy walls of Monticello or Montezillo.

What the Adams-Jefferson friendship and correspondence shows is nothing less than two great men who had reached the height of their intellectual and emotional development and who would, in the course of their conversations, set a pattern of understanding, acceptance, and forgiveness that ranks their letters as a monument to human compassion and grace.

In attempting to understand the scope and complexity of the lives of these great men—diplomats, presidents, philosophers, national heroes—the importance of this series of letters between Adams and Jefferson had sometimes been minimized. There has long been a reasonable desire to "get to the heart" of an historical person, to find some otherwise missed, previously unseen essential quality or action that explains that person and his or her life. The consequence of this pursuit of essentials, a kind of misleading oversimplification and deconstructionism, can only result in an insufficient approach to comprehension. The depth and breadth of their correspondence necessarily overturns any analytical approach based on simplification and reductive "essentialism." A recent reassessment of the founding fathers is a case in point.

The author of a recent history of the American revolutionary leaders described the consequences of Adams's and Jefferson's return from diplomatic service in Europe. After their long years in Europe, the two men, the historian wrote, were "out of synch with things in America. On his return, Jefferson found his countrymen entranced by trade, commerce, and the quest for luxury goods, and eager to embrace policies of public finance and customs of hierarchy and deference.

To his eyes, such things were symptoms of incipient monarchy and aristocracy, the political equivalent of smallpox and the plague, and he responded with all the vehemence, eloquence, and horror of which his humorless, thin-skinned soul was capable."[15] Had the author juxtaposed Mr. Jefferson's magnanimous letter to Adams of October 12, 1823, in which Jefferson forgave his old friend for the harsh criticisms he had read in excerpts of Adams's letters to Cunningham, the term "thin-skinned" would perhaps not have been employed.

The Adams-Jefferson correspondence, and the friendship that it represents, defeats every attempt at "thumbnail sketching" either man—those terse blocks of supposed definitive statements and descriptions by which some authors hope to provide their readers with an accurate and insightful biographical summation.

Though the many negative decades of Adams's historical reputation in the public mind now are apparently receding, that of Mr. Jefferson has been rocked by an old shadow recently made more solid than when it first appeared as a disturbing political smear in 1802.

The shadow of impropriety and hypocrisy that fell across the memory of Mr. Jefferson at the end of the twentieth century is one from which, for some, the third president is unlikely to ever fully emerge. Though Jefferson's historical reputation had previously been a generally and consistently positive (if not entirely enthusiastic) one, events in the late twentieth century have fundamentally and forever challenged Jefferson's legacy. DNA tests that appear to confirm the legitimacy of old, slanderous-appearing accusations involving Jefferson and his slave Sally Hemings have resulted in significant damage to Jefferson's stature in both academic and popular thought.[16]

While Jefferson's memory now suffers a fate worse than that of Adams's, that of the second president has long suffered the slings and arrows of outrageous characterizations. One scholar, in a 2006 article[17] that compares the leadership styles of the first three presidents, acknowledged that his negative portrayal of Adams is in conflict with more positive characterizations from recent biographers such as David McCullough and Joseph Ellis.[18] Admitting "his emphasis on Adams's shortcomings as chief executive" the author suggested that his was nevertheless an accurate portrayal, as opposed to the more positive portraits by overly enthusiastic historians who were mistakenly enraptured and misguided by the wealth of fascinating source materials left to posterity by Adams. "The same qualities of biting honesty, prolix writing, and determined independence that so offended colleagues have endeared Adams to scholars," the historian asserted. "They delight in his vivid quotations, exhaustive documentation, and utter inability to hide his feelings or cover his tracks. He is such a remarkably instructive and cooperative historical source precisely because he was so difficult for most of his contemporaries to work with."[19]

The political careers of Adams and Jefferson, their successes and errors, have generated a depth and breadth of opinion not only wide-ranging and long-lived, but entirely disparate, from worshipful veneration to insulting dismissal, to disgust and anger. Their complexity prevents either of them from being readily "pigeonholed," "thumbnailed,"or even easily understood. One segment alone of their long lives is not sufficient a sample from which to assume general truths. Jefferson and Adams knew full well that some historians would indulge in these types of over-simplified characterizations of them. Knowing that their letters to each other would likely be posthumously published, their correspondence took on a far greater importance to them in that it would always stand as explanation and counterargument to future critics whose thumbnails were smaller and sharper than they ought to be.

"You and I ought not to die before we have explained ourselves to each other,"[20] Adams wrote, early into their renewed friendship. There was much to be hashed out between the two, old friends now brought back together after over a decade of silence. Some water runs slow under the bridges of life—their letters did much to move the stream along, swifter and with fewer obstructions. There is much discussion, friendly debate, an abundance of mutual respect and affection, and sometimes heated words amid all the explanations. They reviewed their lives together through letters, and smoothed out the rough edges and misunderstandings that still remained as best they could. In much the same way that Adams and Jefferson were writing to one another, they were also documenting *themselves* for future generations.

Their correspondence is a record of a deep friendship marked by profound affection between two of America's greatest men, leaders of their generation, and founders of a new democratic republic never seen before in the history of governments and humanity. Adams and Jefferson worked closely together as members of the Continental Congress, then later as fellow diplomats representing the United States at the seats of government of Great Britain and France. Adams returned to the United States from his post as first minister to London in 1788, followed by Jefferson a year later as revolution shattered France. Jefferson had been the second American minister to the Court of Louis XVI (Benjamin Franklin had been the first) when he returned home from Europe in 1789, and was appointed secretary of state in Washington's administration soon thereafter.[21]

Adams's departure from Europe brought a flurry of affection and regrets from both Jefferson and Adams at their impending separation (which would be short-lived). "There are but two Circumstances, which will be regretted by me, when I leave Europe," Adams wrote. "One is the opportunity Searching any questions . . . in any books that may be wanted, and the other will be the Interruption of that intimate Correspondence with you, which is one of the most agreeable Events in my Life."[22] When Jefferson first heard of Adams's decision to return to America (and to take Abigail with him, of course) Jefferson wrote, "I learn with real pain the resolution you have taken of quitting Europe . . . I shall now feel bewidowed."[23]

Jefferson's friendship and professional association with John Adams also included Abigail Adams. A brilliant and articulate woman, Jefferson wrote to Abigail just as he did with any of his great and close friends. Bound by mutual affection and common purposes while in Europe, Abigail and Jefferson had by then already shared a long correspondence characterized by deep friendship that would later be put painfully aside due to political differences and personal hurts. As their departure for America approached, Jefferson saw their leaving as the beginning of an era for him that he expected would be one of unhappiness and loneliness. "I have considered you while in London as my neighbor, and look forward to the moment of your departure from thence as to an epoch of much regret and concern for me," Jefferson wrote from Paris to Abigail in London. "Insulated and friendless on this side of the globe, with such an ocean between me and everything to which I am attached the days will seem long which are to be counted over before I too am to rejoin my native country."[24]

Commenting late in 1787 on the political upheavals in France that would soon explode as the French Revolution, and later prove to be the foundations of the greatest challenge of his administration, Adams observed, "All Europe resounds with Projects for reviving, States and Assemblies, I think: and France is taking the lead.—How such assemblies will mix, with Simple Monarchies, is the question." Suggesting that such a mix (between popular government and monarchism) was not possible, Adams presciently concluded that "attempts to reconcile Contradictions will not succeed, and to think of Reinstituting Republics, as absurdly constituted as were the most which the world has seen, would be to revive Confusion and Carnage, which must again End in despotism."[25] Adams prepared for his return to the United States and closed his letter to Jefferson of December 10, 1787, "with the tenderest Affection of Friendship."[26] After his arrival in Braintree (a part of which would later be incorporated into a new town called "Quincy") in January 1798, Adams reiterated his deep connection with Jefferson by closing a short official letter of introduction for "John Coffin Jones, Esqr, an eminent Merchant of Boston and a late Member of the Legislature from that Town," by asserting that "I am with an affection that can never die, your Friend and Servant, John Adams."[27]

Acknowledging Adams's letter of introduction for Mr. Jones, Jefferson informed him from Paris, on May 10, 1789, that he intended to use the man as a "channel of evidencing to you how much I esteem whatever comes from you." Jefferson closed the letter affectionately, including his expectations of the near future. "Present me affectionately to Mrs. Adams, Colonel and Mrs. Smith.[28] I hope to see you all this summer, and to return this fall to my prison;[29] for all Europe would be a prison to me, were it ten times as big. Adieu my dear friend."[30]

Jefferson's views of the likely outcome of the French Revolution and the possibility of war between England and France were quite

different, and not nearly as accurate as those of his diplomatic colleague and friend. "The lunacy of the king of England will probably
place the affairs of that country under a regency; and as regencies
are generally pacific, we may expect that they will concur with this
country (France) in an unwillingness to enter into war," Jefferson
wrote to Adams on December 5, 1788. "The internal tranquility of
this country (France), which had never been so far compromitted as
to produce bloodshed, was entirely reestablished by the announcing
of the States general early in the next year, the reestablishment of
the parliament and the substitution of Mr. Neckar in the department
of finance instead of the Archbishop of Sens."[31] The attack on the
Bastille and the attendant bloodshed which accompanied that significant moment of victory for the French revolutionaries occurred only
some eight months after Jefferson had written his hopeful letter of
December 5, 1788. The horrific brutality and murders at the Bastille
marked the centrality of violence, and social and civic upheaval which
would become so characteristic of the French Revolution—an eventual whirlwind of horrors from which the United States had escaped
during its Revolution. The political changes that eventually engulfed
France soon would affect all of Europe, including Great Britain, and
the United States. In fact, relations with France, and the serious possibility of war with that country, America's first ally, would be the
central challenge of John Adams's presidency (1797–1801).

French maritime and diplomatic policies toward the United
States (and the Adams administration's responses to them) would
be the foremost among those issues that separated the two American
national political parties of the day, the Federalists and Democratic-Republicans (often known as "Republicans," and later the Democratic Party). As leaders of their respective parties,[32] Adams and
Jefferson, though president and vice president respectively, did not
view matters regarding France eye-to-eye. The two old friends, who
had said goodbye to one another in Europe in 1788 with such affection, soon became bitter political opponents.

Though he was vice president during Adams's presidency, Jefferson was not at all in accord with administration policies toward
France. Very much a Francophile, Jefferson was a devotee of French

wines, architecture, cuisine, culture, history, etc., while Adams and his fellow Federalists were not. The "Ancien Regime" of Louis XVI, (essentially, monarchist pre-revolutionary France) whose military and financial support had been so important to American victory over the British during the American Revolution, was, by the time Adams became president, eradicated—and Louis himself executed by the National Convention in 1793.

When Adams took his oath of office in March 1797, France and Great Britain were then at war, one of numerous conflicts involving revolutionary France and her neighbors (including also Austria, Prussia, Italy, Spain, Russia, and others). President Washington's policy had been one of neutrality, which Adams as his loyal successor promised to continue. Though serving as Adams's vice president, Jefferson did not agree with this approach to France or England. Americans remembered with affection and appreciation the significant financial and military aid that France had provided to the revolutionaries of 1776. Many believed that the United States would not have gained its independence from Great Britain without the aid of pre-revolutionary France.

The anti-monarchy Revolution in France was watched very closely in the United States particularly because so many Americans felt a natural friendship for France. Support for the French Revolution was then common among Americans. However, by Adams' inauguration, the cruelty, violence, and militarism of the Revolution in France had turned respect and support to revulsion and dismay among a majority of Americans including President Adams—though not Vice President Jefferson.

Support and affection for France, the great indispensable ally of the Revolution (and a fellow republic), and opposition to Great Britain—the hated despotic "mother country"—were at the core of Democratic-Republican foreign policy thinking. Federalist ambivalence and antipathy toward France since the French revolution, and apparent interest in normalization of relations (particularly trade) with Great Britain, were positions that Jefferson and his many republican allies could not abide. These incompatible positions would bring the country to a fever pitch of internal partisan enmity during the Adams administration. The cataclysmic political shifts in France and across Europe, combined with differences in domestic politics and national policy, created a growing divide between Adams and Jefferson that neither affection nor friendship could bridge. In a letter years later to his friend and fellow signer of the Declaration of Independence, Dr. Benjamin Rush of Philadelphia, Adams complained bitterly of the damage that the French Revolution had done to his friendship with Jefferson and to the country.

"I have reason to remember these things, for I have heard him assert them and enlarge upon them with the utmost astonishment. I have reason to remember them moreover, because these were the first topicks upon which we ever differed in opinions upon political subjects."[33] During the final year of Jefferson's second term, and eight years after his own presidency had ended, Adams regretfully and bitterly wrote, "I have reason to remember them too because his opinions recommended him to the French Revolutionary Government and Nation, and especially to all the Friends, Ambassadors, Consuls and other agents as well as to all other Frenchman in America, even to Talleyrand and the Duke de Liancourt, who all exerted all their influence and all their Praises to exalt Mr. Jefferson over my shoulders, and to run me down as an Aristocrat and a Monarchist. I have reason to remember it too because my opinion of the French Revolution, produced a coldness towards me in all my old Revolutionary Friends, and an Inclination towards Mr. Jefferson, which broke out in violent Invectives and false imputations upon me and in flattering Panegyricks upon Mr. Jefferson, till they ended in a consignment of me forever to private Life and the elevation of him to the President's Chair. My writings were but a Pretext. They knew that neither Aristocracy or Monarchy were recommended to this Country in any of them."[34]

The support of pre-revolutionary France had been a significant determinant in the outcome of the American Revolution (if not the deciding factor); the posture of France toward America would then necessarily be significant during the Washington and Adams administrations.

Adams and Jefferson were both aware that many of the early revolutionary leaders in France had looked to the American Revolution as a model, with particular emphasis on the American Constitution. Adams and Jefferson were heroes and guides to many of them. As founders of the American Republic and both having had diplomatic experience in France, Adams as envoy, Jefferson as minister, few men in American leadership circles could have been more interested in the course of the French Revolution—and in a better position to understand it.

As their own Revolution had been anti-monarchical, and strongly republican, they had more than merely philosophical ties to the upheavals in France. They had certainly hoped that the concepts of democracy and representative, constitutional government would spread and create new popular republican revolutions. Though minister to France Jefferson had believed as late as 1786 that the French people were happier with their King and government than Englishmen were with theirs, and viewed the convening of the Estates-General in 1789 as indicative of a return to a more stable political environment in France, he also knew from direct observation that poverty, economic conditions, and class inequality were devastating problems.[35]

Jefferson's travels through France's wine regions in the early part of 1787 provided him with a thorough knowledge of *les vins de France* and an eye-opening understanding of the circumstances of the people who worked in the vineyards and made the wines that he came to revere. At many of the chateaux Jefferson visited, where some of the finest wines in the world were produced, he observed extreme poverty. The shocking disparity of living and working conditions in the vineyard regions between the lower and aristocratic classes later produced a red harvest of rebellion and political upheavals.[36]

The extreme changes that the Revolution created in France and across Europe—from the convening of the Estates-General in 1789 to the end of the Revolution with the coronation of Napoleon Bonaparte as Emperor of France in 1804—were rivaled by the speed and unexpectedness of their arrival. Even the great observer, scholar, and diplomat Thomas Jefferson, though he had served as American Commissioner, then later as minister to France from 1784 and 1789, was astounded at the seismic changes that the Revolution brought to French society and government.

In a 1786 letter to Abigail Adams posted from Paris, Jefferson wrote of the tranquility and political stability of the French capital.

"Here we have singing, dauncing, laugh, and merriment. No assassinations, no treasons, rebellions nor other dark deeds," Jefferson observed. Though he had not seen them coming, enough dark deeds would soon occur in Paris and across France (and beyond) to horrify much of the world.

"When our king[37] goes out, they fall down and kiss the earth where he has trodden: and then they go to kissing one another. And this is the truest wisdom. They have as much happiness in one year as an Englishman in ten,"[38] Jefferson assured Abigail Adams, who was then living in London at the Court of St. James. His extensive travels in the French wine regions less than a year later introduced him to a less sanguine side of France, most certainly a very different *terroir* compared to the salons and diplomatic finery of the French capital.

The pre-revolutionary period in France is described by one author as essentially an upheaval waiting to happen. "Two percent of the population, the clergy and nobility, owned or controlled ninety-eight percent of the nation's wealth."[39] This extreme disparity of wealth distribution did not go unnoticed by Jefferson. "I was much an enemy of monarchies before I came to Europe," Jefferson wrote to President Washington two days after returning to Paris from his vineyard tour across France, Germany, and Italy. "I am now 10,000 times more so."[40]

Less than a year before the fall of the Bastille Jefferson had suggested to Adams that the convening of the Estates-General was an indication of the reestablishment of "internal tranquility" in France.[41] Eight months later the French monarchy would be all but overthrown, and there is good reason to believe that the king's earlier vigorous support of the American revolutionaries had been instrumental in his fall. An insightful historian of the French Revolution observed that "when Louis XVI allied with republican rebels who had proclaimed no taxation without representation, his subjects could scarcely help reflecting on why this principle was not deemed appropriate in France."[42]

Jefferson, like most observers, was caught flatfooted as the Revolution swept across France. Fewer still had any conception of the vast scope and reach that the upheavals in France would cause. During his second term as president, Jefferson admitted to a friend from his Parisian ministry days that he had "had no apprehension that the tempest, of which I saw the beginning, was to spread over such an extent of space and time."[43]

The French Revolution would reshape the map of Europe and directly influence American domestic and foreign policy. For Adams, it would play a central role in the course of his administration; for Jefferson it would be, among other things, part and parcel of a growing divergence in worldviews and politics between himself and his great friend Adams. Actions of both men that would later have significant impacts on American political life, national policy, and on their friendship would be directed by how they viewed the French Revolution. For one it was glorious (though regrettably but forgivably violent and bloody); for the other, little less than an appalling catastrophe. These diverging views would set the two friends on alternate paths whose future points of convergence soon became impossible for either man to see.

"The French nation has been awakened by our revolution," Jefferson wrote to Washington in late 1788.[44] Adams later summarized his cynical feelings of responsibility for the Revolution in France. "Have I not been employed in mischief all my days?" Adams asked his friend Dr. Rush. "Did not the American Revolution produce the French Revolution? And did not the French Revolution produce all the calamities and desolations to the human race and the whole globe ever since? I meant well, however."[45] France was their first revolutionary offspring, and a problem child it surely had become.[46]

3

"I Would Have Seen Half the Earth Desolated"

WHEN THE REVOLUTION came to France and swept away the old order of that society at every level, it had a devastating rippling effect across Europe, and then across the Atlantic to the new United States. The details of the Revolution, its personalities and myriad events of importance, controversy, and violence have been exhaustively documented. Most likely to be missed however in the extensive historical analysis of that period is the impact that the French Revolution had on the people and political leadership of the early American Republic. By 1797, President Adams and his then apparently still friendly political opponent, Vice President Jefferson, initially disagreed about the meaning of the Revolution in France, and diverged further as to the correct American posture toward the new French Republic.

Long before their final breach during Adams's presidency, preceded and followed by open antagonisms, Jefferson and Adams had explained their differences in letters. Reacting to Shay's Rebellion in Massachusetts in 1787, Jefferson had written from Paris to Abigail, who was horrified by the rebellion. Jefferson reassured her that "the spirit of resistance to government is so valuable on certain occasions, that I wish it to be always kept alive . . . I like a little rebellion now and then."[1]

Later that same year, during discussions regarding the ratification of the Constitution, Adams described to Jefferson his perspective on the nature of their political differences. His comments are the essential arguments against Jeffersonian-Republican populism and were typical of federalist thought. "You are afraid of the one—I, of the few. We agree perfectly that the many should have a full fair and perfect Representation," Adams explained. "You are Apprehensive of Monarchy; I, of Aristocracy."[2] Adams's fear of aristocracy, his support for a strong central executive, and his often public criticism of the populist, anti–monarchist political opposition lent credence to the idea, later leveraged heavily by Adams's political enemies, that he was a secret monarchist. Adams would refute this accusation for decades with mixed though generally negative results. Only much later, in his letters to Jefferson, was Adams finally and thoroughly convincing in smashing (even to Jefferson's satisfaction) the false accusations of his supposed monarchist tendencies.

When the French Revolution began, it was widely supported in the United States. Jefferson embraced it because it seemed to him (and to many others) something of a continuity of the American revolutionary model; entirely populist and, eventually, thoroughly anti-monarch. Adams was much less enamored with the Revolution particularly after the execution of the French King. For Adams, the Revolution in France seemed to embody his worst fears of anarchy and the brutality of mob rule. By the time of his presidency he was absolutely leery of it—not so for his vice president.

Jefferson did not agree with Adams that violence, even the excesses of the French Revolution (much of which was institutionally sanctioned), necessarily then negated the validity of the republican goals of that populist uprising. He was far more forgiving of the revolutionaries in France than his old friend. Moreover, Jefferson believed that violence, and even the murders of innocents, were justifiable sacrifices for the success of the Revolution. Jefferson's statements in favor of armed revolt and his acceptance of violence to further republican revolutions have a chilly quality to them that have caused controversy and even disillusion for some students of history.

Adams could certainly get his ire going and his rhetoric in a froth to match particularly when he considered perceived injustices against him or his historical reputation; his unfortunate letters to William Cunningham are illustrative. According to one of Jefferson's leading biographers, Adams "like Jefferson, . . . was prone to exaggerated statements, indulging in them in public as well as private to the confusion of others regarding his actual political philosophy of a balanced government, but he showed remarkable prevision regarding the course of events in France."[3] While Jefferson viewed violence in France as an unpleasant but sometimes necessary component of the entirety of the very salutary shifts that entailed the Revolution, Adams saw violence in the Revolution as a profoundly disturbing and inherent negative characteristic of it. One historian, author of a popular late twentieth-century history of the French Revolution, echoed Adams and Edmund Burke when he wrote, "in some depressingly unavoidable sense, violence *was* the Revolution itself."[4]

Jefferson's enthusiasm for the French Revolution and his acceptance of its violence would cause confusion later for many Americans struggling to understand Jefferson's complicated character. Adams's rhetorical excesses have long been understood as key traits of the second president; Jefferson's highly charged rhetoric (which, as with Adams, would negatively affect some of his most important friendships and associations) continue to cause confusion about him, however.

In a letter to William Smith (later John Adams's son-in-law), then in Paris, Jefferson wrote enthusiastically of the tax revolt (later called Shay's Rebellion) that had occurred in Massachusetts in 1787. "God forbid we should ever be 20 years without such a rebellion," Jefferson wrote. "What country can preserve it's [sic] liberties if their rulers are not warned from time to time that their people preserve the spirit of resistance? Let them take arms. The remedy is to set them right as to facts, pardon & pacify them. What signify a few lives lost in a century or two? The tree of liberty must be refreshed from time to time with the blood of patriots & tyrants. It is it's [sic]

natural manure.''[5] Jefferson believed that Revolution, and the message of popular empowerment that such revolts send to rulers, were
an important bulwark against (and response to) tyranny. Jefferson
ensconced the right to rebel in the preamble to the Declaration of
Independence.[6] His was not simply a disinterested support for revolution, nor however was he unappreciative of the costs and risks. Jefferson's was a longer view of governments and revolutions—he saw
the horrors that some popular revolutions bring with them (particularly the French example) as sometimes necessary excesses that are
acceptable when, in the course of time and as a result of revolution,
despotism is replaced by the rule of the people. A letter of Jefferson's
to his friend and then American *Charge d'Affairs* in France, William
Short, further illuminates the third president's views.

Once Jefferson's personal secretary in Paris, Short was often
Jefferson's guest at Monticello. Their relationship was unusually
close for that of employee and employer; Jefferson once described
Short as his "adopted son."[7] While serving as secretary of state
under Washington after his return from Paris, Jefferson had both a
professional and personal interest in the reports of his close friend,
then serving as the American representative at Paris. When a string
of heated communications critical of the excesses of the French
revolutionaries was received from Short late in 1792, through both
official and private channels, Jefferson replied stridently and with
rebukes. Of his many thousands of letters, his early 1793 reply to
William Short is extraordinary for its sharp wording.[8]

The institutional, political, and cultural upheavals of the Revolution in France up to late 1792 had made a significant impact on
Short. His proximity to events, particularly the September Massacres
of that year, must certainly have been at the center of Short's loss
of faith in the political tidal shifts then occurring in France. These
events prompted many, not only Short, to reexamine the course of
the Revolution. One modern historian wrote of the hundreds of
prison murders that occurred across Paris during the first days of
that September, toward which the leaders of the revolutionary government shamefully turned a blind eye,[9] as ". . . the event which
more than almost any other exposed a central truth of the French

Revolution: its dependence on organized killing to accomplish political ends. For however virtuous the principles of the kingless France were supposed to be, their power to command allegiance depended, from the very beginning, on the spectacle of death."[10] This idea of the French revolutionaries killing political enemies, nonconformists, and the innocent for political purposes would be confirmed again and again in the coming months and years.

Short's condemnation of the horrific events of September 1792 is echoed by another historian from the early twentieth century. "Words should hardly be defiled by describing the horrors of those September days," the appalled author wrote, "when a horde of savages, men and women in their outward form but animals within, frenzied with the lust of blood, surged from prison to prison, massacring the helpless crowds of prisoners . . . which have left bloodstains on the history of France never to be washed out."[11] These atrocities did not happen without those writers and agitators who had set the stage for them with their heated, extreme, and so often hyperbolic rhetoric of fear, hatred, partisanship, and justifications of (political) violence. The seeds of hatred and violence had been planted for decades and generations with crushing tax burdens, extreme political and social inequality, and the *lettres de cachet* from the king that sent any man or woman in the country to prison (without trial) on the whimsy alone of the king. In addition, Paris had been rife with rumors of widespread impending prison breaks by nobles, non-juring priests, criminals, and sundry opponents of the Revolution, which would be, it was feared, followed by murderous attacks against patriots and their families across the city. These frightening whispers of impending counter-revolutionary violence fueled the fears (even to hysteria) of those who supported the new government.[12] "Danton must be blamed, like Camille Desmoulins and Marat,[13] for working upon the imagination of a people already hysterical with fear and hatred," the historian of more than a century ago wrote, "and afterwards for condoning and slurring over atrocities which dragged the revolutionary ideals of liberty and justice through the shambles of barbarous revenge."[14] The partisanship of some in the new United States was also, at this time, sometimes extraordinary and excessive though the consequences of participation for French and American opinion-makers were altogether of a different magnitude.

By the summer of 1789—amid economic crisis, wide-spread frustrations over unfulfilled promises of reform, the convening of the Estates-General, and a growing popular antipathy toward the monarchy (based largely on enlightenment concepts of liberty and democracy, frustration at the slow pace of reforms, and widespread agitation for significant and effective changes)—France had become a proverbial powder keg. The republican zeal of one man lit the flame of revolution and war that would engulf France and finally much of Europe—and enmesh the United States in an almost impossible diplomatic conundrum, a challenge that John Adams would be required to navigate and resolve.

Camille Desmoulins was the torchbearer. He and his fellow revolutionary leaders, as astutely described by one early twentieth-century biographer, were eventually "overwhelmed by that monster which they themselves had helped to arose."[15] The revolutionary trajectory of this hot-headed, talented, fanatical, muckraking journalist/polemicist is an illustration in miniature of the convulsions of the first years of the Revolution and its eventual failure—and the collapse of the highest hopes of Republicans everywhere.

The dismissal of the popular Finance Minister Jacques Necker by direct order of the King (and Necker's swift, unceremonious departure from the country) early in July 1789 was seen by French Republicans and reformers as a clear signal from the monarchy that it was becoming less tolerant toward republicanism. Upon hearing the news of this dramatic dismissal and shift in royal opinion against reform, a previously unknown twenty-nine-year-old provincial lawyer from Guise—and former schoolmate of future Jacobin leader Maximilien Robespierre—Camille Desmoulins, climbed atop a table outside the Café Foy in the Palais Royale, then the social hub of Paris. Thousands of people were there strolling, chatting, and enjoying the mid-July sun when, for a brief critical moment, all eyes were on Camille Desmoulins.

Noted for a self-admitted stammer, on that day he had no such difficulties. Apparently carried away with revolutionary fervor he whipped the crowd into a frenzy of anger and insurrection.

"Citizens!" he cried, "you know that the whole nation had demanded that Necker should be preserved to it! I have just returned from Versailles—Necker is dismissed! This dismissal is the tocsin of the St. Bartholomew of the patriots. Tonight, the Swiss and German battalions will come forth from the Champs de Mars to massacre us. There is not a moment to lose! We have only one resource; it is to arm ourselves instantly, and to put on cockades by which we may recognize one another."[16]

Green leaves were torn from nearby trees to make cockades, the color of hope according to Camille. Then, pulling two pistols from under his coat he continued his impassioned call/harangue to resistance and defiance. "My friends! the police are here! They observe, they watch me. Well, then, it is I who call my brethren to liberty! But I will not fall alive into the hands of the police! Let all good citizens imitate me! To arms! To arms!"[17]

Two days later, July fourteenth, elements of this very same crowd, now armed, increased in numbers, and stoked to a hot pitch of revolutionary anger, attacked the Bastille—hated for generations as the great symbol of monarchist tyranny—and started a revolution. The fall of that royal prison, now marked every year in France as Bastille Day, is considered the first explosion of popular violence of the French Revolution. It would not be the last.

Poverty stricken, Desmoulins quickly turned from the path of public oration and began a career as a republican polemicist, pamphleteer, and revolutionary. Mistakenly described by a later writer as "the greatest journalist of the Revolution, and indeed the greatest journalist France had ever produced"; though Camille was certainly neither, he was no stranger to overheated rhetoric and pandering to the masses.[18] Pamphlet sales brought him out of poverty and earned him a well-deserved reputation as a man unafraid to go, rhetorically, "toe to toe" with anyone. Less putridly bloodthirsty than some of his fellow radical revolutionary pamphleteers such as Hebert and Marat, both of whom would come to bad ends, Camille was no stranger to the dark waters of recommending and defending acts of malice and violence (for political ends) to his readers.

Desmoulins's first pamphlet, "La France Libre," laid out the stakes of the Revolution and the high price that some would necessarily be forced to pay. "Never was richer booty offered to conqueror," he wrote. "Forty thousand palaces, hotels, castles, two-fifths of the estates of France to be distributed as the prize of your valour. The nation shall be purged, and strangers, bad citizens, all those who prefer their private interest to the general good, shall be exterminated."[19] Those who did not properly follow the republican path might find themselves strung up on a public lantern post. Such was the tone of Camille when he self-identified in his writings as "*le procureur-general de la lantern*." The implications of his paraphrasing of an old Latin proverb containing the phrase, "those who do evil hate the light" as "rascals do not like the lantern,"[20] was not easily mistaken.

Desmoulins was soon courted by the top leadership of the Revolution—first by Mirabeau, then Danton, and then Robespierre. His impeccable credentials as a dedicated republican revolutionary propagandist were oddly juxtaposed with a romantic and tender heart. Only much later would he fully understand the power of his published words.

No other important leader of the French Revolution drama other than Camille Desmoulins was known at the time by their first name only. His almost childlike enthusiasm had long allowed him a certain indulgence for his personal and rhetorical excesses. This however was not a *carte blanche*.

As most of the population of France during the time of the Revolution was illiterate, there is some question as to who was reading Camille's erudite and classical allusion-heavy publications. His pamphlets were selling and generating revenue for him, but were his ideas so attractive as to be somehow disseminated to (and accepted by) the masses of unread and unlettered *citoyens* who formed the core of the Parisian urban mob of the Revolution? Camille believed that "the people" supported him.

During his last minutes Camille called for their aid. Gathered in their thousands to watch him die they did nothing but heap scorn and derision upon him. Perhaps he had had a sense that something like this would be the final scene; at his trial he had declared without humility, "I am thirty-three, the age of the Sansculotte Jesus; a critical age for every patriot."[21]

At the age of thirty Camille married in Paris toward the end of 1790.[22] Among the sixty signers of the Desmoulins's marriage contract were Brissot and Robespierre. It soon became clear however that, in Paris and across France, "there was a force stronger than love—private and public fear."[23] When, three years later, he was called before his fellow Jacobins on December 14, 1793, Camille declared that of the sixty witnesses at his wedding he had then "only two friends left, Robespierre and Danton. All the others have either emigrated or been guillotined."[24]

On August 10, 1792, a mob attacked the royal family then living at the Tuileries Palace. There the loyal Swiss Guards were massacred almost to a man, and many hundreds of the attackers were also killed. The King and his family were taken to The Temple (a centuries-old fortress constructed by the Knights Templar) as prisoners; the monarchy had fallen. An historian, writing at the close of the eighteenth century, described Camille as having "materially assisted (in) the success of the insurrectionists in August, by preparing the public mind for acts of barbarity."[25] Camille was elected to the Convention as a representative from Paris and quickly appointed by Danton, then minister of justice, as his secretary.

Events now passed for many in France at a seemingly accelerated rate.[26] Madame Roland, one of the leading Girondins, noted this in 1792 shortly after the royal family's failed attempt to flee France, when she wrote to a friend, "We are living through ten years in twenty-four hours; events and emotions are jumbled together and follow each other with a singular rapidity."[27]

The trial of Louis began in January, 1793—the outcome a fairly apparent foregone conclusion to all. One of the more enthusiastic proponents of the death sentence was Camille.

His speech at the Convention in support of execution (a rare public pronouncement) was, to one early nineteenth-century historian, "so violent in its language that it reveals an unbalanced and hysterical mind."[28] One of his more favorable biographers wrote, "the violence of his language on this occasion is quite indefensible, at least if we are to judge the men of that day by the ordinary rules which govern conduct amongst a civilized people."[29]

Camille then put his pen to work to diminish and destroy two influential political factions in the Convention, the Hebertists and the Girondins. Robespierre himself reviewed many of Desmoulins's pamphlets prior to publication. The Hebertists were seen by the Jacobins as too extreme—excessively agitating with outrageous rhetoric in their own publications for more political violence by the masses and a continued association with the sans-culottes mobs. Camille rhetorically laid into them. The Hebertists, including Hebert himself, were eventually guillotined. The Girondins, who were more forgiving of the king, more favorable to a de-centralized approach to the development of the revolutionary state, and strong proponents of foreign war—faired as poorly.

Under extreme pressure from within and without the Jacobins became intolerant of views other than their own. One noted historian of the Revolution saw Robespierre's excesses more as the function of a fanatical utopian's fear and rigidity than of any personal vendetta. "His enemies must be destroyed," he wrote of Robespierre, "not because he hated them, but because he loved France."[30] The Jacobin leadership and the Revolution itself were moving to a point at which, according to a leading modern historian, "all criticism and all social or political deviation were suspect by definition."[31]

Several months after Jefferson wrote his harsh reply to William Short's less than zealous report from Paris, Robespierre's fellow Jacobin and colleague on the Committee of Public Safety, Louis-Antoine Saint-Just, addressed the Convention. Those great dreams of universal political rights, equality, and fraternity that had illuminated the opening of the republican Revolution in France had by then devolved into a system of intolerance, cruelty, and excess that far surpassed the worst of Louis XVI's mild (if not beneficent, in comparison) rule. "Every party is then criminal," Saint-Just ominously declared, "because it is a form of isolation from the people and the popular societies, a form of independence from the government. Every faction is then criminal, because it tends to divide the citizens; every faction is criminal because it neutralizes the power of public virtue. The solidity of our Republic is in the very nature of things. The sovereignty of the people demands that the people be unified; it is therefore opposed to factions, and all faction is a criminal attack upon sovereignty."[32] Those in opposition had got their warning.

One of the leading Girondins was Jacques Pierre Brissot, a witness at Camille's wedding, a leading member of the Convention, and a Jacobin. In two important publications including "History of the Brissotins" (one of the most financially successful of the revolutionary pamphlets) and "Brissot Unmasked" (January/February 1792) Camille attacked the Girondins and Brissot personally. An early (and favorable) biographer of Desmoulins described "Brissot Unmasked" as "a collection of calumnies, of petty gossip, and of murderous outbursts."[33] Brissot attempted to counter-attack in his own publication but with no success.

"This man calls himself a patriot only in order to calumniate patriotism," Brissot wrote of his former friend.[34] Camille's reply, "Brissot Unmasked," had a singular purpose which was "to assail, and, if possible, to destroy, Brissot's reputation."[35]

According to one late nineteenth-century author, Camille attacked "the whole Gironde with a variety of charges built on such bases as plausibly interwoven extracts from documents and speeches, and unfair inferences from private meetings and conversations."[36] "We will see," Camille declared, challenging Brissot directly, "how you will sustain the offensive warfare which you are so fond of using yourself."[37] Camille dramatically used the name of his target (his one-time wedding guest) as a verb for stealing. "I warn you that you shall not succeed in your attempt to *brissoter* my reputation," Camille wrote, "it is I who will tear the mask from your face . . ."[38]

These political combat pamphlets of Brissot and Desmoulins, like those of less notable authors, were widely read, or at least widely sold. If Camille did not then fully appreciate that his challenges, allegations, and accusations came with consequences—he soon learned.

Almost a century later an historian wrote dismissively of Desmoulins that he "was envious, and loved to cast filth upon all superiority, whether of grade or intellect."[39] More a purveyor of rigid republican dogmas and biting animadversions than a journalist (in

the manner that the term is commonly understood today), Camille
was not however without a softer, more human side. In fact, it is for
his humanity far more than his political attack rhetoric that he is now
mainly recalled. Another late nineteenth-century author wrote that
Camille "would weep over the victim his pen had destroyed."[40]

The rhetorical battle between Camille and his old friend Brissot
occurred early in 1792. The monarchy of France then had but several
months of existence remaining. One of its last official acts was to dismiss those Girondin ministers that the king had previously appointed.
By early 1793 the king himself was condemned to death. Brissot and
the Girondins were dismissed from the Convention due to demands
made by pro-Hebertist sans-culotte mobs. In late July, Camille's
friend Robespierre was voted onto the powerful Committee of Public
Safety. (Danton was then removed from that Committee.) Later in
the year the queen was executed. She was harassed and hounded by
bloodthirsty, hateful mobs all the way to the steps of the scaffold.

The Revolution was advancing in big strides, and those previously given notice by Saint-Just who did not heed his warning would
soon, unbeknownst to them, face consequences. Everything seemed
to be changing rapidly; even the Gregorian calendar was eliminated
and replaced with a republican version. For Camille, the month of
Brumaire, of the Year Two of the Republic (late October 1793),
brought such a shock of realization and regret that the foundations of
his rigid republican worldview would be cracked to their foundations.
Once-respected members of the government, Brissot and his fellow
Girondin leaders came to trial early in Brumaire, Year Two of the
Revolution. This period of revolutionary tribunals, the almost constant public use of the guillotine to execute political opponents and
suspects of all stripe, came to be known as the Terror.

Camille attended the trial but apparently did not fully understand
the high stakes that were involved. He sat near the jury beside Vilate,
a juror of the Revolutionary Tribunal.[41] One Desmoulins biographer
provided the following statement from Vilate's memoirs with assurances to the reader that there is "no reason to doubt the authenticity"
of his account:

I was seated with Camille Desmoulins on the bench placed before
the table of the jury. When they returned from their deliberation,
Camille advanced to speak to Antonelle, who came in one of the
last. Surprised at the alteration in his face, Camille said to him,
rather loud: "I pity you; yours are terrible functions"; then, hearing the declaration of the jury, he threw himself into my arms in
distress and agony of mind: "Oh, my God, my God! It is I who kill
them! My 'Brissot Unmasked'! Oh, my God, this has destroyed
them!" As the accused returned to hear their sentence all eyes were
turned on them; the most profound silence reigned throughout the
hall: the public prosecutor concluded with the sentence of death.
The unfortunate Camille, fainting, losing his consciousness, faltered out these words: "I am going, I am going, I must go out!" He
could not.[42]

Danton had a similar reaction. Soon after the trial he and Camille
were walking near the River Seine in the fading light of early evening. The sunlight on the water caused Danton to stop in his tracks.
"'Look,' said Danton, and as he spoke Camille saw that his friend's
eyes were filled with tears, 'Look at all that blood! The Seine flows
with blood! Ah! too much blood has been spilt. Come, take up your
pen, write and ask for clemency. I will support you!'"[43] According
to one historian, "from that time both Danton and Desmoulins were
different men."[44]

Camille quickly launched a new publication, "Le Vieux Cordelier," in whose pages he criticized the course of the Revolution and
called for a "Committee of Clemency." His stunning change of tone
did not go unnoticed.

It was generally understood that those who appeared before the
Revolutionary Tribunal as defendants almost always received a sentence of death. In fact, there were only two possible outcomes at the
Tribunal: death or acquittal. After Desmoulins's third issue Robespierre likely understood that Camille's calls for compassion were a
direct threat to the continuation of the Terror and therefore to him, its
most strident proponent.

In early January 1794, Camille was called before the Jacobin Club to explain his new attitude of compassion and his abandonment of Jacobin orthodoxy. The Jacobin Club had long been something of a debating society for leading members of the revolutionary movement and government. Robespierre took the podium and, though harshly attacking and condemning him and his recommendations that opposed the Terror, offered Camille a costly way out.[45]

"Camille promised to abjure the political heresies, the erroneous, ill-sounding propositions which cover all the pages of the 'Vieux Cordelier.' . . . His writings are dangerous," Robespierre proclaimed to his fellow Jacobins, "they nourish the hopes of our enemies and favour public malignity . . . The writings of Camille are condemnable . . . Camille is a spoilt child who has good dispositions, but whom bad company have misled. It is necessary to protest against his numbers, which Brissot himself would not have dared to avow, and to preserve Desmoulins in the midst of us. I demand, in consequence, that the numbers of Camille's paper shall be burnt in the Society."[46]

"Burning is not answering!" Desmoulins replied. The issues of "Le Vieux Cordelier" were then read aloud in the Jacobin Club.

Robespierre then said, "if thou hadst not been Camille, we should not have had so much indulgence for thee."[47] Robespierre had offered his old friend a way out—a way back to Jacobin-approved revolutionary respectability—but only if he would abandon his pride, self-respect, and new sense of duty in opposing the violent, unforgiving monster that he had helped to create. To his credit, Desmoulins did not break.

Previously, Camille had publicly criticized Saint-Just, a member of the Committee of Public Safety (a notorious fanatic, and one of Robespierre's closest associates). At the time, Desmoulins boldly and injudiciously declared that " . . . this young man carries his head as if it were the corner-stone of the Republic, or the Sacred Host."[48] Later, Camille ominously asked a friend, "Do you think that, for such an excellent jest he could wish to take my life?"[49]

The truth of all that he had done and said finally came to him. "How could I have supposed that certain witticisms in my writings at the expense of colleagues who had provoked me would wipe out the remembrance of my services?" he wrote to his wife from prison. "I do not conceal from myself that I die the victim of these sarcasms, and of my friendship for Danton."[50]

The seventh and final issue of "Le Vieux Cordelier" appeared in March, 1794. "I contend that we have never been so enslaved as since we have called ourselves Republicans," he wrote."[51] The Revolution in France had all but imploded.

Desmoulins, Danton, and several others of the so-called "indulgents" were, after a sham political trial, convicted of crimes against the state and executed by guillotine on April 5, 1794. In her grief, Camille's wife Lucille had gone to the prison where Camille was held and tried to see him. Her appeal to Robespierre for charity and forgiveness for Camille, despite her reminding him that he had attended their wedding and was the protector of their infant child, fell on deaf ears. Less than a month later she too was brought before the Revolutionary Tribunal. Convicted after an absurd trial characterized by unproven charges of conspiracy and counter-revolution, she was brought to the same scaffold as Camille and decapitated. Communications to Robespierre asking for clemency from Lucille's mother also received no response. From the prison to the scaffold Lucille Desmoulins shared a tumbril with the widow of Jacques Hebert (who had been guillotined with his fellow "Hebertists" only two weeks before Camille, Danton, and others of the "Dantonists/ Indulgents" group).

Many in the immense Parisian crowds who enjoyed watching public executions—they had many opportunities during those times to do so—commented on Lucille's beauty, bravery, and strength of character. One Camille biographer described her there as "dressed all in white, as though for a bridal, and with a white handkerchief passed over her head and tied under her chin."[52] Few such observations regarding bravery and calmness were made about Camille as he travelled on the tumbril to his death. Some witnesses stated that he rent his shirt to pieces in his struggles, frustration, and anger. This is in sharp contrast to the self-control of Danton who, just prior to the blade, instructed the executioner to be sure to display his severed head to the ghoulish crowd.

While in prison awaiting execution Lucille Desmoulins had sent a note with locks of her hair to her mother. "Good-night, dearest mother," she wrote. "A tear drops from my eyes; it is for you. I am going to sleep in peace and innocence."[53] She is supposed to have said at some point during that day, "They have assassinated the best of men. If I did not hate them for that I should bless them for the service they have done me this day."[54] Lucille Desmoulins was twenty-three years old at the time of her execution.

When one of her fellow condemned prisoners had attempted to comfort her she stopped him. "Look at my face," she calmly said. "Is it that of a woman who needs to be comforted?"[55] Supporters of the Revolution in France widely held the belief that their Revolution, if successful, would be the beginning of a global movement of democracy and universal liberty.

These views went hand-in-hand with an extreme exaggeration of the importance of events in France after the fall of the Bastille. What was happening in France was not then merely of significance to Frenchmen, but impacted the entire world. Perhaps Lucille Desmoulins needed no comforting because, for her, the earth no longer could claim a hold on her—Camille, her great love, had been stolen from her, and the Revolution that both of them had so strongly supported had failed.

Representative of this view is a statement made by Jean-Marie Roland, a Girondin leader. After escaping Paris, he committed suicide late in 1793 when he was informed that his wife, the renowned Madame Roland, had been executed with the Girondin leadership. In a conversation between Charles Barbaroux (another noted Girondin guillotined in 1794), and M. Roland, Barbaroux recalled that "Roland asked me what I thought of France, and of the means of saving her. I opened my heart to him, and in return he said to me . . . 'If liberty perish in France, it is for ever lost for all the rest of the world; all the hopes of the philosophers are deceived; a tyranny the most cruel [sic] will fall upon the earth.'"[56]

In Philadelphia, Thomas Jefferson was watching events in France with concern and compassion but without condemnation. After the slaughter at the Tuileries, the September Massacres, and the execution of the King (which occurred two weeks after Jefferson wrote his letter of reproach to William Short) many friends of the Revolution outside of France were repulsed into silence and even outright opposition. Many lovers of liberty such as Adams, and foreigners on the ground observing events directly such as William Short and others, recoiled at the political violence occurring in France. Jefferson had no such qualms, agreeing as he did so closely with Roland's assessment of the importance of the Revolution. Roland, Desmoulins, and Jefferson all believed with an absolute certainty that the Revolution was all-important and that horrific deeds could be justified for assuring its success.

Jefferson was extraordinarily critical in his early 1793 reply to his friend William Short, who was then in Paris as the United States' diplomatic representative to France. In this letter Jefferson reiterated his support for the Jacobins and justified their crimes by explaining that extraordinarily important causes sometimes require, and result in, unpleasant events and consequences. Over time there would be other causes too that Jefferson supported (or opposed) as heartily, and that evoked similarly heightened emotions and language.

On display throughout the tragedy of the Revolution—the experience of Camille and Lucille Desmoulins particularly illustrative—was the power of rhetoric. Jefferson, a master of the written word, fully understood this. But he sometimes was no master of himself and got caught up, as did many others, in the authority of an attractive and definitive idea.

Perhaps Jefferson's reaction would have been different had he remained in Paris and seen all of those horrors with his own eyes, as had William Short. Disturbingly, one gets the impression that he may well have kept on, regardless.

The Revolution in France was, for Jefferson, simply too important to fail. For him, those unfortunate "martyrs" (and victims) who fell, by fair means or foul, to ensure its success were essentially "collateral damage" in one of the most important events in the history of the world. For Jefferson, voluntary and involuntary sacrifices were all necessary (though sometimes unfortunate) components of the globally critical event that was the Revolution in France. Jefferson's views are as clear as if illuminated by the light of the street lanterns of Paris.

"The tone of your letters had for some time given me pain, on account of the extreme warmth with which they censured the proceedings of the Jacobins of France," Jefferson complained to Short. Jefferson considered the Jacobins the "Republican patriots" of the French Revolution, and perhaps therefore reacted emotionally to Short's criticism of them.

Jefferson acknowledged that the early revolutionary experiment in France of retaining the monarchy had been unsuccessful, but further explained that the Jacobins had taken necessary actions (which later included regicide) to secure the Revolution. "The experiment failed completely, and would have brought on the reestablishment of despotism had it been pursued. The Jacobins saw this, and that the expunging that officer was of absolute necessity. And the Nation was with them in opinion," Jefferson wrote on January 3, 1793.[57]

Jefferson informed Short that he "deplore(d) as much as anybody," that both the guilty and innocent had fallen in the Revolution in France, "& (I) shall deplore some of them to the day of my death."[58] He mourned the murdered innocents as if they had "fallen in battle." Jefferson believed that the popular Revolution in France, "the arm of the people" as he called it—while inexact, was not as "blind as balls and bombs but," he admitted, "blind to a certain degree." Writing as the revolutionary that he was, and using almost the same words as Roland,[59] Jefferson continued, "The liberty of the whole earth was depending on the issue of the contest, and was ever such a prize won with so little innocent blood?"[60]

For Jefferson, the cause of the French Revolution was of much greater importance than it was for most Americans, including his close friend and subordinate in government, Mr. Short. Jefferson had come to see the revolutionary republic in France, even while its leaders committed government-sanctioned murder of political opponents, as a critically important ally in the global fight against monarchy and tyranny. He likely would have agreed with Jacobin leader Robespierre's seemingly counterintuitive assertion that "the revolutionary government was 'the despotism of liberty against tyranny.'"[61]

In his lengthy letter to Short, Jefferson disturbingly asserted that, "my own affections have been deeply wounded by some of the martyrs to this cause, but rather than it should have failed, I would have seen half the earth desolated. Were there but an Adam & an Eve left in every country, & left free, it would be better than as it now is."[62] When Jefferson's emotions and republican pique were aroused he, like Adams, did not mince words. His style would later have unfortunate consequences, much in the same way that Adams's sometimes unrestrained, bombastic expressions of opinion had done for him.[63]

Jefferson accurately suggested to Short that his continuing support of the French revolutionary cause was reflective of the mood of the American people. "They are," Jefferson wrote of his views, "really those of ninety-nine in an [sic] hundred of our citizens. The universal feasts, and rejoicings which have lately been had on account of the successes of the French showed the genuine effusions of their hearts."[64] He was not then exaggerating about American support of the Revolution in France. Within three years however, by the time Adams became president and Jefferson vice president, most of this widespread American support would be gone.

One modern historian has taken particular umbrage with Jefferson's language in this letter to Short, and suggests that Jefferson was instructing Short to "accept that there was no limit (except the sparing of two persons per nation) to the slaughter that might legitimately be perpetrated in the holy cause of freedom."[65] Jefferson's hyperbole is matched in turn by the historian's own excessive rhetoric via removal of the original historical context. "Those in the culture of the modern American militias who see themselves as at war, or on the verge of war, with the federal government are fanatical believers in liberty, as Jefferson was. Jefferson condoned French revolutionary atrocities on a far greater scale, numerically, than the 1995 massacre in Oklahoma City."[66] The rhetoric that Adams and Jefferson employed in their private correspondence, occasionally much to their dismay and later regret, would serve as both important resources for later historians, and the basis for confusion as to who these men truly were.

There is a danger for students of history in ascribing excessive importance to one letter, or even a small percentage of an historical person's communications, and suggesting that from these limited sources the key to the sum total of that person's character can be acquired. Both Adams and Jefferson were extremely complex and occasionally contrarian personalities—any suggestion that a small minority of their letters are the very keys to unlocking the mystery and complexity of their characters will likely lead to erroneous conclusions.

Eric Hoffer, in his important study of mass movements, *The True Believer*, wrote, "the generation that made the French Revolution had an extravagant conception of the omnipotence of man's reason and the boundless range of his intelligence."[67] Jefferson certainly was a supporter of these ideas. The committing of violent acts of murder, however, is in no way a demonstration of "man's reason and the boundless range of his intelligence."

It is important that a difference is strongly specified in this context involving Jefferson between insane, murderous acts of *individuals* (e.g., the Oklahoma City bombing) and the insane, murderous acts of individuals *working within* the context of an anti-tyranny/anti-monarchy (e.g., republican) mass movement that is "legitimized" by universal or near universal suffrage. (In this context the term "insane" is not used in a clinical diagnostic sense but rather as in common parlance.) Jefferson supported the French Revolution so vigorously, despite all the horrors that had been committed by French Republicans, because he believed that the Revolution itself was a reflection of the will of the French people toward freedom, justice, and liberty. The Estates-General consisted of representatives who had been elected from every province (later "departments") of France in free and open elections that involved universally enthusiastic participation by the electorate. The *cahiers*, lists of complaints and desires for reform composed at the most local of political levels, were written for the eye of the King and sent to him from every corner of France as part of the process of forming the Estates-General. These *cahiers* were meant to be the foundation of discussions on national reform. The nationwide elections and the *cahiers* were convincing evidence to Jefferson and many others that the majority of the people of France were desirous of sweeping governmental, economic, and societal reforms.

The Estates-General later became the National Assembly and then the National Convention. Jefferson believed that this final form of national political body, the Convention, was representative of the people of France and thus—through them—their wishes. Most of the desires for reform specified in the *cahiers* unfortunately went unheeded, which fueled the revolutionary spirit all the more. Jefferson's belief in reason and his faith in the intelligence of the masses could not be easily swayed, nor would it ever be. His championing of the French Revolution even after the Terror of the Jacobins was related in large part to his fervent beliefs in the enduring truth and value of human reason. The fact that Jefferson's faith therein, even after the epic violence of the public executions of "counter-revolutionaries," and innocents such as Lucille Desmoulins, and the resultant reaction executions of Robespierre and his closest supporters and followers, is evidence of the semi-religious nature of his beliefs.

Dumas Malone, a leading Jefferson biographer,[68] fully appreciated the gravity of the statements made by Jefferson to Short and to William Smith (expressing support for "Shay's Rebellion" in Massachusetts), and the mistaken conclusions that less careful analysts might reach because of them. "He would certainly have said no such thing in public, and he could hardly have been expected to anticipate that private words of his would be quoted to schoolboys in later generations, seized upon by political partisans, or exploited by reckless demagogues," Malone wrote of Jefferson's letter to Short.[69]

It is the responsibility of students of history to weigh in full balance the entirety of a person's known experiences, written records, and actions to come to a reasonably accurate conclusion about their character—famous, influential, or otherwise. "Whether the measured judgments of a responsible statesman or the unrestrained private language of the same man should be regarded as the better index of his true sentiments is perhaps an unanswerable question," Malone cautioned. "And both must be taken into account by anyone seeking to arrive at truth."[70]

In his controversial 1996 study of Jefferson and the French Revolution, Connor Cruise O'Brien wrote, "the Jefferson who made a cult of the French Revolution provides aid and comfort not just to the far right in government but to the most ferocious militant extremists. In the paroxysms of his enthusiasm for the French Revolution, in January of 1793, Jefferson laid down the principle that there are (virtually) no limits to the slaughter that may legitimately be perpetrated in the name of liberty."[71] Had Jefferson been the extremist, justifier of all revolutionary violence as a means-to-an-end monster that some historians such as O'Brien suggest—how could the puritan John Adams, no friend of the Revolution in France, have kept, throughout his long life, such undying affection for him? Either Mr. O'Brien overstated his case, or John Adams was wrong.

What is perhaps most interesting is that over the course of their lifetimes, and through all the political differences that separated them, Jefferson and Adams eventually found each other again and reestablished their deep friendship. Adams's fond feelings for Jefferson in 1786 (long before their rift), as expressed by his closing a particular letter with "in great haste yours forever,"[72] is reflected much later on May 1, 1812 (post rift), with Adams closing his letter of that day, "I am still as I ever have been and ever shall be with great Esteem and regard your Friend,"[73] and again soon thereafter with, "I am, and shall be for life, your Friend."[74] This lifetime of affection and respect from Adams for Jefferson, even surviving a ten-year rift of total non-communication between them, is instructive of the nature of Jefferson's character at least in so far as his closest associates and friends understood him. How do those writers who dismiss Jefferson as an extremist with little regard for human life balance this characterization against Adams's deep affection and respect? A simplified, though strongly worded view of these complex men is sure to fall as insufficient (if not inaccurate) when the full weight of the courses of their lives, associations, and actions are reviewed and assessed.

Perhaps the simplest explanation for Jefferson's strong negative reaction to William Smith and William Short in favor of revolution in general, and of Jacobin France specifically, comes from a want of imagination. "When Jefferson said that the tree of liberty needs frequently to be watered with blood, and that rebellion is a good thing and necessary in the political world," one late nineteenth-century

Adams biographer wrote, "he showed that he lacked the constructive power to conceive a government which should be at once firm enough for civil order and elastic and changeable enough for liberty."[75]

Every generation writes its own histories, often reaching different conclusions from those who came before. What is seen as a minor failure of character by a late nineteenth-century historian, for example, can be viewed as a streak of barbarism and extremism by an historian one hundred years later. Our interpretations will change but the truth of the matter will not; it is our responsibility to weigh the evidence and to see and know the difference between the shadows of our prisms and the sometimes-dim light of historical truth. If the characterization of Thomas Jefferson as a heartless extremist is accurate, as some recent historians suggest, on what basis then did John Adams—the opposite of a populist extremist, and a deeply religious man—construct his profound affection for Jefferson? The multi-decade correspondence between Jefferson and Adams, and the full weight of the massive records left behind by them would suggest that Mr. Adams's respect and admiration for Jefferson were not misplaced.

Jefferson and Adams disagreed about the Revolution in France until the last years of their lives. Adams's early enthusiasm for the Revolution had disappeared along with that of most of the American people by the end of Washington's second term and Adams's election to the presidency in 1796. Jefferson's affection for France's Revolution, and for France in general, so clearly evident in his letter to Short, never faltered. When popular American support for the French and the institutional violence of that Revolution had evaporated and American policy shifted toward Great Britain, Jefferson did not shift with the majority view.

Adams, along with most Americans in and out of government, viewed the French Revolution with legitimate fear, apprehension, and revulsion; for them the French had taken a violent and destructive course that the American precedent had thankfully avoided. These failures and excesses were considered inexcusable by Adams and his fellow Federalists; and as French militarism expanded, their former ally became a serious potential enemy. Jefferson saw the Revolution in a very different way—excusing the violence by viewing the Revolution as far greater in importance than even the American experiment in which he had been so instrumental. Jefferson felt far more personally involved with and thus perhaps more attached to the French Revolution than did most Americans.

Though he strongly criticized Short, Jefferson also excused him for his negative opinions of the Revolution in France because, Jefferson wrote, "I know your republicanism to be pure, and that it is no decay of that which has embittered you against its votaries in France, but too great a sensibility at the partial evil which its object has been accomplished there."[76] Had Jefferson determined instead that Short's republican credentials were damaged by his horrified reaction to French revolutionary excesses, would Jefferson's response to Short have been quite different, and harsher? From all the evidence available regarding Jefferson's fanatical support for the Jacobin cause, the answer would most probably have been in the affirmative.

Three years after receipt of Short's disappointing communication from France, Jefferson received a package from Adams dated January 31, 1796. A letter and a book were enclosed. In the letter the future second president ominously asserted that, where relations with France were concerned, "reasoning has been all lost."[77] Jefferson replied at the end of February thanking Adams for "forwarding Mr. D'Ivernois' book on the French revolution. I receive everything with respect that comes from him. But it is on politics, a subject I never loved, and now hate."[78]

Jefferson's declaration of hatred for politics might seem disingenuous, or written for effect. When he wrote his response to Adams he had already achieved a long list of political accomplishments, offices, and honors including service in the Continental Congress, governor of Virginia, minister to France, and secretary of state (and later vice president, then president). These do not appear to be the accomplishments of a man who "never loved" and "now hates" politics. In support of the idea that Jefferson's assertion to Adams was in fact a truthful one is his later letter to Benjamin Stoddart.

"In my retirement I shall certainly divorce myself from all part in political affairs," Jefferson wrote in early 1809. "To get rid of them is the principal object of my retirement, and the first thing necessary to the happiness which, you justly observe, it is in vain to look for in any other situation."[79] As further support of the contention that Jefferson was not exaggerating to Adams when he claimed to hate politics, there is his letter to a correspondent written in 1793, in which Jefferson described the activities of politics as "hated occupations."[80] It is perhaps within this context of Jefferson's self-admitted and seemingly contradictory hatred of politics that his critical letter to William Short, and his "tree of liberty" letter to William Smith, can both best be understood.

One of the central themes found in the Jefferson-Adams correspondence, among many disparate subjects of discussion that showed both men at their ease as aging philosophers and statesmen, is the idea of just and effective government. This balance between justice and effectiveness (sometimes described as power, or authority of the state) was one of the essential points of contention between Federalists and Republicans.

Jefferson considered involvement in politics as a means to an end (the goal being the eradication of tyranny and the victory of democracy/republicanism), not a means in and of itself. The mundane functions of politics and the sometimes repetitive and tiresome daily duties of the politician were not attractive to him. Politics provided the tools that Jefferson needed in order to accomplish the revolutionary goals that motivated him. Politics then was something of a necessary evil to Jefferson and not a path of pleasure or the simple pursuit of personal power and honors. When his political goals had been met or he felt that he had done as much as he could do, he was eager to be done with it. He was not unaware however of the sometimes high personal costs of political engagement.

Jefferson knew that few who engaged in politics remained unaffected by the rising bitterness and partisanship of the times.[81] In a letter to Timothy Pickering he claimed that he would not allow his personal relationships to be impacted by political differences. This was the very same Timothy Pickering who had been secretary of state under Washington and Adams until dismissed by Adams toward the end of his administration over policy disagreements regarding France.

Adams had sharply criticized Pickering in the unfortunate correspondence with William Cunningham. Deeply hurt by Adams's negative comments, Pickering wrote an entire book in reply.[82] During
Jefferson's retirement years, while he was deeply involved in epistolary discussions of politics, history, and philosophy with Pickering's
nemesis Adams, it was to Pickering that Jefferson wrote that he "never
suffered a political to become a personal difference."[83] Perhaps, as he
wrote to Pickering, Jefferson may have been thinking of Adams and
their long friendship that had been broken for more than a decade by
political differences.

Jefferson accepted, as some others did not, that there would be
a bloody cost to revolution and the destruction of monarchist despotism. This acceptance of the human price of freedom made Jefferson
sometimes appear harsher and perhaps more callous than he truly
was. Having laid his life on the line in the American Revolution Jefferson expected that others, for *their* revolutions, would do the same.
This harsh calculus was applied to France specifically. In a letter to
Lafayette written after Jefferson's return to the US from France, the
then secretary of state wrote, "we are not to expect to be translated
from despotism to liberty in a feather-bed." Informing Lafayette
that he had "never feared for the ultimate result" of the Revolution
in France, he had however "feared for you (Lafayette) personally."
Noting the importance that he ascribed to Lafayette relative to the
Revolution in France, Jefferson concluded that if anything were to
happen to him the cost to France would be "oceans of blood, and
years of confusion and anarchy."[84] This was a premonition perhaps
on Jefferson's part but also an understandably dramatic flourish in
communicating with his friend who was deeply involved in revolutionary activities in the heart of Paris. Blood did flow in France and
across Europe, and confusion and conflict reached across the Atlantic, too. Jefferson however did not seem able or inclined to prognos-
ticate about the effect that the French Revolution would have on the
United States nor the lengths to which he would go to support it.

Jefferson (as well as Adams) had been very hopeful that the
ideals of the American Revolution would spread across the world,
and that liberty and freedom would become a reality for millions.

The Revolution that they were instrumental in creating ignited the French Revolution, which would eventually make its way back across the Atlantic to its point of origin. Jefferson had hoped that the concepts of freedom, republicanism, and anti-monarchism that he espoused in the American Revolution would find new vistas in which to flourish. His wishes were more than met in France but with an unexpectedly high price—the French revolutionaries were just as fervently expansionist in their ideas of revolution as Jefferson had been. The winds that once swept from America to Europe in the exciting and dark days of 1776 would return in a cold, bitter rush during the presidency of Jefferson's friend, John Adams. Jefferson, then the vice president, did what he could to support the Revolution. His support for the revolutionary French Republic cost him the trust of his friend, the president, and contributed significantly to the end of their long friendship. It also raised disturbing questions about Jefferson himself.

4

"The Universal Destroyer"

For men like Washington and Adams who valued order and stability, the bloody surge of the Revolution in France was cause for great concern. Washington's famous *Farewell Address* that was delivered to the American people in the form of posted broadsides and published in newspapers included strong warnings against international alliances based on anything other than national self-interest. When Adams took office he promised to construct his foreign policy with this *realpolitik* worldview as a firm foundation—most particularly as relations with England and France were concerned. As he began his presidency Adams had no misconceptions about the difficulties he would face.

In a letter to Abigail describing his inauguration (she was overseeing the farm in Quincy and missed the proceedings) the new president wrote that he thought he had heard President Washington ominously say, "Ay, I am fairly out, and you are fairly in! See which one of us will be the happiest!"[1]

By the inauguration of Adams as second president in March 1797 (with Jefferson as conflicted vice president), the Revolution in France had semi-stabilized. The "Directory," an executive, council-style government of five men, with one member replaced yearly,[2] ruled the country. Its focus was both expansionist, and defensive. Its other major concern, domestic stability, was never quite successfully managed. The National Convention had overthrown Robespierre and Jacobinism several years previously. When Adams took office, the Directory system was less than two years old. (It would be the last form of "revolutionary government" in France before Napoleon.)

French matters very swiftly divided President Adams and Vice President Jefferson. Ten years previously Jefferson had described his thinking process in a letter to Adams. Jefferson wrote that he "suspects an error in (his) process of reasoning" whenever "the same facts impress us differently." Though only ten years had passed since Jefferson made his declaration of reliance on Adams's judgment, perhaps, like Madame Roland and others, Jefferson experienced the passing of that decade as accelerated time. Extraordinary and stressful periods seem to have the effect for some of compressing time so that for Jefferson this decade may have seemed for him as if he had experienced the passage of, for example, eighty years. There is, however, no evidence other than conjecture to suggest that this is the case. While it is clear that Jefferson's letter to Adams in which he declared his dependence on Adams's logic survived, for Vice President Jefferson it was as if the letter—and its contents—had already been long forgotten and turned to dust.[3]

The French Revolution was extraordinary in its scope and character. It was founded upon the desire for an idealized country and society: a purpose that was appealing to many within and without France. Its ambitious goals surpassed mere politics. The Revolution and its essential ideas of governmental, societal, and economic restructuring recognized no national boundaries. Its universality terrified the aristocratic and clerical classes across Europe. Ironically, it also was seen as a threat by many (and later by most) Americans.

"All political and civil revolutions have been confined to a single country. The French Revolution had no country; one of its leading effects appeared to be to efface national boundaries from the map,"[4] Alexis De Tocqueville wrote. A renowned historian and analyst of the American Revolution, De Tocqueville later turned his insightful gaze toward his own country's catastrophic political upheavals. Just as De Tocqueville's analysis of American national character and early civic development has long been held in high esteem, his observations on the French Revolution are equally as valuable. Regarding the supranational character of the French Revolution and its associated ideas, he wrote, "It united and divided men, in spite of law, traditions, characters, language; converted enemies into fellow countrymen, and brothers into foes; or, rather, to speak more precisely, it created, far above particular nationalities, an intellectual country that was common to all, and in which every human creature could obtain rights of citizenship."[5]

De Tocqueville observed that the unifying nature of the French Revolution made it more similar to a religious, rather than any political, revolution that had preceded it. "Therefore," he wrote, "those who wish to examine the French Revolution by the light of analogy must compare it with religious revolutions."[6] The religious component of the Revolution is borne out by both the fervor with which the Revolution swept away ideas, people, institutions, and national boundaries, and the subsequent fostering of a rigid orthodoxy (depending on which phase of the Revolution one happened to be referring to). There was also the related export of the Revolution and republicanism outside of France.

Proselytizing French diplomats of the revolutionary republic would eventually be considered threats by both Washington and Adams. The perfidy of some of the official representatives of the French Republic in the United States, as well as their associates and American supporters, is likely the reason behind Adams's adoption of the controversial Alien and Sedition Acts. The negative popular reaction to these Acts (which were essentially war measures) was significant in the defeat of Adams for a second term and doubtless contributed to the rise of the vice president who actively but surreptitiously opposed them. Jefferson awkwardly claimed later that though he signed them as vice president he never truly supported them.

While no one was prosecuted under the Alien Act, which, with the associated Alien Enemies Act, authorized the president to expel foreigners suspected of disloyalty during time of war, its intended target was likely French agents and their associates. The Sedition Act allowed the president to prosecute anyone who insulted the president or Congress; one can imagine that this put a chill on the freedom of speech, and enraged the Jeffersonian-Republican opposition who saw themselves as the target of this law.

The anarchic and violent aspects of the Revolution in France, which had alienated William Short, John Adams, and many others, were so immense because "the French Revolution did not aim merely at a change in the old government; it designed to abolish the old form of society."[7] In describing the anarchy that many abroad feared from France and its possible effects on their own countries, De Tocqueville acknowledged the essentially destructive character of the Revolution. It "was bound to assail all forms of established authority together," De Tocqueville explained, "to destroy acknowledged influences; to efface traditions; to substitute new manners and usages for the old ones; in a word, to sweep out of men's minds all the notions which had hitherto commanded respect and obedience."[8]

One of the central reasons why Jefferson and American Republicans supported the French Revolution was that the revolutionaries of France had been inspired by Jefferson's written words. His rhetoric of inalienable rights and mankind's essential equality were representations of concepts that Jefferson did not intend to be reserved for (non-slave) Americans alone. For the French revolutionaries their rebellion against monarchic despotism was eventually meant to uplift not only Frenchman—but all of Europe and beyond.

As might be expected, the revolution-without-limits approach of the revolutionaries in France created suspicion and fear among many people across Europe and in the United States, including supporters of France. The French Revolution was so threatening to some for the very same reason that it was so attractive to others—its universality. "It dealt with the citizen in the abstract, independent of particular social organizations, just as religions deal with mankind in general, independent of time and place. It inquired, not what were the particular rights of French citizens, but what were the general rights and duties of mankind in reference to political concerns," De Tocqueville observed. "It was by thus divesting itself of all that was peculiar to one race or time, and by reverting to natural principles of social order and government, that it became intelligible to all, and susceptible of simultaneous imitation in a hundred different places."[9]

"By seeming to tend rather to the regeneration of the human race than to the reform of France alone, it roused passions such as the most violent political revolutions had been incapable of awakening,"[10] De Tocqueville wrote. The massive and swift changes that the Revolution in France brought, the violent excesses, wars, reforms, new governments, "made the Revolution appear even greater than it was. It appeared the universal destroyer."[11]

There is a great and unfortunate irony that the bloody Revolution in France came to be seen as an existential threat to many, if not most, of the countries of Europe. Fear of expansionist revolutionary France was not limited to the ruling classes alone, who appeared to have the most to lose. The belief in the United States that republican France presented a threat as great to America as Great Britain was widely held as Adams became president in 1797. The armies of the French Republic, swollen by the *levée en masse* to many hundreds of thousands of soldiers under arms, among whose commanders was the extraordinarily successful General Napoleon Bonaparte, would bring war to Britain, Austria, Belgium, Prussia, Russia, Holland, Italy, and others. In a final, bitter insult to the goals of the Revolution Bonaparte would overthrow the French republican government itself and declare himself Emperor in 1804 during Jefferson's first presidential term.

The wars of the French Revolution expanded the martial culture and capabilities of France. The republican goal to export the Revolution (at least) across Europe resulted in a kind of duel to the death with the monarchies of Europe. Reasonably concluding that the proselytizing and fanatical nature of the Revolution would necessarily mean that their monarchic forms of government would likely forever be targets of French revolutionary agitation and aggression, several countries formed coalitions to oppose and defeat France. For the monarchies of Europe nothing short of their own survival motivated them.

Adams as president would find dealing with the Directory particularly challenging because there did not appear to be a consistent foreign policy from Paris to which his administration could definitively and confidently respond. For example, "convinced that the 'victory of liberty over despotism' spelled an end to wars, the National Assembly had resolved in May 1790 that the French nation renounces the initiation of war for the purposes of conquest." The Comte de Mirabeau, its most influential early leader, proclaimed in August that "the moment is not far off when liberty will acquit mankind of the crime of war." Finally, the French Constitution of September 1791 incorporated the renunciation of "war for the purpose of conquest" in Article 6.[12] Such hopeful, if contextually impractical and confusing, sentiments from the revolutionary government of the time did little to facilitate the end of war for France (or any of the countries it attacked). While war for conquest was renounced in the Constitution of late 1791, only months later the opposite message was delivered by Girondin leader, Jacques-Pierre Brissot who said, "a people who have conquered liberty after ten centuries of slavery need war . . . to cleanse liberty from the vices of despotism."[13]

A critical aspect of the tragedies of Brissot and of Lafayette, two early revolutionary leaders who were later overwhelmed by the rapidity of events, was that their direct experiences with American politics made them among the few in French revolutionary leadership circles with a background in, and an understanding of, the value of constitutionalism. Regarding Brissot's capacity to participate in organizing order out of the chaos of the Revolution, an historian of the early revolutionary period wrote that "he was fitted to take an intelligent part in the work of the States-General. He had resided in England, had traveled in America, and probably had a more accurate knowledge of American constitutional methods than any other Frenchman save Lafayette."[14] Brissot's heated rhetoric espousing war can be forgiven somewhat when the fanaticism of those involved directly and indirectly is placed in a wider context. Jefferson did as much in a letter to him written in May 1793: "I continue eternally attached to the principles of your revolution. I hope it will end in the establishment of some firm government, friendly to liberty, & capable of maintaining it. If it does, the world will become inevitably free."[15] Six months later Brissot was dead, swept away to the guillotine by the unforgiving political shifts and torrents of the Revolution.

Brissot's and Lafayette's approach to revolution may have been a bit more American in style than their countrymen were prepared to accept. Distrust and fear became common in Paris as security and stability swiftly broke down; official Terror would eventually be the literal "order of the day." Rapidly changing political circumstances resulted in uncertainty, systemic failures, and fear, so much so that even such essential matters as the provisioning of the city of Paris had partisan political tinges.

The storming of the Bastille in July 1789 and the subsequent upheavals brought the orderly functioning of Paris to a dangerous halt. According to one historian, the city of Paris was soon afterward in dire circumstances. "If nothing was done," he wrote, "within two days there would be no bread."[16] Even when a competent and experienced supply agent was available, for example, he could not—for his own safety—be tasked. "It was impossible to entrust the task to experienced hands like those of M. Doumer. . . . He was associated with the old order, and distrust was so great that to give him authority in this manner would probably have led only to his own destruction. . ."[17]

Distrust of the old order may have brought the people of Paris close to starvation early in the Revolution, but a desire to protect that order certainly prompted some foreign rulers to take action against France. Motivated by the French royal family's unsuccessful attempt to escape the country in 1791 (an event known as "the flight to Varennes"), an international alliance of monarchies was formed to oppose France. The Declaration of Pilnitz, an agreement between Prussia and Austria, was signed in August 1791 as a military warning to France that King Louis was not to be harmed nor excluded from rule. The Pilnitz Declaration had a swift result in that the king was brought into the revolutionary government. This arrangement did not last long however as less than two years passed before King Louis XVI and his queen, Marie-Antoinette, were executed by guillotine. Pilnitz was but the first of several international coalitions formed to oppose the Revolution in France. "When the principal sovereigns of Germany proclaimed at Pilnitz, in 1791, that all the powers of Europe were menaced by the danger which threatened royalty in France, they said what was true, but at bottom they were far from thinking so,"

Alexis De Tocqueville wrote in 1854. They "thought they knew—that the French Revolution was a mere local and ephemeral accident, which might be turned to account." They were profoundly mistaken. De Tocqueville described the signatories of Pilnitz and other monarchs of Europe at that time, as "ready . . . for every thing except that which was going to happen."[18]

Few anywhere understood how extensive, comprehensive, and shocking the Revolution in France would become. Jefferson did not see, nor did Adams (though he was closer to the mark); even Lafayette, the French nobleman who, prior to the Revolution in his own country, had gone to America to fight for American liberty, was completely unaware of—and unprepared for—the massive upheavals that would overtake France. As a major general in the American army and aide to George Washington, he became a national hero in both America and France. With his republican credentials unassailable, Lafayette returned to France to play a significant role but soon found himself and his American/Jeffersonian-inspired constitutional goals (that involved the retention of the king as head of state in some capacity) frustrated and finally defeated. Lafayette, too—like Brissot and so many others—would be swept away by the machine of universal destruction that the Revolution became.

An early leader of the Revolution in France, and a close associate and friend of American minister to France, Thomas Jefferson, Lafayette's dream of a new republican France based on constitutionally defined rights, and one linked with an officially diminished yet involved monarchy, was quickly subsumed by the radicalism of Jacobinism and the influence of the Parisian sans-culottes. "All these ingredients combined will lead [us] gradually, without major upheaval, to an independent representation," Lafayette hopefully wrote in an October 1787 letter to Washington, "hence to a diminution of royal authority."[19] Perhaps Lafayette, once one of the wealthiest nobles in all of Europe, had become overly optimistic as a consequence of his experiences in the American Revolution.

The leaders of the republican rebellion in the British colonies (most particularly Jefferson) hoped that their brand of constitutional republicanism would be exported, and that monarchies across Europe would be replaced by it. After Lafayette's return to France, his early revolutionary activities there were inspired by the American model and by his personal association with Jefferson as the American minister in Paris. Lafayette saw this as an extension and continuation of his revolutionary activities in America. After Lafayette ordered that the Bastille be destroyed, he penned a letter to his great friend and former commander, George Washington. Lafayette included the main key to the Bastille along with his letter, explaining that "it is a tribute Which I owe as a Son to My Adoptive father, as an aid de camp to My General, as a Missionary of liberty to its Patriarch."[20]

In the early days of the French Revolution, French and American revolutionaries shared the desire for a "diminution" of the monarchy in France. Lafayette's overly hopeful and idealistic plans for cooperation and compromise with the King were eventually, along with their messenger, soundly rejected in France. In early 1792, then in command of a French army on the French-Austrian border defending against a feared invasion by the Pilnitz signatories, Lafayette wrote to Washington, "I Always Consider Myself, my dear General, as one of Your lieutenants on a detached command."[21] It should come as no surprise that Lafayette would have then, in the midst of such difficult and threatening circumstances, thought back to his successful days with Washington.

As he composed his letter to Washington at his headquarters on the Austrian border, with war clouds growing and his own circumstances in France failing, Lafayette's thoughts appeared to return to his experiences in America. His recollection of a signal victory in 1778 over an overwhelmingly superior force of British and Hessians at Barren Hill, fought while on detached service as a trusted lieutenant of General Washington, perhaps filled his mind with happier thoughts.[22]

There would be no stunning escape from encircling forces for Lafayette like that at Barren Hill—the French monarchy would be overthrown within months and a Jacobin arrest warrant would prompt him to abandon his army and flee France. From revered revolutionary leader to a hunted man, Lafayette's fall was extraordinary and, much like the shifting winds of the Revolution itself, seemingly too swift.

The ideas of compromise and cooperation that Lafayette had champi-
oned were annihilated and a shocking new phase of the Revolution in
France began. Seven months after his letter to Washington, Lafayette
was arrested by Austrian troops to whom he had defected. The once-
great hero of France, in whose person the hopes and dreams of constitutionalists resided, would spend the next five years as a prisoner,
under often harsh confinement, of several monarchist governments.

When the Revolution swept over France and brought war to
Europe it came to most observers as a stunning, unexpected, unprec-
edented shock. Summarizing the magnitude of the Revolution, De
Tocqueville wrote,

> Meanwhile, the Revolution pursued its course. It was not till the
> strange and terrible physiognomy of the monster's head was visi-
> ble; till it destroyed civil as well as political institutions, manners,
> customs, laws, and even the mother tongue; till, having dashed in
> pieces the machine of government, it shook the foundations of soci-
> ety, and seemed anxious to assail even God himself; till it over-
> flowed the frontier, and, by dint of methods unknown before . . .
> overthrew the landmarks of empires, broke crowns, and crushed
> subjects.[23]

In the early days, the Revolution's challenge to the stability and existence of European monarchies was not fully understood by most
observers. "The sovereigns and statesmen began to see what they had
taken for a mere every-day accident in history was an event so new,
so contrary to all former experience, so widespread, so monstrous
and incomprehensible, that the human mind was lost in endeavoring
to examine it," De Tocqueville wrote.[24] The ruling powers of Europe
determined that war against France and the destruction of the Revolution were necessary if their legitimacy to rule were to survive.
However, much to the horror of the rulers of Europe and many others,
the militarism of revolutionary France would not be concluded with
the demise of the Revolution.

At the end of the Revolution, marked by Napoleon's rise to power
from servant of the Revolution to dictator in 1804, the new monarch/
dictator/emperor of France embraced the idea of the necessity of war-

fare even surpassing that of his predecessors. Napoleon believed that
aggressive war was obligatory and unavoidable simply because, as he
put it, "between the old monarchies and the young republic the spirit
of hostilities must always exist."[25] The universality of the revolutionary message and the expansionist militarism that had been created
to sustain and spread it ". . . led them (European monarchs)" as one
historian observed, "to resist to the utmost, or if defeated and forced
to sign peace treaties, to repudiate them at the first opportunity and to
mobilize all resources until they finally overcame him (Bonaparte)."[26]
For the monarchies of Europe the French Revolution presented a
literal and immediate challenge to their survival and—whether it
was headed by a temporary constitution, councils, communes, sans-
culottes mobs, Jacobins, Girondins, Directory, or finally, warlord/
emperor/dictator—there was little alternative left to them but to fight
the revolutionary, and later the Napoleonic, hordes of France.

In America, however, the Revolution in France was applauded—
at first, and was seen by most citizens as a natural by-product of 1776.
Hadn't Lafayette, the much-loved aide to Washington and hero of the
American Revolution, returned to France to work for the founding
of a similar constitutional republic in his homeland, and risked his
life once again? In the early days of the French Revolution, most
Americans viewed France as a new, and most welcome, sister republic.
France had, after all, been instrumental in helping the American
revolutionaries secure their independence from Great Britain.
The overwhelming support in the new United States for its "sister
republic" would not outlast the destruction of the friendly monarchist
government of Louis XVI that had sent ships, men, and money to
aid America's War for Independence. The significant financial and
military support that the French monarchy gave to the United States
played an important part in the eventual economic failures that would
help to bring revolution to France.

Ironically, it had been monarchist Bourbon France that had sent so
much treasure and military power to American shores to help American anti-monarchist revolutionaries fight the British. Most American
leaders understood that it was in the interest of the royal government
of France to support the American revolutionaries as a lever against

their traditional British enemy; the loss of Britain's colonies could not but help the French. This concept of national self-interest, which is the foundation of a classic and icily pragmatic view of international relationships (later understood as "realpolitik"), would be the core of Washington's, and later Adams's, national policy toward revolutionary France. Jefferson and his new party, the Democratic-Republicans, did not share this view.

The decline of American popular and official support for revolutionary France would increase internal American political disagreements and partisanship, as well as become a focal point in the growing crisis between the newly independent American Republic and its once-beloved former ally.

5

"Their Virtuous Enterprise"

B Y THE SUMMER of 1824, much of John Adams's rancor and ill will
had mellowed. One of the great events of that year for him, Jefferson,
and for the entire country was the return of their friend Lafayette to
America. Welcomed back by an adoring and thankful country, fully
aware that the success of the United States had been significantly
aided by his efforts and sacrifices, Lafayette was feted everywhere he
travelled as a great friend of America and the last surviving general
of the Revolution. Lafayette knew that this national tour would be
the last time he would see his aging friends Adams and Jefferson. In
August, he paid his respects to Adams.

Charles Francis Adams, later a noted diplomat, historian, and
author, was there, too, as witness to this important event. Following
in the footsteps of his father, John Quincy, and those of his grandfather, Charles Francis, then a young man of seventeen, was already
an assiduous diarist. According to him, General Lafayette arrived at
Peace field with a small entourage early in the afternoon of Sunday,
August 29, 1824. Adams's grandson noted that the aging general and
hero appeared surprised at how "feeble" Adams had become and
"was affected somewhat."[1] The young man was observant of everyone during the visit, particularly noting that his grandfather appeared
". . . rather more striking now than ever, certainly more agreeable, as

his asperity of temper is worn away."[2] Charles Francis was introduced to Lafayette but the diarist included no details of their conversation. Most interesting is the young Adams's impressions. "I had the honour of an introduction to the Marquis and that was all," wrote young Adams. "He is a mincing man in his manners, he has much ease and grace and knows the proper side of men. His lot is an enviable one, on the whole, as without being an extremely great man, he has received honors which are the lot of only a few."[3]

It is impossible to determine if Charles Francis Adams's less than overwhelmingly positive impression of the great hero of the Revolution was informed somehow by anything his grandfather might have said to him. Charles Francis did not explain what he thought was the difference between an "extremely great man" and someone slightly less so. The implication from the young Adams is that he felt Lafayette to be "great," but not so in the "extreme." This limited or semi-greatness is one of the most endearing and attractive qualities of Lafayette's character. As with John Adams and Thomas Jefferson, none of the revolutionary generation was without their flaws and foibles.

They were also not without the damages and changes that time had brought to them. After the visit, John Adams, then in his late eighties, concluded that he had been "highly delighted" with it, though his remark, "that was not the Lafayette that I knew," is made almost delightful only by Lafayette's similar observation that "that was not the John Adams I knew."[4]

When Lafayette made his way to Monticello in early November, similar reactions occurred. Lafayette was then sixty-seven and Jefferson eighty-one. James Madison, who was there at Monticello on the day of Lafayette's visit, observed of Lafayette that he had "so much increased in bulk and changed in aspect that I should not have known him."[5] For Jefferson, the passage of time, and changes in appearance, could not cause him to mistake his great friend and co-Republican with whom he had worked so closely in Paris in those hopeful days prior to the Revolution there.

While serving as American minister to France, Jefferson had been active in advising the early revolutionaries, particularly Lafayette. At least one strategy meeting was held at Jefferson's residence at the Hôtel de Langeac.[6] As Jefferson was a diplomatic official in the very early days of the American Republic he may not have been given extensively detailed instructions (if any) as to how to comport himself in the capital city of a friendly country in the midst of a possible looming revolution. It is unlikely today that an American Ambassador would host revolutionaries at his official residence during the early days (or any days) of a national upheaval in the capital of a *friendly* country.

Jefferson favored the republican Revolution in France though it had been the monarchist government which had so significantly aided with men and money the Americans in their own Revolution against England. Lafayette, an early constitutionalist revolutionary, visited him (along with several fellow activists). An important subject of discussion was the direction that the Revolution in France, then in its planning stages, should take.

The Marquis and his revolutionary friends wanted to create a constitutional republic on the American example, while Jefferson was more cautious. The American minister suggested a model closer to that of Great Britain which included the retention of the monarch (at least temporarily). The document that would lay out these revolutionary plans was to be the *Declaration of the Rights of Man and of the Citizen*. While his role was advisory to the French constitutional group, "Jefferson's influence on the Marquis in this regard was probably greater than appears in any formal record."[7]

United by a belief of the universality of republicanism, Lafayette and Jefferson had a long and special friendship—two revolutionary fighters whose shared goal had been nothing less than to change the world. When Lafayette arrived at Monticello and stepped from his carriage in the late autumn of 1824, mutual recognition was immediate, "Ah, Jefferson! Ah, Lafayette!"[8]

As a way to gain further insight into the man that Jefferson was it is important to examine, as with Adams, how he interacted privately with his friends. Most people, notable or not, have mixed feelings about their friends—Jefferson was no exception. Jefferson was not one to withhold his feelings, positive or negative, at least under the protective cover of a US Postal Service stamp and an envelope's seal. These sometimes harsh private critiques of friends by Jefferson are important insights into his often contrary nature, a character in its fullness and complexity that has caused consternation, confusion, and anger since long before his death two years after Lafayette's visit in 1824.

In a remarkable 1787 letter written from Paris to his political confidante and friend James Madison, Jefferson shared his positive and negative opinions of both Adams and Lafayette. Jefferson did not mince words in his private correspondence, expecting forbearance from those to whom he wrote, and safety from prying eyes in the sealed envelopes of the time. In a vein of criticism similar to that of Adams's communications to Cunningham, Jefferson provided biting (though mixed) character sketches and observations of both men to Madison who had then "returned into Congress."[9] When this letter was written Adams was minister to Great Britain in London, Jefferson was in Paris as minister to France, and Lafayette was a representative of the nobles to the Estates-General in Paris during the early period of the Revolution in France. As with much of Jefferson's correspondence the letter is a lengthy one.

The verbosity of this letter is worthy of comment because Jefferson had painfully injured his wrist in a fall only several months before.[10] The injury was slow to heal and particularly vexing to him since it affected almost everything (in his view) but for his ability to write. It would be an overly simple perspective to suggest that Jefferson's criticism of Adams and Lafayette, both of whom Jefferson respected and considered friends, could have been related in some way to his injured wrist and the ongoing discomfiture that it caused. More insightful perhaps is that Jefferson thought it important enough to ignore the pain in his wrist to write a lengthy letter of essential character analysis to Madison.[11]

Jefferson's occasionally harsh—though privately expressed—views of friends and colleagues, in this case meant for Madison's eyes alone, reflect an ongoing desire to confidentially speak his truth to his friends in a way that, considered by readers outside the correspondence, might seem mean-spirited. This "backstabbing" of individuals with whom Jefferson had ongoing cordial associations and friendships, both before and after his criticisms, has prompted some later historians to view Jefferson as disingenuous or false. There is little to defend in the sometimes bitter rhetoric that Jefferson shared with friends regarding other friends except to say that such private correspondences were meant simply to be just that, private; and the views and conclusions that later students of Jefferson formulated regarding these communications ought to be viewed by modern readers with a respectful caution. While such disturbing personal criticisms do provide a fuller view of the man, they should not be overly weighted amidst thousands of letters and thousands more of public documents and utterances, nor considered to be definitive insights into the essential nature of his character.

Jefferson's enduring appeal, despite recent controversies regarding his likely long-term sexual relationship with his slave Sally Hemings, is founded in large part on his extraordinary complexity. A man is not defined by a single component of his character. Jefferson continued important friendships with both Lafayette and Adams (not inclusive of their ten-year hiatus of silence). Jefferson's trust of confidentiality between himself and his friends would almost universally be honored, though not without a few unpleasant exceptions.

In a lengthy letter to Madison dated from Paris, January 30, 1787, Jefferson covered a number of important political considerations. He weighed the value of three types of government—no government, systems in which the people have a say (more so in America and less so in England), and "governments of force," which were most all other monarchies and other republics. The second option was clearly the favored one "as the mass of mankind under that, enjoys a precious degree of liberty and happiness." But the benefits of republicanism also had "its evils too," which Jefferson identified specifically as "the turbulence to which it is subject."[12] A strong case could be made that Jefferson's own statements and actions contributed significantly to this turbulence in the United States as well as his later partisan statements and actions while secretary of state, vice president, and president.

Perhaps Jefferson ought to be forgiven for his mixed views of close friends, and for his privately sharing his opinions of them, and put that and every other issue of disputation and discord into that great bucket of "turbulence" that necessarily is filled when humans are able to express their views without the bitter strong arm of the despot preventing them their free expressions. Republicanism is necessarily disputatious and turbulent because people in such a society have the freedom and the right to express most any view and opinion they wish.

This letter of Jefferson to Madison is oftquoted for the singular line that "a little rebellion, now and then, is a good thing, and as necessary in the political world as storms in the physical."[13] More strongly still, Jefferson wrote that occasional rebellions against even republican governments are "a medicine necessary for the sound health of government."[14] Jefferson's appreciation for the value of rebellion explains in large part his support of the French Revolution, but did not diminish his equal appreciation for the stabilization and perfection of his own revolutionary experiment at home. In pursuit of this pragmatic course Jefferson provided these private character sketches of Adams and Lafayette specifically for the increase of Madison's knowledge and effectiveness in his role in Congress. "As you are now returned into Congress it will become of importance that you should form a just estimate of certain public characters," Jefferson wrote to his political colleague and friend. "On which, therefore I will give you such notes, as my knolege [sic] of them has furnished me with. You will compare them with the materials you are otherwise possessed of, and decide on a view of the whole."[15] His mixed critique of Adams has already been described,[16] while that of Lafayette is as equally insightful and only slightly less disturbing.

Jefferson was highly complementary of Lafayette, noting his "zeal," "good sense," and rising popularity. Speculating that one day "he will be of the ministry," Jefferson does not neglect to mention his "foible" which is "a canine appetite for popularity and fame."[17] Perhaps his point was that men who *seek* fame for itself may make decisions that are better suited for the results of press and adoration than they might be for the furtherance of the Revolution then building in France. Jefferson's doubts about Lafayette however, did not diminish his affection and respect for him. As something of a bridge between the American and French revolutions, Lafayette's importance could not be overturned for Jefferson by any concerns about his character foibles. Jefferson would stand with Lafayette as he would for France itself.

Jefferson's affection for France was as strong as his distaste for England and its king, sentiments that were of course shared by Adams. The great difference between Adams and Jefferson in this regard was their worldview and sense of political realities. After the founding of the United States, Jefferson remained a dedicated revolutionary, with France being his particular focus; Adams continued as the great American patriot and politician focused (politically) primarily on American matters. Later, their paths would diverge on this issue of France with Jefferson's revolutionary predilections guiding his decisions—which were sometimes in opposition to the *realpolitik* of both Washington and Adams.

"Nothing should be spared on our part, to attach this country (France) to us," he wrote in his lengthy letter to Madison of late January 1787. "Its inhabitants love us more, I think, than they do any other nation on earth."[18] France's strong support of America's revolutionary efforts and its ongoing opposition to Great Britain made France endlessly attractive to Jefferson. Not long after Jefferson wrote his letter to Madison, the French king would be overthrown and executed, and the Revolution there take on a much darker and more sinister character than almost anything seen in the American War for Independence.

New revolutionary governments would appear in France and the strong, favorable connection that most Americans had had for France diminished, so that by the time Adams was president and Jefferson his not-so-cooperative vice president, the period of amicable relations between France and the United States was but a swiftly fading memory. Jefferson would be good to his word to Madison and spared little on his part to keep France and the new American Republic linked, particularly against their common British foe.

In a letter to Jefferson dated December 6, 1787, Adams wrote of his views of the new American Constitution and of the powers of the president as he would have preferred them explaining that he would have "given more Power to the president and less to the Senate."[19] Adams viewed the presidency as a unifying force in the new government so long as the office was a sufficiently powerful and independent one. Suggesting that nomination and appointment authority should be held alone by the president, with assistance only by a "Privy Council of his own creation," Adams explained that "not a Vote or Voice would I have given to the Senate or any Senator, unless he were of the Privy Council."[20] Adams's preference for a strong executive, typical of the federalist position, tends to suggest a belief in a strong individual with great authority at the center of government. This is the essence of the monarchist complaints against Adams by Republicans, and Jefferson himself. "You are apprehensive the President when chosen, will be chosen again and again as long as he lives. So much the better as it appears to me," Adams unfortunately and controversially declared.[21] While Adams defended this view of potentially lifelong presidents as a counterbalance to elections, which he feared,[22] it is not difficult to understand why Jefferson and other Republicans saw a taint of monarchist ideas in Adams's writings and thought.[23]

In fact, Adams's letter to Jefferson of December 6, 1787, has been cited by one enterprising historian as a key moment between the two—when Jefferson realized that perhaps Adams was not the republican revolutionary that he had once thought. This letter from Adams, among others, according to the historian, "brought to the surface differences so striking that Jefferson must have been jarred by them."[24] It is impossible to know Jefferson's reaction to Adams's letter of December sixth because his only response to it was to acknowledge its receipt. Jefferson's lack of response cannot be seen as telling in and of itself as both men were then overwhelmed with their diplomatic duties, and extensive official and private correspondence. Jefferson, certainly more so than Adams (especially during their later correspondence post-1811), carefully chose the points to which he responded; Jefferson rarely replied to letters acknowledging and responding to every point, question, or comment.

Jefferson may have viewed Adams's lack of enthusiasm for republicanism as anti-republican heresy and taken action on account of it. One historian has suggested that Jefferson may have caused the suppression of the French translation of Adams's 1787 political analysis tome, *A Defence of the Constitutions of Government of the United States of America*, to minimize its potential damage to the Revolution.[25] "In tackling these difficult questions," another historian explained, "Adams studied the histories of various ancient, medieval, and modern republics as though he were a natural scientist conducting experiments."[26] Adams approached politics and governmental organization using historical and comparative analysis very much like a modern-day political scientist. "A learned and heavy work" in three volumes, the *Defence* was intended by Adams as a "political guide for his countrymen . . . and a critique of democracy," which Adams "like the Greek philosophers, equated with mob-government."[27] As one of the founders of the United States and a dedicated supporter of constitutional government, Adams was by no means an aristocrat nor a monarchist.[28] But his balanced and analytical approach to government was not then the popular view, and his conclusions were not at all in accord with the republicanism espoused by the French revolutionaries and, more importantly, by Jefferson and his supporters.

There had been some correspondence between the two while Jefferson remained in Paris about finding a suitable publisher for Adams's book, though no French translation ever appeared during Jefferson's tenure there.[29] Perhaps Jefferson had prematurely offered to help Adams to find a French translator and publisher before he had read the book, then changed his mind once he had. To explain Jefferson's early enthusiasm for Adams's book one historian suggests that "Jefferson apparently had not read the *Defence* closely."[30] However, this is likely not the case, as Jefferson wrote to Adams on February 23, 1787, that he had "read your book with infinite satisfaction and improvement. It will do great good in America. It's learning and it's [sic] good sense will I hope make it an institute for our politicians, old as well as young."[31] Perhaps this was Jefferson overstating his respect for Adams and expanding upon his earlier deference that "in the course of our joint services that I think right when I think with you."[32] More than likely it is Jefferson being honest; he *had* read the book just as he said that he had—he even challenged one of Adams's points (and cited the page number), stating that "there is one opinion in it however, which I will ask you to reconsider, because it appears to me not entirely accurate, and not likely to do good."[33] The failure of a translation of Adams's *Defence* to appear in France—though Jefferson had promised his assistance in procuring a translator and publisher—ought not to be thought of as evidence by which an indictment of Jefferson for overzealous protection of the French Revolution at the expense of his friendship with Adams could be made.

There is no evidence now available that would support the theory that Jefferson had "connive(d) at such a suppression."[34] However, Jefferson's strongly held revolutionary views and deep support for the French Revolution being known, it is not outside the realm of the possible that Jefferson did block the French translation of Adams's book. No defense of Jefferson is required as this theory is built entirely on conjecture and thus cannot be considered definitive or conclusive. It should be noted however that Jefferson's revolutionary beliefs were all-consuming and that he would not necessarily have seen the blocking of a translation of Adams's book as a personal affront to his friend and colleague. Jefferson separated political views and friendship throughout his life and sustained a great affection for Adams in particular through many years of strident political differences. Jefferson's desire to walk the fine line between friendship and political partisanship was not altogether successful however, as the decade of silence between him and Adams attests.

Adams's opposition to republicanism is generally understood to be a key element of the political differences between Adams and Jefferson. This disagreement, which would later result in over ten years of chilly silence between these great old friends, was made more potent through its linkage with their differences about the Revolution in France. Adams's preference for the British monarchy over the French Revolutionary Directory during his presidency seemed to confirm these suspicions for Jefferson. Certainly, Adams's detractors and critics asserted, support of the Jay Treaty with London was additional confirmation of Adams's preference for England versus France; there would be more.

There was much more to what was thought at the time to be Adams's supposed "monarchist tendencies" than met the eye, particularly relative to the difficult years of conflict with revolutionary France that occurred during his presidency. Little more fodder for criticism of Adams was then needed by Jefferson, Madison, or any of Adams's many political opponents. Despite Adams's numerous attempts to explain his political views in ways that would convince his critics, and which would quiet what, in his view, were their ridiculous association of him and monarchism, Adams was never quite successful. "Adams had always demonstrated outright genius at making himself misunderstood on the seminal political issues of his time," one Adams biographer observed.[35]

There was likely no political issue at that moment more seminal than the struggle between republicanism and monarchy; this was after all the very conflict that characterized the American Revolution itself. Since Adams's unintentionally controversial letter to Jefferson of early December 1787 came during a time of heavy diplomatic activity for both men, amidst a flurry of planning by Adams for his return to the United States from London, there is little surprise then in Jefferson's decision to not respond substantively to Adams's comments except to acknowledge receipt.[36]

This political rift came to light long before the Adams-Jefferson administration began in 1797. Jefferson viewed their conflicts as ideological/philosophical while Adams would later come to see them in the context of party and excessive partisanship and alarming ambition on the part of his soon-to-be former friend. Jefferson regarded his own actions as simply an extension of his revolutionary fervor, whose goal was to rescue the American Revolution from being derailed from its republican populist course by the Federalists (led by Hamilton, Washington, and Adams).

Adams and Jefferson came to be identified as leading representatives of two divergent views of government within the United States; the former for a strong center, the latter for populist republicanism in its many forms both pragmatic and utopian. The two rising political parties that represented these views, Federalists and Democratic-Republicans (later known as Democrats though often referred to during that period as simply "Republicans"), would completely change the landscape of American politics forever.

Jefferson's support of the Revolution in France, regardless of its excesses and violence, was linked to his opposition of "monarchism." He was completely opposed to monarchism in its literal form, particularly in England and France, but he also used the term as a dysphemism for any government in which, in his estimation, excessive powers were held at the center, putting him directly at ideological odds with federalism, and with Adams.

As president, Jefferson eventually would have the opportunity to implement his revolutionary concepts via national foreign policy. During the Embargo Acts period of his second term, he inadvertently brought the new country closest to its first bout with secession. The Embargo Acts were, in a sense, an official embrace by Jefferson of what he had all his life opposed—an overly strong central authority. These economic and diplomatic policies were meant to pressure European states and were not symptomatic of a shift in the republican views that Jefferson had long held, though many critics believed that is exactly what they were. Rather, Jefferson had meant for them to facilitate another revolution—this time in international relations.

Some historians have suggested that the Embargo Acts so strongly supported by Jefferson, despite extreme domestic opposition, and the serious economic hardships that they caused at home, represented the lowest point of either of his two terms as chief executive. Having been instrumental in a world-shaking revolution at home, and actively supportive of a second one in France, it is reasonable to consider that Jefferson, the indefatigable inventor and revolutionary, would desire a similar revolution in how nations interacted.

The new revolution in international affairs was to be the Embargo Acts, a policy signed into law late in 1807 intended to pressure England and France to discontinue their harassment of American ships, British impressments of American sailors, and seizures of goods and vessels by both. Jefferson saw the Embargo Acts as an economic and diplomatic alternative to war with England or France. "We have to choose between the alternatives of Embargo and war," Jefferson wrote to Thomas Lehré in November 1808. "There is indeed one and only one other; that is submission and tribute."[37] The act would eventually bar not only imports from the two warring states but ban American commercial exports *in toto*.[38] The intended consequences of the embargo, to influence the foreign policy of France and England in favor of the desires of the United States by causing them economic inconvenience (and worse), did not come to fruition.

The unintended consequences of this policy of economic coercion (or war-by-other-means[39]) were dramatic economic suffering in the US, and the birth of a secession movement based mainly in the New England states where seagoing commerce, devastated by the embargo, was its lifeblood. Only months before the lifting of the embargo in March 1809, Jefferson acknowledged that his revolutionary policy had created "opposition . . . in one quarter . . ." that "amounted almost to rebellion and treason."[40] Very much like the ineffective cotton embargo implemented by the Confederate States to bully European governments into intervening on their behalf (and thus have access to the Southern cotton supply) during the Civil War fifty years later (a policy described as "King Cotton" diplomacy[41]), Jefferson's experiment would ultimately fail. It failed very simply because more damage was done to Americans than was done to anyone associated with France and England.

What Jefferson had attempted unsuccessfully with the embargo in 1807–1808 was similar to Adams's success in avoiding war with France ten years before. Both presidents were required by circumstances to deal with France and England as major issues of their administrations. Their purpose in both cases was to keep the United States out of a European war. Both were successful in that goal but paid a high personal price, as the reputation of both men suffered greatly. Had the Embargo Acts come during Jefferson's first term rather than the second, it is likely that he would not have been re-elected. This was the fate of President Adams's hopes for a second term—dashed upon the rocks of the French Revolution. Long before Jefferson's unsuccessful efforts to pressure post-revolutionary Napoleonic France and monarchical Britain by withholding from them

American commerce, his friend Lafayette's dream of a French constitutional republic had been shattered. Lafayette himself languished in prisons for years despite the intercession of American diplomats and a dramatic though unsuccessful rescue attempt by American expatriates in Europe.

In early March 1793, Washington instructed Jefferson to write a letter of consolation to Lafayette's wife, the Marquise, to express the president's sympathy for Lafayette's ongoing imprisonment in Austria. Jefferson's pro-revolutionary viewpoint is clear: "My affection to his nation and to himself are unabated and, notwithstanding the line of separation which has been unfortunately drawn between them," Jefferson wrote for Washington, "I am confident that both have been led on by a pure love of liberty . . . I shall deem that among the most consoling moments of my life which shall see them united in the end, as they were in the beginning of their virtuous enterprise."[42] Though all American patriotic hearts went out to Lafayette there was little that could be done to ameliorate his suffering or to end his imprisonment. For Jefferson, however, his old friend was simply another victim in the great drama of French revolutionary development whose difficulties and pains were necessary sacrifices for the ultimate victory of the Revolution. Though Jefferson had great patience for the excesses of the Revolution, his stoicism did not extend to one of his more vociferous and influential domestic political opponents.

Bitter disagreements with Alexander Hamilton, leading Federalist, former major general, military aide to Washington during the Revolution, and secretary of the treasury, would cause Jefferson much frustration and grief. Jefferson's personal annoyance with Hamilton significantly contributed to the former's resignation from Washington's Cabinet. Strongly opposed to Hamilton's centralization of the American economy, and bitterly aggravated by his character and methods, Jefferson was united with Adams in his strong dislike of Hamilton. In fact, it had been Adams's strident personal criticism of Hamilton (who had died tragically in a duel with Aaron Burr in 1804) that set the correspondence with Cunningham on its negative and dangerous path.

Trusting his deepest thoughts to the mails, though occasionally harshly critical, Jefferson was no different than Adams in his desire to both unburden himself and honestly share his strong opinions with others. It would be this very honesty—prompted by Jefferson's republicanism and revolutionary fervor—that would bring the breach with Adams out into the open and demonstrate to the country at large that a rift was widening in the highest leadership circles of the new nation.

6

"I Know You Too Well to Fear"

As VICE PRESIDENT to George Washington, Adams's responsibilities did not necessitate the idleness of his creative pen. Finding the time to analyze the writings of seventeenth-century Italian political scientist and diplomat Henrico Caterino Davila, and then offer up arguments against republicanism and the French Revolution, Adams proudly had his efforts published during 1790 as a series of essays in the *Pennsylvania Gazette*. Ever desirous of expanding his fame and reputation as more than a lawyer, politician, and diplomat, Adams was determined to show his countrymen that he was very much a scientist of politics (the term "political scientist" not yet having been coined).[1] With their strong arguments for formality and balance in government, titles, and containing vigorous opposition to republicanism, and the French Revolution in particular, Adams's essays were, much to his surprise, not well-received.

The reaction to the *Davila* essays was, as described by one Adams biographer, a "storm."[2] In fact the reaction was so widespread and negative that the editor of the *Gazette* decided to discontinue publication of them. For an editor of a newspaper in the capital city to inform the vice president that he would no longer run his essays certainly suggests the overwhelmingly negative response that Adams's *Davila* writings had evoked. "The idols of the day were 'equality' and the

French Revolution. Adams had undertaken to attack both."[3] Adams was widely criticized as a monarchist—even his revolutionary credentials were questioned. It was feared by some observers, including Jefferson, that Adams had left the "revolutionary reservation," and was openly supporting aristocracy and monarchism.

Adams's strong personal motive to do and say what he thought right regardless of the popularity of the position that he espoused—no matter what the perceptions of him might be—translated often during his life as a kind of tone-deafness to the most popular themes and issues of the day. Likely thinking that his essays would expand his intellectual reputation as well as shape public opinion through persuasive arguments against republican populism, Adams was stunned at the controversy and the damage to his personal reputation.[4]

Late in 1790, Edmund Burke, an Irish member of the British Parliament and once a strong defender of America in that body, published *Reflections on the French Revolution.* A powerful criticism and indictment of the French Revolution and a defense of British constitutionalism, Burke's book was almost immediately popular and influential. Erudite and articulately written, *Reflections* was widely read and quickly became a critically important rallying point for anti-Republicans in Europe and elsewhere. Thomas Paine, then living in Paris, one of the most important pamphleteers of the American Revolution, read Burke's book and wrote a pro-revolution pamphlet of his own in response. The result, published the following year, was *Rights of Man: Being an Answer to Mr. Burke's Attack on the French Revolution.*

Jefferson received a copy of Paine's pamphlet from Madison, who requested that Jefferson send it along to a certain printer for publication in America, which he did. Along with the pamphlet Jefferson included a note to the printer. In the note Jefferson wrote, "I am extremely pleased to find it will be reprinted here, and that something is at length to be publickly said against the political heresies which have sprung up among us."[5] When Paine's pamphlet was printed soon thereafter, Jefferson's note to the publisher was included as a foreword. Jefferson explained later that inclusion of his comments in the printed version of the pamphlet had not been his intent. One biographer of Washington asserts unreservedly that Jefferson had "intended his comments to remain private,"[6] though there is no evidence for this other than Jefferson's post-publication *mea culpas*. Jefferson, of course, could have cautioned the American printer that his comments were not meant for publication—a simple additional note that he failed to include. A more cynical perspective is that Jefferson was ambivalent about the publication of his comments; perhaps Jefferson thought that if they were not published that would be acceptable, but if they were—he could deny any responsibility for their publication, and challenge any suggestion that they were meant for any eyes other than the printer's.

A firestorm of controversy erupted upon the publication of *Rights of Man* with Jefferson's foreword. Believing (not unreasonably) that both the president and the vice president would see themselves and their policies as the "political heresies" referenced in his comments, Jefferson, then secretary of state, swiftly sent along letters of explanation and apology to both Washington and Adams. Jefferson's fervor had got the better of him, and now his relationships with both men were at risk.

But the publication of his comments in the Paine pamphlet had also set him up in a very public light as the leading opponent of the Federalists and their policies. This significant public self-identification (whether inadvertent or not) by Jefferson as an active republican revolutionary and oppositional voice *within* the government certainly was important in the development of Jefferson as the standard-bearer for the infant Democratic-Republican Party. It is easy to ascribe double-dealing to Jefferson in this controversy, as the publication of his comments, in the long-term, were a significant boost to his political career. There is little reason to doubt however, in view of Jefferson's letters of explanation and apology to Adams and Washington, and his comments of regret to others, that his protestations of regret were anything other than genuine.

Jefferson's first "humble pie" letter was to Washington, dated May 8, 1791. At the time, as Jefferson was the secretary of state, writing to the president first would have been formally correct. Jefferson admitted to Washington that Adams's *Davila* essays were the target of his negative comments but that "nothing was ever further from my thoughts than to become myself the contradictor before the public."[7] His comments in the Paine pamphlet were published to his "great astonishment," he wrote, and the incident had only exploded due to the "indiscretion of a printer."[8] Jefferson then embarked upon an unfortunate and strongly worded lecture of political principles and the anti-constitutional views to be found in Adams's *Davila* publications. Jefferson's language in this letter to President Washington turns highly charged and extraordinarily partisan. Sounding a slightly discordant note more like a revolutionary firebrand than a penitent subordinate, Secretary of State Jefferson mixed pride and anger with regret in a rhetorical ballet that some later reviewers found both excessive and bizarre. A modern reader could be forgiven for finding Jefferson's tone inappropriate.

Acknowledging that Adams would likely consider himself the target of his criticism and take offense from it, Jefferson swiftly abandoned his opening conciliatory tone. One might get the impression that Jefferson, in his enthusiasm for Paine's pamphlet, had forgotten to whom the letter he was writing was addressed.

Critics of Paine and opponents of the Revolution were motivated by fear, Jefferson wrote. "Their real fear, however, is that this popular and republican pamphlet, taking wonderfully, is likely at a single stroke, to wipe out all the unconstitutional doctrines which their bell-weather [sic], 'Davila,' has been preaching for a twelvemonth." Jefferson closed the letter with an assertion of his mortification at the publication of his comments, the public controversy they had caused, and his "abhorrence of dispute."[9] There is no record of a response from President Washington.

There is a clear sense from this letter that Jefferson was truly mortified at the public controversy his comments had created, though his companion self-justifications suggest that his partisan views, like Adams's in the Cunningham correspondence, had perhaps clouded his judgment. Jefferson was correct to identify Adams and his *Davila* essays as perhaps representing the most public and scholarly/substantive opposition to Paine's *Rights of Man* pamphlet and to revolutionary republicanism in general. The lines of partisanship now were being drawn more starkly between Jefferson and his old friend Adams, and this latest eruption would make their growing political differences all the more clear. Adams for his part would come to see Jefferson as the instigator and facilitator of the growing abyss between them.

In a letter to President Washington from his friend and personal secretary Tobias Lear, dated May 8, 1791 (the same date that Jefferson affixed to his own letter to Washington), Lear explained clearly that Jefferson's comments were drawing a strong political line between the secretary of state and Vice President Adams. "This publication of Mr. Jefferson's sentiments respecting Mr. Paine's pamphlet will set him in direct opposition to Mr. Adams's political tenets," Lear wrote. He further explained how deeply their differences ran. "I had myself an opportunity of hearing Mr. Adams's sentiments on it one day soon after the first copies of it arrived in this place. I was at the Vice-President's house, and while there Dr. and Mrs. Rush came in. The conversation turned upon this book, and Dr. Rush asked the Vice-President what he thought of it. After a little hesitation," continued Lear, "he laid his hand upon his breast, and said in a very solemn manner, 'I detest that book and its tendency, from the bottom of my heart.'"[10]

Two months later Jefferson took up his pen to address the matter directly to Adams. His letter to Adams of July 17, 1791, reiterates Jefferson's attestations of how, to his horror, his favorable comments about the Paine pamphlet, and his criticism of "political heresies," had ended up in the printed version of it. He told Adams of the same series of events that he had previously explained to Washington, in fact using almost the same verbiage. Jefferson described himself as "thunderstruck" to see his comments published which had been meant, as he claimed, to be only for the eyes of the printer and not for the general public.[11] Jefferson appealed to Adams's feelings of friendship and assured him that the comments had not been intended for public view. Jefferson did not admit to Adams, as he had to Washington, that the target of his negative words had been Adams's *Davila* essays. Most importantly, perhaps, is Jefferson's assertion that their differences of opinion regarding government were known to both. As would be made clear later to Jefferson, this was, however, not at all how Adams understood the situation.

"That you and I differ in our ideas of the best forms of government, is well known to us both; but we have differed as friends should
do, respecting the purity of each other's motives, and confining our
difference of opinion to private conversation," Jefferson declared.
Then, simultaneously both overreaching and understating, Jefferson
suggested that no harm would come of it because of their long friendship, and Adams's superb character. "The friendship and confidence
which have so long existed between us required this explanation
from me, and I know you too well to fear any misconstruction of the
motives of it."[12] Adams's response was swift.

Writing less than two weeks later on July twenty-ninth, Adams
accepted Jefferson's explanation of the events that resulted in his
provocative and critical comments being made public. "I give full
credit to your relation of the manner in which your note was written and prefixed to the Philadelphia edition of Mr. Paines [sic] pamphlet on the rights of man," Adams comfortingly wrote.[13] Adams
complained in this lengthy letter that editors of newspapers around
the country had seen in Jefferson's comments a direct attack on himself, but did not directly accuse Jefferson of targeting him. Adams
also wrote that Jefferson's introductory comments to Paine's pamphlet were "generally considered as a direct and open personal attack
upon me, by countenancing the false interpretation of my Writings as
favouring the introduction of hereditary Monarchy and Aristocracy
into this Country. The Question every where was, What Heresies are
intended by the Secretary of State?"[14] Adams pointedly asked.

While Jefferson claimed to be "mortified" at the affair, even
"thunderstruck" by it, Adams's reaction was similarly vehement
though he made special pains to communicate that he did not believe
that their friendship was in imminent peril. Adams appeared to sense
that a dangerous rift founded upon a general misinterpretation of his
writings and political beliefs (a misinterpretation apparently shared
by Jefferson) was growing between the two old friends and revolutionary colleagues.

Denying Jefferson's assertion that it was "well known" to both
that they differed in their views on the "best forms of government,"
Adams complained that he had been targeted and misrepresented

unfairly. His July twenty-ninth response to Jefferson included a detailed defense of his views, and a reiteration of his affection for Jefferson—despite the growing popular animosity against him that Jefferson's endorsement of Paine's pamphlet had seemed to confirm. "It was high time that you and I should come to an explanation with each other. The friendship that has subsisted for fifteen Years between Us without the smallest interruption, and until this occasion without the slightest Suspicion, ever has been and still is, very dear to my heart. There is no office I would not resign, rather than give a just occasion to one friend to forsake me," Adams wrote.[15]

There is a strong sense in Adams's reaction to Jefferson of his deep feelings of friendship for him, but there is also a nagging sense of impending loss and sadness. Though Jefferson did not specifically admit to him that Adams had been the target of his inflammatory *Rights of Man* comments (as he had clearly stated in his letter to Washington), Adams reacted as if he were certain that he had been the intended subject of criticism. Quoting directly from Jefferson's letter to him of the seventeenth, Adams wrote,

> You observe, "that You and I differ in our ideas of the best form of Government is well known to us both." But, my dear Sir, you will give me leave to say, that I do not know this. I know not what your Idea is of the best form of Government. You and I have never had a serious conversation together that I can recollect concerning the nature of Government. The very transient hints that have passed between Us have been jocular and superficial, without ever coming to an explanation.[16]

While Adams may have been speaking the literal truth that no such discussions had occurred between the two, their divergent views on the Revolution in France and Jefferson's opposition to key federalist concepts of centralization of authority, at least, were by then clear to both men. Adams himself had furthered the informal (and public) discourse by publishing the *Davila* essays, which were antipodal to the core concepts of French revolutionary (and Jeffersonian) republicanism. Though no formal discussion had occurred, as Adams noted, Jefferson likely felt that no such discussion was necessary.

"If you suppose that I have or ever had a design or desire, of attempting to introduce a Government of King, Lords, and Commons, or in other Words an hereditary Executive, or an hereditary Senate, either into the Government of the United States or that of any Individual State, in this Country," Adams wrote strongly, "you are mistaken."[17] Adams challenged Jefferson to produce any example from his written work, public or private, in which he had suggested such things. No record of any response by Jefferson to Adams's challenge exists. There is some not so small irony in the fact that on the same day Adams was writing his letter of self-defense, and appreciation for their long friendship, Jefferson was writing quite a different letter to Thomas Paine.

Jefferson reiterated to Paine, in a letter dated July 29, 1791, in the same way he had already done with Washington, that Adams's works were the "heresies" that were unidentified in his controversial preface. Appreciating Paine for having written *Rights of Man*, Jefferson proceeded to describe the effect of its publication.

> That has been much read here, with avidity and pleasure. A writer under the signature of Publicola has attacked it. A host of champions entered the arena immediately in your defence . . . The discussion excited the public attention, recalled it to the 'Defence of the American constitutions' and the 'Discourses on Davila,' which it had kindly passed over without censure in the moment, and very general expressions of their sense have been now drawn forth; & I thank god that they appear firm in their republicanism, notwithstanding the contrary hopes & assertions of a sect here, high in names, but small in numbers. These had flattered themselves that the silence of the people under the 'Defence' and 'Davila' was a symptom of their conversion to the doctrine of king, lords, & commons. They are checked at least by your pamphlet, & the people confirmed in their good old faith.[18]

Though Jefferson had been unreserved in his communications to both Washington and Paine that Adams had indeed been his target, he made no similar admission to Adams himself. Known for his self-admitted disdain of direct confrontation, perhaps Jefferson's purpose in not being forthright and entirely honest with Adams on the matter was to avoid the rift that would almost certainly have occurred. That Adams would let the matter drop is a testament to his character as well as to his affection and esteem for Jefferson; Adams's forgiveness would not go unrepaid.

The purpose of Jefferson's letter to Adams of August 30, 1791, was to put the matter to rest. He reiterated his innocence, but had the temerity to add that the controversy had actually been caused by the defenders of Adams and their criticism of Jefferson rather than by Jefferson's comments themselves. Jefferson bizarrely concluded that he was therefore innocent of any wrongdoing and, much like Adams's view of himself in the matter, something of a victim.

Little is added favorably to Jefferson's historical reputation by this letter to Adams. A common view of Jefferson is that he was a deeply contradictory man—distant and aloof, according to some scholars—a determined political and personal manipulator, an emotionally challenged man who withheld his deepest and most essential personal truths. This negative view is enhanced by a close reading of his letter to Adams of the thirtieth of August.[19] This highly critical interpretation of Jefferson, a viewpoint now more popular than in previous generations, is an oversimplified approach to an extraordinarily brilliant and multifaceted person whose better nature was sometimes subsumed by personal pride, emotional limitations, and by his deep affection for revolutionary political principles.

Adams's public rejection of French revolutionary republicanism and his private fear of elections (a fear that Adams had shared with Jefferson in a letter several years previously) were the central political apostasies to which Jefferson obliquely alluded. Later events during Adams's administration confirmed these opinions for Jefferson. Though he did not inform Adams that it had indeed been his (Adams's) published writings that were the targets of his *Rights of Man* "heresies" comments, Adams must have surely sensed that their political views were no longer in accord.

Jefferson opened his August 30, 1797, reply to Adams with an acknowledgment and appreciation of Adams's gracious though challenging letter of the twenty-ninth. Jefferson then moved quickly to his own defense. "The importance which you still seem to allow to my note,[20] and the effect you suppose it to have had tho unintentional in me, induce me to shew [sic] you that it really had no effect."[21] It is a strange-sounding argument that denies the legitimacy of Adams's reaction as essentially unfounded, and seems to be a way in which Jefferson was denying that it was he who had been the cause of discord in their long friendship. The real instigator of the difficulty and controversy had not been he, Jefferson asserted, but rather a very public and determined defender of Adams by the name of "Publicola." Many at the time thought that Publicola was in fact Adams himself, taking to the public papers to mount an anonymous defense, though Adams denied this. Jefferson did not then know that Publicola was John Quincy Adams who had taken it upon himself to defend his father's writings before the public- a defense undertaken entirely without his father's knowledge or involvement.

Jefferson asserted that when Paine's pamphlet was published, "not a word ever appeared in the public papers here on the subject for more than a month; and I am certain not a word on the subject would ever have been said had not a writer, under the name of Publicola, at length undertaken to attack Mr. Paine's principles, which were the principles of the citizens of the U.S."[22] According to Jefferson, it had been Publicola's response to Paine's pamphlet and to Jefferson's comments rather than the original comments themselves, which had caused the controversy and thus the ensuing bitter public attacks against Adams. "As soon as Publicola attacked Paine, swarms appeared in his defence," Jefferson noted. "To Publicola then, and not in the least degree to my note, this whole contest is to be ascribed and all its consequences."[23]

"As long as Paine's pamphlet stood on it's [sic] own feet, and on my note, it was unnoticed," Jefferson disingenuously averred. A new pamphlet by Paine would not have gone unnoticed (and certainly not by critics) for long, especially when accompanied by provocative comments written by the secretary of state. To Washington, Jefferson had admitted that his target had been Adams's *Davila* essays, though with Adams he took a very different approach. In light of his admissions to Washington and Paine, Jefferson's proposal to Adams, that no blame "not in the least degree" should be ascribed to him in the matter, is a dissembling performance.

"Indeed it was impossible that my note should occasion your name to be brought into question; for so far from naming you, I had not even in view any writing which I might suppose to be yours, and the opinions I alluded to were principally those I had heard in common conversation from a sect aiming at the subversion of the present government to bring their favorite form of a king, lords, and commons," Jefferson falsely proclaimed. Definitive though his assertions of innocence appeared, and perhaps meant to forcefully nudge the door of the controversy closed with some finality, the matter would not be so readily concluded.

Jefferson was determined that Adams should accept him as blameless in the affair. "Thus I hope, my dear Sir, that you will see me to have been as innocent *in effect* [emphasis in original] as I was in intention,"[24] proclaimed Jefferson preparatory to declaring the matter closed. "The business is now over, and I hope it's [sic] effects are over, and that our friendship will never be suffered to be committed, whatever uses others may think proper to make of our names."[25]

Jefferson's purpose in this awkward letter appears to have been to save his friendship with Adams—by withholding the truth and shifting blame from himself to others. He was exceedingly aware that he and Adams had diverged onto different and not complimentary political roads. Though their political paths were no longer parallel and, for a long time, would not converge here-or-there, Adams's (previously cited) letter to Jefferson of July twenty-ninth showed that Adams had no desire whatever in allowing political differences to ruin their friendship.

No further discussion of Jefferson's *Rights of Man* comments, or the response by Publicola and the ensuing controversies, passed between Adams and Jefferson. After Jefferson's August letter of self-defense in the Paine comments matter, their correspondence slowed to a trickle. Two years later, at the conclusion of 1793, Jefferson resigned as secretary of state citing in part his hatred of politics.

The temporarily retired public servant retreated to Monticello to his much-loved farms and books. In replying to an April 1794 letter with which Adams had sent a book in French about European politics, Jefferson wrote, "the difference of my present and past situation is such as to leave me nothing to regret but that my retirement has been postponed four years too long."[26] Adams responded several weeks later and mentioned that Chief Justice John Jay had been sent to London with extraordinary ministerial powers "to try if he can find any Way to reconcile our honour with Peace."[27] This was the first hint of a rapprochement with Great Britain that would later be solidified as the Jay Treaty.

This agreement, so favorable to England and consequentially the cause of great bitterness in France (and among American Francophiles such as Jefferson and most Republicans), would become a serious point of contention between the two most important American political parties (which Adams and Jefferson in time came to represent). In his May 1794 letter Adams had reiterated his animosity toward "Aristocratical Government." Warning that involvement in the war between England and revolutionary France would be detrimental to the United States, a belief that both men shared, Adams wrote that "those who dread Monarchy and Aristocracy and at the same time Advocate War are the most inconsistent of all men."[28] Their letters now rested for much longer before a reply was written and mailed. A new phase of their lives was rapidly approaching; Adams and Jefferson would soon be linked again professionally and in a way that would bring frustration to both.

Desiring retirement, President Washington had declined a third term, thus creating the need for the first American presidential election in which candidates from opposing parties vied for the prize. Adams was the leading candidate for the Federalists, Jefferson for the Democratic-Republicans. During the 1796 election campaign both Jefferson and Adams kept a public silence and did no personal campaigning (as was the practice of the time). Their surrogates and supporters attacked and defended in the press. Washington also kept silent as to his preferred successor. The public political discourse during the election was often heated and unpleasant to both Adams and Jefferson, which prompted a later letter to President Adams from Jefferson acknowledging the same. Finally, the tally was read in the House with Adams victorious by a slight margin. One noted historian explained the process: "Each elector was required to cast two ballots of equal value, so the candidate with a plurality would be President and the second highest would win the Vice Presidency, whether or not the two were compatible in ideas or ideals."[29]

The result of the election dictated that the leaders of the two opposing parties would run the government together. Though Adams and Jefferson were old friends, they were now increasingly political rivals. The election of 1796 was the last time that the president and vice president were selected in this manner due to obvious ideological conflicts that might (and did) arise. President Adams had before him the very same challenge that had faced his predecessor: the country's relationship with France. Unlike Washington, Adams would not have the full support of his vice president.

Peaceful relations between France and the United States were viewed by the soon-to-retire Washington as the core of the foreign policy of the country, as well being central to its domestic tranquility. "The nature of the relationship would determine every aspect of American policy toward England and Spain as well as toward France," one noted biographer of Washington wrote. "Even more, it would cut the contour of American politics and throw long shadows into every corner of the Federal Union."[30] Adams concurred with this view and determined to take the same course as that laid out by Washington. The second president would soon be required to focus all of his energies on avoiding American involvement in the war between England and France, following diligently the model that Washington had communicated in his *Farewell Address*. This approach was not altogether satisfactory to Adams's vice president, however. Though he disagreed with President Adams on most essential political matters, Vice President Jefferson was not at all disappointed to occupy the second chair in the government rather than the first.

Early in his tenure as vice president in the Adams administration, Jefferson wrote to James Sullivan, then the attorney general of Massachusetts and later governor of that state, that "neither the splendor, nor the power, nor the difficulties, nor the fame or defamation, as may happen, attached to the first magistracy, have any attractions for me," proclaimed Jefferson. "The helm of a free government is always arduous, & never was ours more so, than at a moment when two friendly people are likely to be committed in war by the ill temper of their administrations."[31] Jefferson had on several occasions mentioned his dislike of politics—though he had answered whenever the call to serve arrived. But he also knew that the issue of France, and support or opposition to the Revolution there, would be a serious dividing line in American politics, if not the central issue. For President Adams, the success or failure of relations with France would determine that of his presidency just as the same concerns had determined the latter part of Washington's tenure.

Adams and Jefferson, however, were not Washington—what could be forgiven the man "first in war, first in peace, and first in the hearts of his countrymen" (from eulogy of Washington by Henry "Light Horse Harry" Lee) could not be forgiven them. For Jefferson (a republican revolutionary and supporter of France), 1796 was not likely the most propitious time for him to be president; the vice presidency was a comfortable alternative. There was a viable opposition party to be built which, at a more advantageous time in (hopefully) the near future, would perhaps be ready to win the reins of government. The creation of a legitimate and popularly supported opposition was critically important to Jefferson as the views of the Federalists were, to him, "political heresies."

At the close of 1796, Jefferson wrote a letter of congratulations to the generally expected next president, his old friend and colleague, John Adams. The election cycle had by then not yet concluded though Jefferson assumed from what he had seen in the Philadelphia public papers that Adams was, though not yet officially declared, the winner of the election. This was something of a concession and congratulatory letter from Jefferson with well wishes and assurances of support and continued friendship. There is much affection and respect in this letter of December twenty-eighth, though its most intriguing aspect is not Jefferson's consideration for Adams but rather the fact that Adams never saw it.

This unsent letter began with an observation by Jefferson that the press was characterizing the new president and vice president as far from a unified leadership team. "The public and the public papers have been much occupied lately in placing us in a point of opposition to each other," Jefferson wrote. "I trust with confidence that less of it has been felt by ourselves personally."[32] This slightly disingenuous appeal to Adams's friendship ignored the fact that it was Jefferson himself who had set the tone of conflict and partisanship between the two old friends which the "public and the public papers" were then referencing. Jefferson characterized himself as reveling in his mountaintop political isolation at Monticello and his lack of unawareness, by choice, of events in the wider world—most particularly at the nation's capital. "In the retired canton where I am, I learn little of what is passing: pamphlets I see never; papers but a few; and the fewer the happier," he wrote, feigning a disinterest which Adams, if he had seen the letter, would perhaps have shrugged off as his friend's affectation for being above, and uninvolved in, the political brawls of the presidential election. Jefferson most assuredly retained a strong interest in politics, particularly republican concerns, and his knowledge of the election (and his defeat to Adams) likely originated within his own social and political network, rather than the public press.

Jefferson wrote that he had expected an Adams victory but that the outcome was exactly as he had hoped it would be. This assertion of acceptance of his defeat in the election is supported by Jefferson's letter to James Sullivan, written little more than a week later. While Jefferson's tone to Adams is unmistakably benign, distinguished, and considerate if not solicitous, that of the Sullivan letter is quite different and carries little of the friendly feeling found in his December twenty-eighth letter to Adams (which was never sent). "I have never one single moment expected a different issue: and tho' I know I shall not be believed, yet it is not the less true that I have never wished it," Jefferson wrote in that unsent letter to Adams.[33]

Though not a sailor and with limited experience of ocean travel, Jefferson often used metaphors of ocean storms and transatlantic voyages to convey feelings of challenges and overcoming adversity. This is a common theme throughout the correspondence between the two men over the years. "I leave to others the sublime delights of riding in the storm, better pleased with sound sleep and a warm birth below, with the society of neighbors, friends and fellow laborers of the earth, than of spies and sycophants. No one then will congratulate you with purer disinterestedness than myself," Jefferson had assured Adams.[34]

Those who knew Jefferson best understood that these fancies of excessive humility and ersatz noninvolvement on Jefferson's part were something of an epistolary and literary affectation which they came to accept, and ignore simultaneously. Jefferson's allusion to spies was a direct reference to both Adams's and Jefferson's "archfriend," Alexander Hamilton.[35] The political machinations of Hamilton in undermining Adams's most senior advisors would result in controversy and frustration for Adams during his administration. However, it would be during the first administration of Jefferson that the many intrigues and conflicts surrounding the influential federalist leader and former secretary of the treasury would come to a disturbing and fatal conclusion.

Continuing in the vein of accepting the election outcome, Jefferson, in his unsent letter, explained to Adams that he had "no ambition to govern men. It is a painful and thankless office." His own difficult experience as governor of Virginia during the American Revolution would suggest that this comment is an honest one. However, "governing men" under less controversial and more advantageous circumstances, not presented by the complex and challenging political environment of late 1796, would not be an opportunity that he would eschew in the future. Jefferson concluded his letter to Adams with assertions of friendship and a wish that Adams would be successful in keeping the country in a state of peace. "I devoutly wish you may be able to shun for us this war by which our agriculture, commerce and credit will be destroyed." The two men were very much in accord on this point, though later events might suggest otherwise. Adams had every intention of making American neutrality in the war of the great powers of Europe the central concern of his administration; this had been Washington's policy and so it would be President Adams's policy as well.

Adams approached his friend and vice president for help on this critical issue to which both had earlier asserted their dedication; Jefferson demurred, and their growing rift expanded once again. In the meantime, Jefferson wished his old friend and new chief success and predicted that if Adams were to be successful "the glory will be all your own."[36]

Adams never saw this letter because Jefferson had sent it first to Madison for review. Madison recommended that Jefferson suppress the letter, which he did. Madison may have missed the subtext of Jefferson's conclusion, however, which was a regretful, deeply honest homage to his long association with Adams. It seems likely that it was these references to past friendly relations and an exuberant flourish of wishes for a successful administration that Madison, Jefferson's friend and political advisor, could not abide.

"That your administration may be filled with glory, and happiness to yourself and advantage to us," Jefferson concluded, "is the sincere wish of one who tho', in the course of our own voyage thro' life, various little incidents have happened or been contrived to separate us, retains still for you the solid esteem of the moments when we were working for our independence, and sentiments of respect and affectionate attachment."[37] The time was swiftly approaching when Jefferson's political beliefs, at odds with those of his friend Adams, would prompt actions that created haunting doubts in Adams of Jefferson's reliability, and of their friendship.

Jefferson pursued new "various little incidents" which soon put a cold seal to their friendship for over a decade. His request of Madison to review and comment on the advisability of sending the congratulatory letter to Adams is indicative of both Jefferson's political self-awareness, and an unspoken acknowledgment that he was treading a fine line between friendship and partisan political positioning. It is to Jefferson's credit that he attempted to do this, but something of a shame that he chose political calculations over his true affection for the new president and his longtime friend.

James Madison and Jefferson were two-of-a-kind: brilliant Virginians, and staunch Republicans. Their friendship was largely utilitarian, though marked by strong mutual respect. Both were rigidly ideologically opposed to the ruling Federalists, and desirous of creating a substantive republican opposition. Madison occasionally, at Jefferson's behest, reviewed the latter's correspondence and provided his opinion as to whether or not the intended recipient should receive it. One historian wrote,

In the politics of both Virginia and the nation, James Madison early became one of Jefferson's protagonists, defending him against criticism and offering helpful advice when it was sought. Tactful and discreet, Madison never presumed on his friendship. A more cautious and less ebullient man than Jefferson, Madison sometimes gave counsel which proved beneficial in checking Jefferson's enthusiasm. The two friends were eternally on the alert to combat tendencies opposed to the democratic principles which they espoused.[38]

Three days after writing his congratulatory letter to Adams, Jefferson sent it along to Madison for his approval. "I enclose it open for your perusal," wrote Jefferson, "not only that you may possess the actual state of dispositions between us, but that if anything should render the delivery of it ineligible in your opinion, you may return it to me."[39] Madison responded on the fifteenth of January, 1797: Do not send the letter to Adams.

Madison made his case with a list of six reasons of varying consideration as to why the letter should remain unsent to Adams. The sixth reason was the most politically pragmatic and partisan. It is not known which item on the list Jefferson found most convincing as he did not comment back to Madison. "Considering the probability that Mr. A.'s course of administration may force an opposition to it from the Republican quarter," Madison wrote, "& the general uncertainty of the posture which our affairs may take, there may be real embarrassments from giving written possession to him, of the degree of compliment & confidence which your personal delicacy & friendship have suggested."[40]

Jefferson retained a copy of the unsent letter. The new vice president's fastidious record keeping has been a great boon to later students; his is the only copy extant of this important communication to his great friend Adams that was suppressed for political considerations. Students of Adams and Jefferson can only wonder if anything might have been different between the two friends had this amiable and appreciative letter been sent instead of quashed. The answer must suggest itself in the negative in light of later events. It is important to note that Jefferson's decision to defer to Madison was almost entirely political in nature. As a fellow republican partisan in opposition to the Federalist Party of Adams, Madison reasonably determined that Jefferson—as the *de facto* leader of the Democratic-Republican opposition—should not be seen to profess too much personal support for Adams in case the letter were to somehow find its way to the public's view.

Though Jefferson's impolitic letter of support to Adams was suppressed in accordance to Madison's recommendation, another letter from Jefferson to Madison dated less than two weeks prior had a significantly positive impact on Adams. "If a tie vote should force the election into the House of Representatives, Jefferson told Madison on the seventeenth, 'I pray you and authorize you fully to solicit on my behalf that Mr. Adams be preferred. He has always been my senior from the commencement of our public life, and the expression of the public will being equal, this circumstance ought to give him the preference.'"[41] In a letter to Abigail written soon after learning of Jefferson's comments to Madison, Adams wrote, "It is considered as Evidence of his determination to accept (the vice presidency), of his Friendship for me—And of his modesty and Moderation."[42]

The contrary nature of Jefferson's accession to the idea of being vice president rather than the chief executive had a dual track—friendship and respect for Adams, and a pragmatic acknowledgement of the political realities and risks of serving as president during a time of national crisis. Duality is a theme often repeated in Jefferson's life and is seen time and again in his writings and behavior. Fostering the concept of republicanism and universal rights for most all citizens while simultaneously refusing to vigorously oppose the slavery system in the South is a sure illustration of Jefferson's conflicted nature. When it became known that a congressional vote on the presidential election was unnecessary and that Adams had won, Jefferson must have understood that the subordinate role he had accepted would be an increasingly difficult, if not impossible one.

Jefferson's position, as vice president to a chief executive whose party he and his Democratic-Republican supporters ideologically opposed on both domestic and foreign matters, was profoundly difficult. His appeal to Madison's pragmatically political review of his letter to Adams was a tacit admission of the dilemma of his conflicted role as the second-highest government officer in the country, while at the same time being the leader of the opposition party. Jefferson's concurrence with Madison's recommendation to suppress the letter of support to Adams was a crucial moment in the political maturation of Jefferson and the next step in the growing rift between him and the president.

No other vice president in American history has been in a similarly frustrating and dangerously conflicted role as was Jefferson. With his divided loyalties, and the necessity to constantly review his actions in relation to his inherently oppositional roles, the possibilities for a misstep (or worse) on Jefferson's part were very real.

7

"We Came to Fifth Street, Where Our Road Separated"

PRESIDENT WASHINGTON'S *FAREWELL Address* appeared in the Philadelphia *Daily American Advertiser* on September 19, 1796. On the day of its publication, Washington left Philadelphia for his home at Mount Vernon.[1] It was soon reprinted in newspapers and in pamphlet form across the new country. Washington never delivered the address as a speech, preferring publication of it over oratory. In this seminal address the first president announced that he would not seek a third term, and warned of factionalism and partisanship. The *Farewell* laid out a worldview in which the United States must maintain its neutrality relative to the conflict between England and France. Washington's warnings and strongly worded recommendations for the future set the stage for both the presidential election that soon followed, and the foreign policy of John Adams who, as president, would loyally and vigorously continue on Washington's path.

In a direct warning to partisans of both England and France, Washington asserted, "there can be no greater error than to expect or calculate upon real favors from nation to nation. It is an illusion, which experience must cure, which a just pride ought to discard." Relative to the ongoing war between those countries, his position was a firm neutrality. "In relation to the still subsisting war in Europe . . . I was well satisfied that our country, under all the circumstances of the case, had a right to take, and was bound in duty and interest to take, a neutral position. Having taken it, I determined, as far as should depend upon me, to maintain it, with moderation, perseverance, and firmness."

Washington did not write this important final public document of his presidency alone; Hamilton and Madison, two noted political partisans with opposing views, assisted him. Hamilton, the former secretary of the treasury, was a powerful and dogmatic Federalist. Madison, a Republican, was famous for his efforts to support and ratify the Constitution, as well as his friendship and political association with Jefferson. The wisdom of Washington in selecting two such powerful, but politically opposite, intellects to collaborate on this most important address is born out in the *Farewell*'s discussion of the dangers of political partisanship.

"I have already intimated to you the danger of parties in the State, with particular reference to the founding of them on geographical discriminations. Let me now take a more comprehensive view, and warn you in the most solemn manner against the baneful effects of the spirit of party generally. This spirit, unfortunately, is inseparable from our nature, having its root in the strongest passions of the human mind. It exists under different shapes in all governments, more or less stifled, controlled, or repressed; but, in those of the popular form, it is seen in its greatest rankness, and is truly their worst enemy."[2]

As the great military hero of the Revolution, Washington had been perhaps the only person who could unify all the factions and parties, north and south, behind him and the new national government. His second term saw the erosion of this once powerful unity. It was this rising partisanship, which had often manifested in unbridled personal criticism of Washington that, in large part, prompted that brave and sensitive man to retire to Mount Vernon and the private life of a gentleman farmer. Some Republicans, in their zeal against any contagion of monarchism, considered another Washington presidential term as potentially imperiling American republicanism and thus the new democracy itself. Jefferson too shared in this fear of the popular investment of too much prestige and power in a single person (Washington) which would thus directly or indirectly facilitate the reintroduction of monarchist and aristocratic principles and forms into the democracy.

One of Adams's biographers noted that both Adams and Washington saw themselves as unifiers, above party squabbles. "Adams saw himself, like Washington, as a national leader, a reconciler of parties and factions, the President of Federalists and Republicans alike, and his policies and actions can best be understood in the light of such a conception of the presidency."[3] Adams spoke of this theme in his inaugural address. Not only would partisanship and the growing divide between Federalists and Republicans receive Adams's attention, however. A simmering diplomatic crisis with France that had begun in late 1794 would soon come to a head as, only a week before Adams's inauguration, the Senate had ratified a treaty of commerce with Britain then commonly known as "Jay's Treaty." The stipulations of the treaty would significantly affect both domestic politics and foreign policy during Adams's administration.

In the war between England and France, which was then being waged almost entirely at sea, the dual goals of President Washington had been to protect American shipping from both warring parties, and to stop the British from impressing American sailors. His purpose in sustaining a strong neutrality was to avoid involvement in a European conflict for which the United States was not prepared. Perhaps even more critically, the country was divided as to which belligerent to support.

Both political parties had their preference; Federalists were strongly opposed to France while Jefferson and the Republicans supported it—regardless of the horrors that had transpired during the Revolution, and despite France's aggressive naval and economic posture toward the United States. This American bifurcation of support, Federalists for England and Republicans for France, would be a central issue of separation and contention between the parties during the entirety of Adams's term.

The Jay Treaty was viewed by revolutionary France as an affront, and clear evidence that the United States had taken a pro-British position in the war. Though Washington had preferred a strict neutrality, the aggressive actions of France had, despite British offenses against American shipping and sailors, essentially pushed him into the arms of England. "Finally Washington, because of the rumors of an insurrection, in which Fauchet (a French diplomat in the United States) was implicated, was forced to approve the Jay Treaty although he had asserted it need cause no alarm in France,"[4] one historian asserted. Washington's hope that France would take no offense over the new treaty with England was proven to be a fantasy. His successor would be required to contend with the consequences.

In a letter to John Quincy written several weeks after his inauguration, Adams wrote, "My entrance into office is marked by a misunderstanding with France, which I shall endeavor to reconcile. But not at the cost of 'too much humiliation.'" Adams assured his son, "America is not SCARED."[5] At that time, only a month had passed since Adams had attended his inauguration alone, with most of the event's fanfare reserved for admiring celebrations of Washington and a general regret at the departure of the first president from the national stage. The president-elect had by no means been ignored, however; Adams's dignified deportment and hopeful inauguration address earned him many compliments.

A sensitive and complicated man, Adams slept little the evening prior to his oath-taking ceremony. Likely affected by the seriousness of the challenges and the heavy burden of responsibility that lay before him, Adams presented an almost dour countenance through much of the proceedings, though his attire bespoke a unity of self-awareness and celebration. One of Jefferson's premier biographers described Adams as "resplendent" in "light drab or pearl-colored cloth and wearing a sword and cockade."[6] There was certainly a profound mix of feelings at the inauguration ceremonies of President-elect Adams at Congress Hall in Philadelphia. Jefferson, too, was moved by the solemnity and importance of the moment, complimenting the new president in a short speech after his own swearing in as vice president. "The exercises of the inauguration itself, on Saturday, March 4, were pervaded by an equally amicable and sportsmanlike spirit. Jefferson's brief speech in the Senate chamber, following his taking of the oath some time after 10am, was characteristically felicitous,"[7] Jefferson biographer Dumas Malone wrote.

Jefferson generally exercised great care regarding the language and tone he used in public utterances. As the leader of the opposition party and now the vice president, Jefferson's complimentary tone was an important symbol of unity for the country. "He meant what he said when he spoke of the 'eminent character' whose talents and integrity had been known and revered by him for many years and with whom he had enjoyed 'a cordial and uninterrupted friendship,'"[8] Malone wrote of the occasion.

Adams's dour expression was perhaps a result not only of his feelings of personal loss at the absence of Abigail or any member of his family at his inauguration, but also might have reflected a sense of foreboding. The difficulties he would soon face were in part self-created. His public writings, and private correspondence with Jefferson in particular, in which he defended the British Constitution and aristocracy (as opposed to monarchy which he loathed) had by then set a tone of suspicion against Adams in a sizable segment of the American population. The predominant, and growing, popular concept of American government as Adams took office was of the republican type, quite contrary to Adams's somewhat British-tinged (anti-republican) federalism. Adams's slim victory over Jefferson in the 1796 election had not been an indicator of general favoritism for federalism among the voting public. While he was out-of-step with the masses of American citizens in his support of a concept of the aristocracy of quality, he was wholly true to himself. His choice of attire at the inaugural, for example, which was an embodiment of his support for formalities and public honors (for those worthy to receive them), was the result of his paying homage to his concepts of the trappings of government and governing—as well as the limitations of his own purse.

The result of Adams's traditionally informed formality and outward accouterments of authority, which Jefferson and his followers preferred to be eliminated from the public sphere as a demonstration of egalitarianism and popularism, was a general misunderstanding of Adams's real views of government and of the Constitution. Jefferson's simple attire was certainly a (populist) political statement in

cloth, while Adams's more formal and flashy clothing also appeared
to signal a different political perspective.

Adams's inaugural attire was both a political statement and a consequence of his reduced financial resources. Never an extraordinarily
wealthy man (exclusive of his large land holdings at Quincy), Adams
had little financial means when he took office. His lack of ready cash
required him to press into service his old fine clothing from his years
of diplomatic service as minister to Great Britain, and as American
envoy to France. Necessarily refined and far more fashionable in a
European sense than what most Americans wore, Adams's old ministerial clothing added to the popular perception that Adams was an
elitist, a monarchist, and aristocrat.

"Many criticized Vice President John Adams in his first years
in office because of the opulence of his attire. In response, he complained that he was wearing the only clothes he had, the clothes
that he had worn while he was American minister in Britain in the
1780s; he could not afford a new wardrobe," a recent historian of the
early republic period observed.[9] When one sees the beauty and size
of Adams's Peace field home in Quincy, this description of Adams
as financially stressed may seem a slight stretch though the "Old
House," as it came to be known, was not considered an opulent home.
In comparison to Monticello, Montezillo was fairly humble. Abigail
herself, however, confirmed the difficulties of their financial situation.

Less than three weeks after the inauguration, Abigail, then in
Quincy, reported to John that she had been visited twice by the tax
collector. "Yesterday the collector calld upon me for the 2d Time. I
told him I could not pay him, but that I would in the course of the
Month, relying upon the post of this day. He observed if I could not
pay, who could? I told him I had not the money. I could have added
that I had but one solitary 5 dollors [sic] bill in my command."[10]
Adams's writings, which had inadvertently supplied so much ideological ammunition for the republican opposition seemed to be
confirmed for many critics by his overly ostentatious apparel—particularly when compared to the simple garb of Jefferson. The truth
of the matter was perhaps much simpler; as Abigail's report of her
inability to pay the tax collector shows, Adams likely had little cash

with which to purchase a new, more fashionable, and less "monarchist" wardrobe.

In a letter to Abigail written the day after the inauguration, Adams described the event and his feelings. With a bit of characteristic New England humor, Adams wrote that he thought that he had heard Washington wrly express pleasure at leaving the presidency.[11] Adams noted that while most eyes at the ceremony were clouded with tears, few of them were produced out of joy for Adams's accession to the nation's highest post. Adams's self-doubt and concern for the future caused one historian to confuse the new president's dark mood as representative of the character of the event itself, noting that "four days later, the new President was still dwelling upon the sadness and gloom of the occasion."[12] While the departure of Washington from public life was certainly the cause of "gloom" among many at the event, Adams himself played little or no role in arousing such melancholy. Writing again to Abigail several days later, Adams acknowledged the many tears shed. "It is the general report that there has been more weeping than there has ever been at the representation of any tragedy."[13]

Adams's observations of apparent sadness and high emotions in the crowd at Congress Hall seemed to feed his sense of self-doubt. As his confidante and foil, Abigail soon received a full report of his reactions to the profound and emotional scenes. Adams had often shared feelings of self-doubt with his wife, and historians with a psychological bent have long discussed the nature of these feelings. Lack of self-esteem is common among sensitive and creative people. Rather than bringing to the fore a confident reminder of past accomplishments and qualifications for future success for such individuals, acceptance of greater responsibility might produce instead feelings of inadequacy, self-doubt, and inordinate and unreaslistic fears.

The inauguration of Adams was a bittersweet event for all in attendance, as everyone knew that they were witness to the next step in the development of their young country. Events of great importance, such as a presidential inaugural, often have multiple layers of meaning, as Adams acknowledged in his report of the ceremony to Abigail. "Whether it was from grief or joy, whether from the loss of their beloved President, or from the accession of an unbeloved one, or from the pleasure of exchanging Presidents without tumult, or from the novelty of the thing, or from the sublimity of it arising out of the multitude present, or whatever the cause, I know not."[14] Adams was himself mystified by all the tears as "no one descends to particulars to say why or wherefore; I am, therefore, left to suppose that it is all grief for the loss of their beloved." This is a reasonable response and view, but it is also colored by Adams's self-doubt. "Perhaps," the new president darkly wrote to Abigail, "there is little danger of my having such another scene to feel or behold."[15] The new first lady's reply was insightful and comforting. "The solemnity of the Scene in which you was [sic] the principle actor, the dignified Speech delivered previous to the oath of office, the presence of the Great Friend and Father of his Country who presented himself to the publick as a pledge for his Successor, could not fail to inspire into the minds and Hearts of all present, the strongest Emotions of tenderness," she wrote. "Nor do I wonder that it found its way to their Eyes."[16] Speculating further about the public mood, Abigail noted, "the publick have exhausted themselves upon your predecessor. They must take breath, and recollect themselves, before they can bestow even merited praise."[17] Abigail's urging of patience, and her recommendation that he keep things in context and wait for the praise that was his due, must have come as a great comfort to Adams who, not a week into his presidential term, was already suggesting that it would likely be his last.

Adams's inaugural address touched on many of the same themes that Washington had discussed in his *Farewell Address*. Paying tribute to the service of Washington and the great example he had set, and reiterating his predecessor's warning against partisanship, Adams laid out a long list of principles and promises which, when delivered from the presidential podium, was likely more powerful and affecting than its complex constructions appear on the printed page. One of the items on the new president's list was an acknowledgement of his affection for France "and a sincere desire to preserve the friendship which has been so much for the honor and interest of both nations."[18] He also described the "natural enemies" of the Constitution as "the spirit of sophistry, the spirit of party, the spirit of intrigue, the profligacy of corruption, and the pestilence of foreign influence." With the conclusion of Adams's inaugural address the tone of the new administration was now clearly set.

Adams was immediately faced with two great questions—how would France respond to the recently ratified Jay Treaty with England, that is, could war with France be avoided? Just as important was the second: How much cooperation and support could he expect from his old friend, political rival, and now vice president, Thomas Jefferson?

Two days before the inauguration Jefferson had arrived in Philadelphia and paid a visit to Adams, a gesture which Adams returned the following day. No record survives of what was discussed.[19] Jefferson's visit demonstrated a sense of propriety and respect which Adams reciprocated. Perhaps, as they faced governing together, their long friendship could overcome the growing political chasm between them.

In the days following the inauguration the president and vice president shared the same boarding house, prompting Justice William Paterson to observe to a friend, "I am much pleased that Mr. Adams and Mr. Jefferson lodge together. The thing carried conciliation and healing with it, and may have a happy effect on parties. Indeed, my dear sir, it is high time we should be done with parties."[20] Many in the capital and elsewhere were keenly aware of the growing conflicts (of which few approved) between the parties. A nineteenth-century biographer of Adams made note of the bitter partisanship of the 1790s that had personally stung both Washington and Adams. Most Americans viewed Washington, certainly throughout his first term, as the great unifier of the country, a man beyond personal criticism and calumny. By the end of his second and final term, the partisan criticism against him had become both personally painful and involved accusations and language that previously would never have been publicly associated with him. As party differences increased, the decorum, awe, and general respect that had prevented public attacks against his policies and character had mainly fallen away. After Washington's retirement, Adams would be the first in line to receive this new kind of bitter political attack driven by party allegiances. One Adams biographer noted,

> If the Republicans so abused Washington, whom we venerate, what would they not say against John Adams? Poor Adams, if not really more sensitive than Washington, seemed to be so, and could not conceal his irritation and wrath. That delighted his tormentors the more. It was an age of coarse vituperation, as well as of bitter political hatreds and groundless suspicions.[21]

Every age since, it seems, has had its periods of vituperation and coarse political rhetoric. It would appear also that partisanship and the public expression of bitter, negative feelings are elements of human nature, and therefore also an undeniable yet unfortunate truth of democracy. Perhaps the greatest fear common to all the Founders was a rift within the Union; a breakdown of the unity of common identity as Americans that had so characterized the revolutionary years. The building blocks of disunion are constructed upon such partisan foundations.

In one of his post-presidency essays published in the *Boston Patriot*, Adams described a meeting between him and Jefferson on the day before his (Adams's) inauguration. "I sought and obtained an interview with Mr. Jefferson," he wrote. "Though by this time I differed from him in opinion by the whole horizon concerning the practicability and success of the French revolution, and some other points, I had no reason to think that he differed materially from me with regard to our national Constitution."[22] Adams was only partially correct in this; he had proven himself to Jefferson to be much less the populist republican partisan than Jefferson preferred. Jefferson's strong views against monarchism and aristocracy, and his deep dislike of the British, in contrast to his vigorous support of France—a view in particular which Adams did not share—made President Adams a target for obstructionism and, later, political defeat.

During this meeting with his soon-to-be vice president the day before the inauguration (which Adams erroneously later recalled as having occurred "the morning after my inauguration"[23]), Adams and Jefferson discussed the conflict with France and how it should be handled. Adams asked Jefferson if he would consider returning to France on a diplomatic mission though he acknowledged that the Constitution might prevent the vice president from undertaking such a task.

According to Adams, Jefferson replied that even without consideration of constitutional limitations on such a plan, he was "so sick of residing in Europe, that I believe I shall never go there again." Accepting Jefferson's negative reaction, Adams recommended that perhaps Madison might go instead. "What do you think of sending Mr. Madison?" Adams asked. "Do you think he would accept an appointment?" Jefferson replied, "I do not know. Washington wanted to appoint him some time ago, and kept a place open for him a long time; but he never could get him to say that he would go."[24] This conversation would mark the end of their professional relationship, and set them on a path that would culminate in a period of ten years of mutual silence.

After their discussion about the mission to France, Adams retrospectively wrote in the *Boston Patriot*, Jefferson and he "parted as good friends as we had always lived; but we consulted very little together afterwards. Party violence[25] soon rendered it impracticable, or at least useless."[26] Adams was not altogether forthcoming in his *Boston Patriot* essay, however.

Adams had also told Jefferson in detail about his broad plans to respond to "the situation of our affairs with France."[27] As issues relating to France would soon be at the center of Adams's administration, these conversations have a very important place in American political and diplomatic history, as well as in the story of the friendship of Adams and Jefferson. Jefferson's recollections of this meeting, and another one that occurred two days after the inauguration, add further revelations.

"He found me alone in my room," Jefferson wrote of Adams's visit to him on the day before the inauguration. Explaining to Jefferson his concerns about the pressing challenge of France, Adams thought that a "rupture with that nation" would "convulse the attachments of this country." To avoid such an outcome he told Jefferson that he had decided to send a diplomatic mission to the Directory, the revolutionary government of France then in power. Adams acknowledged that the Constitution might not allow Jefferson to be included in the mission, and reasonable prudence regarding continuance of the government made the appointment unlikely. "It would have been the first wish of his heart to have got me to go there (France), but that he supposed it was out of the question, as it did not seem justifiable for him to send away the person destined to take his place in case of accident to himself," Jefferson wrote in his personal notes of the conversation. Adams then mentioned that the public's perception of Jefferson as opposition leader would also have to be considered in choosing another man for the mission to France. Adams told Jefferson that he thought it would not be "decent to remove from competition one who was a rival in the public favor."[28]

Adams's acknowledgement of the complexity of their professional relationship, while simultaneously being leaders of opposing political parties, appears to have been Adams's signal to Jefferson to walk with him on the middle path of loyalty to the government and the Constitution and cooperation with him and the administration of which he was an important part. Adams clearly wanted to diminish the party differences between them and work together as a unified team as much as was possible. This was something of an invitation from Adams to Jefferson to unite with him and abandon any conflicting loyalties that Jefferson may have had.

There is a sense of disappointment in Adams's later realization that Jefferson had embarked on a road that the two could not travel together, and which was entirely divergent from his own. This metaphor of an approaching fork in the road would be played out on the streets of Philadelphia three days later.

"I think it was on Monday the 6th of March, Mr. Adams and myself met at dinner at General Washington's, and we happened, in the evening, to rise from table and come away together," Jefferson wrote in the notes for his memoirs. As they exited Washington's house and walked along the street together Jefferson told Adams that Madison had declined Adams's offer to go to France. This was not unexpected, and Adams replied that since their talk several days before "some objections to that nomination had been raised which he had not contemplated."[29] Jefferson perceived this response by Adams as excuse making, though federalist members of his cabinet had indeed made objections about the offer to Madison. "We came to Fifth street, where our road separated, his being down Market street, mine along Fifth, and we took leave: and he never after that said one word to me on the subject, or ever consulted me as to any measures of the government."[30] One noted historian described this night walk from the President's House (Washington's official home), and leave-taking in the cool darkness of an early March Philadelphia evening as "the end of an era."[31]

Jefferson understood that Adams, though he desired to minimize party passions, was himself under pressure from partisan Federalists in his cabinet. The vice president viewed Adams's recommendation of Madison for the mission to France as an indication that Adams was trying to "steer impartially between the parties." Jefferson speculated that, because the first meeting of Adams's cabinet had occurred earlier in the day, Adams "on expressing ideas of this kind, he had been at once diverted from them, and returned to his former party views."[32] Jefferson's beliefs about the extent of Adams's party partisanship were unfairly exaggerated, at least when compared against his own strongly held republican views.

Jefferson found a convenient synergy between his party-building goals and his interpretation of the constitutional definition of his new role as vice president. In an early 1797 letter, dated several months prior to the dinner at Washington's and the ominous evening walk with Adams, Jefferson wrote to Madison that he believed his duties as vice president were very limited. Adams, Jefferson wrote, had hoped to administer the government "in concurrence with me." This could not be possible, however, due to Jefferson's rigid constitutional interpretation of his vice presidential role. Jefferson explained to Madison, "As to duty, the constitution will know me only as the member of a legislative body: and its principle is, that of the separation of legislative, executive, and judiciary functions, except in cases specified."[33] Jefferson's sense of obligation to his interpretation of the Constitution in this regard, and his inclination to obstruct the federalist political agenda, certainly encouraged his non-participation in activities of the "executive cabinet."

It seems likely that Adams had been made aware of Jefferson's views of his limited role as vice president, and the limitations that he had set upon himself in so far as cooperation with Adams and other Federalists was concerned. There were mixed purposes between these two old friends now embarking on separate roads—Adams to avoid a war with revolutionary France, Jefferson to build his party and rid the government of federalist "heresies." While party-building would become an inordinately large (and soon to be unfortunate) focus of Jefferson's attentions, there was still the matter of the crisis with France that threatened to engulf both countries in a disastrous and costly war, a war that both the president and vice president wanted very much to avoid.

Jefferson's assertion that, after their walk together on March sixth, Adams never again "consulted" with him on matters of the government may not be as forthcoming a statement as it first appears. Later events strongly suggest that though Adams may not have asked for Jefferson's views on governing he may well have issued orders to his vice president—orders that Jefferson would have been glad to accept.

There are strong reasons to believe that Adams directed Jefferson to undertake a *domestic* diplomatic mission with France. Jefferson had already expressed his lack of interest in travelling to Paris, and had argued that the Constitution would not allow it. Adams perhaps determined on a different course—one that would hopefully accomplish essentially the same goals; and, for Jefferson's benefit, only local roads would be travelled. There is no discussion of this mission either in Jefferson's or Adams's extant writings. That the mission did occur is an undeniable part of the historical record. These events are known to history not via the voluminous records of Jefferson or Adams but due only to a French diplomat's official reports.

Jefferson's notion of early March that the involvement of a vice president in a diplomatic capacity was disallowed by the Constitution was apparently an interpretation with which the president concurred. This is a reasonable explanation for the silence of both men on the matter. Adams likely never knew the truth of his vice president's controversial performance, nor of his personal attacks on Adams himself, as over a hundred years passed before the truth became known. Jefferson's purposeful misapplication of this extraordinary domestic diplomatic mission, whether he had taken it upon himself or been authorized by President Adams, materially affected American relations with France for the worse, and created a new crisis that would shock the American people and bring the two countries perilously close to war.

Jefferson's anti-federalist and pro-French partisanship was not limited to obstructionism of administration policy, but also included employing the dubious talents of a bitter anti-federalist writer whose loyalty to Jefferson would be short-lived. The same biting invective that characterized the writings of this man, which were at first aimed at Adams and the Federalists, would later be turned against Jefferson and result in a stain on his reputation that two hundred years have not dissipated.

Jefferson's unfortunate association with muckraking, anti-federalist pamphleteer James Callender began in June, and though it started quietly enough, would later bring considerable controversy to Jefferson. Recognizing in Callender a powerful voice against the Federalists that he could use to rally support for his republican goals, Jefferson's confidence in that opinionated and troubled author would be short-lived. The greatest controversy of his life, one that still shadows his reputation—that he had had an affair with one of his slaves and fathered children with her—originated from an allegation written by Callender. One of Jefferson's biographers described Jefferson's mistaken encouragement of Callender's inflammatory, hostile articles and anti-federalist pamphlets in this way: "He was to have abundant reason to regret this instance of letting a great end—the attainment and preservation of popular representative government—justify what he must have known were dubious means."[34] Jefferson's unfortunate dalliance with Callender is illustrative of the end-justifies-the-means choices that Jefferson sometimes made to further his political goals and oppose those of his old friend Adams.

There is a strong theme in Jefferson's character of the "true believer"—that is, his unshakable belief that his goals and motives were loftier and more morally correct than those of his opponents. While those with similarly overinflated certitude in the value and accuracy of their political views sometimes make decisions that are outside the law and contrary to accepted ideas of correct behavior, as Jefferson did do in the case of his domestic diplomatic mission with the French Consul in Philadelphia, the outcomes were not always favorable and the costs high.

The consequences of his support of Callender would, in the long term, be limited to the devastating personal damage that it had on Jefferson's reputation. His failure however to apparently implement his domestic diplomatic mission in good faith would, at least in the short term, have catastrophic results for the Republican Party and for the cause of peace with France. Jefferson's opportunity for direct diplomacy with an official representative of the French government, which he unfortunately combined with partisan political subterfuge/warfare against Adams and the Federalists, would have to wait however, as another embarrassing domestic political controversy involving Jefferson quite suddenly arose.

"My letters inform me that Mr. Adams speaks of me with great friendship," Jefferson wrote to Madison in January 1797. "I saw that our ancient friendship was affected by a little leaven, produced partly by his constitution, partly by the contrivance of others, yet I never felt a diminution of confidence in his integrity, and retained a solid affection for him."[35] Jefferson's private assertions of affection for his longtime friend and now superior in government would become rarer and eventually entirely disappear for a long hiatus. Worse still a personal letter written by Jefferson surfaced in public soon after the inauguration that would eclipse his supposedly inadvertently printed preface to Paine's *Rights of Man*, and temporarily devastate his public reputation.

Jefferson's relationship with Adams would suffer further from this breach of trust by one of Jefferson's friends and, as a direct result, too, no invitations to dinner from General Washington would ever again be sent to Jefferson. As this newest controversy involving Jefferson's private political opinions that he had meant only for the eyes of a trusted friend was about to burst into the public mind, affairs of France, for the moment, took precedence once again.

Having his wish to not participate in executive operations of the government granted, Jefferson focused on his duties as presiding officer of the Senate. He explained to Madison that this was the extent of his role as vice president. Finding that official demands on his time were thus not excessive, Jefferson accepted the presidency of the American Philosophical Society.[36] Benjamin Franklin, a former diplomatic colleague of Jefferson's in France, had once held the same office.

Jefferson's immense intellectual hunger and activity required constant stimulus for which he went to great pains throughout his life to assure were available to him. Matters of scholarship would often occupy his mind and time while Adams toiled with the more mundane problems of governing. Due to Jefferson's inclination (one might say instead "insistence") for a limited role in the administration, Adams essentially had a part-time vice president. Adams's realization that Jefferson's priorities were not focused on those matters of national government where they ought to be kept Jefferson, in the main, out of the central circles of national authority. Jefferson's noninvolvement did not go unnoticed.

One of Abigail's greatest frustrations with her husband during times of separation, particularly when Adams had been in Europe for many years prior to her arrival there, were his sometimes short (or delayed) letters. With Abigail in Quincy and John ensconced at the capital in Philadelphia this theme would be repeated a number of times. On May 13, 1797, John Adams sent a two-page letter (short by her standards) complaining of the weather, his new work "most of which is new to me," and urging her to leave Massachusetts and join him at the President's House. John and Abigail were a spectacular couple, perfect the one for the other, mutually complimentary in demeanor, character, and intellect. Their mutual love and respect leap off the pages of their letters; their voluminous correspondence is a treasure trove of the inner thoughts and mutual affections of an important political and romantic relationship central to the Revolution and early development of the nation. Among his observations to Abigail of the situation at Philadelphia on March 13, 1797, was this simple but loaded statement: "Mr. Jefferson has been here and is gone off to day for Virginia. He is as he was."[37]

Due to the long distance between Philadelphia and Quincy, Abigail's reply was not swift. On the twenty-third she received four letters from John written on four different days; she replied two days later. Once close friends with Jefferson, in penning her response Abigail perhaps remembered their fond association in Paris while Adams and Jefferson served there together. After she and John Adams moved to London from France Abigail had formed a deep bond of parental affection with Jefferson's daughter Polly. The young girl and her slave companion Sally Hemings had rested in London at the Adams's home on their journey to Paris to join Jefferson—then American minister to France. Abigail's anger toward Jefferson as shown in her response to John's four letters was both personal and political.[38] "There is one observation in your Letter which struck me as meaning more than is exprest," she wrote. "J. is as he was! Can he still be a devotee to a cause and to a people, run mad, without, any wish for Peace, without any desire after a rational system of Government, and whose thirst for power and absolute dominion is become Gluttonous? Can it be?"[39] Abigail's response encapsulated her frustration at what she saw as a kind of abandonment, if not betrayal, by someone for whom she had once had a great affection and respect. Since her husband was now the president and Jefferson his vice president—though more importantly his most serious political opponent—Abigail couldn't help but see Jefferson's opposition and obstructionism as more than simply about politics. For her, and later for her husband, Jefferson's lack of support and active opposition were clearly *personal* matters. Her allusion to Jefferson's support of the French Revolution, which both she and John strongly opposed, cannot be missed.

Prior to Jefferson's departure from Monticello for the inauguration ceremony, he had received an ominous letter. Charles Cotesworth Pinckney, the newest American ambassador to the Directory at Paris, had been rejected by the French government.[40] A widely respected former major general in the revolutionary army, Pinckney had gone to France to replace the previous ambassador, James Monroe, who had been removed from that post by Washington. Apparently, the mails to Philadelphia were not as swift as those directed to the mountain home of Mr. Jefferson because word of Pinckney's rough handling by the French had by then not yet arrived in Philadelphia. "Not only had Pinckney not been received, he had been jockeyed and insulted and ordered to quit French soil. In addition French frigates had seized American ships in the West Indies."[41] Soon enough however, word of Pinckney's rejection, as well as the French aggression against American vessels, became known to Adams. The brewing conflict with France had suddenly taken a dangerous and dark turn. The president quickly determined to send a new diplomatic mission to America's once most important ally.

Jefferson had already refused such an assignment on both personal preference and constitutional grounds; Madison had also demurred. Regardless, a mission to Paris would have to be named and sent on its way to France rapidly.

Jefferson viewed the growing conflict between England and France as an opportunity to spread republicanism to the mother country. In a letter to Edmund Randolph, Jefferson wrote, "Nothing can establish firmly the republican principles of our (own) government but an establishment of them in England. France will be the apostle of this."[42] The growing stresses around the matter of France and the future of its Revolution would soon find the vice president in a personal conflict of loyalties. Before this great crisis occurred however, more pressing matters of state and a new, and most unpleasant controversy caused by the poor judgment of a friend exposed Jefferson's unfortunate rhetoric, partisanship, and sense of indignance to the world and further split the nation on partisan lines.

8

"Conceal the Lever"

JEFFERSON'S ENTHUSIASM FOR republicanism, and revolution to foment it, was not isolated to him alone; officers of the French revolutionary government were equally interested in expanding both French-style republicanism and French power. This expansionist view put France and the United States in direct conflict because one of the targets of French revolutionary agitation was America itself.

Inappropriate (and unfriendly) activities of French diplomatic officials in the United States and later by the Directory itself (particularly where American shipping was involved) were strong motivators in forcing President Washington to take action against France. Both the open and covert hostility of that country finally pushed Washington to move the United States diplomatically closer to the British via the Jay Treaty. In fact, the immediate purpose of the *Farewell Address*, according to one noted scholar of the period, was "to strike a powerful blow against French intermeddling in American affairs."[1] The reaction of Pierre-Auguste Adet, the French Ambassador to the United States, to Washington's *Farewell* was anything but favorable.

Adet made his anger at Washington's Address quite clear in a letter to the French Foreign Ministry. "You will have noticed the lies it contains, the insolent tone that governs it, the immorality which characterizes it. You will have had no difficulty in recognizing the author of a piece extolling ingratitude, showing it as a virtue necessary to the happiness of States, presenting interest as the only counsel which governments ought to follow in the course of their negotiations, putting aside honor and glory."[2]

Though American minister to France, James Monroe had erroneously assured the French government that the Jay Treaty would not be ratified, the Directory had already set its aggressive tone toward the United States. French foreign minister Charles Delacroix declared in a report to the Directory that President Washington had to be replaced by someone favorable to France, and that revolution should be fomented in the United States. He also made certain that French diplomats would be empowered to assure that these outcomes came to pass. "A friend of France must succeed him in that eminent office," Delacroix asserted. "We must raise up the people and at the same time conceal the lever by which we do so . . . I propose to the Executive Directory to authorize me to send orders and instructions to our minister plenipotentiary at Philadelphia to use all the means in his power in the United States to bring about the right kind of revolution (*l'heureuse Révolution*) and Washington's replacement, which, assuring to the Americans their independence, will break off treaties [sic] made with England and maintain those which unite them to the French Republic."[3]

The growing favoritism of the American government toward Great Britain prior to Adams's presidency was a direct result of French hostility to American commercial interests and ongoing pressure from French diplomats in the United States. French anger at the United States government was ironically therefore a direct result of hostile actions by the French themselves, which in turn then caused American diplomatic moves toward England. Driving French annoyance and disappointment with the United States were pre-Revolution expectations of American indebtedness to France by which the French believed that the United States should continue to be bound; but to which the Americans, for their part, particularly since the murder of Louis XVI and the overthrow of the friendly Bourbon monarchy, no longer felt obligated.

The old feelings of obligation to France for that country's assistance during the American Revolution had, for many in the United States, been overturned first by the execution of the King, and then by the aggressive, expansionist posture of the French revolutionary government. The official newspaper of the French government, the *Moniteur*, asserted that "France had a right to expect more from the United States than any other country, for she is their true mother country since she has secured to them their liberty and independence."[4] The bitterness of official revolutionary France toward the United States drove French foreign policy throughout Adams's term, and forced him to walk a fine line between preparing for, and avoiding, war with that country. Jefferson never seemed to grasp the finesse of Adams's dual path with regard to France.[5]

Jefferson's opposition to Adams's apparent contradictory occasional martial rhetoric (in conjunction with actual buildup of military strength to prepare for possible war with France) mixed with diplomacy was founded upon his dislike of Britain and his affection for revolutionary France. Jefferson believed that a war against either European power was not then in the interest of the United States, though a war against France would be far worse for republicanism.

Not at all shy about a war with Great Britain, Jefferson was specifically opposed to the favorable approach that the United States was taking toward that country at the expense of the American relationship with France. French bitterness toward the United States had been further exacerbated by the ratification of the Jay Treaty with England, an event which the American minister to Paris had repeatedly assured the Directory would never occur.

One nineteenth-century historian wrote of the November 1794 ratification of the Jay Treaty that it "awakened a deep feeling of indignation, and, eventually of resentment. To that instrument may, immediately, be traced the unjust acts of the French government."[6] France's bitter and hostile reaction to America's closer relations with Britain, particularly upon the signing and then later ratification of the Jay Treaty, was no doubt due in large part because of false expectations created by American minister to France, James Monroe.

Historian Samuel Flagg Bemis believed that the purpose of Monroe's diplomatic mission to Paris had been to offset the treaty negotiation mission of John Jay to London. Monroe's purpose was to minimize and deflect the likely negative reaction in Paris to Jay's mission. A supporter of Jefferson with a strong aversion to John Jay, Monroe appears to have been a wise political selection to ameliorate French concerns about any treaty with England that might result from Jay's diplomacy to London. "To mask this mission," Bemis wrote, "they sent to France the pro–French Republican senator from Virginia, James Monroe, an old opponent of Jay's diplomacy since 1786, who considered Jay's mission as mischievous and in the Senate voted against his confirmation."[7] Washington and his advisors would have cause to regret their decision to send Monroe to France, however, as Monroe was appparently motivated by the same partisan spirit that inspired Jefferson.

Monroe's official defense of the Jay Treaty at Paris did not meet the expectations of President Washington. Worse still, Monroe apparently participated in unofficial conversations with French officials, which the American minister "did not reveal to his own government."[8] Monroe offered to acquaint, unofficially, his French hosts with the "real dispositions of my countrymen."[9] Bemis wrote, "He [Monroe] certainly led the French government to believe that any treaty of amity between the United States and Great Britain would never be ratified. When it was known that a treaty had been signed, Monroe repeated this assurance."[10] Citing a letter that Monroe wrote to the Secretary of State (then Edmund Randolph), Bemis shows that Monroe had been true to his orders in this one regard, repeating to the French that they had no cause for concern about the Jay Treaty. "I assured them, generally, as I had done before, that I was satisfied the treaty contained in it nothing which could give them uneasiness; but if it did, and especially if it weakened our connexion with France, it would certainly be disapproved in America."[11] Monroe had however overstepped his authority in assuring the French government that the treaty he had been sent to explain and defend would not be ratified. Even worse, Monroe had "led them in Paris to believe that the people would overthrow the administration of President Washington as a result of the treaty, that better things might be expected after the election of 1796."[12]

Washington understandably recalled Monroe from his post in Paris, thus opening the position to be soon thereafter filled, almost momentarily, by Charles Cotesworth Pinkney. It would seem that the early leaders of the United States were far more forgiving than is commonly known; Monroe was not set aside for his apparent disregard to his instructions and disloyalty to President Washington and the administration. With his reputation unscathed by his activities in France, Monroe later became the fifth president of the United States. Jefferson's questionable activities as vice president would soon however overshadow even those of former minister to France Monroe.

With the recall of Monroe and the ratification of the Jay Treaty, the French Directory was in no mood to show courtesies to the American government. "The French authorities, offended at this change and at the ratification of Jay's treaty in spite of their remonstrances, while they dismissed Monroe with great ovations, refused to receive the new ambassador sent in his place, at the same time issuing decrees and orders highly injurious to American commerce."[13] The removal of Monroe, a highly popular man in Paris despite his failed assurances regarding the Jay Treaty, was, from the perspective of at least one French diplomat, yet another illustration of American ineptitude in dealing with France. "Louis-Guillaume Otto, formerly charge d'affaires in the United States, characterized Monroe's recall as 'the most unpardonable . . . of all the many political blunders, made on both sides the Atlantic these six years past.'"[14]

From the American government's perspective the recall of Monroe had been unavoidable. Under the circumstances his personal popularity among his French hosts was irrelevant. Among the French, it was commonly believed that the political parties in the United States represented a British bloc (Federalists) and a French bloc (Republicans). Bolstered by this widely accepted yet mistakenly over-simplified conception of American politics, the reaction to the recall of Republican Monroe by his federalist superiors was more negative than it otherwise should have been. The French foreign minister chose to view the recall of Monroe in a domestic American political context when, in a letter to Adet, he accused Washington of replacing Monroe simply to discredit the Republicans.[15]

In such a highly charged diplomatic environment in which French purposes and American goals were completely at odds, the arrival of

Federalist Pinckney in Paris to replace the Republican Monroe was seen by many officials in France as little more than a ploy by Washington to diminish his political opponents at home. This misunderstanding of American politics was at the center of French actions, and was noted by insightful French Foreign Ministry official Louis-Guillaume Otto. "Our agents wished to see only two political parties in the United States, the French party and the English party; but there is a middle party, much larger, composed of the most estimable men of the two other parties," Otto wrote in 1797. "This party, whose existence we have not even suspected, is the American party which loves its country above all and for whom preferences either for France or England are only accessory and often passing affections."[16] Having spent over a decade living in the United States (1779–1792), Otto was well qualified to make such penetrating observations about American politics. One scholar described him as a man "notable for his ability as a diplomat, his remarkable learning, and sterling integrity."[17] His knowledgeable reports on American issues were a font of accurate information and analysis for his seniors in the foreign ministry at Paris. Though French Minister Adet in Philadelphia appears to have fully understood Washington's *Farewell Address* concept of "national interest," rather than alliances, as the central driver of American foreign policy, his colleagues in Paris did not.

Foreign Minister Charles Delacroix had told Monroe that "the Directory has seen in Jay's Treaty 'a derogation of the friendship which unites the United States and the Republic'"[18] which could perhaps explain to some degree Monroe's repeated (but mistaken) assurances to the French that the treaty with England would not be ratified. Adet immediately opposed Charles Cotesworth Pinckney's appointment. In an October 1796 letter to Delacroix at Paris, Adet wrote, "You know that their protestations of friendship are false and that their caresses are faithless. You will recall that in our misfortunes they have insulted and betrayed us and that, if today they pay the Republic a too just tribute of admiration, if they appear to share as friends its success and triumphs, fear alone dictates a language that their hearts deny."[19] Adet's letter did not fall on deaf ears. Delacroix announced to Monroe early in December 1796 that France would "no longer recognize nor receive a minister pleni-potentiary from the United States."[20] Foreign Minister Adet's suspicions of American motives were not limited to the government of the United States alone but were also targeted toward one of France's greatest champions in America, Thomas Jefferson. A diplomat and scientist, and strongly patriotic, Adet was confused as to the real pro-France motivations of Jefferson. The senior French diplomat in the United States at that time perhaps believed that Jefferson's views and those described in Washington's *Farewell Address* were one and the same.

"Mr. Jefferson likes us because he detests England; he seeks to draw near to us because he fears us less than England; but tomorrow he might change his opinion about us if England should cease to inspire his fear," Adet provocatively reported to the foreign ministry at Paris. "Although Jefferson is the friend of liberty and of science, although he is an admirer of the efforts we have made to cast off our shackles and to clear away the cloud of ignorance which weighs down the human race, Jefferson, I say, is an American, and as such, he cannot sincerely be our friend." Adet concluded his over-the-top report with this dramatic assertion: "An American is the born enemy of all the peoples of Europe."[21]

Adet was clearly confused about Washington's *reapolitik*, Jefferson's unabashed support for France, and his deep dislike of England. In truth, there was little or no cause for Adet to be concerned about Jefferson's affections for France, or suspicious that he harbored some (never expressed) secret endearment for England (which he did not); Jefferson no more supported the Jay Treaty than did his friend Monroe.

France had a true friend in Jefferson. Adet's official correspondence that placed such serious doubts on Jefferson's support for France must have greatly confused his superiors in Paris. Most importantly perhaps is the clarity of Adet's distrust of Americans in general—if *bon ami* Thomas Jefferson was suspected by French officials, then certainly no American could be beyond suspicion. One respected historian of the period described Adet's influence on American-French relations as "baneful."[22]

The Directory made its displeasure known about the ratification of the Jay Treaty and Monroe's recall by suspending Foreign Minister

Adet's diplomatic mission to the United States. This act essentially severed diplomatic relations between Paris and Philadelphia.[23] The French also increased their harassments of American shipping and confiscations of goods from American-flagged vessels, which soon grew into an undeclared economic and naval war against the United States. Some historians have characterized the French depredations against American naval commerce during this time, prior to the Convention of 1800 (Treaty of Mortefontaine), as the "Quasi-War." This is an accurate term due to French diplomatic and military hostility, resulting in significant American financial losses, and naval combats between French and American ships—though no formal declaration of war from either nation was ever issued. The absence of an official declaration of a state of war between France and the United States, and the sometimes baffling actions of the French government, did little to create an environment of clarity for President Adams.

Between 1793 and 1799 numerous hostile decrees against American commerce were announced by the Directory. These decrees caused great confusion in the United States as they were often amended and/or repealed within a short span of time. In addition, the exact stipulations of these decrees were sometimes not completely understood.[24] What remained a constant however was that, with the ratification of the Jay Treaty, French vessels increased their attacks on American ships and confiscated more American goods as contraband on the high seas.[25] The aggression of France against American shipping was so extensive that by the time Adams and Jefferson were inaugurated, France had already seized "three hundred American merchant ships."[26] The economic cost of these seizures was not insignificant. One historian of the period wrote, "American shipping losses in Europe and the West Indies amounted to $12,149,306.10 between 1793 and 1800."[27]

Pinckney's harsh and disrespectful treatment at the hands of his French hosts, swift official rejection, and finally his insulting ejection from the country came as a disturbing surprise to the Adams administration. Perhaps most alarming (and confounding) was that Pinckney's official instructions, which were conciliatory and friendly, had received such a bitter and aggressive rebuke. Pinckney's "Letter of Credence" to the French government stated that his mission was "to maintain that good understanding, which, from the commencement of the alliance, had subsisted between the two nations, and to efface unfavourable impressions, banish suspicions and restore that cordiality which was at once the evidence and pledge of a friendly union."[28] The Adams administration then embarked upon a dual response to France, an approach that Jefferson did not approve: The country would make ready for war, but continue with diplomacy to try to avoid it, if at all possible.

The government of France reasonably suspected that American preparations for war would include additional cooperation with England—which they hoped to avert. In fact, perhaps surprisingly, American requests for munitions and naval support had been sent to the British.[29] Otto, the French Foreign Ministry analyst, believed that a war with the United States was not in France's best interests, nor would it likely be one that, in the long term, France would win. "Their sailors, much more able than those of England, will become the scourge of all nations that Great Britain wishes to attack," Otto wrote in a mid-1797 report about American affairs to Delacroix. "The most experienced sailors, provisions, fish, lumber, naval supplies, which they furnish will be for the exclusive use of the enemy of France, and there will remain to us only the regret that we have erected the structure of American independence that it might contribute to the destruction of our commerce and our colonies."[30]

Adams's reaction to the disrespectful treatment of Pinckney, and the official insult against the United States that it represented, was to call a joint session of Congress on May 16, 1797. In his remarks to the combined House, Adams strongly denounced the actions of France. "The refusal on the part of France to receive our minister is, then, the denial of a right," Adams declared, "but the refusal to receive him until we have acceded to their demands without discussion and without investigation is to treat us neither as allies nor as friends, nor as a sovereign state."[31] The president also acknowledged what the French diplomatists already knew, that there was an ongoing attempt by the agents of revolutionary France to corrupt and use the American political system to foment rebellion against the government. Adams declared that France was attempting "to separate the people of the United States from the Government, to persuade them that they have different affections, principles, and interests from those of their fellow citizens whom they themselves have chosen to manage their common concerns, and thus to produce divisions fatal to our peace." Asserting that the French government "had inflicted a wound in the American breast" (which Adams continued to hope could be healed), he acknowledged that, with the suspension of Adet's mission, no official diplomatic ties existed between the government of the United States and that of France.

Adams further asked the Congress if "the means of general-defense ought not to be increased by an addition to the regular artillery and cavalry, and by arrangements for forming a provisional army."[32] Agitations within the United States by French officials, attacks against American shipping by French navy ships, and finally the rejection of the American minister to Paris had brought the president of the United States to public talk of preparations for war with its once most important friend and ally. Jefferson's response to Adams's speech was, not surprisingly, devoid of positivity.

"I consider the calling of Congress so out of season an experiment of the new administration to see how far & on what lines they could count on its support," Jefferson suspiciously wrote to a friend several weeks after the address.[33] Despite Jefferson's private objections, the American government certainly had just cause to publicly discuss preparations for (defensive) war with France. In his reaction to Adams's speech to the joint House, Jefferson also included statements that one of his most respected biographers described as "questionable value-judgments," including the suggestion that Adams's speech might "endanger the peace of the country."[34] Jefferson's private letter of bitter complaint against Adams did not remain confidential for long.

According to one of Adams's leading biographers, some "busybodies" informed the president of the text of Jefferson's letter.[35] Adams's reaction was understandably far from sanguine. Replying in a letter to an admirer/busybody, Adams asserted that Jefferson's criticisms were "evidence of a mind soured, yet seeking for popularity, and eaten to a honeycomb with ambition, yet weak, confused, uninformed, and ignorant."[36] Jefferson's criticism during a time of national crisis had a profound and negative effect on Adams. Knowledge of this letter marked for Adams, according to one of Jefferson's most respected biographers, "the cessation of personal friendliness" toward Jefferson.[37] The vice president's strident criticism of Adams's speech, in combination with events soon to come, set Adams on a completely divergent path both politically and personally from Jefferson and effectively prompted a lengthy denouement of their friendship lasting many years.

"You can witness for me how loath I have been to give him up," Adams wrote to his son John Quincy in early November 1797. "It is with much reluctance that I am obliged to look upon him as a man whose mind is warped by prejudice and so blinded by ignorance as to be unfit for the office he holds. However wise and scientific as philosopher, as a politician he is a child and the dupe of party!"[38] Jefferson's bitter opposition signaled a new phase in Adams's political life and an apparent unhappy conclusion to the friendship that Adams had long considered one of the most important of his life. There is a deep sadness evident in Adams's announcement to John Quincy of his reluctance to "give up" Jefferson, and an understandable anger at having to make such a personally painful decision to separate himself from his vice president and once-cherished friend.

Though high-level official diplomatic relations between the United States and France had been severed with Adet's recall, lower-level channels remained open. After Adet's exit, Phillipe André Joseph de Létombe arrived at Philadelphia in May 1797 as French consul general. Létombe quickly "informed Adams and Jefferson that France did not intend a rupture and that all could be put right if America would send a minister whose character guaranteed a change of attitude toward France."[39] Back in Paris, former minister to the United States Adet recommended, ironically on the basis of French national interest, that diplomatic relations between France and the United States be normalized quickly, "as the means of settling differences which it is not in our interests to prolong."[40] Adet also advised that the new representative(s) sent to France by America be received, and that discussions should be "frank."[41] The stage appeared to be almost set for a peaceful conclusion—neither country wanted war, and both appeared to be willing to negotiate.

Adams, with his cabinet, determined to send a diplomatic delegation of three to Paris. The purpose of their mission was to normalize relations, and prevent open war with France.

Pinckney (a Federalist), the American minister to France (recently rejected by Paris), then in Holland, was selected to return to Paris. The remaining two members of the mission were to be Virginia Federalist John Marshall (later Secretary of State, and Chief Justice of the Supreme Court), and Republican Elbridge Gerry of Massachusetts.[42] As the sole Republican in the mission much of the responsibility of this new diplomatic effort would be thrust upon Gerry.[43]

The Adams administration hoped that the French could not mistake the seriousness of the American government in wanting to resolve the crisis between the two countries; not only had one accomplished man been sent to Paris to represent the United States—there would be three. However, before the triple commission to France could be sent on its way for high-level discussions that, it was hoped, would reduce the tensions between the two countries, stop French naval attacks, and normalize relations, a new and ugly partisan controversy involving Jefferson suddenly appeared.

In late April 1796, Jefferson had written a lengthy letter to his friend, then in Italy, Phillip Mazzei. An early and strong supporter of American independence, Mazzei had authored two pro-American pamphlets that had been published in Italy. Mazzei, a onetime wine merchant, became great friends with Jefferson, as both men desired to bring viticulture to American shores. But their plans to start a vineyard and winery were interrupted, and ultimately cancelled, by British advances into Virginia during the Revolution. Adams had, during his ministerial years in Europe, also corresponded with the Italian patriot—with more than several friendly but formal letters between them extant. Mazzei later immigrated to the United States but eventually returned to Italy where he died after a long and eventful life. But for Jefferson's unfortunate letter the importance of Mazzei has generally been overlooked; it was he who had recommended the phrase "all men are created equal," which Jefferson later included in the Declaration of Independence.[44]

After Mazzei returned to Europe, Jefferson wrote occasional letters to keep his Republican friend informed of events in the United States. Jefferson was apparently quite agitated and frustrated about the Jay Treaty when he wrote a private letter to him on April 24, 1796. Much to his discomfiture, Jefferson's letter to Mazzei of late April did not remain private for very long.

Perhaps overly enthusiastic upon receipt of this highly charged letter from his renowned republican friend in the United States, Mazzei imprudently decided to share Jefferson's quite personal and politically explosive thoughts with others.[45] Mazzei copied a number of paragraphs from Jefferson's letter (retaining the original wording), then sent these copies to several friends. One of the recipients was "the Dutch banker Jacob Van Staphorst, who rebuked Mazzei for his lack of 'prudence and delicacy' in allowing the personal correspondence of a friend to be circulated without his permission."[46] Another friend, upon receiving Mazzei's transcription of the extracts of Jefferson's letter, translated the paragraphs into French. Soon enough, the official organ of the French revolutionary republic, the *Moniteur,* received the French translation from channels that are as yet unknown. That newspaper published the French version of Jefferson's letter in full in January 1797. The editors of the *Moniteur* also added several paragraphs of editorial comment that were highly unfavorable toward American policies. Jefferson's luck with such things being consistently poor, as was Adams's in similar circumstances, a copy of the *Moniteur* containing Jefferson's letter made its way to Noah Webster.

The noted author of the first American Dictionary, Webster was an ardent foe of Jefferson. Worse for Jefferson, Webster was then the editor of the strongly federalist New York newspaper *Minerva.* On May 2, 1797, Webster published an English translation of the extracts of Jefferson's letter from the French *Moniteur*, as well as the critical editorial comments. It was not long before the *Minerva* bombshell made its way from New York to nearby Philadelphia. Jefferson was thunderstruck at the savage attacks that quickly sprang up against him from partisan federalist newspapers. He would never quite see the end to the controversy that the publication of this private letter to Mazzei created.

Madison "sagaciously remarked many years later, allowances 'ought to be made for a habit in Mr. Jefferson as in others of great genius of expressing in strong and round terms, impressions of the moment.'"[47] Jefferson and Adams shared this trait of genius—and that of occasionally using strong expressions and charged rhetoric to express personal opinions that were highly critical of others. One recent political historian suggested that, because of the Mazzei letter, "Jefferson made himself the brunt of attack and embarrassment, the victim of his own careless pen."[48] This seems an unfair criticism as Jefferson's letter had been a personal one written to a longtime friend, a letter that he reasonably expected would remain private.

Jefferson's frustrated expectation of privacy regarding his controversial letter to Mazzei was not unreasonable; such concepts of trust and confidentiality are among the hallmarks of friendship and intimacy. This situation is in sharp contrast to Jefferson's favorable comments about Paine's *Rights of Man* that he had sent to a publisher with whom there was no long-standing relationship of trust nor friendship and with which he did not attach a specific enjoinder that his comments were not for publication and were to be considered confidential. Without a specific instruction that his comments were not for publication, there could be no reasonable expectation on Jefferson's part that the publisher/printer of the Paine pamphlet would abandon such a marketing gift as positive comments from one of the leading politicians in the country. Neither Adams nor Jefferson ought to be criticized too heavily for what they wrote privately to correspondents from whom they reasonably expected protection of their private thoughts. Regardless of expectations, reasonable or otherwise, these private expressions sometimes brought unintended consequences.

As a result of the publication of excerpts from this private letter, Jefferson found himself in the center of a whirlwind of personal and public controversy. The segments which Jefferson's friend Mazzei caused to appear upon the international scene, and then published in the United States in Noah Webster's federalist *Minerva,* are reproduced below.

Our political situation is prodigiously changed since you left us. Instead of that noble love of liberty, and that republican government, which carried us triumphantly thro the dangers of the war, an Anglo-Monarchico-Aristocratic party has arisen.—Their avowed object is to impose on us the *substance*, as they have already given us the *form*, of the British government. Nevertheless, the principal body of our citizens remain faithful to republican principles. All our proprietors of lands are friendly to those principles, as also the mass of men of talents. We have against us (republicans) the *Executive Power*, the *Judiciary Power*, (two of the three branches of our government) *all the officers of government, all who are seeking offices, all timid men who prefer the calm of despotism to the tempestuous sea of liberty, the British merchants and the Americans who trade on British capitals, the speculators, persons interested in the bank and the public funds.* [Establishments invented with views of corruption, and to assimilate us to the British model in its corrupt parts.]

I should give you a fever, if I should name the apostates who have embraced these heresies; men who were Solomons in council, and Sampsons in combat, but whose hair has been cut off by the whore England.

They would wrest from us that liberty which we have obtained by so much labor and peril; but we shall preserve it. Our mass of weight and riches is so powerful, that we have nothing to fear from any attempt against us by force. It is sufficient that we guard ourselves, and that *we break the lilliputian ties* by which they have bound us, in the first slumbers which succeeded our labors. It suffices that we arrest the progress of that system of ingratitude and injustice towards France, from which they would alienate us, to bring us under British influence, &c.[49]

Clearly, the harsh and partisan language that Jefferson had used, language which he thought would never reach an audience greater than the person to whom it was intended, was aimed at the federalist administration of Washington and Adams. There is no evidence that Adams ever wrote of this controversy to anyone, except perhaps obliquely in his letter to John Quincy (quoted previously) in which Adams remarked of Jefferson several months later that he was "loath to give him up." Washington, likely seeing himself as the intended target of Jefferson's wrath, had a far stronger reaction. Jefferson later explained that his reference to "Sampsons" and "Solomons" was not about Washington but was reserved specifically for the Society of the Cincinnati, an organization of American Revolutionary War officers of some political power and influence, that Jefferson considered a potential threat to republicanism if unchecked.

Jefferson's opposition to the Cincinnati was long-standing, and based firmly on republican principles that any society of elites, such as an organization of Revolutionary War officers, could be destructive of fundamental democratic principles. When he first arrived in Paris, Jefferson had sent a letter of warning to Washington about the Society. "I have never heard a person in Europe, learned or unlearned, express his thoughts on this institution, who did not consider it as dishonorable and destructive to our governments," Jefferson wrote, "and that every writing which has come out since my arrival here, in which it is mentioned, considers it, even as now reformed, as the germ whose development is one day to destroy the fabric we have reared."[50]

Jefferson later explained, in a lengthy letter to Martin Van Buren, why he thought that Washington could not have believed that the term "Samsons in the field" was a reference to him personally, rather than the Society of the Cincinnati. "Disapproving thus of the institution as much as I did," Jefferson wrote of Washington's rejection of the Society, "and conscious that I knew him to do so, he could never suppose that I meant to include him among the Samsons in the field, whose object was to draw over us the *form*, as they made the letter say, of the British government, and especially its aristocratic member, an hereditary house of lords."[51] Jefferson reiterated to Van Buren that Washington "knew that I meant it for the Cincinnati generally, and that from what had passed between us at the commencement of that institution, I could not mean to include him."[52] Jefferson made a great effort to show that the publication of the Mazzei letter had caused no damage to his relationship with Washington. He explained to Van

Buren that their lack of visits and, in fact, of any correspondence in the wake of the publication of the letter was simply because neither of them had anything to say to the other:

> My last parting with General Washington was at the inauguration of Mr Adams, in March, 1797, and was warmly affectionate; and I never had any reason to believe any change on his part, as there certainly was none on mine. But one session of Congress intervened between that and his death, the year following, in my passage to and from which, as it happened to be not convenient to call on him, I never had another opportunity; and as to the cessation of correspondence observed during that short interval, no particular circumstance occurred for epistolary communication, and both of us were too much oppressed with letter-writing, to trouble, either the other, with a letter about nothing.[53]

Perhaps it is best to take Jefferson at his word on this account as Washington, the very representation of federalism, other than Hamilton, would not have been a person to whom Jefferson would have flown for conversation on matters of the day. After Washington's retirement there was really little that might have prompted a discussion between them, differing as they did on fundamental matters of politics. As they had no mutual propensity to discuss daily matters, discussions that are almost universally fostered by a desire to share time and views between friends, Jefferson's assertions then to Van Buren, though awkward in appearance, are understandable.

There remains a lingering controversy on the matter however: that the Mazzei letter *did* profoundly negatively affect the Jefferson/Washington relationship. One Jefferson biographer suggests strongly, in concurrence with his subject's view, that Washington felt no personal offense from the criticisms in the Mazzei letter. "He either, therefore, did not apply them to himself, or he did not consider them proofs of unfriendliness. Adopting either supposition, the inference is unavoidable that the Mazzei letter produced no rupture or even alienation between him and its writer."[54]

An alternative and far more radical view is that "after this disagreeable incident they never saw each other again. On several

occasions Jefferson passed the door of Mount Vernon without calling."[55] While the truth of Washington's reaction to the Mazzei letter
may lie somewhere between these perspectives, this explanation of
the consequences of the Mazzei letter, however, does not appear to
be sustainable.

A recent biographer of Noah Webster wrote, "the letter to Mazzei
cost Jefferson all influence he might have had in the Adams administration, and France all hope of obtaining military support from the
American government. With all hopes of alliance shattered, France
broke relations with the United States and expelled the American
ambassador Charles Pinckney."[56] This suggestion that the Mazzei letter is somehow linked with American-French relations, the rejection
of Pinckney, and the supposed failure of France to acquire military
aid against England from the United States is not supported by the
historical record. Any possibility of a renewed alliance between the
US and France had long before been extinguished by the Jay Treaty,
the actions of French diplomats, and by subsequent naval attacks
on American commerce; the Mazzei letter was not a consideration
at all. Finally, Jefferson had already alienated himself from Adams
by his refusal to participate in Cabinet discussions. By the time the
Mazzei letter was printed in Webster's *Minerva* in May 1797, Jefferson had *already* lost "all influence he might have had" within the
administration.

The allegations and insults that Jefferson included in his letter
to Mazzei were concepts that were fully understood in France. Jefferson's letter was published in the *Moniteur* not to demonstrate any
change in policy on the part of the French government, but rather
to leverage Jefferson's rhetoric to criticize Adams and the Federalists. Policy makers in France had no need of the contents of Jefferson's private letters to tell them what they already believed—that
the Adams administration was hostile to France and pro-British.
Regardless of the publication of an obviously private communication
from Jefferson in the official organ of the French government, it was
already understood in Paris (though this fact had escaped the notice
of France's onetime chief representative at Philadelphia, Adet) that
Jefferson indeed was a true friend of the Revolution. Later events

would prove the point. Jefferson's affection for revolutionary France remained strong. In contrast to his positive view of France, Jefferson's opinion of Noah Webster was quite the opposite.

"Tho' I view Webster as a mere pedagogue, of very limited understanding and very strong prejudices and party passions, yet as editor of a paper and as of the Newhaven association, he may be worth striking," President Jefferson wrote to Madison, then secretary of state, several years later.[57]

The controversy that resulted from the Mazzei letter never fully died away during Jefferson's lifetime; partisan opponents raised the issue as a weighted sledge against him again and again over time. Another aspect of the Mazzei letter debacle remains alive to this day.

According to at least one author, Washington and Jefferson had written several strongly worded letters to each other on the matter. "An overseer at Mount Vernon," Mr. Albin Rawlins, who claimed to have seen these letters, described them as having made the "hair rise on his head," and that the wording of them was such that "it must produce a duel."[58] Unfortunately, these letters, if they ever existed, were supposedly destroyed by Washington's private secretary, Tobias Lear, after the death of the first president.

Harvard alumnus Tobias Lear had come to Washington's attention by way of strong recommendations from Benjamin Lincoln, a Revolutionary War general and president of Harvard University. He became Washington's private secretary, and tutor to Washington's adopted children. Later, he became Washington's aide with a colonel's rank when the retired general was offered command of the Provisional Army in 1798, the army Adams ordered to be formed in preparation for a possible war with France. Washington considered Lear a member of his family. Consequently, he was trusted with Washington's most important correspondence and business activities.

When Washington was stricken in mid-December 1799, Lear held him in his arms, and recorded Washington's final words. With the permission of Martha Washington, Lear's letter describing the death of Washington acted as official notification to President Adams, who later read the entire letter to the Congress.[59] Lear held Washington's private papers for over a year after his death; the fate of the first president's papers during that year became a matter of some controversy, and resulted in ugly allegations. Jefferson was not unaware of these supposed angry letters between himself and Washington.

Timothy Pickering, the former secretary of state who had been dismissed by Adams in the closing months of his administration (May 1800), a onetime member of Washington's cabinet, and avowed Federalist, published a bitter pamphlet in 1824 within which he attacked both Adams and Jefferson. Most significantly, Pickering included allegations that he claimed were told to him twenty years previously by a "Doctor Stuart," a man known to both Jefferson and Washington, regarding the aftermath of the publication of the Mazzei letter. "In what manner the latter [Jefferson] humbled himself, and appeased the just resentment of Washington, will never be known, as, some time after his death, the correspondence was not to be found, and a diary for an important period of his Presidency was also missing,"[60] Pickering alleged. Buried within the allegation itself are several unstated assertions: that a correspondence relating to the Mazzei letter had occurred between Jefferson and Washington; that the correspondence would be viewed as unfavorable to Jefferson; and that the correspondence was purposefully and deliberately destroyed to shield Jefferson. Tobias Lear, Washington's trusted secretary and friend, had been in possession of the documents after the death of the president. Lear was a known supporter of Jefferson—therefore by implication, some believed that Tobias Lear must have got rid of these incriminating letters.

One of Jefferson's leading biographers of the nineteenth century, Henry Randall, a defender of Jefferson, concluded that no such correspondence between Jefferson and Washington had ever existed. To support this contention Randall referenced a discussion between him and Jared Sparks, later president of Harvard University. Sparks had, prior to the publication of Randall's biography of Jefferson, published *The Writings of George Washington* in twelve volumes. Mr. Sparks had had full access to Washington's papers and correspondence during the writing of this monumental work.[61] Sparks's response to Randall on the matter is illuminating, and goes a long way in quashing Pickering's allegations as fantasy. In a letter to Randall, Sparks wrote, "In regard to the report or suspicion which for some time existed, that a portion of the correspondence between Washington and Jefferson was abstracted from Washington's papers by Mr. Lear . . . I had found no evidence in support of it among the papers as they came into my hands." In conclusion, Sparks asserted, "no positive proof has ever been adduced," and that the allegations against Lear (and Jefferson) in the matter were "entirely destitute of foundation."[62] Another eminent historian of the early republic period, Richard Hildreth, writing in 1863, also found that evidence was "wholly insufficient" to support the allegations.[63] Sparks and Hildreth, two noted historians of the period and of the people in question, both dismissed the controversy as without merit. Despite Hildreth's and Randall's dismissal of the controversy as unsupported by any evidence, Pickering's allegations would not easily be silenced.

The issue arose again in the early twentieth century due to the efforts of another distinguished historian and archivist of great reputation, Worthington C. Ford.[64] Chief of the Manuscripts Division at the Library of Congress, and later president of the American Historical Association, Mr. Ford attempted to definitively correct the historical record on this matter in 1902.

In a lengthy letter to the editor of *The Nation* magazine, Ford hoped to put a closure to the controversy. "It has been known that, after Washington's death, Tobias Lear permitted Alexander Hamilton to withdraw from his papers certain letters and documents,"[65] Ford wrote. There is little controversy as to the truth of Lear's dubious involvement with Hamilton regarding Washington's papers. Correspondence is extant between them within which Lear offered to remove certain papers relevant to the former secretary of the treasury. "It was also rumored that Jefferson enjoyed the same privilege and used it to destroy all evidence of an interchange of caustic letters between Washington and himself," Ford continued. "At intervals this rumor reappears, with variations and embroideries, and has almost attained the dignity of an historical fact."[66] Ford was certainly in a position to know of the matter first hand, having had full access to Washington's papers (most importantly the first president's letterbooks), as had Sparks before him.[67] Stating definitively that he had found no evidence of "mutilation" in Washington's letterbooks, historian/archivist Ford identifies George Washington Parke Custis, one of Washington's adopted children and last surviving member of the immediate family, as responsible for sustaining the myth of the allegations against Lear and Jefferson.[68]

Describing Custis as a man "possessed of an inordinate vanity," and "depending for his position and reputation on his connection with Washington," Ford did not consider him "a reliable witness on any question concerning his guardian."[69] Ford cites an 1832 letter of Custis's in which Custis states that Tobias Lear had exclaimed to him "There were letters!"[70]

According to Ford, Custis also claimed that, in conversation with Lear soon afterward, Lear had assured him that he would write a letter to him regarding the matter which, Custis explained, Lear never did. Custis asserted that Washington's personal secretary, Albin Rawlins, had also proclaimed that the letters existed. "Rawlins, when questioned, declared that there were *three letters* on the part of Washington, the first courteous, & a mere letter of enquiry.[71] To this was returned an answer in the usually elegant style of Mr. Jefferson, who was assuredly the most finished epistolary writer of the age in which he flourished," Custis wrote. "In the second, the old Chief pressed the Philosopher home, bringing him to the point of guilty or not guilty. The answer was said to be couched in terms of conciliation, spoke much of ancient friendship, and of the long and happy intercourse & kindly reminiscences of by gone days. The last letter of Washington, to use the words of Rawlins, was awfull [sic], so that R declared, my hand trembled as I wrote it down."[72]

Custis certainly created quite an expectation in the recipient of his letter that the Washington/Jefferson letters were real, that people in-the-know had spoken of it first hand, and that the truth would soon be revealed. "The subject of the letters will be found at large & treated from facts only, in my *Recollections & Private Memoirs of the Life & Character of George Washington*," Custis promised.[73] Stating regretfully that the book was "too long delayed from the American public," he closed the letter with the exciting assertion that the Washington/Jefferson letters relating to the Mazzei controversy were real, and that the *"letters of Washington were of no friendly character."*[74]

Ford, harshly critical of Custis in his letter to *The Nation,* wrote that though Custis "believed his own story . . . his own evidence is against him."[75] The book that Custis had promised would include information about the letters was published posthumously in 1859, Custis having died two years previously. The book contained no mention of Mazzei, nor of the letters that supposedly passed between Washington and Jefferson on the matter. Another edition appeared the following year and, again, no mention of Mazzei nor of the supposedly heated letters was included. Ford reasonably concludes that because Custis did not produce the evidence he had promised, and Ford himself had found no evidence of tampering with Washington's letterbooks, that "it is safe to reject the whole story."[76]

Finally, there is the denial of Jefferson himself. In an unusually lengthy 1824 letter to Martin Van Buren (other sections of this letter previously quoted), Jefferson categorically denied that any such correspondence between Washington and himself regarding the Mazzei letter had occurred. "The correspondence could not be found, indeed, because it had never existed. I do affirm that there never passed a word, written or verbal, directly or indirectly, between General Washington and myself on the subject of that letter," Jefferson wrote.[77] Continuing his defense, as seen in other letters by Jefferson on the subject, that his use of the term "Samsons" was a reference to the Society of the Cincinnati and not to Washington, Jefferson explained to Van Buren (later eighth president of the United States) that Washington

> would never have degraded himself so far as to take to himself the imputation in that letter on the "Samsons in combat." The whole story is a fabrication, and I defy the framers of it, and all mankind, to produce a scrip of a pen between General Washington and myself on the subject, or any other evidence more worthy of credit than the suspicions, suppositions and presumptions of the two persons here quoting and quoted for it.

Jefferson closed his refutation with an attack on his detractors, Doctor Stuart, and Timothy Pickering.

> With Doctor Stuart I had not much acquaintance. I supposed him
> to be an honest man, knew him to be a very weak one, and, like
> Mr. Pickering, very prone to antipathies, boiling with party pas-
> sions, and under the dominion of these readily welcoming fancies
> for facts. But come the story from whomsoever it might, it is an
> unqualified falsehood.[78]

Jefferson's resolute self-defense has the ring of truth to it; no evidence has ever been produced to disprove his definitive assertions of
innocence in the matter. Partisans and embittered former colleagues
were not alone in keeping alive the fiction of the supposed missing
Washington-Jefferson letters. Several modern authors have given
redence to these alleged but elusive (likely non-existent) Washington-
Jefferson letters as if they are a matter of the utmost urgency and, by
their excited rhetoric and surety of language, tend to legitimize them
as historical fact just as Ford had warned over a century ago.

As of this writing, there is one biography of Tobias Lear. Written
by Ray Brighton, a New Hampshire historian and former newspaper journalist and editor, *The Checkered Career of Tobias Lear* was
published in 1985. As the only biography of Lear, Brighton's book
is important in that, for some readers, it carries, simply by its existence, the weight of authority. Brighton asserts that the letters were
most likely real, and that Lear destroyed them to benefit Jefferson and
himself. After Washington's death, Lear was in Federal employment
(until his death by suicide in October 1816), which Brighton suggests could have been the fulfillment of a *quid pro quo* arrangement
between Lear and Jefferson that involved the disposal of the supposed
Washington-Jefferson letters.

Brighton and others have suggested that when John Marshall,
then chief justice of the United States, received the General's papers
from Lear, which were to be the foundation of Marshall's multivol-
ume biography of Washington, that Marshall "must have also been
disturbed by the abrupt termination of letters between Washington
and Jefferson."[79] Mr. Brighton, however, provides no citation to
substantiate this theory of Marshall's supposed upset. It should be
noted for context that Adams's and Jefferson's correspondence also

"abruptly terminated" around this same time; no suggestion that any of their letters had therefore been destroyed has ever been advanced.

It is true that Lear had made an offer to Alexander Hamilton to remove certain of Washington's papers. Such an offer then legitimately suggests that Lear *could* have done the same for Jefferson. "Lear showed his willingness to remove any papers Hamilton might want suppressed," Brighton wrote. "What he pulled out at Hamilton's behest isn't known. Once again, if Lear was willing to so serve Hamilton, to what extremes would he have gone for Jefferson, whose political principles he had adopted? And for what reward?"[80] Lear's subsequent and lengthy government employment during Jefferson's administrations appears to Mr. Brighton (at least circumstantially) to imply that an arrangement of some kind *could* have been made between them.

No evidence, however, is presented by Mr. Brighton to substantiate the allegation. In answering the rhetorical question, "What happened?" Brighton, to his credit, replies, "Conjecture is the only possible vehicle, rickety as it may be."[81] Mr. Brighton, though he acknowledges that his argument is based entirely on conjecture, continued anyway to build his speculative case against Jefferson. "Once their existence is accepted," Brighton wrote leadingly of the letters, "only Jefferson could have suffered from their being made public."[82] There is, however, no basis, other than the "conjecture" that Brighton has already characterized as "rickety," upon which to accept that the letters were ever written.

As has already been established by the statements of two eminent historians who both had access to Washington's letterbooks, no tampering or destruction of the contents was found by either. In addition, George Washington Parke Custis's failure to write of the letters in his book, despite his promise to do so, adds significantly to the conclusion that these supposedly highly charged letters between Washington and Jefferson never actually existed.

Regardless of his admission that the case for the letters was entirely conjectural and circumstantial, Brighton charged ahead and asserted definitively that "Lear saw to it that an acrimonious exchange of letters between Washington and Jefferson, over the Mazzei letter, never saw the light of day."[83] Brighton certainly had a particular and strong opinion on the matter and had no hesitation in stating it though he had also admitted that his view was based entirely on "conjecture." Lear's only biographer makes no mention of the firsthand findings of Sparks and Ford, the views of Randall, Jefferson's denial, nor of G.W.P. Custis's failure to "deliver the goods." This failure to present to the reader alternative views by those involved in the matter and in the best position to materially add to the discussion reduces the value of Mr. Brighton's "conjecture" to dubious at best. The lack of thoroughness in the Lear biography on this issue has unfortunately not dissuaded several recent authors from using Brighton's conjectures as a definitive source on this matter.

Richard Zacks, in *The Pirate Coast* (2005), asserts that the Jefferson-Washington letters, which Sparks and Ford (both eminent historians and archivists) discount as fantasy and which G.W.P. Custis failed to produce as he had promised, were, nevertheless, real. "Six key letters—that might have added a chapter to American history—were gone," author Zacks claims.[84] Unfortunately for Mr. Zacks (and his readers), there is no evidence at all that these letters ever existed. Zacks also astoundingly asserts that Lear "had burned the president's letters."[85] (Mr. Brighton's biography of Lear is mentioned both in the body and the endnotes of *The Pirate Coast*.) Mr. Zacks is not the only recent author to indulge in the "Lear did it" theory. Another recent author repeats the circumstantial case that the letters existed, that Lear destroyed them, and implied that Jefferson and Lear had had a mutually beneficial arrangement.

Joseph Wheelan, in *Jefferson's War: America's First War on Terror 1801–1805* (2003), also cites Brighton in his section on the alleged bitter correspondence between Jefferson and Washington. "While it will never be known whether Lear and Jefferson had an agreement about the letters, Jefferson and Madison made sure Lear had a government job for the rest of his short, eventful life," Wheelan wrote, dragging Madison into the controversy. Suggesting that "publication of the letters very likely would have cost Jefferson the election"[86] of 1800 against Adams, thus providing a strong motive for Lear and Jefferson to destroy the letters, Wheelan does not acknowledge that there is no evidence for the existence of the letters. Mr. Brighton wrote that his allegations against Lear were based in "conjecture" and thus "rickety," which then must mean that the assertions of those authors who carry forward Brighton's allegations are also, at best, "rickety." While the controversy about Lear's supposed destruction of likely nonexistent letters between Washington and Jefferson certainly makes for dramatic copy, it must be reiterated that there is no evidence at all to support any of the key aspects of the story. It must be concluded then, regardless of the definitive-sounding statements of several modern authors to the contrary (including Tobias Lear's sole biographer), in accord with Jefferson's assertions, that no letters between Jefferson and Washington relative to the Mazzei letter had ever existed.

When the Mazzei controversy erupted in May 1797, the correspondence between Adams and Jefferson had by then almost entirely ceased. In fact, during Adams's administration, no letters passed between them. There are likely two reasons for this, first is that they were in almost constant proximity of one another as president and vice president, respectively, thus making the effort of letter writing unnecessary; second, as their rift continued to expand there was little purpose in corresponding. Much like Jefferson's explanation to Van Buren of his lack of correspondence or interaction with Washington post-Mazzei, Jefferson and Adams did not write to one another because they no longer had anything to discuss. "Both of us were too much oppressed with letter writing, to trouble, either the other, with a letter about nothing," Jefferson had written to Van Buren about his lack of communications with Washington.[87] While it is clear that no evidence exists to support the contention that a heated correspondence between Jefferson and Washington had occurred in the aftermath of the publication of the Mazzei letter, the political damage of the controversy to Jefferson was surprisingly minimal.

Regardless of the criticism leveled against him, Jefferson would follow Adams to the chief executive's chair.[88] Like Adams's unhappy experience with the Cunningham correspondence, perhaps Jefferson learned a painful lesson from the Mazzei episode. Jefferson's comfort in sharing his deepest thoughts with his friends by letter had however been dealt a harsh blow.

During his first term as president, Jefferson sent to his friend Benjamin Rush "a syllabus or outline of such an estimate of the comparative merits of Christianity, as I wished to see executed by some one of more leisure and information for the task than myself. This I now send to you, as the only discharge of my promise I can probably ever execute, and in confiding it to you, I know it will not be exposed to the malignant perversions of those who make every word from me a text for new misrepresentations and calumnies."[89] This "syllabus or outline" would later be expanded by Jefferson and finally become known as the "Jefferson Bible."[90]

There could have been few subjects more controversial in the United States at that time than a critique, or reassessment of, Christianity. While Jefferson, like Adams, never lost the ability to trust his friends, it was understandable that Jefferson would remind Rush of the difficulties he had experienced at the hands of another friend who had "exposed" his personal, and controversial, views to the public. Rush, an honest and religious man who shared Jefferson's iconoclast views, kept Jefferson's letter and enclosure confidential.

Rush later wrote to Adams, a mutual friend, "I may perhaps give you my creed . . . It is a compound of the orthodoxy and heterodoxy of most of our Christian churches."[91] Jefferson chose his confidante well both for his openness to controversial religious concepts and for his loyal and honorable character. Much later, Rush would demonstrate again that Jefferson's confidence in him had not been misplaced. Due to the trust he had earned from both Adams and Jefferson, Benjamin Rush would play a central role in both of their lives.

Adams did not comment directly to Jefferson about the Mazzei letter. In fact, when he and Jefferson resumed their friendship and extensive correspondence at the end of 1811, neither ever mentioned it. The forgiveness that Jefferson would show later to Adams, relative to the harsh rhetoric the latter had used in the Cunningham correspondence, Adams previously had done for Jefferson by his silence at the Mazzei letter debacle. It would have been perfectly understandable had Adams taken offense at the harsh criticisms of "heresies" in the American government against which Jefferson had railed in his unfortunate letter to Mazzei. Jefferson, after all, had admitted to Washington and to Thomas Paine (though not to Adams) that it had been to Adams's "heresies" that he referred when he had used the same term in the preface to Paine's *Rights of Man* pamphlet five years previously. Adams could not then have known that his public silence about this unfortunate matter would pay important dividends much later.

9

"All Doors Wide Open"

As the controversy over the Mazzei letter played out, Adams continued to try to resolve the crisis with France diplomatically. Gerry and Marshall would soon arrive in Paris and meet Charles Pinckney, already waiting, to begin their diplomatic mission with the French government. In a letter of support to Gerry, Jefferson wrote, "I do sincerely wish with you that we could take our stand on a ground perfectly neutral and independent towards all nations."[1] Despite Jefferson's apparent sincerity, Gerry already had suspicions about his motives. Jefferson's support of France was widely known and, as would be seen later, Gerry had good cause to doubt his seemingly sincere wishes favoring "neutrality."

In a letter to Abigail Adams written prior to the election of 1796, Gerry had presciently written that he thought Jefferson "not entirely free from a disposition to intrigue."[2] The month after his letter of support to Gerry in 1797, Jefferson wrote to Edward Rutledge, a fellow signer of the Declaration (as was Gerry). Jefferson surpassed his earlier comments to Gerry about neutrality in his letter to Rutledge and presented a strong case for noninvolvement with both France and England. "Our countrymen have divided themselves by such strong affections to the French and the English that nothing will secure us internally but a divorce from both nations; and this must be the object of every real American, and its attainment is practicable without much self-denial," Jefferson wrote. "But for this, peace is necessary."[3] The vice president's stated goals—to be both independent of France and England, *and* neutral in their wide-ranging conflict on land and sea—adds a large question mark to his activities during May and June of the same year. Three days after writing to Gerry espousing neutrality, Jefferson called on Phillipe Létombe, the French consul in Philadelphia.

They met privately on four occasions, described by Létombe later in official dispatches to the French Foreign Ministry. Their first meeting was on May 16, 1797, three days after Jefferson had written to Gerry about neutrality, and, more importantly, on the very same day that President Adams addressed a joint session of Congress. The subject of Adams's speech that day was the rejection of Pinckney and the escalating crisis with France.

In his speech, Adams made conciliatory gestures to France but also announced "arrangements for forming a provisional army." These military preparations were meant to influence relations with France, as well as to meet a French invasion which many feared, particularly during the following year.[4] Adams also told the Congress that French attempts to alienate the American people from the government "ought to be repelled with a decision which shall convince France and the world that we are not a degraded people, humiliated under a colonial spirit of fear and sense of inferiority, fitted to be the miserable instruments of foreign influence, and regardless of national honor, character, and interest."[5]

The timing of Adams's speech and Jefferson's first meeting with the French consul in Philadelphia is of more than passing interest, though it is not known if Jefferson met with Létombe prior to or following the speech. Did Adams send Jefferson on a domestic diplomatic mission to meet with the French representative, or did Jefferson, angered by Adams's sometimes aggressive tone in the speech, take it upon himself to "drop in" on M. Létombe? It would have been exceedingly convenient for Jefferson to walk from Congress Hall, where Adams delivered his speeches, at the corner of Chestnut and 6th to Létombe's office located on South 12th Street, between Market and Chestnut, less than a mile distant.[6] If Jefferson had travelled from his lodgings at Francis's boarding house adjacent to the popular Indian Queen Hotel, on 4th Street, south of Market, to call upon the French representative, the journey to Létombe's office would have added little more than a few minutes to his likely customary route as Jefferson lived but two blocks from Congress Hall while he served as vice president.[7]

It is not known whether Jefferson travelled on horseback, by coach, or on foot to visit with Létombe; the manner of conveyance he took to get to the French consul's office is not relevant as it is unlikely that he could have made these visits and remained unnoticed on every occasion. The public nature of these visits and the friendly open-ended invitation from Jefferson to Létombe that he should feel welcome to "drop in" on the vice president whenever he wished suggests that their meetings were not at all "secret," as some historians have speculated.

Both Jefferson and Madison had refused the president's invitation/request several months before to go to Paris as American diplomatic representatives. Since Adet's departure (and the severance of diplomatic relations between the US and France which his leaving represented), Consul Létombe was therefore the senior French diplomatic representative in the United States, though at a lower rank than minister. Sending the vice president to meet with Létombe could be seen as a reasonable (though unacknowledged) back channel attempt on Adams's part to express American desires for the restoration of normal relations with France. (Such back channels would be used by the United States and France to great effect later.) Jefferson would certainly have concurred in such a mission.

For Jefferson, the idea of meeting with the French consul without the aggravation and danger of a return to Europe (which Jefferson had said he would never do again), and at a location within minutes of his own residence, would have been highly appealing. For the shared purpose of both Adams and Jefferson to ensure peace between France and the United States, such a series of meetings was perhaps seen by both as potentially beneficial and impossible to ignore. The situation was so convenient that it would have been perhaps more surprising if these meetings, or something similar to them, hadn't occurred.

If this mission occurred with Adams's approval, his purpose most certainly would have been to communicate to the French consul (and thus the government of France) that the president and vice president were united in their earnest desire for peace.[8]

Thus began a flurry of overlapping presidential speeches and Jefferson/Létombe meetings that appear to have been purposefully coordinated. In addition to Adams's firm desire for peace with France, he also likely wished for another message to be conveyed by his representative: If normalization of relations was not possible and cessation of French naval attacks could not be assured, there would be war. So that the diplomatic and public messages were in synch, Adams reiterated this duality via strategically timed speeches and addresses. France could make no mistake on the matter—there would be peace or there would be war, the choice was theirs.

Jefferson had three more meetings with the French diplomat; the first on May 30, the second on June 5, and the third on June 6. The clustering of these meetings within a week's time suggests a concerted effort on the part of Jefferson to make some headway with the French diplomat. The key question is—was Jefferson acting in an official capacity, or was he meeting with Létombe for his own purposes? While Jefferson's social calendar was clearly full during that week, Adams was also very busy during this brief period in exerting influence as president to pressure the French into fruitful discussions. Within the same week that Jefferson met Létombe on three occasions, Adams delivered three speeches (literally two speeches, and one "Reply to the House" letter that was read aloud in Congress) all relating to France.

On May 31, one day after Jefferson's second meeting with the French consul, Adams announced the triple commission to Congress. (Francis Dana, chief justice of the Supreme Court of the State of Massachusetts, was one of the original three but had to withdraw, and was replaced by Gerry.) Adams made it quite clear that his purpose in sending the three diplomats was normalization of relations with France. "After mature deliberation on the critical situation of our relations with France, which have long engaged my most serious attention, I have determined on these nominations of persons to negotiate with the French Republic to dissipate umbrages, to remove prejudices, to rectify errors, and adjust all differences by a treaty between the two powers."[9] Then, on June 2, 1797, Adams addressed the House of Representatives telling them that "it is now with extreme regret we find the measures of the French Republic tending to endanger a situation so desirable and interesting to our country,"[10] Adams said. "Although it is the earnest wish of our hearts that peace may be maintained with the French Republic and with all the world," Adams proclaimed, "we feel the full force of that indignity which has been offered our country in the rejection of its minister." Mixing conciliatory language, expressions for peace with France, and the feelings of grievance in the United States at the treatment of Pinckney, Adams warned everyone that if France's belligerence continued there would be consequences. "Fully, however, impressed with the uncertainty of the result, we shall prepare to meet with fortitude any unfavorable events which may occur, and to extricate ourselves from their consequences with all the skill we possess and all the efforts in our power."[11] This speech, which clearly delineated Adams's "carrots and sticks" approach to France, was delivered three days before Jefferson's third meeting with Létombe. Finally, in a short "Reply" of June third to the House of Representatives, which had sent an official letter of approval and support to Adams regarding his speech of the previous day, the president again addressed the issue of France.[12] Adams wrote in reply:

> I pray you, gentlemen, to believe and to communicate such assurance to our constituents that no event which I can foresee to be attainable by any exertions in the discharge of my duties can afford me so much cordial satisfaction as to conduct a negotiation with the French Republic to a removal of prejudices, a correction of errors, a dissipation of umbrages, an accommodation of all differences, and a restoration of harmony and affection to the mutual satisfaction of

both nations . . . And whenever the legitimate organs of intercourse shall be restored and the real sentiments of the two Governments can be candidly communicated to each other, although strongly impressed with the necessity of collecting ourselves into a manly posture of defense, I nevertheless entertain an encouraging confidence that a mutual spirit of conciliation, a disposition to compensate injuries and accommodate each other in all our relations and connections, will produce an agreement to a treaty consistent with the engagements, rights, duties; and honor of both nations.[13]

Once again Adams reiterated his dual policy of negotiations with France and preparations for war; Adams's language however was unmistakably weighted toward peace and normalization. Revolutionary France had clearly become the central issue of Adams's presidency (in fact, he had inherited it from Washington), with his public and private comments so often touching on the situation in some way. Adams sent his Reply to the House the day after his speech of June second. Three days later Jefferson met Létombe for the third time, followed *the next day*, June 6, 1797, by their fourth and final meeting. The close proximity in time between Adams's four speeches in which relations with France played a central role, and Jefferson's meetings with Létombe which occurred during the same time frame, it is highly likely that the speeches and the vice president's visits to the French consul in Philadelphia were intricately and directly related.

Perhaps the purpose of Jefferson's mission, if in fact he had been authorized by Adams to meet with Létombe (as it appears that he was), was to prepare the way for the arrival in Paris of the three American ministers, Pinckney, Marshall, and Gerry, and to assure for them a favorable welcome.[14] Only a few comments made by Jefferson during his private meetings with the French consul are known to history. These several statements must represent but a fraction of the conversations that transpired between the vice president and M. Létombe. Later, Létombe reported to his superiors that Jefferson had told him to "not hesitate to drop in on him anytime I liked."[15] It would seem then that their meetings had been quite successful indeed.[16]

The Jefferson/Létombe meetings are described by one historian as a "a secret campaign" by Jefferson "to sabotage Adams in French eyes."[17] Another historian of the period describes them as "clandestine conversations" that "verged on treason."[18] In his diplomatic dispatches to Paris, Létombe reported that Jefferson had said that Adams "'is vain, suspicious, and stubborn, of an excessive self-regard, taking counsel with nobody.' Jefferson predicted to Létombe that Adams would last only one term and urged the French to invade England. In the most brazen display of disloyalty, he advised the French to stall any American envoys sent to Paris: 'Listen to them and then drag out the negotiations at length and mollify them by the urbanity of the proceedings.'"[19] Jefferson also told the French diplomat that "it is for France, great, generous, at the summit of her glory, to pretend to take no notice, to be patient, to precipitate nothing, and all will return to order."[20] The vice president assured Létombe that Adams would be a one-term president, that he had won the chief executive's office by a mere three-vote margin, and that "the system of the United States will change" when Adams was out of office.[21] One biographer of Marshall wrote, "Jefferson apparently had no doubts about an eventual French victory, and he thought the best course for the United States was to delay negotiations until then."[22] Elbridge Gerry's suspicions about Jefferson's claims of wanting American neutrality had been well-founded.

Philadelphia was then not a great or large city, in comparison to London or Paris. It is difficult to conceive that Jefferson, the world-renowned vice president of the United States and key architect of the American Revolution, could have visited the French consul at his official residence in the national capital on four occasions without being observed—nor that those meetings would not have been made known to President Adams. The relationship in time of these meetings in conjunction with Adams's speeches about France, and the unlikelihood of Jefferson's four visits to the French consul's office all remaining unobserved (and not reported to Adams)—suggest strongly that these were sanctioned as opposed to "secret" meetings as several historians have theorized.

Dumas Malone, one of Jefferson's most respected biographers, struggled to defend the vice president's actions. "His goals and fears for the country are clear enough, but something further should be asked about the means he employed while occupying what he had expected to find a 'tranquil and unannoying station.'"[23] Malone asserts, "the best short answer is that he rarely did as much of a partisan nature as his political enemies claimed, and that, in keeping as much as possible out of sight, he followed not only the dictates of his own nature but also those of the existing situation."[24] Malone's assertion that Jefferson rarely did "much of a partisan nature" is, even when *only* the discussions with Létombe are considered, inexact at best.

A recent biographer of John Adams also took a less than critical view of Jefferson's meetings with Létombe. "The truth, it happens," the noted historian wrote, "was that Adams and Jefferson both wanted peace with France and each was working to attain that objective, though in their decidedly different ways."[25] Jefferson's personal and political criticisms of Adams spoken *in private* to a foreign official of a country with which the United States might potentially soon be at war, and his stunning recommendation that the American diplomatic mission to France should be obstructed, are extraordinary and disturbing matters. These inflammatory and disloyal statements by Jefferson, whose purpose appears to have been to directly undermine the plans, policies, and existence of the Adams administration, were far too serious to explain away with only a terse dismissal of them.

It is unlikely that President Adams could have been unaware of Jefferson's activities, as the many "do gooders" and "busy bodies" that circled most of the high leadership of the early republic would certainly have informed Adams as to Jefferson's meetings with Létombe. It is more likely however that Adams was fully aware of these meetings (though not what transpired during them) because he had authorized them.

Those few unfortunate details of Jefferson's conversations with Létombe that survived remained unknown until long after the deaths of all concerned. Létombe's official diplomatic correspondence was published for the first time in the United States in 1904 by the American Historical Association (entirely in the original French).[26] That these meetings occurred, and that Jefferson made stunning and disloyal statements, as recorded by the French Consul Létombe and reported by him to his superiors in Paris, is historical fact; the total silence of Adams (and of Jefferson) regarding them presents, however, something of a mystery.

There is no mention of Jefferson's meetings with Létombe in any of Adams's writings, public or private. If Adams did not authorize these meetings, it is difficult to conceive that he was unaware of them. These meetings were not likely the stuff of cloak and dagger. Adams and Jefferson both desired peace with France. It is reasonable to conclude that Adams himself authorized Jefferson's meetings with Létombe.[27]

Could there have been a better representative of America than Jefferson, a noted Republican and enthusiastic supporter of the French Revolution, to approach the highest-ranking French diplomat in the United States for the purposes of discussing peace and normalization? If Adams agreed with Jefferson's March assessment that a diplomatic mission to France undertaken by the vice president was excluded under the Constitution, he apparently made a determination to press ahead with the Létombe/Jefferson meetings regardless.[28] This could explain the permanent silence of both Jefferson and Adams on the matter. Looking back on his attempts to repair the breach with France, Adams wrote, "But I would not foreclose myself from sending a minister to France, if I saw an opening for it consistent with our honor; in short, that I would leave both doors and all doors wide open for a negotiation."[29] Whose door could have been more convenient than Létombe's; and who better to send to knock upon it than that great friend of the French Republic, Thomas Jefferson?

Had he known of them, Adams would not have condoned those insults and personal criticisms that Jefferson expressed to Létombe; nor would he have accepted without comment and/or official censure Jefferson's undermining of the mission of the triple commission to Paris. The sensitivities of Adams were widely known, if not infamous. He was aware of these character flaws and worked throughout his life to minimize the difficulties that they caused, particularly his "vanity." A scandal eclipsing that of the Mazzei letter would certainly have occurred if the details of Jefferson's meetings with Létombe were known during his lifetime. Had Consul Létombe's meeting notes been released during Jefferson's lifetime, could he have been victorious over Adams in the election of 1800? If they had been released during his presidency could he have avoided impeachment?

The Létombe-Jefferson meetings considerably influenced French policy toward the United States. They also played a significant role in ultimately derailing the mission of the three American diplomats who were then preparing to travel to Paris.

"The three Commissioners will be very much at sea in Paris . . . I believe them to be expecting an unpleasant reception. . . . I am certain that nothing will throw them off balance as much as a polite but cold reception, infrequent, vague and private meetings and no foreseeable end to the talks," Létombe wrote to Delacroix in Paris, alluding to Jefferson's recommendations as to how the American diplomats should be handled.[30] The mistaken idea then in vogue in the French government that the Republican (i.e., "Democratic-Republicans") and Federalist parties were merely partisan pro- and anti-French blocs, respectively, had been essentially substantiated, if not confirmed, by Jefferson's comments to Létombe. One historian of the era wrote, "Létombe, after the departure of Adet writes to the home-government of his frequent confidential talks with Jefferson and mentions that the 'Republican party supported by our victories is gaining in this country.'"[31] The belief among the French diplomatic and foreign policy community that French successes were causally related to the rise of Jefferson's party in the United States was a serious, though understandable, miscalculation. Circumstances would later disabuse them of this fundamental misjudgment of American society and politics.

Adams viewed his presidential role as leader-of-the-nation rather than as a "party man" serving as chief executive. He approached his presidential functions as "certainly not that of a partisan. It was simply that the Executive's was the hand that held the scales: it was all a matter of balance."[32] Washington and Hamilton had "believed," according to one leading historian, "that with the system of checks and balances in the new government, party politics was unnecessary for the preservation of ordered liberty. The rise of an opposition they identified with a faction opposed not only to the policies of the administration but to the new national government itself. They connected this faction with the French government and its agents."[33]

Adams's beliefs were very much in line with those of his predecessor. Deeply troubled by Jefferson's partisanship, Adams believed that it undermined both Jefferson's effectiveness as a national leader, as well as the foundations of their long friendship. Washington's and Adams's distrust of opposition parties as being likely oppositional to the government itself was an unfortunate generalization that tended to mischaracterize political opposition as a form of disloyalty.

If Adams had known of Jefferson's harsh criticisms against him, and those comments and recommendations that were undermining of his presidency (as reported by the French Consul himself to Paris), Adams would certainly have discussed it publicly or to Abigail, at least, in his private letters. The issue would also surely have been raised in the correspondence with Cunningham, which consisted in large part of Adams's politically oriented complaints, or in his *Boston Patriot* essays on similar matters. The subject might also have been alluded to during the lengthy Adams-Jefferson correspondence many years later, if such a correspondence could even have been possible. As there is no evidence that Adams ever mentioned these meetings in public or private, there is a good possibility that he was unaware of what had been said between Jefferson and Létombe. While Jefferson was meeting with the French consul in Philadelphia, across the Atlantic the diplomatic situation was rapidly changing. There would be serious consequences for the three American Commissioners soon to arrive in Paris, and for the country they represented.

Little more than a month after Jefferson's last known meeting with Létombe, Foreign Minister Charles Delacroix was suddenly dismissed. His replacement, as of July 17, 1797, was the hardworking, self-aggrandizing, brilliant, greedy, cunning manipulator (and later, renowned diplomat), *bon vivant*-without-scruples Charles Maurice de Talleyrand-Périgord.[34]

An extraordinary character in the history of France and of European statecraft, Talleyrand, the Bishop of Autun, had embraced much of the anti-Catholic church policy of the Revolution including state control of church properties. He was elected to the Estates-General and became an early adoptee of republicanism (while hedging his bets by quietly retaining a favorable view toward monarchism). Though he continued to support the idea that the monarchy should be retained in some form, he was, as his character would suggest, extremely flexible on the matter, bowing as a sturdy tree to the extraordinary fierce winds of change blowing across revolutionary France. As republican fanaticism and intolerance for royalists, non-jurer clergy, and aristocrats grew during the increasingly authoritarian rule of the French revolutionary government, Talleryrand fled France for England. Wisely waiting many hours for a passport,[35] which Danton himself acquired for him, before leaving the country late in 1792, the controversial refugee from France eventually made himself obnoxious to the British Prime Minister, William Pitt.

Talleyrand's not surprising, yet ill-judged, associations with English Republicans finally pushed the British government, highly nervous about its own vocal revolutionaries (such as Dr. Priestley), to react. Expelled from England in 1794, Talleyrand made his way to Philadelphia. Within a month of his arrival, in accordance with the laws of Pennsylvania, Talleyrand swore an oath of allegiance to the State of Pennsylvania and the United States of America on May 19, 1794.[36] The oath included this promise: "I will be faithful and bear true allegiance to the Commonwealth of Pennsylvania, and to the United States of America, and that I will not at any time willfully and knowingly do any matter or thing prejudicial to the freedom and independence thereof."[37] Another aristocratic French refugee, Lucie de la Tour du Pin, whose mother had been one of Marie Antoinette's Ladies-in-Waiting, landed in Boston soon after Talleyrand's arrival in Philadelphia. La Tour du Pin had known Talleyrand well in Paris. They would soon meet again in upstate New York.

A courageous and insightful woman whose father was guillotined during the Terror of the Jacobins shortly before her arrival in America, La Tour du Pin's straightforward memoir is considered a classic of the French Revolution and Napoleonic Empire periods in France.[38] Her concise character sketch of Talleyrand goes a long way in illustrating this cynical, yet extraordinary man who later became a key player in the drama of John Adams's presidency. Writing years later of their meeting at her family's rough farmhouse near Troy, New York, La Tour du Pin wrote,

> Monsieur de Talleyrand was amiable as he has always been for me, without any variation, with that charm of conversation which no one has ever possessed to a greater degree than himself . . . He had known me since my childhood, and therefore assumed a sort of paternal and gracious tone which was very charming. I regretted sincerely to find so many reasons for not holding him in esteem, but I could not avoid forgetting my disagreeable recollections when I had passed an hour in listening to him. As he had no moral value himself, by singular contrast, he had a horror of that which was evil in others. To listen to him without knowing him, you would have believed that he was a worthy man.[39]

With firsthand experience of American affairs, having lived in the United States between early 1794 and mid-1796 and, in fact, an American citizen—Talleyrand had sworn (and signed) an oath of allegiance—his appointment later to the highest office of the French Foreign Ministry "was hailed as marking a new era in Franco-American relations."[40] Initially—among those who did not know of him personally, of his questionable reputation, or, perhaps most importantly, of his views on America's predilection to affinity and kinship with England—there was good reason to consider Talleyrand's appointment as potentially beneficial to the United States. "Talleyrand himself knew the United States and its politics intimately. He had lived in America for the better part of two years, and in most of his public speeches and private business ventures had analyzed the United States and its relations with Great Britain and France."[41] In addition to his own experiences in the United States to draw upon, a number of Talleyrand's colleagues in the French diplomatic service also were widely knowledgeable on American political affairs.

Talleyrand had available the experience of French diplomats who had served in the United States or lived there after the outbreak of war with Great Britain in 1793, namely, Joseph Fauchet, Pierre Adet, Louis Otto, and Charles de la Forest. The former French consul in

New York and schoolmate of Talleyrand, Alexandre Hauterive, soon took up duties assisting Talleyrand in preparing foreign policy statements. One of Talleyrand's private secretaries, Louis Paul d'Autremont, had lived in Asylum, Pennsylvania, and returned to France with Talleyrand.[42] With the new foreign minister, and many of his subordinates, having had direct American experience a more accurate understanding of American domestic politics should therefore have been prevalent in French government counsels, at least in the Foreign Ministry.

Jefferson's inappropriate comments to Létombe had unfortunately provided further substantiation to many in the diplomatic services of France that the two most influential American political parties were, in fact, little more than French and British sympathy blocs which could be manipulated. Regardless of the Francophile or Anglophile character and rhetoric of these parties, the consensus in America was that neutrality in the conflict between England and France was the best course for the United States. The argument for American neutrality had been clearly and powerfully delineated by Washington, and then also by Adams, who, as Washington's successor, became its champion. The leaders of France were aware of this policy, of course; they foresaw little consequence for France however in failing to respect it, and chose to ignore it instead.

"A month before Talleyrand's induction into office, Otto presented for the consideration of the Minister of Foreign Affairs an extended report on the relations between the United States and France,"[43] noted historian James Alton James wrote early in the twentieth century. Talleyrand would certainly have seen Otto's report. In it Otto described the disappointing and confrontational behavior of Genet (French Ambassador to the United States prior to Adet) toward the United States government. James wrote that "this unusual conduct on the part of a foreign minister who had not been presented to the government and whose mission had received no official recognition: became more insulting when Genet accused Americans of ingratitude, and attacked the government in the newspapers with the aim of provoking revolution." Historian James explained further, "in such conduct, Otto stated, there was a failure to comprehend that while many Americans were applauding the successes of the French Revolution they were insisting on a policy of neutrality on the part of their government, a policy which was at the time equally desirable for both France and the United States."[44]

Otto's report demonstrated that the cause of the difficulties existing between France and the United States was in the main the fault of actions by French official representatives as by any on the part of the American government. Despite the clear evidence of French provocation, which was known in the diplomatic circles at Paris, the new foreign minister's agenda did not take this into account. The new relationship between England and the United States via the Jay Treaty was a growing risk to France, as was Adams's dual policy of negotiation and preparations for war. However, there was little that the United States could do against France in the short term to prevent, or effectively retaliate against, French naval depredations (or most any other hostile act that France might undertake).[45] This imbalance of force did little to encourage the leadership in Paris to arrange for a speedy reconciliation between the US and France.

Talleyrand was fully aware that President Adams desired peace with the French Republic. In an October 1797 *Memoir*, Talleyrand alluded to Adams's May 16 speech to the joint House that "beneath these accusations and the arrogance of the rest of the speech, a strong desire for reconciliation can be detected as well as firm intentions to seek out all possible means."[46] Regardless of the clarity of Adams's expressed determination for normalization and reconciliation with France, the new foreign minister in Paris felt little inspiration to reciprocate. Canny and calculating, Talleryrand was aware that in delaying a resolution to the crisis (a situation for the French that then had little of the character of a crisis) for as long as possible, benefits for both France and himself could be painlessly and inexpensively acquired. This, then, would be the highly charged political environment in which the three American ministers to France would soon find themselves.

Talleyrand had a great deal more on his mind than mere public service *seulement* when he accepted his new post. "When after months of intrigue to displace Delacroix and get the Foreign Ministry for himself, the news of his appointment came at last on July 18, 1797, Talleyrand was delirious with joy. 'I'll hold the job,' he exulted over and over, 'I have to make an immense fortune out of it, a really immense fortune.'"[47] With the new French foreign minister's purposes, a sometimes lopsided mixture of personal wealth accrual in awkward combination with the fulfillment of his official duties, the fortunes of the American Commissioners were seriously threatened. What was in store for Pinckney, Marshall, and Gerry would be recalcitrance, rudeness, and obstruction.

The confusion in the highest circles of the French Foreign Ministry regarding the true nature of the American political landscape was directly influenced by Jefferson's partisan and disloyal statements to Létombe. With their misconceptions of American domestic politics seemingly confirmed by Jefferson's bashing of Adams, and his recommendations to Létombe on how France should best scuttle the American diplomatic mission to France, the official reception that the American diplomats received in Paris is not surprising.

"Perhaps the most arrogant and insulting taunt given to our country was [sic] the words of Talleyrand's agents to the American envoys in 1798 when they declared that 'the diplomatic skill of France and the means which she possesses in your country are sufficient to enable her with the French party in America to throw the blame of a rupture of negotiations on the Federalists as you call yourselves but on the British party as France calls you and you may be sure it will be done.'"[48] Such rhetoric fit very nicely into the French policy of diplomatic brinksmanship; the conflicting messages likely confused their American counterparts, and obscured their true purposes.

With the advent of Talleyrand, American government officials soon faced a more complex milieu of conflicting signals. French attacks on American shipping, the rejection of Pinckney, and the bitter departure/recall of French Ambassador Adet, were decidedly negative and confrontational events. In a letter to Létombe dated late August and September 1, 1797, early in his tenure as foreign minister, Talleyrand appeared to be prepared to set a more conciliatory tone, however. Talleyrand wrote that "he allowed that the rejection of Pinckney and its consequences were 'regrettable' and 'involved nothing personal against Mr. Pinckney' and could be 'repaired,' and that 'we shall do everything necessary when the commissioners arrive to exhibit fully our peaceful intentions.'"[49]

It is hardly surprising that Talleyrand was not entirely truthful with Létombe; the foreign minister of France failed to mention to his subordinate either his plans for brinksmanship or his goal of making "an immense fortune" from his office.[50] Nor did Talleyrand hint that he believed that the people of the United States were decidedly pro-British in their feeling, despite having fought a revolution to gain their independence from England. In a letter to his friend Lord Lansdowne written in 1795, likely as a reaction to the Jay Treaty, Talleyrand wrote, "without France they would never have gained independence," "America is English to the core," and, "Americans are inclined to favor the English."[51] Despite Talleyrand's questionable character and motives, there was still cause for some optimism.

The observations of John Marshall, made during his voyage to Europe, appear to suggest that Talleyrand's letter to Létombe of late August/early September signified something much more than an empty rhetorical promise to resolve the conflict. In a letter to Washington dated September 15, 1797, Marshall described the non-threatening character of multiple interceptions of his ship by French navy vessels. "By the ships of war which met us we were three times visited and the conduct of those who came on board was such as would proceed from general orders to pursue a system calculated to conciliate America."[52] Though Marshall considered the friendly manner of the French sailors he met when his ship was boarded during the transatlantic crossing as positive signs, his optimism proved to be short-lived.

A staunch Federalist, Marshall did not share Jefferson's views of the French Revolution. "The same day the liberty of the press was abolish'd by a line, property taken away by another and personal security destroy'd by a sentence of transportation against men unheard and untried. All this is stiled the triumph of liberty and of the constitution," Marshall wrote to Washington about conditions in

France.[53] Writing to Washington later from Paris, Marshall's earlier shipboard hopefulness had evaporated. "Might I be permitted to hazard an opinion it would be that the Atlantic only can save us, and that no consideration will be sufficiently powerful to check the extremities to which the temper of this government will carry it, but an apprehension that we may be thrown into the arms of Britain."[54] Even before meeting with his French counterparts, Marshall felt a strong sense of gloom about the upcoming negotiations; his negative premonitions were swiftly confirmed.

By early October 1797, the three American diplomats had assembled in Paris and were met there, briefly and unofficially, by Talleyrand. As the weeks passed no official meetings occurred, nor were the Americans formally presented to the Directory. On the eighteenth of October, a representative of Talleyrand called upon Pinckney. The agent, a Monsieur Hottinger, privately stated to Pinckney that some members of the Executive Directory had been offended by remarks made by President Adams in his May sixteenth speech, and that only a transfer of monies could alleviate their displeasure. Pinckney was informed that a sizable loan would be required to be paid by the United States government to the French Republic, and a "private douceur" (bribe) of 1,200,000 French livres (approximately 240,000 US dollars, at that time) must be paid to Talleyrand directly.[55] Additional unofficial representatives of Talleyrand hounded, cajoled, and annoyed the American diplomats in the following weeks.

The American delegation was soon informed that without the required financial "apology" for Adams's speech, or at least the delivery to France from the United States government (in the form of a complex transfer of debt) of almost 13 million dollars, no official reception of the diplomats by the government of France would occur. The Americans were reminded that the bribe "must be a separate and additional sum."[56] Finally, in a meeting alone with Gerry, who had known Talleyrand during his time in America, the French foreign minister pressed the American representative about payment of the "loan." Gerry replied that neither he nor his two colleagues had the necessary authorizations to negotiate a loan to France, whereupon Talleyrand demanded, "Then assume them, and make a loan."[57]

Offended at the inhospitable treatment and denial to them, as a delegation, of direct access to the French foreign minister, and angered at meeting only his supposed intermediaries (none of whom showed credentials, contrary to diplomatic protocol), the American ministers refused to make any agreement regarding loans or bribes without first consulting their superiors at Philadelphia. They sent no less than six encoded copies of a report of their experiences in France to Adams in at least the same number of ships (to assure that at least one copy was received).[58] As the reports made their long journey to Philadelphia, several months of inactivity in Paris followed which included intrigues and delays on the part of the French Foreign Ministry. With growing frustration at French demands, and insulted at the petty iniquities of the French government, Elbridge Gerry determined to take a new approach—he invited Talleyrand to dinner.

Gerry's hope that a less formal environment would allow the American diplomats to air their grievances directly to Talleyrand and perhaps break the impasse was quickly frustrated. Gerry's late December dinner party was not a success.[59] Soon after this disappointing attempt at gastronomic relations, the French government, in January 1798, issued a belligerent proclamation which stated that any ship that landed at any English port (or at any English colony) would be denied entry to any French port, and that any ships carrying any English merchandise were to be considered valid "prizes" for French privateers. Rightfully seeing this new proclamation as a direct and serious threat against American commerce and a purposeful expansion of tensions between France and the United States, Pinckney and Marshall drafted a protest against the new law, which Gerry refused to sign. Gerry's refusal to cooperate with his colleagues essentially shattered the triple commission.

Pinckney and Marshall, both Federalists (and Marshall a defender of the Jay Treaty), refused to palliate the French after this latest insult and threat. Gerry, a Jeffersonian-Republican, was less inclined to answer the new provocation with a strong response and had demonstrated a greater willingness to be flexible and deferential to the French. Seeing that the American delegation was splitting over their response to the belligerent French Proclamation, Talleyrand determined to finish the job. The French foreign minister asked the Directory for permission (which was granted) to "pass over" Pinckney and Marshall, "and to deal with Gerry alone."[60] Talleyrand justified this request by noting, "since the Americans were accredited, 'jointly and severally, envoys extraordinary and ministers plenipotentiary,'" therefore dealing with only one of the three American ministers was permissible.[61]

Early in March 1798, Marshall wrote a dire letter to Washington stating, "before this reaches you it will be known universally in America, that scarcely a hope remains of accommodating on principles consistent with justice, or even with the independence of our country, the differences subsisting between France and the United States." Informing Washington that the French had not negotiated in good faith, and that only American acquiescence to French demands would result in the diplomats being officially received, Marshall warned Washington that if America did not give France the loan which they demanded, he and his colleagues "will be order'd out of France and a nominal as well as actual war will be commenc'd against the United States."[62] Ten days later, Marshall and his colleagues received an official response to a letter they had sent to Talleyrand in January. Talleyrand's heavy-handed reply, which he also "sent to Létombe with instructions to give it all possible publicity," advanced the French diplomatic brinksmanship crisis to the next level.[63]

Once again complaining of America's new relationship with England, including accusations of treaty violations, Talleyrand heatedly declared that France would no longer deal with Pinckney and Marshall, but only Gerry. The purpose of this letter, which insulted Pinckney and Marshall and put Elbridge Gerry in a very uncomfortable, if not impossible position, was to split the American delegation.

The foreign minister's letter was a not-so-subtle demand of Pinckney and Marshall, but not Gerry, to leave France. Loyal and patriotic, Gerry believed that he had no option but to remain in Paris despite Talleyrand's denunciations of his diplomatic colleagues. The lone Republican in the American delegation, Gerry explained later that he had stayed behind in Paris "because Talleyrand told him France would declare war if he left."[64]

After much aggravation and delay Marshall was finally able to leave France in mid-April; Pinckney received permission to remain in the south of France for several months.[65] As the only remaining member of the American triple commission to both not be expelled and to remain in the French capital, Elbridge Gerry's "conduct aroused a storm of protest at home."[66]

In a lengthy letter of explanation to Jefferson written in 1801, Gerry wrote, "Mr. Talleyrand had early in the spring declared to me in the name of the Directory, that my departure from Paris would bring on an immediate rupture, & as there had been no instance of an official declaration made by the directory which had not been carried into effect, I have no doubt of it in this instance."[67] With the foreign minister of France promising war if he should depart, Gerry remained in France essentially under duress. Aware of the damage that his remaining in Paris might do to his reputation in the United States, Gerry announced that though he remained, he was no longer acting as an accredited minister.

Gerry informed his French hosts that, due to the expulsion of his colleagues, he was therefore remaining in France as but a private citizen and thus treating in "an individual capacity." This diplomatic counterattack/parry from Gerry greatly frustrated Talleyrand.[68] Several months later Gerry attempted to leave the country but with little success. "My frequent applications for a passport . . . have been altogether unnoticed," Gerry complained to Talleyrand early in July 1798.[69] Talleyrand's outrageous, improper demands and disrespectful treatment of the three American representatives became widely known in the United States. American reaction to events in Paris would overturn Talleyrand's brinksmanship, and stun France.

On March 5, 1798, Adams announced in a Message to the Senate and House that dispatches from the American Commissioners in Paris had been received the previous day. Adams dramatically informed the Congress that because all the dispatches were encoded there would be some delay in releasing them, with one exception (that had been written in plain language, that is uncoded). "The contents of this letter are of so much importance to be immediately made known to Congress and to the public," Adams declared, "especially to the mercantile part of our fellow-citizens, that I have thought it my duty to communicate them to both Houses without loss of time."[70] The president's republican opponents however viewed the speech and the delayed release of the encrypted letters from the American diplomats with suspicion.

On March 19, Adams followed up with a more detailed public message, though the dispatches were still not yet released. Adams's strong tone of conciliation, previously commonplace in prior speeches, was noticeably muted. Using language that appears to show that Adams had read Marshall's letter to Washington of March 8, the president dramatically announced to the country that the diplomatic mission to France had failed.

> After a careful review of the whole subject, with the aid of all the information I have received, I can discern nothing which could have insured or contributed to success that has been omitted on my part, and nothing further which can be attempted consistently with maxims for which our country has contended at every hazard, and which constitute the basis of our national sovereignty.[71]

Adams's tone strongly suggested that the conciliatory component of his dual policy of diplomacy with France, that of negotiations and war preparations, had been unsuccessful. Acknowledging publicly that the situation with France had further deteriorated, President Adams informed the Congress that the restrictions on American vessels, which had until then prevented them from arming against French attacks, were no longer in force. "The present state of things is so essentially different from that in which instructions were given to the collectors to restrain vessels of the United States from sailing in an armed condition that the principle on which those orders were issued has ceased to exist," President Adams said.[72] Republican reaction to this speech was one of deep concern that the federalist administration was pushing the country unnecessarily, in their view, toward war with France. Because Adams had not yet released the dispatches from the American ministers in France, the Republican opposition was ignorant as to the true situation. Regardless of not knowing the contents of the dispatches, and likely motivated by a deep suspicion as to the

Administration's motives in not immediately releasing them, Jefferson responded to Adams's speech with a letter to Madison on March twenty-first in which he described the March nineteenth brief Message to the House as "the insane message."

Jefferson also recommended to Madison that Republicans should oppose Adams's withdrawal of the "executive prohibition to arm, that Congress should pass a legislative one."[73] As the leader of the opposition, though still a senior member of the administration, Jefferson's recommendation to Madison to empower Congress at the expense of the Federalist-controlled executive appears to be a reasonable and legitimate, though strongly partisan, strategy. He would have only several weeks however in which to organize opposition to Adams's new tougher posture.

On the day prior to Jefferson's letter of complaint to Madison about Adam's speech Abigail Adams wrote to her sister, Mary Cranch, in Quincy, Massachusetts. She presciently and ominously complained of Jefferson's (and his supporters') seemingly endless opposition to President Adams. "We have renewed information that their System is, to calumniate the President, his family, his administration, until they oblige him to resign, and then they will Reign triumphant, headed by the Man of the People."[74] The First Lady's sarcasm was based in large part on the perception that she shared with her husband that Jefferson's extreme republicanism and anti-administration viewpoint had superseded and overturned their long-standing friendship.

Several days later in a letter to her son-in-law, Abigail continued to vent her frustration at Jefferson's virulent opposition. "How different is the situation of the President from that of Washington? The Vice President never combined with a party against him and his administration, he never intrigued with Foreign Ministers or foreign courts against his own government and country."[75] Abigail's reference to Jefferson's "intrigue with Foreign Ministers" suggests that Abigail may have been aware of Jefferson's meetings with Létombe (though Létombe's title was consul rather than minister). As it is unlikely that John Adams knew the true nature of Jefferson's conversations during his private sessions with French Consul Létombe, Abigail was also most likely unaware. The First Lady did however view Jefferson as an active threat rather than as a supportive old friend who happened to have opposing political views.

Driven by their belief that Adams was leading them into a needless war with France, and not yet aware of the devastating contents of the official communications from the American delegation, Republicans around the country loudly agitated for the swift release of the encrypted dispatches. The House voted on April second to call for the president to release the documents. Amidst the clamor for them, and all the criticism from the Republicans regarding them, Adams could not have been more pleased to comply. The dispatches were released the following day. In a short Message sent to the Senate and House on April 3, 1798, Adams announced,

> In compliance with the request of the House of Representatives expressed in their resolution of the 2nd of this month, I transmit to both Houses those instructions to and dispatches from the envoys extraordinary of the United States to the French Republic which were mentioned in my message of the 19th of March last, omitting only some names and a few expressions descriptive of the persons.[76]

Requesting that the Members of the House "deliberate on the consequences of their publication," Adams was likely fully aware that the release of the dispatches would signal a stunning political victory over Jefferson and his republican supporters.[77] One Adams biographer wrote of the highly charged political atmosphere, "He would have been less than human if he had not enjoyed the consternation of his political enemies. It is not, perhaps, going too far to call it panic; certainly it was demoralization."[78] Jefferson quickly realized the error that the Republicans had made in prematurely criticizing Adams prior to the release of the dispatches.

The names that Adams had said were omitted from the dispatches were those of the French agents who had unofficially met with the American delegation. These representatives of Talleyrand had communicated the French foreign minister's demands for delivery of a large loan to France, and payment of a *douceur* to him (for the building of his "immense fortune"), as preconditions to official talks with the government of France. In the decrypted dispatches released to Congress, and thus to the American people, the names of these men were replaced with the letters X, Y, and Z.

10

"A Civil War Was Expected"

JEFFERSON DESCRIBED THE release of the "XYZ dispatches" as "such a shock on the republican mind, as has never been seen since our independence."[1] The immediate consequence to the Republicans of the revelations from France was a general disillusionment. "Many of their boldest leaders left for home; others went over openly to the Federalists,"[2] Jefferson observed to Madison.

The Republicans had dangerously miscalculated; in light of the dispatches from the American diplomats in Paris, whose contents were so unfavorable to France, some of the defenders of the Revolution in America began to doubt their support for the French Republic. Recognizing the likely impact of the XYZ documents, former President Washington correctly predicted that the French government would soon see "the spirit and policy of this country rising with resistance and that they have falsely calculated upon support from a large part of the country thereof."[3]

Talleyrand, for all his blustering and demands made on the American ministers, must have then realized that the winds of public opinion in the United States had just then radically shifted, and were no longer blowing favorably for the ship of France. The French foreign minister quickly shifted from aggressive brinksmanship to damage control. One of his first responses was to publish (unsigned) "an elaborate refutation of the envoys' letters."[4] In a letter to Barras, the senior member of the Directory, Talleyrand defended his actions.

> They seem to me to be within the bounds of the moderation we should display; they are not too offensive to Mr. Gerry of whom we are desirous of making use, but severe enough against his colleagues . . . They are very nettling to Mr. Adams, whose liberticide policy they unmask, as a whole encouraging for our friends in America. I believe that this was required. Moreover, the refutation is complete.[5]

The French Foreign Minister's absurd and arrogant emphasis on sparing offense to Gerry, while heaping it upon his two federalist colleagues, fulfilled little purpose due to Gerry's refusal to cooperate. Talleyrand realized, despite his self-defenses, that he had overstepped—he quickly began investigating alternative paths to a resolution of the crisis that he himself had created. Before Talleyrand could find other avenues of approach to President Adams, however, the political situation in the United States had dramatically changed.

Deeply offended at the treatment of the American ministers by Talleyrand and his surrogates, the American polity forgot their differences and united against France, and behind President Adams. "For the first time since the beginning of the French Revolution, a majority of Americans now seriously questioned the political motives of their Gallic ally," one historian wrote of the American reaction. "Many Americans' former love for revolutionary France had turned to disbelief, disgust, and revulsion as a result of the XYZ Affair."[6] Meetings whose purpose was to express approval of Adams and anger at France were held across the country. Many of these political rallies occurred in Virginia, which had long been a bastion of republicanism and support for the French Republic.[7] Calls for unity, a strong American response, and enthusiasm for President Adams were often heard at these patriotic gatherings which occurred in every state of the Union.

Adams soon found himself overwhelmed with petitions of support from across the young republic. All of these addresses to the president received a personal response from Adams, either in the form of a stump speech to those delivering them, or via a letter.[8] Hundreds of addresses arrived at the capital.[9] "The hostile and disrespectful behavior of France was all the more disturbing because until recently she had been America's closest friend and ally. Those sending resolutions frequently emphasized this point, and mentioned the bonds of friendship that had existed between the two republics," one historian wrote of the addresses.[10]

Most Americans had (until the release of the dispatches) thought of France and the United States as natural friends and allies. Many addresses expressed strong feelings of betrayal. "She once fought for liberty—she now contends for dominion" was the opinion communicated by the Massachusetts legislature regarding France in its address to Adams.[11] Adams's observation that the French "ought to have known us better"[12] is certainly pertinent as Talleyrand and his senior staff had had more than enough direct knowledge of the culture and political situation in America. However, the French government was not entirely without friends in the United States, the vice president himself being one of the most dedicated.

Several days after the release of the XYZ dispatches, Jefferson proclaimed to Madison that the French had misread the motives of American Republicans, "whom they so far mistake, as to presume an attachment to France and hatred to the federal party, and not the love of their country, to be their first passion."[13] Jefferson's harsh confidential criticism of Adams and the policies of the Federalists had been understood by Létombe and his colleagues as indicative of a "hatred to the federal party" as a "first passion" on Jefferson's part. As Jefferson was the recognized leader of the republican opposition, it seems not an unreasonable assumption on the part of Létombe, and then Talleyrand himself, to consider Jefferson's personal views as representative of those of his party and followers. Jefferson's dual role of vice president and partisan leader of the opposition confused many, including, apparently, officials of the French Foreign Ministry.

Jefferson described the release of the XYZ dispatches as causing "a state of astonishment" in the "public mind;" his own reaction must certainly have been similar.[14] A general shift of support across the country toward the anti-France, federalist position, and

President Adams swiftly occured. This result was in direct opposition to the goals of Jefferson and his Francophile followers who
viewed England as the greatest enemy of the United States, and of
republicanism. There would be consequences for Adams, too, and
for relations between the two countries. An opportunity for redemp-
tion of a sort, however, soon presented itself to Jefferson, despite
the extensive political damage that his party had suffered.

Regardless of the overwhelming and enthusiastic bipartisan support for Adams personally, and general calls for strong retaliation
against France, the president remained hopeful that a diplomatic solution to the ongoing crisis could still be found. Adams was walking a
fine line between peace and war as the population, reinvigorated and
angry, united behind him. "In the spring of 1798 he took precaution-
ary measures, and he sought to strengthen American forces by aug-
menting the fleet and by creating a new national army. Yet he did not
want war," one noted historian wrote of the crisis.

> For the first time he even spoke of soldiers in less than compli-
> mentary terms, and he advised some college students against
> enlisting in the new army. He also warned the citizenry not to be
> 'dazzled' by martial splendors. Adams additionally denigrated
> those who clamored for war. He called them the 'worst Enemies'
> of the Republic.[15]

While the anger of the American people continued to grow, and the
political divisions between Federalist and Republican were, at least,
temporarily minimized, Talleyrand sent a new consul to represent
France in the United States.

"During the month of May 1798, Victor Du Pont, formerly French
consul at Charleston, was sent as Consul General to the United States.
President Adams refused him an exequatur, and after an interview
with Jefferson he returned to France."[16] There should be little surprise
that Jefferson granted Du Pont "an interview" as the rejected French
consul was the son of Pierre Samuel du Pont de Nemours, a noted
French Republican whom Jefferson had known since his service as
American minister to France. In fact, "the ripe friendship between
these two notable liberals ended only with the death of the elder in

1817."[17] If Talleyrand had hoped to leverage Jefferson's friendship with the new consul general's father, his plans were swiftly quashed. Worse still for Talleyrand was that on his return to France the younger Du Pont submitted a report to the foreign minister in which "he demonstrated that it would be to the interest of France by all means within its power to avoid war with the United States," a noted historian wrote. "Talleyrand had asked for facts and Du Pont replied that there were so many it was hard to make a choice, since the acts of violence, brigandage, and piracy committed by French cruisers or under the French flag in American seas would fill many volumes."[18] Likely influenced by his meeting with Jefferson at the end of his abbreviated diplomatic posting in the United States, Du Pont informed Talleyrand that the consequence of an American alliance with Great Britain against France would certainly be the loss to France of American commerce.[19] Perhaps even worse than that however for revolutionary France was that America would be lost to the international anti-monarchy, republican movement which the leaders of France believed they were then leading.

Du Pont also informed Talleyrand "that a war between the two republics would cause the United States to sacrifice their liberty through an alliance with Great Britain and would enhance the maritime strength of the latter power."[20] Neither wishing to provide advantages to France's most bitter enemy (Great Britain) nor of losing access to American commerce, Talleryrand began to be convinced that the days of French brinksmanship with the United States must end. Doubtless impressed by Adams's angry reaction to the XYZ dispatches, and the overwhelming anti-French sentiment that had arose in the United States, and likely moved by Du Pont's report and recommendations, Talleyrand finally embarked on a plan to reach a peaceful resolution of the crisis with Adams. Accomplishing such a denouement however, to a crisis that he had recklessly and needlessly prolonged and escalated, would prove to be more difficult than Talleyrand had likely expected.

French responsibility for the crisis was clear to Victor Du Pont, to Otto, and to other French diplomats, and certainly was a viewpoint not foreign to the three American ministers to Paris. The majority of

Americans who had read or were familiar with the contents of the XYZ dispatches concurred with Otto and Du Pont. Immune to the rising anti-French feeling that swept the country in the aftermath of the release of the American diplomats' decrypted reports, Jefferson's support for the Revolution in France remained solid. In a letter to his longtime friend, Pierre Du Pont de Nemours, Victor Du Pont's father, written four years later during his first presidential term, Jefferson wrote,

> I am told that Talleyrand is personally hostile to us. This I suppose, has been occasioned by the XYZ history. But he should consider that that was the artifice of a party, willing to sacrifice him to the consolidation of their power: That this nation has done him justice by dismissing them; that those in power [now], are precisely those who disbelieved that story, and saw in it nothing but an attempt to deceive our country . . .[21]

Jefferson's self-serving explanation to Du Pont de Nemours posited that the XYZ affair was the result of partisan anti-French machinations by Adams and the Federalist Party, and that those "who disbelieved the story" (as if to suggest that the dispatches themselves contained falsehoods or were fraudulent) were rewarded with political power and that Adams, who had not "disbelieved the story" had rightfully been rejected by the American people.

Though the disrespectful treatment of the American diplomats by their French hosts could have been used as a *cassus belli* by Adams to go to war with France, he continued to pursue peace. He was fully aware (as was Jefferson) that a war with France would be to no advantage to the United States and was likely unwinnable. If indeed he was a good (or better) and able leader; it was a war he had to avoid, if at all possible. Once the popular clamor for war had reached a fever pitch after the release of the XYZ dispatches, avoiding war became all the more difficult, and would likely carry a serious political cost for Adams.

Abjuring an emotional reaction to the crisis he continued his dual pursuit of peace and reluctant preparations for war; a legitimate and reasonable dual path. Jefferson's characterization, in his letter to Du Pont, of Adams's actions as entirely political—to "sacrifice" Talleyrand to consolidate his and his party's power and to "deceive" the country (perhaps then to gain advantage over those opposing the Federalists)—is an unfair and unrealistic "spin" on Jefferson's part. Jefferson's is a cynical and disingenuous view not supported by documentation or events.

The XYZ dispatches confirmed for most of the country, including many Republicans, but not for Jefferson, that France's belligerence and intransigence were at the heart of the conflict between the two countries. The mistreatment of the American diplomats was only the most recent, and potentially most dangerous, phase.

Jefferson believed that the success of the French Revolution, regardless of its brutality and violence, was essential for the future of the entire world. People who believe that they have the fate of the world in their hands will go to extraordinary lengths to ensure the attainment of their goals. Though he had gone to extreme lengths to assist the Revolution in France, they were all for naught as Napoleon Bonaparte's 18–19 Brumaire, 1799 coup finally destroyed the French republican dream.

Throughout the crisis with France during Adams's presidency, Jefferson's self-assurance that only his pro-France/anti-Great Britain view was the correct one, and that those who disagreed were therefore dangerous to the country, made Adams's situation all the more difficult. The vagueries and confusions of European conflicts and shifting international alliances that would see Britain and the United States linked by a treaty of amity and trade (an agreement that further alienated France from the United States) during Adams's administration would, little more than a decade later, see a British invasion. Though the War of 1812, during the presidency of his friend and fellow Republican James Madison, may appear to validate Jefferson's anti-British views of 1798, they ought not to suggest prescience on his part. That monarchical Britain was inherently opposed to American republicanism (and vice-versa), a view strongly held by Jefferson and many others, it does not necessarily follow as an absolute consequence that war between Britain and the United States must then be inevitable or unavoidable.

Supported by a massive surge of popular indignation against France in the wake of the XYZ revelations and a sense of national support for him personally, Adams would take the conflict to a new level. His three ministers to France having been harassed, disrespected, abused, and obstructed, the diplomatic path to resolve the crisis with France appeared closed. With French intransigence and belligerence the two most powerful forces in the crisis, Adams had no option remaining to him but to refocus his energies on the other half of his dual policy: prepare for war.

On June 13, 1798, Congress approved the "Act to Suspend the Commercial Intercourse between the United States and France, and the Dependencies Thereof." In addition to severing trade relations between the two countries, it also barred French vessels from American waters "unless driven there by distress of weather or in want of provisions."[22] Though Adams was piloting the country toward a new, stronger, and more belligerent course with France, the harsh language of the new policy also included a path for France to end the difficulties without war.

> That if, before the next session of Congress, the government of France, and all persons acting by or under their authority, shall clearly disavow, and shall be found to refrain from the aggressions, depredations and hostilities which have been, and are by them encouraged and maintained against the vessels and other property of the citizens of the United States, and against their national rights and sovereignty, in violation of the faith of treaties, and the laws of nations, and shall thereby acknowledge the just claims of the United States to be considered as in all respects neutral, and unconnected in the present European war, if the same shall be continued, then and thereupon it shall be lawful for the President of the United States, being well ascertained of the premises, to remit and discontinue the prohibitions and restraints hereby enacted and declared.[23]

As if to reiterate the new emphasis on military preparations, additional Amendments were added to this measure by the president over the following several months. Though the door to peace and normalization was always held open by Adams, the ongoing aggressions and "depredations" of France necessitated the building of a legitimate military capability.

The publication of the XYZ documents resulted not only in a national swell of support for Adams and disgust and anger at France, it also brought about an extraordinarily swift warship construction effort. "Outraged by this affront to national honor, on 27 April 1798 Congress authorized the President to acquire, arm, and man no more than twelve vessels, of up to twenty-two guns each. Under the terms of this act several vessels were purchased and converted into ships of war."[24] Less than a week later Congress established the Department of the Navy. The following month, Adams authorized American merchant ships to defend themselves

> . . . against any search, restraint or seizure, which shall be attempted upon such vessel, or upon any other vessel, owned, as aforesaid, by the commander or crew of any armed vessel sailing under French colours, or acting, or pretending to act, by, or under the authority of the French republic; and may repel by force any assault or hostility which shall be made or committed, on the part of such French, or pretended French vessel, pursuing such attempt, and may subdue and capture the same; and may also retake any vessel owned, as aforesaid, which may have been captured by any vessel sailing under French colours, or acting, or pretending to act, by or under authority from the French republic.[25]

In early May 1798, former President Washington was offered, and accepted, command of a new provisional army "of ten thousand men,"[26] which was expected to deter any potential invasion by France.[27] Washington accepted command of the new army only with the proviso that Alexander Hamilton would be named as his senior general—likely disgusting both Adams and Jefferson.[28] In June, "only one American naval vessel was deployed," though before the conclusion of hostilities in 1800, "the force available to the navy approached thirty vessels, with some 700 officers and 5,000 seamen."[29]

Late in June 1798, Adams sent another Message to Congress about the American diplomatic mission to France. In supporting

Gerry's refusal to treat with France in any fashion other than as a private citizen (and no longer as an empowered American minister to France), Adams informed Congress that Gerry's new instructions were "to consent to no loans, and therefore the negotiation may be considered at an end."[30] As Gerry was the only member of the triple delegation then remaining at the French capital, there were no opportunities remaining for Talleyrand to officially respond to Adams's Message or to continue even the pretence of negotiations.

Adams concluded his short Message with a promise "to never send another minister to France without assurances that he will be received, respected, and honored as the representative of a great, free, powerful, and independent nation."[31] The June twenty-first Message to Congress was meant to be a clear signal from Adams to the French that their refusal to receive the three American ministers had exhausted the diplomatic component of the ongoing conflict. With diplomacy no longer a viable option, actual warfare became a serious possibility. A war was approaching rapidly which leaders in both Paris and Philadelphia, at least in private, claimed that they did not want.

During this period of frustrations, fear, and rising tensions, the Federalist-controlled Congress passed the Alien and Sedition acts. Mainly targeted against French agitation in the United States, the Sedition Act also was used against republican critics of the government. According to the biography of Adams on the White House's website, the intent of the two acts was two-fold: "to frighten foreign agents out of the country and to stifle the attacks of Republican editors."[32] Adams was noncommittal on the acts, and signed them into law with little fanfare. Jefferson, though vigorously opposed, also signed. Regardless of affixing his signature, Jefferson, with significant assistance from Madison, attempted to defeat the new laws by "planting resolutions in legislatures" of several states that were fiery denunciations of the new legislation.[33]

Jefferson wrote a strongly worded Resolution (but kept his authorship a secret) that passed in the Kentucky legislature. Jefferson's Resolution asserted that the states had the right to nullify, under certain circumstances, Federal law. Employing language that was extraordinarily heated, even when compared with Jefferson's highly charged rhetorical flourishes seen elsewhere, the Kentucky Resolution described the Alien and Sedition acts as likely to result in the dissolution of the Union.

> That these and successive acts of the same character, unless arrested at the threshold, necessarily drive these States into revolution and blood, and will furnish new calumnies against republican government, and new pretexts for those who wish it to be believed that man cannot be governed but by a rod of iron.[34]

Jefferson's hyperbole was too much for Madison however, who found the rhetoric of his party's leader "inflammatory and tried to get the words for nullification withdrawn."[35] Madison submitted his own somewhat less controversial Resolution against the Acts in the Virginia legislature.

Extremely unpopular with Democratic-Republicans, some Federalists including Hamilton believed that the new acts were not quite strong enough. These laws later significantly affected Adams's reelection bid, with many critics a suggesting that the Adams Administration had demonstrated an excessive zeal in dealing with its political opponents and those it viewed as enemies of the nation. Jefferson, constantly walking the razor's edge between his role of vice president and that of the president's greatest political opponent, both signed the law and then did his utmost to oppose it. In a letter to Jefferson written many years later, Adams referenced a letter that Jefferson had written to theologian, scientist, and noted Republican Dr. Joseph Priestley. In his letter to Dr. Priestley, Jefferson had described the Alien Act as "that libel on legislation," prompting Adams to reasonably inquire of Jefferson—

> As your name is subscribed to that law, as Vice President, and mine as President, I know not why you are not as responsible for it as I am . . . Neither of Us were concerned in the formation of it. We were then at War with France: French Spies then swarmed in our Cities and in the Country. Some of them were, intolerably, turbu-

lent, impudent and seditious. To check these was the design of this law.[36]

Fears of French invasion, attacks on American commerce, and widespread anger at French insults had created an environment in which federalist leaders believed that they were obligated to take extraordinary measures to ensure the survival of the new country. Many in both parties believed that the country was under an existential threat from France and its revolutionary agents agitating within the United States. In the opposing camp, led by the vice president, these laws were viewed as existential threats to the Constitution and to republicanism.

The view from France of these American protectionist laws could only have been a confirmation of the obvious—that Americans saw France as a clear and present danger. With American public opinion rising swiftly against France in the wake of the XYZ scandal, and Adams's announcement that the diplomatic component had failed, Talleyrand had no choice but to take a more circuitous route toward a denouement of the conflict.

Talleyrand found his solution in a convenient back channel to President Adams via a close friend of the president's son, John Quincy. The French foreign minister sent Louis Andre Pichon, a former secretary in the Foreign Office and one-time colleague of Fouchet in the United States, to The Hague to "cultivate the acquaintance of William Vans Murray."[37] Murray was a friend of John Quincy Adams, and had succeeded him as American minister to The Hague. Pichon was successful in building a relationship with Murray who at first was "indignant at the Directory" but soon warmed to the French diplomat.[38] In keeping with Talleyrand's desire for personal control over the French diplomatic relationship with the United States, the Pichon-Murray discussions were not divulged to the French minister then serving at The Hague.[39] With the expectation that Murray would relay details of these conversations to his friend John Quincy Adams, who then, in turn, would send them along to his father, Talleyrand sent instructions to Pichon on August fifteenth to "continue unostentatiously to see Mr. Murray," and "to make some impression on the men devoted to the administration of Mr. Adams and to make them doubt at least the justice of the measures he continues to enact in the Legislative Body of the United States."[40] Though he had found a means of communicating with Adams, Talleyrand was not yet ready to abandon efforts to undermine the federalist American president for the sake of peace. It would not be long however before this approach was abandoned and replaced with an altogether different diplomatic tone.

At the end of August 1798, Talleyrand used the Pichon-Murray back channel to reply to Adams's June twenty-first Message to Congress. Talleyrand wrote to Adams, via Pichon-Murray, "the government of the United States believed that France wished to revolutionize it; France believed that the government of the United States wished to throw itself into the arms of England. Let us substitute calm for passion, confidence for suspicion and soon we will be in accord."[41] Disingenuously inquiring as to the source of the conflict, Talleyrand rhetorically (and with a touch of threatening arrogance, too) asked Adams, "What, therefore, is the cause of the misunderstanding, which, if France did not manifest herself more wise, would henceforth induce a violent rupture between the two republics?"[42] The French foreign minister asserted that "neither incompatible interests, nor projects of aggrandizement, divide them," and that "France, in fine, has a double motive, as a nation, and as a republic, not to expose to any hazard the present existence of the United States. Therefore, it never thought of making war against them, nor exciting civil commotions among them."[43] Talleyrand understood that his previous tactics had failed. In a follow-up letter to Adams via Pichon-Murray, he made his intentions to defuse the crisis perfectly clear. Adams had laid out specific conditions in his short June Message to the Congress to which Talleyrand, by August, was prepared to concede. Talleyrand wrote to Adams,

> You were right to assert . . . that, whatever plenipotentiary the government of the United States might send to France, in order to terminate the existing differences between the two countries, would be, and undoubtedly received with the respect due to the representative of a free, independent and powerful nation.[44]

Talleyrand's favorable acknowledgment of Adams's June speech—in which the president had promised Congress that without specific assurances, no American diplomat would ever again be sent to France—was the strongest signal yet that France had no interest in war with America. Though there was reason to believe that peace was in the offing, French and American warships continued to occasionally meet in naval combat—with American commanders more often the victor. These combats could only serve to reiterate to the French that further attacks on American commercial vessels would no longer be without cost.

In early February 1799, Adams sent another Message to the Senate in which he included Talleyrand's conciliatory letter. The president accepted Talleyrand's offer to reopen negotiations with France by sending William Vans Murray from The Hague to Paris as "minister plenipotentiary of the United States to the French Republic."[45] The reaction in the United States to the appointment of Murray was not entirely favorable. This prompted a slight change of plan and another Message to the Senate from Adams in which he explained "that a new modification of the embassy will give more general satisfaction to the Legislature and to the nation; and perhaps better answer the purposes we have in view."[46] A new triple diplomatic mission was therefore announced by Adams, "I now nominate Oliver Ellsworth, esq., chief justice of the United States; Patrick Henry, esq., late governor of Virginia, and William Vans Murray, esq., our minister resident at The Hague."[47] Patrick Henry, the famous Virginia patriot, orator, and politician, declined the honor due to ill health, and was replaced by William Davie, governor of the state of North Carolina and a former officer in the revolutionary army. The inconsistency of the French revolutionary government which had caused considerable confusion among American diplomats since 1789, most recently seen in Directory decrees promulgated then repealed time and again, was revisited fivefold when the Directory itself ceased to exist.[48]

By the time the newly appointed triple commission arrived in Paris, the Directory had been overthrown. "First Consul" Napoleon Bonaparte was the new ruler of France. The Revolution in France had imploded, just as Adams had said that it would. Talleyrand by then had already resigned and been reinstated as foreign minister under Bonaparte. The conciliatory and cooperative tone that Talleyrand had begun to foster toward America during the latter part of the Directory period continued under Napoleon. "The envoys were received by the French government with suitable respect, and three commissioners immediately appointed to treat with them," one historian explained.[49] A Convention between the French Republic and the United States that was submitted to the Senate on December 16, 1800, during the final months of Adams's first and only term, officially ended the "Quasi-War" between France and the United States. The timing of the 18 Brumaire Coup (November 19, 1799) in France, which brought Napoleon Bonaparte to power, was more than favorable to the cause of peace.[50] The Convention, signed formally as the Treaty of Morte-fontaine, stated in Article 1:

> There shall be a firm, inviolable, and universal peace, and a true and sincere Friendship between the French Republic, and the United States of America; and between their respective countries, territories, cities, towns and people without exception of persons or places.[51]

Though their mutual goal to avoid a war with France was finally realized, Jefferson and Adams had not been brought closer by the period of distrust, fear, and conflict just then concluded. Adams considered his management of the crisis with France and its final result as his greatest political and diplomatic triumph; in fact, he believed that it was the greatest accomplishment of his life. His success at avoiding war with France however did not help him to get reelected.

His defeat to Jefferson in the acrimonious election of 1800 created a deep bitterness in Adams. His once-greatest friend, and now most strident political rival, had beaten him; but, even more cruel and unfair, in his view, was that his successful avoidance of war with France had brought him political banishment rather than glory. Adams was resentful at what he considered a lack of appreciation for having successfully done what he believed had been his duty as president—keeping the country out of an almost certainly costly and unwinnable war.

Years later, Adams wrote a lengthy defense of his approach to France to his friend James Lloyd, a federalist Senator from Massachusetts. Prompted by a published correspondence in the *Boston Daily Advertiser* in January 1815 between Lloyd and Virginia Republican Congressman John Randolph, Adams was keen to explain and justify his past actions. Randolph had mentioned Adams in his original letter, and Lloyd did the same in his response to Randolph. Almost completely incapable of avoiding a good rhetorical battle, even one to which he hadn't been invited, or of steering clear of those that involved his historical reputation, Adams indulged that special brand of "vanity" in his letters to Lloyd.

The vanity of Adams, clearly on display in his letters to Lloyd, was much less that of hubris or conceit than a neurotic preoccupation with others' views of him. Adams's excessive (and sometimes self-destructive) concern for his historical reputation, combined with his famous garrulousness that had too often affected his personal and professional relationships, resulted in a misunderstanding of Adams's character, which has yet to be fully corrected.

Just as the contradictions in Jefferson's character and actions continue to confound students of American history and of human behavior, Adams's personality was equally complex. Fully aware that his argumentativeness and strong opinions had created difficulties with others, Adams warned Lloyd that he could not "repent of my 'strong character'."[52] Adams's assertiveness and self-assuredness in his several letters to Lloyd, though he had met him only once, is typical of Adams in that, when given the opportunity to defend his record—or when he created one—he spared no ink. When it came to matters of his administration, and particularly regarding his efforts to avert war with France, Adams's surety was much more than a kind of monomania; it was rather an unsteady and contrary definitiveness. Adams's greatest personality flaw was his need for validation from others. Later in life this need became something of an obsession.

Adams's desire for personal validation, appreciation, and recognition was not simply a kind of weakness of character, but was rather, over the course of time, an unfortunate expression of the essential human need for meaningfulness. The correspondence with Cunningham, for example, had turned out so very badly, mainly due to Adams's overly heated criticisms of others. For many seeking the recognition that they believe rightfully their due, a common strategy includes the diminishment of others. By contrasting their own accomplishments with the lesser actions of those they criticize, the validation seeker believes that he/she has, through sometimes forced comparisons, proven his/her worth. This approach is frought with danger, most notably the alienation of those who are not involved (a correspondent or newspaper reader, for example) and the enmity of those who are. Adams discovered on a number of occasions the hazards that this approach involved.

With Lloyd, Adams successfully kept himself in check in so far as criticism of others was concerned. His effusive descriptions of the successes of his administration to Lloyd appear excessively self-congratulatory, and thus might be seen to close the circle once again around Adams's "vanity." A thoughtful correspondent would perhaps have overlooked these lapses on the retired president's part, and forgiven him for his abiding frustration that so few seemed to hold a positive view of his presidential accomplishments of which he was so proud. Adams did not know Lloyd well. In his introductory flourish, Adams explained,

> The want of familiarity between us, I regret, not only because I have known, esteemed, and I may say, loved your family, from an early age, but, especially, because whatever I have heard or read of your character in life, has given me a respect for your talents and a high esteem for your character.[53]

Such courtesies, and elegant constructions, once so common in early American correspondence, reached a zenith with the second and third presidents.

Lloyd's public criticism of Adams's diplomatic missions to France, particularly in view of the fact that peace had been the result rather than war, was particularly irksome to Adams. In several letters to Lloyd, Adams defended his diplomatic efforts to resolve the conflict with France without war and explained that, even with American anger at France running high at that time, there was little support for actual war. Adams explained to Lloyd that his foremost concern during his presidency was the preservation of the Union.

> You say, Sir, that my missions to France, "the great shade in my Presidential escutcheon paralyzed the public feeling and weakened the foundations of the goodly edifice." I agree, Sir, that they did with that third part of the people who had been averse to the revolution, and who were then, and always, before and since, governed by English prejudices; and who then, and always, before and since, constantly sighed for a war with France and an alliance with Great Britain; but with none others . . .The house would have fallen with a much more violent explosion, if those missions to France had not been instituted.[54]

Adams noted the slim majority in the Electoral College by which he had been elected, "a majority of one, or at most two votes," then followed up with a rhetorical question to Lloyd. "And was this a majority strong enough to support a war, especially against France?"[55] Citing President Madison's difficulties in the then-current war against the British, regardless of the large electoral majority that had brought *him* to office, Adams made a strong case that, for many reasons, avoiding war with France had been the best course fifteen years previously. "Mr. Madison can now scarcely support a war against England, a much more atrocious offender, elected as he was, and supported as he is, by two thirds of the votes."[56]

Adams believed that his leading the country to peace with France, despite popular clamor to fight, had been an extraordinary accomplishment. That few others appeared to see the situation in the same way was a source of deep frustration. "I wish not to fatigue you with too long a letter at once; but, Sir, I will defend my missions to France, as long as I have an eye to direct my hand, or a finger to hold my pen. They were the most disinterested and meritorious actions of my life," Adams declared to Lloyd. "I reflect upon them with so much satisfaction, that I desire no other inscription over my gravestone than: 'Here lies John Adams, who took upon himself the responsibility of the peace with France in the year 1800.'"[57]

"To despatch [sic] all in a few words, a civil war was expected," Adams wrote in his next letter to Lloyd.[58] Adams had done his utmost to avoid war with France, not only because of the expected high costs involved but also due to fears that the stresses of such a war could have resulted in a disruption of the Union itself. In his first letter to Lloyd, Adams mentioned a list of reasons why open war with France would have put the future of the federalist administration and the existence of the Union itself at risk. Adams specifically cited the two state legislatures where Jefferson had opposed the Alien and Sedition acts to illustrate his very dramatic point.

> In this critical state of things, when Virginia and Kentucky, too
> nearly in unison with the other Southern and Western States, were
> menacing a separation; when insurrection was flaming in Penn-
> sylvania . . . had the administration persevered in the war against
> France, it would have been turned out at the election of 1800 by
> two votes to one.[59]

Reiterating the correctness of his actions and tipping his hat to the accusations of "monarchism" which had haunted him for so long, Adams again strongly defended his French diplomacy. Adams wrote in his second letter to Lloyd, dated February 6, 1815:

> My own "missions to France," which you call the "great shade in
> my Presidential escutcheon," I esteem the most splendid diamond
> in my crown; or, if any one thinks this expression too monarchical,
> I will say the most brilliant feather in my cap. To such an extent
> do we differ in opinion. I have always known that my missions to
> France were my error, heresy, and great offence in the judgment,
> prejudices, predilections, and passions of a small party in every
> State; but no gentleman in the fifteen years past has ever publicly
> assailed those missions till your letter to Mr. Randolph.[60]

Such a discussion, and defense, of course merited further instruc-tional letters from the former president. Adams next wrote Lloyd on February seventeenth. Perhaps realizing that his strong language might be misconstrued as personal hostility, Adams reminded Lloyd of his friendly regard, and closed with, "It is not my design nor desire to excite you to a controversy. Be assured, I considered what you said of me, exactly as you intended it, and that in a very friendly light. My wish is equally friendly to give you information of some facts, of which, from your age, I presume you were not aware."[61] Adams viewed the peaceful resolution of the conflict with France as the most important of a string of successes for which he had never received recognition and appreciation.

In another letter to Lloyd written at the close of March 1815, Adams detailed the "happy conclusion of the peace with France in 1801, and its fortunate effects and consequences."[62] In citing the year 1801, Adams acknowledged, without comment, that though the peace with France was arranged through his efforts and under his administration, it was not finalized until Jefferson's administration was in office. "I did not humble France," Adams triumphantly explained, "nor have the combined efforts of emperors and kings humbled her, and, I hope, she never will be humbled below Austria, Russia, or England. But I humbled the French Directory as much as all Europe has humbled Bonaparte."[63] Adams's frustration at what he perceived to be a lack of appreciation for the successes of his administration became a recurring theme in his retirement years. The reiteration of his victories, and complaints about their not being appreciated, did little to raise the former president's reputation with his countrymen. Adams's summation for Lloyd is characteristic of this unfortunate approach.

These sometimes lengthy and heated defenses by Adams are best seen as the consequences of a frustrated patriotism whose decades of loyalty, sacrifice, and labor, in the end, brought unexpected political defeat and endless criticism rather than esteem and honors. Adams declared to Lloyd,

> My labors were indefatigable to compose all difficulties and settle all controversies with all nations, civilized and savage . . . And I had complete and perfect success, and left my country at peace with all the world, upon terms consistent with the honor and interest of the United States, and with all our relations with other nations, and all our obligations by the law of nations or by treaties. This is so

true, that no nation or individual ever uttered a complaint of injury, insult, or offence.[64]

And then, amid all the frustration that resulted from what he saw as a universal lack of understanding and acknowledgement of his efforts and successes as president, there was the memory of his long and turbulent friendship with Jefferson. "As I had been intimately connected with Mr. Jefferson in friendship and affection for five-and-twenty years, I well knew his crude and visionary notions of government as well as his learning, taste, and talent in other arts and sciences,"[65] Adams wrote to Lloyd. When this letter was written, the renewed relationship between Jefferson and Adams had already been underway for several years. His use of the terms "crude and visionary" to Lloyd are not necessarily backstabbing or insulting to Jefferson, though they do show that despite their renewed friendship, Adams and Jefferson certainly did not see eye to eye on issues of government and politics.

The first real indication that Adams gave to the country that the conflict with France was receding had been his Message to the Senate of February 18, 1799, which included Talleyrand's conciliatory letter. Jefferson, as leader of the opposition, was in no way deaf to the fact that Adams had been successful, and that the new French tone of conciliation was a signal that the crisis could be resolved without recourse to war. Though Jefferson desired peace with France he was likely not particularly pleased that the Federalists would get the credit.

In an early 1799 letter to Edmund Pendleton, a Virginia politician and jurist, written the day after Adams's Message to the Senate of the eighteenth of February, Jefferson wrote, "a great event was presented yesterday." In Jefferson's view the conciliatory nature of the French communiqué had undermined the Federalists' desires and machinations for war with France. Describing the gist of Adams's Message for Pendleton, Jefferson criticized the federalist administration, and embraced the self-deluding, inherently oppositional and bizarre view that Talleyrand's new peaceful tone "renders their efforts for war desperate, & silences all further denials of the sincerity of the French government."[66]

After the XYZ dispatches were released, supporters of both parties demanded retaliatory action against France; at that point, pressure on Adams to prepare for war had grown significantly. The success of Adams and the Federalists in avoiding war brought private criticism however from Jefferson instead of rejoicing. In the postscript to his letter to Pendleton, Jefferson wrote,

> The face they will put on this business is, that they have frightened France into a respectful treatment . . . Whereas, in truth, France has been sensible that her measures to prevent the scandalous spectacle of war between the two republics, from the known impossibility of our injuring her, would not be imputed to her as a humiliation.[67]

In his letters to Lloyd, Adams asserted that he hadn't "humbled France," only her aggressive, arrogant, and corrupt leaders. Jefferson's view on these events was completely different, of course. Rather than seeing the aggressions of France as a fundamental cause of the crisis and its continuance, Jefferson saw instead the rhetoric of the federalist "war party" as the key element in the conflict. This view of the federalist administrations of Washington and Adams as the aggressors, and France as the aggrieved "sensible" party whose desire to avoid war was coupled with her wish to avoid "humiliation," is not however supported by the diplomatic records of the time, by the previously belligerent statements and actions of Talleyrand, nor by unprovoked French attacks against American shipping (particularly those that had occurred prior to the ratification of the Jay Treaty).

For the moment, Adams had had a great success in bringing France to a more reasonable posture with the United States. A formal peace with France finally arrived after Jefferson's election a year later. Much later, Jefferson would see the facts in a different light and comingle the parsing of such things with his friendship with Adams, a renewed friendship that would become critically important to both. Jefferson wrote to Adams in 1813,

> About facts, you and I cannot differ; because truth is our mutual guide . . . And if any opinions you may express should be different from mine, I shall receive them with the liberality and indulgence

which I ask for my own, and still cherish with warmth the sentiments of affectionate respect of which I can with so much truth
render you the assurance.[68]

Deliberate confusion and denial of facts for political purposes, that
is, for political leverage, is an old strategy; the mischaracterization of
facts is a tool also used to lever out of power those who currently hold
it. The facts of the French depredations on American shipping made
less impact on Jefferson than the fact that France was a revolutionary
Republic, and that the United States had arranged the Jay Treaty with
England, a monarchy. Jefferson's central political concern was the
advancement of republicanism.

Jefferson later acknowledged that Adams had been both prescient
and correct about the course of the French revolution, a movement
which Jefferson had never stopped supporting. Jefferson's goal to oust
the Federalists from power was fulfilled, though the Revolution in
France would, by then, be dead and replaced with a dictatorship just as
Adams had long before predicted. The political sacrifices that Adams
had made in treating with France in the midst of a massive swell of anti-
French feeling following the XYZ scandal resulted not in his elevation
as a national hero and re-election, but instead brought his defeat.

In his First Inaugural Address Jefferson ironically acknowledged
the dangers of the very same partisanship that had brought him to
office knowing, from his own success with it, that it was an inherent
danger to the continuing stability and existence of the Union. His
opposition to Adams and federalism had been motivated partly by
their profoundly different views on the nature and future of the Revolution in France. When the heat of their political fights, and the rise
and fall of the Revolution in France, had receded into the past, only
then could Jefferson finally assert to Adams that they were bound
together not by partisanship, but by facts.

Years later Jefferson acknowledged that Adams's predictions
of the eventual failure of the French Revolution had been accurate.
"Your prophecies to Dr. Price proved truer than mine; and yet fell
short of the fact, for instead of a million, the destruction of eight
or ten millions of human beings has probably been the effect of

these convulsions," Jefferson wrote to Adams in early 1816. "I did not, in '89, believe they would have lasted so long, nor have cost so much blood. But altho' your prophecy has proved true so far, I hope it does not preclude a better final result."[69] After all, if the idea of popular government were to fail, what then could be the consequence but a return to the tyranny of monarchy, or something even worse?

11

"Mr. Jefferson Said I Was Sensitive, Did He!"

ADAMS EXPECTED THAT reelection to the presidency in the election of 1800 would be his reward for successfully avoiding war with France. In late December 1799, with the election results from South Carolina definitively pointing toward a national republican victory, Adams and his supporters knew that he would lose the election.[1] Though both Jefferson and Adams abstained from campaigning, as was the style of the time—demonstrating that they were above, at least publicly, the muddy waters of political wrangling—their representatives were not so circumspect. Unpleasant and acrimonious, the election of 1800 is infamous for the coarseness and harshness of the insults and allegations laid against one candidate by the camp of the other.

It was understood early on that Adams had been defeated though it was not immediately clear who the next president would be, Jefferson or his running mate, Aaron Burr. Due to a flaw in the Electoral College, a congressional vote was required to determine who, Burr or Jefferson, would be president and vice president. After thirty-six ballots, over seven days of voting, Jefferson was elected.[2]

Almost at the same time that Adams received news of his defeat in South Carolina, and the larger loss that it signaled, the soon-to-be outgoing president learned of the death of his son Charles. "Oh, that I had died for him if that would have relieved him from his faults as well as his disease," Adams wrote to his son Thomas upon hearing the news.[3] Adams's anguish at the death of Charles, a troubled man with a serious alcohol abuse problem, was presaged by years of difficulty and failure which appeared to begin most pronouncedly while he was a student at Harvard.

Enrolled there at the age of fifteen, Charles's school associates were apparently not of the best character. During one Thanksgiving at the Yard, Charles participated in what one of Abigail Adams's recent biographers described as a "riot," during which Charles appeared to take a leadership role; younger brother and fellow Harvard student Thomas Boylston also participated. Having caused some damage on the campus, both boys were fined ten shillings.[4] Another historian, in describing Charles's behavior while at Harvard, wrote that he had been caught "running naked, either solo or with a group, across Harvard Yard."[5]

During a visit to Charles in 1798, the president found his son, according to one Adams biographer, "inextricably in the thrall of alcoholism."[6] Horrified at the disastrous condition of his son, and his numerous failures including the loss of several thousand dollars belonging to John Quincy, Adams could take no more. He wrote to Abigail that Charles was a "madman possessed of the devil."[7] In failing his brothers, his parents, his wife and children, and finally himself, Adams could barely contain his anger, horror, and disappointment at what his son had become.

In a letter of October 12, 1799, to Abigail, Adams proclaimed of his troubled son that he "is a mere rake, buck, blood, and beast . . . I renounce him."[8] John Adams kept this bitter promise; he never saw his son Charles again. Charles's failure to successfully live his life, support his wife and family, and to meet the extraordinarily high standards of effort and success expected by John and Abigail resulted in Charles being lost to himself, his family, and finally lost to history.

That the tragedy of Charles Adams should be forever forgotten was the purpose of the Adams family in denying Charles burial in the family plot at what is now the Hancock burial ground in Quincy, located within walking distance of Peace field. It would seem that the disaster that Charles had made of his life, from his failed law practice to the abandonment of his wife and children, then finally his death by alcohol abuse at the age of thirty had pushed his parents and brothers in their horror, anger, grief, and disappointment to respond with a kind of existential abandonment of their own.

"Charles's fate was so mortifying that his brother Thomas, expressing the family's sentiment, said: 'Let silence reign forever over his tomb.'"[9] There would be few visitors to Charles's lonely grave in "the old Presbyterian burying ground" in New York City, as few would ever know its location.[10] Though saddened, embittered, and, as he would reasonably assert later, seriously distracted with grief by the death of Charles, outgoing President John Adams still had official duties to perform such as preparing the new White House for the arrival of his successor, after just a few months' occupancy. The coming months also involved the transfer of presidential power to the man who had defeated him.

One critically important aspect of the transfer of presidential power was that certain open positions within the government were required to be filled. That is, they could not remain vacant for long. These obligatory appointments, particularly of judges, later became the subject of great contention and controversy. Frustration, grief, executive appointments, and finally haste—rather than triumph and laurels—would mark the sad and ignominious end of Adams's single term as president of the United States.

A friend of Jefferson's, Edward Coles, secretary to President Madison and later governor of Illinois, paid a visit to Adams at Peace field many years later. Coles inquisitively broached the subject of Jefferson's first post-election defeat visit to Adams. This difficult meeting between President-elect Jefferson and outgoing Chief Executive Adams occurred when Congress first met after the election. Coles explained to Adams that Jefferson had told him of the event, and recalled that Jefferson's description of the meeting began with a nervous prelude.

> Knowing Mr. Adams's sensitiveness, and wishing to do nothing to arouse it, he deliberated much as to the proper time for making his

usual call on the president, fearing if he called very soon, it might have the appearance of exulting over him, and if, on the other hand, he delayed it any longer than Mr. Adams thought was usual, his sensitive feelings might construe it into a slight, or the turning a cold shoulder to him, in consequence of his having lost his election. When, finally, he concluded the proper time had arrived, he called on the president, and found him alone.[11]

Jefferson had clearly given much consideration to the proper approach he should take to his old friend and political opponent, even debating with himself as to the timing of his visit. Much to Jefferson's dismay however, Adams was in a sour mood, and whatever Jefferson might say could readily prove the wrong thing. "But the first glimpse of him convinced Mr. Jefferson he had come too soon," Coles told Adams. Recounting the story as it had been told to him by Jefferson, Coles said that "Mr. Adams advanced to him in a hurried and agitated step, and with a tremulous voice, said, 'You have turned me out, you have turned me out!'"

Coles again quoted Jefferson for Adams,

> "I have not turned you out, Mr. Adams, and am glad to avail myself of this occasion to show I have not, and to explain my views on this subject. In consequence," he said, "of a division of opinion existing among our fellow-citizens, as to the proper constitution of our political institutions, and of the wisdom and propriety of certain measures which had been adopted by our Government, that portion of our citizens who approved and advocated one class of these opinions and measures, selected you as their candidate for the Presidency, and their opponents selected me."

Seeing clearly that Adams was upset and agitated, and that he had apparently considered the election results as something of a personal defeat, Jefferson addressed the issue directly.

> "You will see from this," said Mr. Jefferson, "that the late contest was not one of a personal character, between John Adams and Thomas Jefferson, but between the advocates and opponents of certain political opinions and measures, and, therefore, should produce no

unkind feelings between the two men who happened to be placed at the head of the two parties."

Jefferson's reasoned explanation and somewhat dispassionate tone likely fell on deaf ears, however. Coles wrote later that, in describing this meeting to him, Jefferson had said, "Mr. Adams became composed, and they took their seats, and talked on the usual topics of a morning visit."[12] Though the conclusion of the meeting as described by Jefferson to Coles, which Coles shared with Adams in Quincy, suggested a return to normalcy between the two men, that was far from the truth. One considerate visit by the new president to the now former president so close to the date of his defeat could not resolve the pain and frustration that Adams surely then felt. Only years later, and with the active involvement of a particularly persistent mutual friend, would Adams's anger and bitterness at the political fights, perceived betrayals, sly public criticisms and controversies finally melt away. Coles's visit to Peace field during the summer of 1811 had a profound and salutary effect on Adams. Coles wrote,

> When I finished my narrative, Mr. Adams said if I had been present and witnessed the scene, I could not have given a more accurate account of what passed—and promptly added, "Mr. Jefferson said I was sensitive, did he! Well, I was sensitive. But I never heard before that Mr. Jefferson had given a second thought as to the proper time for making the particular visit described."[13]

Jefferson's recollection of the meeting, which he described in a letter to Benjamin Rush, supports Adams's admission to Coles that he had indeed been "sensitive." Jefferson wrote to Rush of Adams's reaction during their post-election meeting:

> "I believe you are right," said he; "that we are but passive instruments, and should not suffer this matter to affect our personal dispositions." . . . But he did not long retain this just view of the subject. I have always believed that the thousand calumnies which the federalists, in bitterness of heart, and mortification at their ejection, daily invented against me, were carried to him by their busy intriguers, and made some impression.[14]

Coles's statement to Adams that Jefferson had agonized about the proper time to first visit the outgoing president was something of a revelation to Adams. This unexpected news of Jefferson's consideration for his then obviously tender feelings would later play an important part in reconciling the two former friends. Years of silence would pass before this reconciliation could happen, and as the days and hours of Adams's residence at the new President's House in Washington dwindled down, Adams's eleventh-hour decisions seemed to overturn Jefferson's thoughtful and comforting, though somewhat impersonal characterization of the election results.

Having lost the presidency, there was little official business remaining for Adams but to fill those vacancies in the judiciary and executive that required presidential recommendations. Many of the open posts were judgeships, which Adams understandably filled with fellow Federalists. As these presidentially appointed judges were to serve for a life-time term, the incoming republican president could do little about them.

Executive appointments and lower-level judiciary positions were however subject to Jefferson's oversight, which he employed by removing some of the men appointed by Adams. "Politics being politics in the eighteenth as in the twentieth century, it was entirely natural that Adams should wish to appoint loyal and deserving Federalists to offices," one of Adams's noted biographers wrote of the matter. "Adams certainly spent a portion of his last evening in the White House signing those commissions which the Senate had acted on that day."[15] Perhaps the most aggravating appointment from Jefferson's perspective might have been that of John Marshall as chief justice of the Supreme Court.

Marshall, a distant cousin, had long been a vocal critic of Jefferson, particularly regarding the Mazzei letter. This appointment would later be seen by many, including Adams (though not Jefferson), as one of the best decisions of his presidency. Writing to Marshall about the appointment years later, Adams declared, "the proudest act of my life was the gift of John Marshall to the people of the United States."[16]

Jefferson later told both Benjamin Rush and Abigail Adams that, of all the things that had transpired between he and Adams, these "midnight appointments" had irked him the most. At the time, Jefferson wrote to a friend, "I have not considered as candid, or even decorous, the crowding of appointments by Mr. Adams after he knew he was making them for his successor and not himself, even to nine o'clock of the night at twelve of which he was to go out of office."[17]

The increased number of US District and Circuit courts that resulted from the Judiciary Act, passed in the last weeks of the Adams administration, required that judges be appointed to fill the newly created positions.[18] The lateness of the passage of this act brought about a delay in finalizing these judicial appointments, so that even up to the last day of the Adams administration, March 3, 1801, the Department of State had not yet signed off on all the appointments. "The law was passed at such a late hour, that, though the appointments for the new judgeships created by it had been previously selected, yet the commissions had not been issued from the Department of State," one nineteenth-century historian explained.[19] Commissions that remained unsigned by midnight would be left open for Jefferson to fill (most likely with men of his own party). It was therefore to Adams's benefit to make as many appointments as he could prior to the end of his presidential authority.

A dramatic story of secretary of state John Marshall and the signing of these delayed judicial commissions late in the evening of March third is told by Rayner in his *Sketches* of Jefferson's life, and by Parton in his *Life of Thomas Jefferson*, both of whom reference Sarah Randolph's (Jefferson's great-granddaughter) book *Domestic Life of Thomas Jefferson* as the source. However, Albert Beveridge, an early twentieth-century biographer of Marshall, believed the story to be "absurd," "third-hand household gossip," and "probably, a myth."[20] Though the following account may be apocryphal, the sentiments it represents add further color to an admittedly already-colorful and difficult presidential transition. The scene as set by Jefferson's great-granddaughter is the office of Secretary of State John Marshall, who had recently been appointed chief justice of the Supreme Court, late in the evening of March 3, 1801.

According to Mrs. Randolph, Jefferson was not unaware of the late-hour signing of judge's commissions that was occurring at the secretary of state's office. Toward the end of the day, therefore, Jefferson gave his pocket watch to the new attorney general, Levi Lincoln of Hingham, Massachusetts, and instructed him to go "at midnight and take possession of the State Department."[21]

> Mr. Lincoln accordingly entered Judge Marshall's office at the appointed time. "I have been ordered by Mr. Jefferson," he said to the Judge, "to take possession of this office and its papers." "Why Mr. Jefferson has not yet qualified," exclaimed the astonished Chief-justice. "Mr. Jefferson considers himself in the light of an executor, bound to take charge of the papers of the Government until he is duly qualified," was the reply. "But it is not yet twelve o'clock," said Judge Marshall taking out his watch. Mr. Lincoln pulled out his, and, showing it to him, said, "This is the President's watch and rules the hour."[22]

In general, Jefferson accepted most of these appointees, although one rejection in particular, that of a certain Mr. Marbury, resulted in extraordinary consequences. The landmark Supreme Court case *Marbury v. Madison* was a direct result of Adams's "last minute" rush to appoint judges (in compliance with the Judiciary Act) in the waning hours of his presidency.

William Marbury was one of those late judicial appointees, and was fully prepared to take up his duties as Justice of the Peace for the District of Columbia. Due to the extreme time constraints under which Marshall (then secretary of state under Adams) was forced to sign the latest of these commissions, Marbury's appointment was not finalized in time. When Jefferson took office (the following day) Marbury, much to his consternation, was one of those Adams-appointed officials that Jefferson refused to commission.

Marbury petitioned the Supreme Court (then under its new Chief Justice Marshall), to issue a writ of *mandamus* to Madison (the new secretary of state) to compel him to deliver up the signed commission, and allow him to take his place as Justice of the Peace for the District of Columbia as per the appointment of former President Adams. While the Marshall court supported the Jefferson administration's decision to not accept Adams's appointment of Marbury, it also took

the opportunity to make a powerful assertion of the power and authority of the Supreme Court itself by declaring that the Court had oversight (or judicial review) of executive and congressional decisions.

Marshall's ruling in the Marbury case established the Supreme
Court's position as a coequal entity, with Congress and the Executive branch, within the constitutional framework of "checks and balances." The Marbury verdict would be the final word in the so-called
"midnight appointments" matter, though it would not be decided until
1803, well into Jefferson's first term. Before the 1803 conclusion of
the case was announced, the immediate consequences of Adams's
"last minute" appointments were felt very strongly by Jefferson as the
newly seated president. The impact of these "midnight appointments"
relative to the already-shattered friendship of Jefferson and Adams
should not be overemphasized.

A recent biographer of Abigail Adams, for example, emphat-
ically wrote that "the midnight appointments finally accomplished
what Adams's electoral defeat had not: they ended his friendship
with the man who had turned him out of office."[23] There is no cause
to doubt that Jefferson was angered over the so-called "midnight
appointments." However, to Adams's thinking, he was already alienated by four years of Jefferson's opposition and obstructionism, both
of which were the seals to the dissolution of their friendship rather
than the so-called "midnight appointments."

Adams had long suffered the slings and arrows of Jefferson's strident opposition; perhaps the midnight appointments are seen most
reasonably in the theoretical light of Adams issuing some minor and
irksome political "payback" for all that Jefferson had said and done.
If Adams's purpose in appointing judges till almost the last hour of
the final full day of his presidency had been partly to aggravate his
former friend, he was successful.

After Adams's exit from Washington City a pall of silence covered their former friendship. Several years passed before an unhappy
event provided an opportunity for a reopening of communications
between Monticello and Montezillo.

The untimely death of Jefferson's daughter Polly (Mary Jefferson
Eppes) in 1804 elicited a compassionate letter of condolence from

Abigail Adams to Jefferson, her first letter to him in many years. Her expression of grief and concern began a correspondence of several months between the two. Husband John remained entirely unaware of these communications until Abigail, upon closing the correspondence to Jefferson, presented the stack of letters to John.

After their mutual grief at the loss of Polly had been discussed, however, mutual recriminations replaced them. At the bottom of Abigail's final letter, dated November 19, 1804, of this tense and ultimately unhappy correspondence, John Adams wrote in a postscript, "The whole of this correspondence was begun and conducted without my knowledge or suspicion. Last evening and this morning at the desire of Mrs. Adams I read the whole. I have no remarks to make upon it at this time and in this place."[24]

Almost ten years passed before another letter from Quincy was sent to Monticello. In this brief correspondence between the former first lady and the current president, once great friends, there were several issues that Abigail hoped would be put to rest—ideally with explanations and apologies from Jefferson, which she ultimately did not receive. For Jefferson, still grieving for his daughter and burdened with the responsibilities of the presidency, there was but one matter from the past for which he hoped to get some accommodation from Mrs. Adams which he, also, would not receive. Jefferson wrote to Abigail on June 13, 1804,

> I can say with truth that one act of Mr. Adams's life, and one only, ever gave me a moment's personal displeasure . . . I did consider his last appointments to office as personally unkind. They were from among my most ardent political enemies, from whom no faithful cooperation could ever be expected, and laid me under the embarrassment of acting thro' men whose views were to defeat mine.[25]

The president added that though he had brooded over the matter "for some little time, and not always resisting the expression of it," he had finally "forgave it cordially, and returned to the same state of esteem and respect for him which had so long subsisted."[26]

There is no small irony in Jefferson's complaint of Adams's late-hour federalist judicial appointees from whom he could expect no "faithful cooperation." More interesting perhaps is his observation that these federalist judges and government bureaucrats held views that "were to defeat mine." Abigail's tough, accusatory responses to these multilayered comments from Jefferson perhaps were motivated by a deep resentment at his complaints. Abigail had not forgotten that it had been their former dear friend and colleague Jefferson, overly enamored with the Revolution in France, and with republicanism in general, who had withheld his own faithful cooperation from John Adams, and had often worked assiduously to defeat Adams's plans and policies, most particularly as they related to American relations with the French Republic.

Years later on the eve of their long-delayed reconciliation, arranged in large part by their mutual friend and fellow signer of the Declaration of Independence Dr. Benjamin Rush, Jefferson complained to Rush of Adams's late-hour appointments. Though many years had passed since the frustrating correspondence with Abigail, Jefferson's bitterness had not diminished.

> The last day of his political power, the last hours, and even beyond the midnight, were employed in filling all offices, and especially permanent ones, with the bitterest federalists, and providing for me the alternative, either to execute the government by my enemies, whose study it would be to thwart and defeat all my measures, or to incur the odium of such numerous removals from office, as might bear me down.[27]

Jefferson did proclaim to Rush, however, just as he had to Abigail Adams, that "a little time and reflection effaced in my mind this temporary dissatisfaction with Mr. Adams, and restored me to that just estimate of his virtues and passions, which a long acquaintance had enabled me to fix."[28] Over a decade after Adams's "midnight appointments" had soured Jefferson's first day in office, Jefferson stated to Rush that he had long before forgiven Adams for this slight. Jefferson also noted to Rush that in the same letter in which Abigail had written her condolences to him on the occasion of the death of his daughter, though she expressed "the tenderest expressions of concern at this event, she carefully avoided a single one of friendship towards

A formal pose of Jefferson in retirement. Portrait by
Gilbert Stuart, 1821.
Courtesy National Gallery of Art, Washington

John Adams looking something much less than confident.
A lithograph by Pendleton's printing company created
circa late 1820s after original portrait by Gilbert Stuart.
*Courtesy of the Library of Congress, Prints and
Photographs Division, LC-USZ62-13002*

Monticello's east portico. An engraving from *Century Magazine*, 1887.
Courtesy of the Library of Congress, Prints and Photographs Division, LC-USZ62-104751

Detail of panoramic view of Monticello. "Monticello Cirkut," photograph by Rufus Holsinger, c.1912.
Courtesy of the Library of Congress, Prints and Photographs Division, LC-USZ62-122242

Peace field in winter, the home of John and Abigail Adams, Quincy, Massachusetts.
Author Photo

John Adams's study at Peace field. Adams died at this desk. Photograph (1961) by Samuel H. Gottscho, 1875–1971.
Courtesy of the Library of Congress, Prints and Photographs Division, LC-G613-77313.

Abigail Adams. Portrait by Gilbert Stuart, c.1800–1815.
Courtesy National Gallery of Art, Washington

John Quincy Adams. Engraving by Durand from Seward's
Life and Public Services of John Quincy Adams, 1856.

Maria Cosway. Color mezzotint by Valentine Green
after self-portrait by Maria Cosway, 1787.
Courtesy National Gallery of Art, Washington

Gilbert du Motier, Marquis de Lafayette, hero of
the United States and France. Frontispiece of *Life of
Lafayette: Including an Account of The Memorable
Revolution of the Three Days of 1830*, Author
Anonymous, 1835.

Camille Desmoulins. Etching by Richard Bentley, in *History of the French Revolution*, Volume 3, by M. A. Theirs, 1838.

Lucille Desmoulins. Etching after portrait by Boilly, c.1790s, in *Paris Revolutionnaire: Vieilles Maisons, Vieux Papiers* by G. Lenotre, 1904.

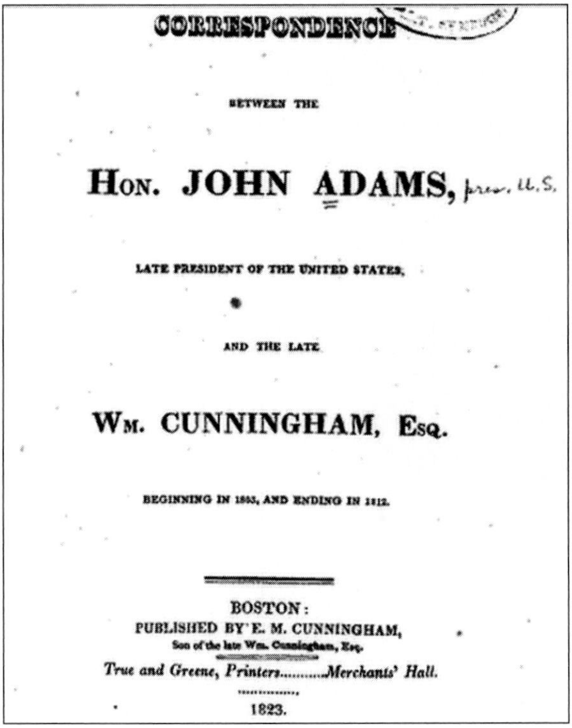

CORRESPONDENCE

BETWEEN THE

Hon. **JOHN ADAMS,** *pres. U.S.*

LATE PRESIDENT OF THE UNITED STATES,

AND THE LATE

WM. CUNNINGHAM, Esq.

BEGINNING IN 1803, AND ENDING IN 1812.

BOSTON:
PUBLISHED BY E. M. CUNNINGHAM,
Son of the late Wm. Cunningham, Esq.
True and Greene, Printers..........Merchants' Hall.

1823.

Title page of the confidential Adams-Cunningham correspondence, published without Adams's permission by Cunningham's son.

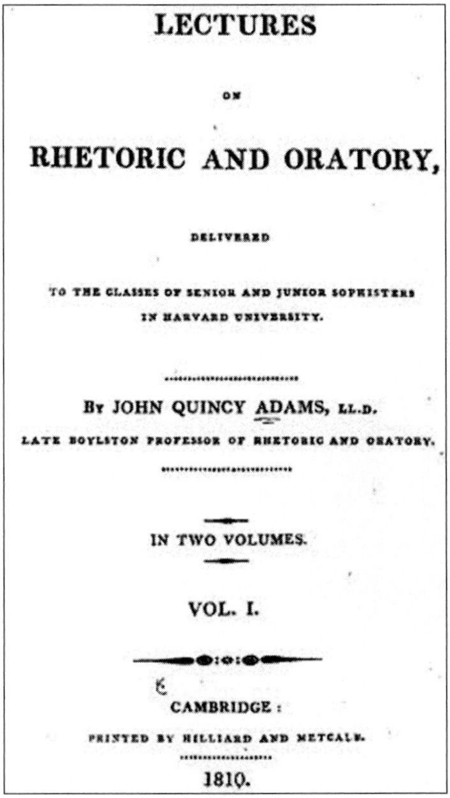

LECTURES

ON

RHETORIC AND ORATORY,

DELIVERED

TO THE CLASSES OF SENIOR AND JUNIOR SOPHISTERS
IN HARVARD UNIVERSITY.

By JOHN QUINCY ADAMS, LL.D.
LATE BOYLSTON PROFESSOR OF RHETORIC AND ORATORY.

IN TWO VOLUMES.

VOL. I.

CAMBRIDGE:
PRINTED BY HILLIARD AND METCALF.

1810.

Title page of a scholarly book written by John Quincy Adams, then professor at Harvard College, and sent as a gift by his father to Thomas Jefferson.

Philip Mazzei. 1980 US Postal Service
commemorative stamp.
Courtesy of osia.org

Tobias Lear. Engraving from William Bixby
and William Samson's *Letters from George
Washington to Tobias Lear*, 1905.

Maximilien Robespierre. From Thiers' *The History of the French Revolution*, 1838.

Louis Antoine de St. Just (Saint-Just). Engraving from Hamel's *Saint-Just-Député De La Convention Nationale*, 1860.

Louis XVI, King of France. Etching and engraving on wove paper by Pierre Adrien Le Beau after Benedict Alphonse Nicolet, 1783 *Courtesy National Gallery of Art, Washington*

Marie Antoinette, Queen of France. From Du Pin Gouvernet's *Recollections of the Revolution and Empire*, 1920.

President's House, Philadelphia. This building, no longer standing, was the residence of Washington and then, for a short time, President John Adams. Lithograph by Breton, c.1830 in *Annals of Philadelphia* by John F. Watson, 1830.

The White House, 1811. From Singleton's *The Story of the White House*, 1907.

John Marshall. Engraving by Charles Balthazar Julien Fevret de Saint-Mémin, 1808.
Courtesy of the Library of Congress, Prints and Photographs Division, LC-USZ62-54940

Charles Cotesworth Pinckney. Engraving after portrait by Chappel, c.1862.
Courtesy of the Library of Congress, Prints and Photographs Division, LC-USZ62-44907

Elbridge Gerry. Engraving by James Barton Longacre, 1847; from a drawing by Vanderlyn.
Courtesy of the Library of Congress, Prints and Photographs Division,LC-USZ62-111790

Lucie de La Tour Du Pin Gouvernet. From Du
Pin Gouvernet's *Recollectionsof the Revolution
and Empire*, 1920.

Charles-Maurice de Talleyrand-Périgord, prince de
Bénévent. Frontispiece of *Life of Prince Talleyrand
with Extracts from His Speeches and Writings* by
Charles K. McHarg, 1857.

Dr. Benjamin Rush. Engraving after portrait by Peale, 1818, in Herring and Longacre's *The National Portrait Gallery of Distinguished Americans*, 1836.

James Madison. Portrait by Gilbert Stuart, c.1821.
Courtesy National Gallery of Art, Washington

Samuel Adams. Jefferson wrote his First Inaugural Address with him in mind. Engraving by Charles Goodman and Robert Piggot, between 1810–1835.
Courtesy of the Library of Congress, LC-USZ62-102271

Thomas Paine. Engraving by Sharp, 1793, after portrait by George Romney.
Courtesy of the Library of Congress, Prints and Photographs Division, LC-USZC4-2542

Dr. Joseph Priestley. From *Joseph Priestley* by T.E. Thorpe, 1906.

Alexander Hamilton. Photograph c.1904 of a mural by Constantino Brumidi in the United States Capitol, Washington, D.C. Portrait created 1855–1870s.
Courtesy of the Library of Congress, Prints and Photographs Division, LC-DIG-det-4a26388

The University of Virginia designed and planned by Jefferson; a view from the south several years prior to the Civil War. Engraving by John Serz, 1856.
Courtesy of University of Virginia Library

John Adams's self-designed bookplate. From *Art and Archaeology: The Arts Through the Ages*, 1920.

Edward Coles. Frontispiece of *Collections of the Illinois State Historical Library* edited by Clarence Walworth Alvord, Vol. 15; Biographical Series, Volume 1, Governor Edward Coles; Sketch of Edward Coles, Second Governor of Illinois and of the Slavery Struggle of 1823–1824 by E. B. Washburne, 1881, 1920.

LIBERTATEM AMICITIAM FIDEM RETINEBIS

D. O. M.

Beneath these Walls	At his Side
Are deposited the Mortal Remains of	Sleeps till the Trump shall Sound
JOHN ADAMS,	**ABIGAIL,**
Son of John and Susanna Boylston Adams.	His beloved and only Wife.
Second President of the United States.	Daughter of William and Elizabeth Quincy Smith.
Born 8 October 1735.	In every Relation of Life a Pattern
On the fourth of July 1776	Of Filial, Conjugal, Maternal and Social Virtue.
He pledged his Life, Fortune and Sacred Honour	Born November 8 1744.
To the INDEPENDENCE OF HIS COUNTRY.	Deceased 28 October 1818.
On the third of September 1783	Aged 74.
He affixed his Seal to the definitive Treaty with Great Britain	Married 25 October 1764.
Which acknowledged that Independence,	During an Union of more than Half a Century
And consummated the Redemption of his Pledge.	They survived in Harmony of Sentiment, Principle and Affection
On the fourth of July 1826	The Tempests of Civil Commotion;
He was summoned	Meeting undaunted, and surmounting
To the Independence of Immortality,	The Terrors and Trials of that Revolution
And to the JUDGMENT OF HIS GOD.	Which secured the Freedom of their Country;
This House will bear witness to his Piety:	Improved the Condition of their Times;
This Town, his Birth-Place, to his Munificence;	And brightened the Prospects of Futurity
History to his Patriotism;	To the Race of Man upon Earth.
Posterity to the Depth and Compass of his Mind.	

PILGRIM,

From Lives thus spent thy earthly Duties learn;
From Fancy's Dreams to active Virtue turn:
Let Freedom, Friendship, Faith, thy Soul engage,
And serve like them, thy Country and thy Age.

Plaque commemorating the lives of John and Abigail Adams in the sanctuary of First Parish Church, Quincy, Massachusetts. A similar plaque commemorates John Quincy Adams and his wife Louisa Catherine. *Photo by author, 2015.*

Thomas Jefferson for the ages. Bronze statue (15 1/4 x 6 9/16 x 4 3/4 in) by Pierre-Jean David d'Angers, 1892.
Courtesy National Gallery of Art, Washington

myself, and even concluded it with the wishes 'of her who *once* took pleasure in subscribing herself your friend, Abigail Adams.'"[29] Jefferson sent along the entire correspondence that he had had with Abigail to Rush to "convince you I have not been wanting either in the desire or the endeavour to remove this misunderstanding. Indeed, I thought it highly disgraceful to us both, as indicating minds not sufficiently elevated to prevent a public competition from affecting our personal friendship."[30]

"Often have I wished to have seen a different course pursued by you," she wrote. "I bear no malice, I cherish no enmity. I would not retaliate if I could."[31] For Abigail, this "misunderstanding" was a deeply painful and personal matter. The tone of her letters—hurt, offended, sad, angry—is that of someone who feels wronged by a friend. Her pain and offense suggested that apologies from Jefferson rather than aloof-sounding, finely tuned logical explanations of personal exculpation could likely have done wonders. Abigail was not mollified by Jefferson's reasoned and detailed defenses of his actions and, in fact, saved her most bitter explosion of anger and dismay for the last letter in the correspondence, to which Jefferson sent no reply. There was little to be gained for Jefferson in responding to that final letter as Abigail declared that it would be her last to him and that the correspondence was closed.

Comments made later to Rush suggest that this abrupt and very definitive conclusion of the correspondence had been frustrating and painful for Jefferson; Abigail's shots had hit their mark. Not withholding any of her anger or pain, and with an honesty characterized by a certain passive-aggressiveness, Abigail wrote in the end that "affection still lingers in the bosom, even after esteem has taken its flight."[32] Relentless in her attacks on Jefferson and his character, Abigail closed her final letter with a bitter accusation that he would do further harm.

> . . . Here Sir may I be permitted to pause, and ask you whether in your ardent zeal, and desire to rectify the mistakes and abuses as you may consider them, of the former administrations, you are not lead into measures still more fatal to the constitution, and more

derogatory to your honour, and independence of Character? Pardon
me Sir if I say, that I fear you are.[33]

Though Jefferson later asserted to Rush that he had forgiven the
Adams's their particular trespasses, identifying specifically the "midnight appointments" as the issue which had annoyed him the most, it
is interesting to note the absence of any introspection or self-awareness on Jefferson's part as to what he may have done, if anything,
to bring about the long rift. Jefferson appears to have viewed these
unfortunate and, as yet, unresolved conflicts as the fallout from "a
public competition" that should not have been allowed to interfere
with personal friendships.

Jefferson's chilly and dispassionate perspective on deeply personal
matters of affection, friendship, anger, resentment, and betrayal, among
other things, had been entirely ineffective in bringing about a resolution.
Long-suffering with his own frustrations and deeply painful personal
losses, yet possessing one of the finest and most vigorous minds on the
planet at that (or any) time, Jefferson would often retreat to a dispassionate, hyper-reasoned approach to his most important relationships.

Unhappy at the turn of events that had brought about his election
defeat, having been "turned out" by his former friend, Adams planned
his departure from Washington. The soon-to-be former second president, then sixty-six years old, expected to embrace a quiet retirement
at his rock-strewn Quincy, Massachusetts, farm, which he did not
expect to be lengthy.

After his departure, Adams never returned to Washington. He
would say later that the death of Charles then still covered him in a
grief that was both devastating and distracting. Busy with the burdens of office and the transition of power, Adams had had little time
to grieve for the once-beloved son who had finally been the cause
of so much pain and disappointment. Grief-stricken for his losses,
Adams had his private coach prepared for the long trip to Massachusetts by the early morning of March fourth—the day of Jefferson's
inaugural. (Abigail had preceded him to Quincy some weeks before.)
Likely emotionally adrift by the absence of Abigail at such a trying time, Adams perhaps indulged the lesser parts of his nature and,

unrestrained by Abigail's good counsel, departed the capital before the commencement of Jefferson's inaugural ceremonies. By the time the inauguration began, Adams was nowhere to be found, having left the city in the early hours of the morning. Adams's precipitate departure from Washington on the eve of Jefferson's inauguration has been described over the years since as "discourteous" at best, but also as a contributing factor in the fall of the Federalist Party itself.[34] One nineteenth-century political analyst wrote of the preparations for Jefferson's first inauguration,

> While these events were transpiring, Mr. Adams was preparing for that precipitate flight from the Capital which gave the last humiliation to his party. He had not the courtesy to stay in Washington for a few hours, and give the éclat of his presence to the inauguration of his successor. Tradition reports that he ordered his carriage to be at the door of the White House at midnight; and we know that, before the dawn of the fourth of March, he had left Washington forever.[35]

Historian Richard Hildreth, in his *History of the United States*, wrote that "this abrupt departure, and the strict non-intercourse kept up for thirteen years between Adams and Jefferson . . . indicates, on the part of Adams, a sense of personal wrong, of the exact nature of which we possess at present no means of judging, except indeed from the charge brought against Jefferson in Adams's confidential correspondence (1804), of 'a want of sincerity, and an inordinate ambition,' as well as of 'a mean thirst for popularity.'"[36]

Jefferson never mentioned Adams's absence at the inaugural ceremonies. Four days later Jefferson forwarded a private letter that had been meant for Adams. The newly inaugurated third president also included a short, friendly, and respectful message to his predecessor and former friend. This letter from Jefferson, written in the third person, strikes a note of respect and courtesy which perhaps Jefferson hoped would tend to ameliorate some of the negative feelings between them after the long political battle that had just concluded. Jefferson wrote to Adams,

> Th Jefferson presents his respects to Mr. Adams and incloses [sic]
> him a letter which came to his hands last night . . . on reading what
> is written within the cover, he concluded it to be a private letter, and
> without opening a single paper within it he folded it up and now has
> the honor to inclose [sic] it to Mr. Adams, with the homage of his
> consideration and respect.[37]

Several weeks later Adams replied from his home in Quincy, Massachusetts, which he sometimes called "Stony Field." Adams responded in kind and included for Jefferson a "letter to one of your Domesticks Joseph Doughtery."

Though both men were known to write extensive and detailed letters when time allowed them, Jefferson's concise note of March 8, 1804, was barely surpassed in length by Adams's brief reply of March twenty-fourth. Adams's response would prove to be the last letter between them for almost a decade.

Adams expressed no bitterness at his election loss and his unexpected retirement from public life in his short letter to Jefferson; that would come later. There was instead sorrow and grief at the death of Charles, and considerate respect for the new chief executive of the United States. Adams also enclosed notices of Charles' funeral. Adams wrote,

> Had you read the Papers inclosed [sic] they might have given you
> a moment of Melancholly or at least of Sympathy with a mourning
> Father . . . They related wholly to the Funeral of a Son who was
> once the delight of my Eyes and a darling of my heart, cutt [sic] off
> in the flower of his days, amidst very flattering Prospects by causes
> which have been the greatest Grief of my heart and the deepest
> affliction of my Life. It is not possible that any thing of the kind
> should happen to you, and I sincerely wish you may never experi-
> ence any thing in any degree resembling it.

Adams wrote to Jefferson as one father to another, but also as the scion of a family that was cursed by its sometimes very negative interactions with alcohol. This affliction of the family did not end with the death of Charles; John Quincy would also have a son similarly afflicted. Over the years, other descendents of John and Abigail would also not be spared. Adams closed the letter on a positive note, however. "This part of the Union is in a state of perfect Tranquility and I see nothing to obscure your prospect of a quiet and prosperous Administration, which I heartily wish you. With great respect I have the honor to be your most obedient and very humble Servant."[38] Jefferson sent no reply.

A great silence then descended between the two former friends, both signers of the Declaration of Independence, fellow Members of the Continental Congress, diplomats to the leading courts of Europe, and fellow founders of the United States of America. With Adams's unceremonious departure from Washington but a recent memory, Jefferson had before him a new and perhaps somewhat unlikely—if not ironic—mission. He would use the occasion of his First Inaugural Address to try to extinguish the passions of political partisanship and unify the country behind him.

As one of the leading political partisans of his era, Jefferson's past conduct and reputation would suggest that this goal, though admirable, would be difficult to achieve. The forces of partisanship and party, which Jefferson had been instrumental in creating and directing, would not so easily disappear from the capital as had the previous president.

12

"We Are All Republicans, We Are All Federalists"

W ITH THE DEFEAT of his old friend Adams, and the resulting diminishment of the Federalist Party, President Jefferson was free to turn the country back to what he considered its proper populist republican path. Jefferson viewed the extreme personal popularity of Washington and the excessive formality of Adams (with the machinations of Hamilton ever in the wings) as dangerous trends too uncomfortably reminiscent of monarchist ways and forms. He was not alone in believing that all the trappings and concepts of monarchism should have been eradicated by the Revolution of '76—even those that were not entirely obvious.

The federalist pro-British viewpoint, which Republicans considered central to America's unnecessarily confrontational relationship with republican France was, for them, a strong strike against Adams, Washington, and the Federalists. In conjunction with the pro-English perspective of the Federalists was their even stronger suspicion about and later rejection of republican France. This negative view of revolutionary France, which was an essential cornerstone of federalist foreign (and occasionally domestic) policy, was in large part based on a rejection of what the French Revolution had become.

In contrast, Jefferson and the Republicans were far more patient on the matter as their's was a much longer view of the French Revolution than was Adams's. The conflict with France that had recently concluded with the Peace Convention of 1800 was seen by Jefferson, as well as by many in France, as caused in large part by the Jay Treaty and the Federalists' rejection of the French Revolution. Jefferson and the Republicans viewed the Revolution in France as a sister republican experiment struggling to find its way. Jefferson considered the Federalists' preference for Great Britain and opposition to France as a kind of unforgivable heresy against the goals of the democratic revolutionary movement which, in his view, forever linked France and the United States.

The simplicity of his Inauguration ceremony, the plain clothing that he wore throughout his two terms, and the elimination of presidential levees (which Adams had held weekly) were, for Jefferson, all part of restoring the populist approach to government and the removal of all semblance of the monarchist system. Jefferson believed that the eradication of all the objectionable forms and styles of British governance had always been central to the purposes of the Revolution of '76. Not all Americans concurred with this widespread eradication of traditions, or of the abandonment of functional and proven approaches and methods.

Adams in particular, with his rationalist and analytical approach to the study of politics, had been completely sanguine to support in politics what worked, and reject what did not. He was prepared to retain, if he had the option (which he did not) some aspects of the English Constitution, while rejecting almost the entirety of the nightmare that was the French Revolution.

The election of 1800, which marked the victory of republicanism and the beginning of the end of federalism, was considered by many, including Jefferson, as an adjunct to the American Revolution. The defeat of the Federalist Party itself was surpassed for Jefferson only by the fact that the ballot box had been the instrument of its demise; a peaceful, and constitutionally compliant accomplishment that set a profound and positive precedent for the future of the American democratic experiment. "The revolution of 1800 was as real a revolution in the principles of our government as that of 1776 was in its form; not effected, indeed, by the sword, as that, but by the rational and peaceable instrument of reform, the suffrage of the people. The nation declared its will by dismissing functionaries of one principle, and electing those of another," Jefferson wrote years later to judge and fellow Virginian, Spencer Roane.[1] The transition from Federalists to Republicans through the vote of the people simply reiterated an essential truth that Jefferson believed to his core, that "the people through all the States are for republican forms, republican principles, simplicity, economy, religious and civil freedoms."[2]

When Jefferson's inaugural ceremony began on March 4, 1801, the temperature was a comfortable 55 degrees F in Washington.[3] Outgoing President John Adams was not there to witness the event or appreciate the pleasant air. Adams's abandonment of Jefferson's inauguration set a pattern of unfortunate and sometimes excessive reactions, which continued off and on for the remainder of his life. Over the coming years Adams's ire, resentment, and bitterness would sometimes explode out of Quincy, doing damage to his reputation though accomplishing little else. Jefferson occasionally was the subject of his anger though he reserved his harshest criticisms and invective for others, most particularly Hamilton. While Adams was tireless and unrelenting in his negative opinion of Hamilton, he and Jefferson shared a thorough lack of affection for the former treasury secretary and federalist leader. In fact, Adams's dislike for Hamilton was rarely tempered even after Hamilton's death in a duel with Jefferson's vice president, Aaron Burr, in 1804. Once describing Hamilton as a "colossus to the anti–republican party," Jefferson had long viewed Hamilton as a threat to the country and to republicanism in general.[4] As Jefferson's presidency began, without the symbolic attendance and approval (if not polite acquiescence) of his vanquished predecessor, Hamilton must then have been far from the new president's thoughts. Former President Adams's end-of-term appointments were however still fresh.

Adams's late-hour appointments of judges and officials directly resulted in a new challenge for Jefferson. Supreme Court Chief Justice Marshall's 1803 ruling in the *Marbury v. Madison* case was a disappointment to both Mr. Marbury and to President Jefferson, though for different reasons. Jefferson considered the new judicial review powers of the high court, as established by Marshall's decision, to be a threat to the new democracy. The third president never accepted this decision as anything but a dangerous error, and a potential disaster to the republic.

Jefferson opposed the newly self-bestowed authority of the Supreme Court because the Court appeared to him to be outside of the checks and balances concept that was central to the Constitution; there were checks against executive and legislative abuse of power— no such checks limited the power of the Supreme Court. Checks and balances had been built into the Constitution for both Congress and the executive as they answered *directly* to the people by elections, and *indirectly* through the legislative oversight authority of their elected representatives. The president could also be held to account by the impeachment power of Congress, another constitutional mechanism by which the people could check executive power through their elected representatives. That Supreme Court judges were appointed for life was of particular concern to Jefferson.

In a letter written many years after the end of his presidency, Jefferson discussed the issue with William Jarvis, a noted merchant from Boston, and later US Chargé d'Affairs at Lisbon, Portugal. Prompted by receipt of a book of essays written by Jarvis,[5] Jefferson observed to the author, "You seem, in pages 84 and 148, to consider judges as the ultimate arbiters of all constitutional questions; a very dangerous doctrine indeed, and one which would place us under the despotism of an oligarchy."[6] Though he admitted to Jarvis that he had not had time to read his book "seriously," Jefferson noted that while judges are honest, though "not more so" than other men, they also have the same "passions for party, for power, and the privileges of their corps." Warning Jarvis that, "with the corruptions of time and party," judges "would become despots," Jefferson expressed a deep concern about the lack of oversight of Supreme Court judges whose authority included review powers over the other two branches of the government. Jefferson explained to Jarvis, "when the legislative or executive functionaries act unconstitutionally, they are responsible to the people in their elective capacity. The exemption of the judges from that is quite dangerous enough."[7]

Jefferson had long believed that the success of the Revolution, and of democracy, resided with the people themselves. He rejected the idea of a powerful tribunal whose members were, in effect, outside of the balance of powers regime as described in the Constitution. "I know no safe depository of the ultimate powers of the society but the people themselves; and if we think them not enlightened enough to exercise their control with a wholesome discretion," Jefferson wrote, "the remedy is not to take it from them, but to inform their discretion by education. This is the true corrective of abuses of constitutional power." Jefferson concluded by reminding Jarvis that "if the three powers[8] maintain their mutual independence on each other it may last long, but not so if either can assume the authorities of the other." Certain in his views, Jefferson asked Jarvis for his "candid re-consideration of this subject, and am sufficiently sure you will form a candid conclusion."[9]

Jefferson's complaint with the new powers of the Court as elucidated by Marshall in the Marbury decision was that the oversight authority of the Court appeared to overturn the model of three separate, but coequal branches of government. The balance between the branches depended upon each being both in service to, and answerable to, the people *and* to one another. Jefferson believed that the proper character of government was that it should be in the service of the people—a concept which required that the government, ideally by design, must be required to answer to the people (through their votes and those of their representatives in Congress). Jefferson's view was that Marshall's Marbury ruling put the judges of the Supreme Court outside of this oversight relationship between the people and government. The Marbury case and Marshall's assertion of Supreme Court constitutional oversight still remain controversial in some circles.

Jefferson's request to Jarvis that he "reconsider" his conclusions suggests that Jefferson felt that his own views on the issue of balance of powers, and of the essential importance of the will of the people in the democratic calculus, were self-evident. However, just as obvious as the importance of the checks and balances paradigm, so, too, was the idea that the pervasiveness of partisanship and party, if not brought under control, could undermine and destroy the republic itself. Jefferson understood that powerful opinions and partisanship, embodied in party loyalties in the political world, were *de rigueur* in a democratic system in which the freedom to assemble and the freedoms of belief and speech were fundamental rights. But Jefferson was also aware that political partisanship could be a threat to the unity of the country, and that the very same partisanship which he himself had used so deftly to defeat Adams could now just as readily be used as a weapon to undermine *his* presidency. Minimizing the power of partisanship, then, but not necessarily of party, would be Jefferson's first self-assigned challenge as chief executive. Jefferson used his First Inaugural Address to set a new, and unlikely, bipartisan tone for the republic.

Jefferson believed that the desire to associate with people of similar beliefs was as common as the innate human need to be free of despotism. Translated to the political milieu of the new United States, this desire to associate became, over a short time, a strong attraction to party and the partisanship that often went with it. "To me then it appears that there have been differences of opinion, and party differences, from the first establishment of governments, to the present day," Jefferson wrote to Adams years later. However, Jefferson suggested, "opinions, which are equally honest on both sides, should not affect personal esteem, or social intercourse."[10] Knowing well that political differences were too often the cause of sometimes painful social ruptures, Jefferson's comment to Adams seems a healthy mix of optimistic, wishful thinking, and the clarity of hindsight.

Though he clearly understood that parties were a necessary component of the political environment, his comments in a letter to fellow signer of the Declaration of Independence, Francis Hopkinson of New Jersey, show that Jefferson's views on the subject had at one time been entirely negative. "If I could not go to heaven but with a party, I would not go there at all," Jefferson wrote from Paris in 1789.[11] At the outset of his presidency, however, Jefferson acknowledged, "wherever there are men, there will be parties; and wherever there are free men they will make themselves heard."[12] This theme of the inevitability (and unavoidability) of parties in a free political environment, and the destructive divisions that they create, would be central to Jefferson's message of unity in his First Inaugural Address.

Jefferson knew that the shaping of political opinion had been instrumental in forming and sustaining the American revolutionary movement that had successfully brought an experimental republican government to the world stage. The shift from rebellion and military operations to a stable civil and political society had required the powerful influence of a national uniter, George Washington. The first president's force of personality, his extraordinary moral character, and example of service and self-sacrifice had set a tone of unity for the country during and after the Revolution. One modern historian described the first president as "indispensable."[13] For Jefferson, as the leading republican politician in the country, Washington's personal popularity eventually became something to be feared.

Jefferson believed that the reverence and affection that most Americans had felt for Washington during the Revolution and into his presidency resulted in an overreliance on, and exaggerated view of, Washington's political opinions. Jefferson viewed Washington's popularity as an insidious threat to the institutions and concepts of democracy, and far too reminiscent (for his comfort) of the "cult of personality" so typical of monarchism and other forms of tyranny. "Such is the popularity of President Washington that the people will support him in whatever he will do or will not do, without appealing to their own reason, or to anything but their feelings towards him," Jefferson wrote several months after Washington's retirement.[14] Jefferson strongly believed that when the people equated the idea and authority of government with any one individual (as he believed had happened with Washington), the republic and American democracy were both then at risk. He was careful in both his administrations to minimize the possibility that the people would associate the person of "Thomas Jefferson" with the government or with democracy itself.

In August 1803, Jefferson received a request from some citizens of Boston to tell them the date of his birthday so that they might make a yearly holiday. The Boston inquirers received the following indirect response from Jefferson via the Attorney General.

With respect to the day on which they wish to fix their anniversary, they may be told, that disapproving myself of transferring the honors and veneration for the great birthday of our Republic to any individual, or of dividing them with individuals, I have declined letting my own birthday be known, and have engaged my family not to communicate it. This has been the uniform answer to every application of the kind.[15]

Henry S. Randall, a nineteenth-century biographer of Jefferson, observed, "accordingly, his birthday was never publicly known until after his death."[16] Jefferson was determined to set the model for correct republican leadership in both dress and official manner, in contrast to the pomp and (British) tradition which Jefferson believed that Adams and Washington had both embraced.

"Monarchism, which has been so falsely miscalled federalism, is dead and buried," Jefferson wrote triumphantly during his first term, "and no day of resurrection will ever dawn upon that."[17] Jefferson's declaration proved to be an accurate one; no federalist candidate would be elected to the presidency after Adams.

Federalism had been defeated by an opposition party led by a populist master of partisanship and political maneuver, a dedicated revolutionary whose view of the meaning of the American Revolution required him to see federalism, its leaders and functionaries, as (political) enemies to be marginalized and defeated. The horrific violence of the French Revolution, as well as the extreme partisanship displayed by both sides during the election of 1800, had shown that separating divergent political opinions from social intercourse and personal esteem was exceedingly difficult, particularly during periods of heightened national tension and crisis. Adams had abandoned the Revolution in France as failed mainly because of its extraordinary violence, while Jefferson held a more patient and ultimately more forgiving perspective—that the goal of popular rule was worth the lives of however many innocents might be lost in the struggle.

As president, Jefferson's goal was to avoid any such similar horrors as had occurred during the Revolution in France, unify the country after a divisive election, and foster a civil, stable, and republican society founded on popular democracy. Having been so deeply involved in partisan politics and knowing from personal experience that political differences often caused breaches in personal relationships, Jefferson hoped to set a new standard for an American revolutionary political culture in which partisan passions did not necessarily lead to social breaks, or to violence.

For Jefferson, the loss of his friendship with Adams appears to have been an acceptable sacrifice, similar, in its way, to the high costs in blood of the French Revolution; all of these losses were unfortunate though ultimately necessary casualties in the long struggle for popular democracy. Now that he held the nation's highest office, heavy sacrifices such as those were no longer acceptable, nor, he believed, should they be necessary.

Before noon on Wednesday, March 4, 1801, President-elect Jefferson left his boarding house and headed to the unfinished capital. Without the distraction of his predecessor's attendance, which had so affected Adams during his inauguration, all eyes were upon the new president. "Let us, then, fellow-citizens, unite with one heart and one mind. Let us restore to social intercourse that harmony and affection without which liberty and even life itself are but dreary things."

Jefferson reminded the country that political opposition was protected, as was the freedom of religion. "And let us reflect that, having banished from our land that religious intolerance under which mankind so long bled and suffered, we have yet gained little if we countenance a political intolerance as despotic, as wicked, and capable of as bitter and bloody persecutions." Advancing his theme of unity, Jefferson asserted that, although political differences would always exist, Americans were united by important common beliefs.

> But every difference of opinion is not a difference of principle. We have called by different names brethren of the same principle. We are all Republicans, we are all Federalists. If there be any among us who would wish to dissolve this Union or to change its republican form, let them stand undisturbed as monuments of the safety with which error of opinion may be tolerated where reason is left free to combat it.

For President Jefferson, the Union itself was a central, essential truth that united both Federalists and Republicans. So long, then, as Federalists and Republicans were united in support of the Constitution and of the Union, there was little cause for earthshaking domestic controversies. "Let us, then, with courage and confidence pursue our own Federal and Republican principles, our attachment to union and representative government," Jefferson declared.

The idea of the Union, considered sacrosanct by both Adams and Jefferson, would later be challenged, and finally abandoned by Jefferson's fellow Virginians and many others across the South. For Adams's descendents and most Northerners however it would be revered and protected at the point of the bayonet. Both Jefferson and Adams viewed the continued existence of the Union as the only foundation upon which all the associated benefits and freedoms that were gained by the Revolution and solidified by the Constitution could be secured for future generations. They believed that the Union should be supported, and continue in perpetuity regardless of domestic political disagreements; no issue must be allowed to shatter the Union of the states. To ensure the continued existence of the Union, a political culture of tolerance was therefore required.

The Constitution was the bulwark of a government of sometimes precarious and imperfect balance. Jefferson believed that the balance had been occasionally threatened—by the judicial review powers elucidated by Marshall in the Marbury decision, and by the Alien and Sedition acts, for example. Despite these and other challenges to the constitutional foundation, he maintained that "this Government, the world's best hope" could exist only so long as did the Union itself.[18]

The challenge of sustaining the Union—which upheld a government and political culture within which opposition was not only supported but encouraged—would become and remain a central concern for the country. Little more than thirty years would pass after the deaths of both Jefferson and Adams when the issue of the existence of the Union became the *essential* question, and a matter of life and death for hundreds of thousands of Americans. Jefferson's deep affection for populist democracy, which in turn had prompted his opposition to the Alien and Sedition acts, as well as his sometimes

strident support of revolutionary France, would have unintended consequences relating to the sustainability of the Union.

The hostility and bitterness of the competition between Republicans and Federalists was a key component in the origins of a
long-standing cycle of inflexibility in American political discourse,
which finally culminated in the shattering of the Union in 1861. Jefferson was certainly not the only American political leader during the
early years of the republic with unwavering surety in the rightness of
his views; his legacy was, however, more profoundly influential than
that of most others.

Jefferson asserted in his First Inaugural Address that it was
"attachment to union and representative government" which united
the opposing parties together under the Constitution.[19] In Jefferson's
perspective, Adams's approach to representative government had
been overly infused with respect for British aristocratic and monarchic forms. It was perfectly legitimate for Jefferson to oppose his old
friend whose views on the forms of government, or any other issue,
he did not share. Such disagreements are the foundation of political
debate, and are supported and encouraged by the Constitution. This
often rancorous first national political disagreement, represented by
Adams and Jefferson, which culminated in the peaceful transition of
political power of one party to its rival, indicated the success of the
constitutional model and of the new American democracy. Though
Jefferson and the Republicans supported the rule of the majority,
a concept fundamental to popular democracy, he also warned the
nation to "bear in mind this sacred principle, that though the will of
the majority is in all cases to prevail, that will to be rightful must be
reasonable."

That the majority opinion must also be "reasonable" was intended
by Jefferson as a check against the potential "tyranny of the majority."
The difficulty, of course, occurs when attempting to determine if the
will of the majority is "reasonable" and how such a determination can
be made. There is no method or measure in the Constitution to decide
the "reasonableness" of a political position—that is a determination
left to the coequal branches of government and to the people (i.e., the
voters) themselves.

Prior to the Marbury decision there had been no body of arbitration with the authority to rule definitively on the constitutional "reasonableness" of a particular law or policy. With the Revolution over and the Constitution the foundation of American political life, the kind of unrestrained opposition that had been so critical in motivating people to embrace the revolutionary cause, an approach which Jefferson had been so adept at, must necessarily be restrained. As president, Jefferson was clear in communicating to the nation that the Union was far too important to be undermined by political partisanship.

While serving as Adams's vice president, Jefferson had created and lead an opposition party that could unseat the Federalists. Jefferson believed that the party of Adams and Washington had abandoned at best, corrupted at worst, the promises and path of populist democracy. As vice president, he could not speak out publicly against Adams's policy regarding France. Jefferson had also quietly opposed the Jay Treaty but to no effect. His opposition to the Alien and Sedition acts prompted him to anonymously draft the Kentucky and Virginia Resolutions, which suggested that a state could cause a Federal law, should it deem it undesirable, to be unenforceable and asserting that "whensoever the general government assumes undelegated powers, its acts are unauthoritative, void, and of no force." This legislation was not only a challenge to Adams but to the edifice of federal authority itself. Delivered by Jefferson through intermediaries, the Resolutions undermined the relationship between the federal government and the states by reasserting in his characterizations the pre-Constitution sovereign status of the states. Jefferson's extremely strong language in his draft of the Kentucky Resolution was toned down however by a Kentucky legislator named Breckinridge for the version that was placed before the Kentucky House.[20] This language by Jefferson was removed from his 1798 draft and not included in the final draft Resolution:

> Where powers are assumed which have not been delegated, a nullification of the act is the rightful remedy: that every State has a natural right in cases not within the compact, (*casus non foederis*,) to nullify of their own authority all assumptions of power by oth-

ers within their limits: that without this right, they would be under the dominion, absolute and unlimited, of whosoever might exercise this right of judgment for them.[21]

Jefferson's rejection of the Alien and Sedition acts did not limit him to the consideration and justification of the nullification concept only, however. Much to Jefferson's disappointment, no other states took up his rallying cry delivered via the legislatures of Kentucky and Virginia. Jefferson had described the Alien Act to Madison as "a most detestable thing,"[22] and wrote later "that the principles already advanced by Virginia & Kentucky are not to be yielded in silence, I presume we all agree."[23] In a letter to Wilson C. Nicholas, a Virginia Senator and later governor of that state, Jefferson wrote that, due to the lack of enthusiasm from the other states, he "thought something essentially necessary to be said, in order to avoid the inference of acquiescence; that a resolution or declaration should be passed." Jefferson laid out three points to Nicholas that were "meant to give a general idea of the complexion & topics of such an instrument." The third item on the list would later be seen as particularly ominous.

. . . expressing in affectionate & conciliatory language our warm attachment to union with our sister states, & to the instrument & principles by which we are united; that we are willing to sacrifice to this everything but the rights of self-government in those important points which we have never yielded, & in which alone we see liberty, safety, & happiness; that not at all disposed to make every measure of error or of wrong, a cause of scission, we are willing to look on with indulgence, & to wait with patience till those passions & delusions shall have passed over, which the federal government have artfully excited to cover its own abuses & conceal it's [sic] designs, fully confident that the good sense of the American people, and their attachment to those very rights which we are now vindicating, will, before it shall be too late, rally with us round the true principles of our federal compact.[24]

No such "resolution or declaration," which clearly implied that secession was a legitimate option to states, was produced by the angry and frustrated vice president, due only to the intercession of Madison. Jefferson explained to Nicholas that Madison "does not concur" and, therefore, Jefferson declared that "from this I readily recede." Jefferson withdrew from his inflammatory plan "not only in deference to his (Madison's) judgment," but also because "we should never think of separation but for repeated and enormous violations."[25] Only Madison's pragmatic and patient counsel brought the overly zealous vice president back from the brink of publicly justifying and recommending disunion.

In a letter to Madison written during the week prior to his letter to Nicholas, Jefferson laid out almost word for word the three-point plan he would describe to Nicholas the following week. There was one striking difference however between Jefferson's three points as they were written for Madison versus the version that he then sent to Nicholas. In the Nicholas version, Jefferson had concluded his third and final point with comments about the "true principles of the federal compact;" not so in his earlier communication to Madison. In that version, dated August 23, 1799, Jefferson had expanded on this third point. It had been Madison's objection to the expanded third point that forced Jefferson to "recede." Jefferson wrote to Madison,

> . . . Before it shall be too late . . . rally with us round the true principles of our federal compact; but determined, were we to be disappointed in this, to sever ourselves from that union we so much value, rather than give up the rights of self government which we have reserved, & in which alone we see liberty, safety, & happiness.[26]

Employing an insightful understatement, one scholar described Madison's influence on his occasionally excessive mentor thusly: "A more cautious and less ebullient man than Jefferson, Madison sometimes gave counsel which proved beneficial in checking Jefferson's enthusiasms."[27] The vice president would soon be president however, and the extreme views that had been palatable to Jefferson while he held the subordinate Executive office would be, from the first day of his administration, far less attractive.

The Kentucky Resolutions of 1798–1799, followed shortly after by a similar but less heated Resolution in Virginia (submitted to that state's legislature by Madison), continued a difficult, divisive, though necessary national discussion about the nature of the relationship between the federal government and the states. The Resolutions, whose purpose had been to oppose the Alien and Sedition acts at the state level (the Jeffersonian-Republicans could not successfully oppose them in the Federalist-controlled Congress), produced long-lasting doubts and questions about federal versus state authority. These questions were never definitively resolved and the seeds of doubt and confusion that were planted by them played an important part in the coming of civil war in 1861. Jefferson's desire to defeat the Alien and Sedition laws led him to publicly suggest extraordinary measures via intermediaries, and even more radical solutions in private which would certainly have been made public but for Madison's intercession.

Jefferson had been guided in his opposition to the Alien and Sedition acts by his reverence for popular representative democracy. His view was that if the federal government had abandoned these essential characteristics of republicanism (and of the Revolution), he was, at least rhetorically, prepared to undo the Union to protect them. It is an important point to emphasize that Jefferson later abandoned his favorable views of secessionism, and expressed his belief (in accord with Adams's) that the survival of American democracy required that the Union must be sustained.

Jefferson's opposition to the Sedition Law in particular was about much more than the protection of republican critics from legal attack by Federalists. The Sedition Law was widely seen as an assault on the First Amendment guarantee of freedom of speech and of the press. In keeping with Jefferson's extraordinarily conflicted and complex nature, once he became president and the Sedition Law had been defeated he attacked the very thing, the freedom of speech, which he had so stoutly defended as vice president.

Little more than two years into his first term, Jefferson's patience with libelous attacks against him by federalist editors had run out. His strong response to federalist editorial attacks was in accord with his view that certain important matters sometimes merited extraordinary actions. In a letter to fellow Republican Thomas McKean, then governor of Pennsylvania, and a fellow signer of the Declaration of Independence, Jefferson wrote, "on the subject of prosecutions, what I say must be entirely confidential."[28] Suggesting to McKean that secrecy was required because "you know the passion for torturing every sentiment & word which comes from me," Jefferson proceeded to lay out a plan that certainly would have excited "passion" had McKean not respected Jefferson's very specific request for confidentiality.

"The federalists having failed in destroying the freedom of the press by their gag-law, seem to have attacked it in an opposite form, that is by pushing it's [sic] licentiousness & and it's lying to such a degree of prostitution as to deprive it of all credit," Jefferson proclaimed to McKean. "And the fact is that so abandoned are the tory presses in this particular that even the least informed of the people have learnt that nothing in a newspaper is to be believed."[29] In order to return "credibility" to the American press, Jefferson suggested essentially the same remedy that the Federalists had employed with the Sedition Act for which he and his party had so excoriated Adams and his party. "This is a dangerous state of things, and the press ought to be restored to it's [sic] credibility if possible," Jefferson declared.

He therefore determined to take action (secretly) to rehabilitate and protect the press, in a sense, from itself. In this regard, what had been unacceptable for Jefferson when he was vice president and leader of the opposition became acceptable, expedient, and necessary when he sat in the president's chair. These attacks on critical editors and writers by both presidents are clearly in direct opposition to the First Amendment of the Constitution.

Jefferson informed McKean that prosecutions should be few and undertaken at the state level "as restraints provided by the laws of the states are sufficient for this if applied." The president also warned that general prosecutions, rather than a picked few, "would look like persecution." Jefferson "had long thought that a few prosecutions of the most prominent offenders would have a wholesome effect in restoring the integrity to the presses." Not surprisingly, Jefferson included an offender's clipping with his letter. "The paper I now inclose [sic] appears to me to offer as good an instance in every respect to make an example of, as can be selected," Jefferson wrote.[30] Having selected his first target, Jefferson's private war against the purveyors of untruth, and those who participated in the eradication of integrity from the American press, went forward. The indictment against Harry Croswell of New York, editor of the federalist *The Wasp*, accused the defendant of

> being a malicious and seditious man, of a depraved mind and wicked and diabolical disposition, and also deceitfully, wickedly, and maliciously devising, contriving and intending, Thomas Jefferson, Esq., President of the United States of America, to detract from, scandalize, traduce, vilify, and to represent him, the said Thomas Jefferson, as unworthy the confidence, respect, and attachment of the people of the said United States . . . and to alienate and withdraw from the said Thomas Jefferson, Esq., President as aforesaid, the obedience, fidelity, and allegiance of the citizens of the state of New York.[31]

The indictment is awkwardly reminiscent of the bases for prosecution of republican writers under the Sedition Act. In July 1803, Croswell "was convicted, at the last circuit court in Columbia County, of printing and publishing a scandalous, malicious and seditious libel upon Thomas Jefferson, the President of the United States."[32] Croswell appealed the conviction. Jefferson's old political enemy and former cabinet colleague, arch-Federalist Alexander Hamilton, signed on as a defense counsel for the appeal; Hamilton waived his fee.

The February 1804 appeal focused on the accuracy/truthfulness of those writings of Croswell's that had been the subject of the indictment and trial the previous year. Hamilton, the great "high Federalist" arguing "freely from the heart," made an impassioned six-hour defense of freedom of the press.[33] If Croswell's statements had been true, Hamilton argued, then they could not be libelous. "I never did think the truth was a crime. I am glad the day is come in which it is to be decided, for my soul has ever abhorred the thought that a free man dared not speak the truth."[34] In a direct allusion to President Jefferson, Hamilton said to the Court, "the most zealous reverers of the people's rights have, when placed on the highest seat of power, become their most deadly oppressors." A free press unfettered by government intrusions and harassment "is necessary to observe the actual conduct of those who are thus raised up," Hamilton asserted to the Court.[35] Although the *pro bono* defense counsel argued long and passionately, with one attendee observing, "It was indeed a most extraordinary effort of human genius . . . (t)here was not, I do believe, a dry eye in the court," the judges on the case were split two against two, and Hamilton lost the case.[36] Though his appeal was lost, Croswell however was not sentenced.[37]

Jefferson's efforts to "rein in" the press and restore it to what he considered "credibility" would ultimately be unsuccessful. Several years after Hamilton's impassioned though unsuccessful defense of press freedoms, Jefferson described his own motives. "As to myself, conscious that there was not a *truth* on earth which I feared should be known, I have lent myself willingly as the subject of a great experiment."[38] Jefferson explained that the purpose of the "experiment" had been to

> prove that an administration, conducting itself with integrity and common understanding, cannot be battered down, even by the falsehoods of a licentious press, and consequently still less by the press, as restrained within the legal & wholesome limits of truth. This experiment was wanting for the world to demonstrate the falsehood of the pretext that freedom of the press is incompatible with orderly government.[39]

Jefferson had somehow concluded that by prosecuting opposition editors and writers, just as his predecessor had done, he would disprove the contention that a free press and orderly government are "incompatible."

Admitting defeat, and reasonably observing that the press is "impotent when it abandons itself to falsehood," Jefferson decided to "leave to others to restore it to it's [sic] true strength, by recalling it within the pale of truth."[40] The relationship of the citizens to the government and, most importantly, the obligations of the government to the people had been described in detail in the Declaration of Independence and in the Constitution. Despite its protections in the founding documents, the freedom of speech and of the press sometimes presents a particular challenge to occasionally sensitive presidents.

While the Sedition Act was enacted under intense domestic and international pressure from revolutionary France (stresses which motivated the Federalists and others who supported the legislation), Jefferson's "experimental" prosecution of Croswell was founded on different challenges and goals. Regardless of the foundations of either effort to muzzle press criticism and free speech rights, both of these efforts were mistaken uses of presidential power and, as the republic was then in its infancy, perhaps that is the most illuminating light in which these measures are best understood. That the offensive legislation was overturned, and that Jefferson quickly desisted, boded well for the future of the country and the Constitution. That it was Alexander Hamilton, despised by both Jefferson and Adams, who warned in court that even the greatest champions of the rights of the people and of liberty in general were susceptible to the abuses of power, further extends the irony of these unfortunate assaults against the press by two champions of democracy in America. The vigilance of the press, in combination with limitations on government interference, is essential to the sustainability of American democracy. Jefferson's "experiment" to influence the press by prosecuting a few "examples" failed mainly due to the protections for speech and press freedoms that he himself had supported. Though Jefferson was active for a time in his opposition to what he considered excesses and lies by editors and writers, he was also a strong supporter of the press.

In defense of his secret campaign to, as he saw it, save the press's credibility from its own abuses, he declared that his actions against the opposition press hadn't been driven by a bruised ego. Proclaiming his "thick skin" against press attacks, Jefferson denied that his actions were of a personal nature. "I have never therefore even contradicted the thousands of calumnies so industriously propagated against myself."[41] There is no irony in Jefferson's having supported the establishment of the *National Intelligencer*.[42]

The greatest responsibility of the press in a free society is the monitoring of the never-ending friction of citizens and government and, most importantly, the actions of those who are elected to represent and to lead. This "watchdog" role is perhaps the most essential contribution of the press to the democracy; it is a critical component of the checks and balances regime. While sometimes unpleasant and worse, this perpetual give-and-take between citizens and government is indicative of a free society and central to the American system.

One of the first things that Jefferson did after his inauguration was to address the matter of the Sedition Law. Jefferson declared in a chilly letter to Abigail Adams,

> I discharged every person under punishment or prosecution under the Sedition Law, because I considered and now consider that law to be a nullity as absolute and as palpable as if Congress had ordered us to fall down and worship a golden image; and that it was as much my duty to arrest its execution in every stage, as it would have been to have rescued from the fiery furnace those who should have been cast into it for refusing to worship their image. It was accordingly done, in every instance . . . without asking what the offenders had done, or against whom they had offended.[43]

Though the Alien Act expired on the final day of the Adams administration, March 3, 1801, the Sedition Act had had a two-year life and expired during the first year of Jefferson's administration. The new president's unwillingness to enforce it effectively nullified it on his first day of office, however.[44] Two associated, but rarely discussed acts, the Naturalization Act and the Alien Enemies Act, had slightly different fates. Congress repealed the Naturalization Act in April 1802, which had required at least fourteen years of residency and five years' notice of intent in order to acquire citizenship.[45] "The Alien Enemies Act of 1798, which is still in force in modified form, authorizes the president to detain, relocate, or deport enemy aliens in time of war."[46]

The expiration of the Alien Act in particular had a personal immediacy for Jefferson. Soon after his ascendency to the presidency, he sent a letter to Dr. Joseph Priestley in which he extended his appreciations and apologies, and an offer to visit at the White House.[47] A widely known republican British émigré iconoclast, clergyman, and scientist, then living in Pennsylvania, Dr. Priestley had been targeted under the now expired law. During the Washington administration vice president Adams had been Priestley's congregant and the two had had a friendly correspondence.

President Jefferson's letter to Priestley, dated March 21, 1801, much more than a simple invitation, was an unburdening summation of the conquest of the republican worldview over that of the federalist. Jefferson's radical politics and philosophy of government were unhindered by any ties of obligations to the past; in his view those who believed in such ties were mistakenly (or perhaps purposefully) obstructing humanity's progress. In the previous administration the greatest champion of the idea that the living are indebted to the past was John Adams.

> Yours is one of the few lives precious to mankind, & for the continuance of which every thinking man is solicitous. Bigots may be an exception. What an effort, my dear Sir, of bigotry in politics and religion have we gone through. The barbarians really flattered themselves they should be able to bring back the times of Vandalism, when ignorance put every thing into the hands of power and priestcraft. All advances in science were proscribed as innovations. They pretended to praise and encourage education but it was to be the education of our ancestors. We were to look backwards not forwards for improvement: the President himself declaring in one of his answers to addresses, that we were never to expect to go beyond them in real science. This was the real ground of all the attacks on you: those who live by mystery and *charlatanerie*, fearing you would render them useless by simplifying the Christian philosophy, the most sublime and benevolent but most perverted system that ever shone on man, endeavored to crush your well-earned and well-deserved fame. But it was the Lilliputians upon Gulliver.[48]

An important difference between the political and humanitarian philosophies of Adams and Jefferson was the way in which they viewed the relationship of the living to the past. The widely held belief that the accumulated knowledge of the past is of inherent value and must be respected prompted many, including Adams, to rely upon it as the only proven foundation astride which new insights should (and could) be constructed. Jefferson alternatively believed that the old concepts of the past had culminated in monarchism, tyranny, and the minimization of the individual; he was therefore fully prepared to abandon the "lessons of the past" and strike out on a new path, one that was unbeholden to a failed history. Jefferson had made assertions in this vein in his draft version of the foundational French revolutionary document *Declaration of the Rights of Man and of the Citizen,* and later discussed these concepts in more detail with his friend Madison. Adams also, much later, would be made familiar with these concepts.

Jefferson believed that Adams's adherence to a traditional perspective of past and present was at best a failure of imagination. For Jefferson, the old ideas had proven ineffective in facilitating human and individual freedom; therefore, they were not to be relied upon. Worse, still, for Jefferson than Adams's intellectual support for a viewpoint that Jefferson rejected, was his former friend's appreciation for some of the forms of the British government, including the Constitution of the United Kingdom. Jefferson particularly hated these traditional trappings of a government that had failed to free humanity from monarchism because, in accord with the goals of the French Revolution to eradicate almost the entirety of the detritus of what the revolutionaries considered a failed past, Jefferson hoped that *all* such things would have no place in the new American system.

While minister to France at Paris, Jefferson had played an active (though legally/ethically questionable) role in assisting the early French revolutionaries to eradicate these old forms of government that he and they deemed dangerous failures. His frustration must have been extreme at seeing them alive in the new American Republic and, perhaps more aggravating, encouraged in the writings of his old friend and fellow revolutionary John Adams.

Jefferson gave significant assistance to Lafayette and his associates in drafting the *Declaration of the Rights of Man and of the Citizen* of 1789. The final article in Jefferson's draft of the document includes a direct challenge to the widely accepted view of the inherent value of the knowledge (and traditions) passed down by previous generations.

> And whereas the progress of enlightenment, the introduction of abuses and the rights of succeeding generations necessitate the revision of all human institutions, constitutional provisions must be made to insure in given cases an extraordinary convocation of the representatives with the sole object to examine and, if necessary, to modify the form of the government.[49]

The draft Declaration, which certainly included Jefferson's input, was clear on the point that moral, political, and legal authority resided with the present and succeeding generations rather than with the accumulated knowledge and experiences of those who had gone before.

Jefferson's was an extraordinarily radical view of civilizational and political development, turning the tradition of respectful deference for the institutions, wisdom, and forms of past generations utterly on its head. The Revolution in France had been so consequential because it not only had swept away the forms of the past, it had also eradicated, though for a relatively short time, respect for, and deference to them as well.

In early September 1789, likely only weeks after composing his draft version of the *Declaration of the Rights of Man and of the Citizen* for Lafayette and his republican colleagues, Jefferson wrote at length to Madison. Jefferson discussed "the question whether one generation of men has a right to bind another" because, though it "seems never to have been started either on this or our side of the water," the issue was "among the fundamental principles of every government." Linking the matter with his activities in Paris, Jefferson wrote that the assertion was essentially an obvious one. "The course of reflection in which we are immersed here on the elementary principles of society has presented this question to my mind; and that no such obligation can be transmitted I think very capable of proof. I set out on this ground which I suppose to be self evident, 'that the earth belongs in usufruct to the living;' that the dead have neither powers nor rights over it." Jefferson then lays out a complex legal argument of how debts incurred by one generation should not be the responsibility of those who follow them. Jefferson's challenge to the concept of generational debt fundamentally shatters the traditional reverence-for-the-previous-generation model as well as the continuity of societal development, so well thought of by Adams and many, if not most, Americans of the time. "On similar ground," Jefferson wrote, "it may be proved that no society can make a perpetual constitution, or even a perpetual law. The earth always belongs to the living generation."[50]

Perhaps overly taken with the extremism of the events unfolding around him in Paris, Jefferson intellectually leapt even further away from the mainstream by suggesting that governments should not be long-lived, asserting that "every constitution, then, and every law, naturally expires at the end of nineteen years. If it be enforced longer, it is an act of force and not of right." In closing this extraordinary letter, whose essential points Madison did not find particularly pragmatic,[51] Jefferson asserted that in establishing such unprecedented laws which were to be founded upon the controversial principle that the living owed little (if anything) to the dead, the new American Republic would be "taking reason for our guide instead of English precedents, the habit of which fetters us, with all the political heresies of a nation, equally remarkable for its encitements from some errors, as long slumbering under others."[52]

Demonstrating the synergy of great ideas being shared by great thinkers at that time, Thomas Paine echoed these same views in his *Rights of Man* published two years later. It is possible that Paine and Jefferson had discussed these issues as the two men were on friendly terms and both had been in Paris at the start of the Revolution there. Restating Jefferson's argument Paine wrote,

> Every age and generation must be as free to act for itself, *in all cases,* as the ages and generations which preceded it. The vanity and presumption of governing beyond the grave, is the most ridiculous and insolent of all tyrannies.[53]

A strong abolitionist, Paine had consistently called for freedom for all men (which included a demand for the eradication of slavery), an idea fundamental to the foundational concepts of America which

Jefferson—despite his leading role in the authorship of the Declaration of Independence—would never fully embrace. Paine wrote, "Man has no property in man; neither has any generation a property in the generations which are to follow."[54]

The controversial ideas of abandoning obligations to the past, which Jefferson had shared with Madison in 1789, and which were later so influentially spread by Paine in his pro-republican pamphlet *Rights of Man* in 1791, were similar in spirit to Dr. Priestley's views on religion and monarchism. Dr. Priestley's unorthodox religious ideas and revolutionary political views had brought him much criticism and personal difficulty in England, all of which precipitated his dramatic and hasty emigration to the United States. Jefferson had an understandably deep appreciation for Priestley's scientific accomplishments, political and religious iconoclasm, and support for the French Revolution.

Widely known for his discovery of oxygen, Priestley wrote and published extensively on religion and science, and spoke publicly in support of republican political ideas. Pro-republican rhetoric was even less well-received in England than it was in the United States during Adams's administration. As a maverick Unitarian religious leader who rejected the validity of the Trinity, as had Adams and Jefferson, and a vocal proponent of the French Revolution, Priestley's radical religious and political views (and activities) came to be seen by many in his home city of Birmingham, England, as a direct challenge to the social and political order of the day.[55] "Priestley was caricatured and denounced," one historian wrote. "Abhorred by defenders of the religious establishment and feared as an agent of reform by government officials whose fortunes were tied to the continuation of the current system, Priestley became a target in a mounting national hysteria."[56] The rising hatred and distrust in England of supporters of the Revolution in France, who were reasonably believed to be anti-monarchists and threats to the political and social order in Great Britain, reached a fiery explosion for Priestley during the summer of 1791. On July 14, 1791, Priestley and his family were driven out of their burning home and forced to flee Birmingham, chased by a drunken, incendiary mob. With his meetinghouse, private home, and personal laboratory torched and destroyed, Priestley relocated to London, then finally to Pennsylvania.

Arriving in Philadelphia in mid-1794, Priestley began to preach Unitarianism to large and admiring audiences. One observant parishioner wrote, "the congregations that attended were so numerous that the house could not contain them, so that as many were obliged to stand as were to sit, and even the door-ways were crowded with people. Mr. Vice President Adams was among the regular attendants."[57] In a letter to a friend dated January 1797, Priestley hopefully wrote that Adams would soon be president and Jefferson vice president and that "there is no doubt they will act very harmoniously together, which will greatly abate the animosity of both parties. But such is the temper and habit of this country, that if any thing be once decided, though by a single fair vote, all contention instantly ceases, and all will join with the majority."[58] Dr. Priestley soon discovered that the political environment in America was far less tolerant of dissent in the latter part of the Adams administration than he had expected, and that harmony and acquiescence to the majority view in the United States were as difficult to see as had been oxygen in his laboratory.

Several days before the inauguration of Jefferson, Priestley wrote in a letter to a clergyman friend that "the violence of the other party,[59] and the extremes to which they were prepared to go, are hardly credible. I myself . . . was in more danger than I imagined, as I find it was under deliberation to send me out of the country under the Alien Act." Priestley knew that at least one high official of the Adams administration desired to expel him, but that his old congregant John Adams had likely prevented it. "It was certainly the wish of the Secretary of State, and other officers of the government, but I imagined that Mr. Adams had revolted at it."[60]

With the election of Jefferson, Priestley must have been greatly relieved, and perhaps felt a renewed confidence that he no longer faced expulsion or harassment by the new republican government. Several weeks after writing to a friend of his realization that he had been in serious personal danger due to his republican politics and resident alien status, he received an invitation to the White House from President Jefferson.

Unsurprisingly, Jefferson had been in a celebratory mood when he wrote his letter to Priestley. There is a mark of triumph and joy in it, and a delight that the Revolution which he had feared had been driven off its proper course by Adams and his party was back on track.

"As the storm is now subsiding, and the horizon becoming serene, it is pleasant to consider the phenomenon with attention. We can no longer say there is nothing new under the sun. For this whole chapter in the history of man is new" Jefferson wrote.

Jefferson closed his letter with an invitation to Priestley to the new executive mansion in Washington—the house that Adams had inhabited for only a short time. "I should be much gratified with the possession of a guest I so much esteem, and should claim a right to lodge you, should you make the excursion" from Philadelphia, Jefferson wrote.[61] Over the next several years until Priestley's death in 1804, the two men continued a lively correspondence, much of which involved discussions of Jefferson's desire to create a university in Virginia.[62] Ill health however was likely the reason Priestley never made the trip from his home in Pennsylvania to visit Jefferson and the new presidential mansion.

Jefferson was not alone in his view that many of the official acts of the Adams presidency were evidence that the Revolution in America had strayed from its intended path. Jefferson's election and reelection would appear to substantiate the observation that a preponderance of Americans were in agreement with Jefferson. It would be Jefferson's purpose to bring republicanism back to the fore and minimize, as much as he could, what he and his supporters perceived to have been anti–republican excesses and errors by the central government during Washington's second term, and under Adams's defeated administration.

The election of Jefferson was, for Jefferson and Republicans, a renewal of the Revolution. Early in his first term Jefferson looked back to another Adams who had been instrumental in bringing about the separation from England. A week after his invitation to Priestley, Jefferson sent a similar communication to Samuel Adams, a cousin of John Adams. Unlike his old friend John Adams, the third president believed that Samuel Adams had never wavered from the proper path of republicanism; Jefferson's election to the presidency was the perfect ocassion on which to personally acknowledge and thank Sam Adams for his more than significant contributions to the Revolution.

Jefferson had had many influences in the course of his developing concepts of republicanism. Once he attained the executive mansion and defeated federalism, which he had considered an existential threat to the populist, republican character of the Revolution, Jefferson's thoughts swiftly returned to some of the men who had informed his revolutionary views. Jefferson's superb and heartfelt letter to Samuel Adams (written only weeks after his inauguration) shows the contradictions and complexities of the third president, and his deep and abiding affection for some of those fellow revolutionaries with whom he had worked to change the world.

Samuel Adams was in retirement and ill health in Massachusetts when Jefferson was inaugurated in 1801. Never successful financially, Adams had "lived the greater part of his life in poverty" and long before had been overshadowed on the national stage by his cousin John, in particular, as well as by many of his fellow signers of the Declaration of Independence. Sam Adams's influence on the Revolution, and love of republicanism, had not been forgotten by Jefferson, however.[63]

Having been one of the originators of the pre-Revolution Committees of Correspondence, a key organizer of the Boston Tea Party, and later an important proponent of independence as a delegate from Massachusetts in the first and second Continental Congresses, Sam Adams had been in Jefferson's thoughts when he composed his First Inaugural Address. Adams was then retired some years from public life (and in poor financial and physical health) after serving as lieutenant governor, then governor (1794–1797) of Massachusetts. Adams had previously played a major role in both the drafting and passage of the Articles of Confederation. Often criticized for his strict adherence to Puritanism, as well as for his personal eccentricities, Sam Adams was also a strong Jeffersonian-Republican.

With Jefferson focused on the importance of both the Union and the Constitution in his first inaugural speech, the president had not likely forgotten Samuel Adams's extraordinary speech to Congress in support of the Declaration of Independence, delivered on August 1, 1776, in Philadelphia. Though the Declaration of Independence had already been approved in July, the document itself was still unsigned on the day that Adams gave his stirring speech. It did not remain unsigned for long.[64]

Adams's first of August speech is now ranked among the greatest orations of the world and was doubtless an effective and eloquent exhortation to his fellow members of Congress to continue the struggle against Great Britain—and to accept nothing less than independence. "Our Union is now complete; our constitution composed, established, and approved. You are now the guardians of your own liberties," Adams triumphantly declared to Congress, though the Revolution itself would not be over for another seven years. "We may justly address you, as the *decemviri* did the Romans, and say, 'Nothing that we propose can pass into a law without your consent. Be yourselves, O Americans, the authors of those laws on which your happiness depends.'"[65] Adams's deep appreciation for the involvement of the people in the new American democracy perhaps made him a special favorite to Jefferson.

Adams argued that those who live in the present should not be abused and harassed by the tyrannies and injustices ensconced in law by those who preceded them, nor dictated to by the protectors of those ancient codes against whom Americans then had no recourse. Adams dramatically declared to his congressional colleagues,

> Ye darkeners of counsel, who would make the property, lives, and religion of millions depend on the evasive interpretations of musty parchments, who would send us to antiquated charters of uncertain and contradictory meaning, to prove that the present generation are not bound to be victims to cruel and unforgiving despotism, tell us whether our pious and generous ancestors bequeathed to us the miserable privilege of having the rewards of our honesty, industry, the fruits of those fields which they purchased and bled for, wrested from us at the will of men over whom we have no check.[66]

Adams's speech was a powerful justification for separation from England and was meant to bolster the hearts of those in Congress who were to affix their signatures to the Declaration of Independence. Signing the document was a brave and extraordinary act of official rebellion against England that, if the Revolution were to be lost, would likely have cost the signatories their lives. Adams's eloquent argument that the present generation should not be burdened by the errors or crimes or bad laws of the past would later be essentially the same argument that Jefferson would make in his controversial "usufruct of the living" letter to Madison.

Samuel Adams's influence on Jefferson's political thought had clearly been profound. In his late March 1801 letter to his old friend and colleague, his mentor, Jefferson wrote that, in addition to having had him in mind when composing his (First) inaugural address, the speech had, in fact, been written *for* him.

"I addressed a letter to you, my very dear & antient [sic] friend, on the 4th of March," Jefferson wrote to Adams several weeks later referring to his inaugural address, "not indeed to you by name, but through the medium of some of my fellow citizens, whom occasion called on me to address."[67] After establishing that the speech had been directed at him, Jefferson proceeded to explain that it had also been written with Adams's expectations and standards in mind. "In meditating the matter of the address, I often asked myself, is this exactly in the spirit of the patriarch of liberty, Samuel Adams? Is it as he would express it? Will he approve of it?" Acknowledging that he was aware of the bitter criticisms that had been made against Adams over the years, Jefferson wrote of those who had "avoided, insulted, frowned on" him; "Father, forgive them, for they know not what they do," Jefferson dramatically wrote.

Employing one of his favorite metaphors, Jefferson compared the country to a ship, and told Adams that "though the ship was not rigged for the service she was put on," referring to the several years of rule by Adams's cousin, John, "the storm is over, and we are in port." Jefferson told Sam Adams that, since the country was now reclaimed from federalist leadership, "we will show the smoothness of her motions on her republican tack." Declaring himself dedicated to an end of partisanship, "an entire oblivion to past feuds," Jefferson told Adams that he would "sacrifice everything but principle to procure it."

Jefferson likely had similar thoughts about eradicating partisanship in mind when he wrote to Elbridge Gerry on the same day that he composed his letter to Samuel Adams. "It will be a great blessing to our country if we can once more restore harmony and social love among its citizens," Jefferson wrote to Gerry. "I confess, as to myself, it is almost the first object of my heart, and one to which I would sacrifice everything but principle. With the people I have hopes of effecting it. But their Coryphaei are incurables. I expect little from them."[68] Having experienced so much criticism for his actions as a diplomat in Paris during John Adams's presidency, Gerry would certainly have welcomed a return to political "harmony." Reiterating a promise he had also made to Samuel Adams, Jefferson assured Gerry that "the right of opinion shall suffer no invasion from me."

Jefferson was no stranger to the power of ideas, as he had long been one of its greatest advocates. Though he was not interested in quashing opposition rhetoric simply because it was not in accord with his views, he likely was, just as he had asserted to New York Governor McKean when suggesting the prosecution of select federalist editors, interested in reestablishing credibility in the American press. Jefferson finally abandoned his plan as unworkable, though his desire to curtail libel and slander in the press had certainly been a reasonable one.

There is a utopian quality about many of Jefferson's views of how "the people" should comport themselves within the new representative democracy. Though Jefferson's experimental campaign to stamp out slanderous attacks against him in the American press was excessive and inappropriate, it was however mild in comparison to the government of Great Britain's response to opposition writers, such as Thomas Paine.

Jefferson was ultimately unsuccessful in finding a balance between checking what he considered abuses in the press, and avoiding what could reasonably be interpreted as harassment and censorship of the opposition. The issues, rights, and responsibilities around press freedoms are less nebulous now than they were in Jefferson's time, though the issue is not at all a dead one. Jefferson targeted editors who, in his opinion, had published lies and slanders about him. He viewed these kinds of personal attacks as purposeful attempts to delegitimize him as president; such criticisms in his view were thus potentially threatening to both his presidency (and the office itself) and the democracy. Jefferson did not pursue editors and writers because he disagreed with their politics.

The freedoms enjoyed by the American press in the early United States, though challenged and tested by both Adams and Jefferson, did not exist in England. Writers whose works were considered by the government to be in opposition could be, and were, arrested and prosecuted for sedition or worse. This is exactly what happened to Thomas Paine.

The same message of republicanism and individual freedom that Thomas Paine had employed to such great effect prior to and during the American Revolution produced similar results in France. Hoping that the 1789 Revolution there would be as successful as its American forebearer had been, Paine made his way to Paris in 1792 to lend his support.

Paine had been living in England since the end of the American Revolution. The publication of the *Rights of Man* caused great controversy there, and resulted in serious legal charges against him. He wisely determined, for his own safety, to leave England. His last-minute escape to France had left him with only twenty minutes from the time his boat left the dock at Dover to the arrival there of British officials there with a warrant for his arrest.[69] Paine was convicted in absentia of slanderous libel in 1792. He never returned to England.

His arrival at Calais, France, was celebrated by a triumphant greeting of soldiers "drawn up to receive him at the city gate . . . and the crowd shouted '*Vive Thomas Paine, vivent les Droits de L'homme!*'" His departure from that country years later would be much quieter, and involve neither fetes nor bon voyages.[70] Paine, the great champion of republicanism, had already, prior to his arrival in France, been made a citizen of the republic and elected (in absentia) to the National Assembly. The honor of citizenship in the new republic had also been conferred on a number of other non-French Republicans including Washington, Hamilton, Priestley, and others.[71] When Paine arrived in Paris and took his seat at the National Convention, "the colors of France, America, and England [were] entwined behind his chair."[72] Though Paine's knowledge of French was minimal, as a revolutionary with global republican goals similar to those of Jefferson, he had been inexorably drawn to France. He had been visiting in Paris when the Bastille fell. Lafayette, one of the leaders in that bloody drama, which proved to be but a taste of much more violent and unpleasant events to follow, gave the key of the fallen fortress to Paine to present it as a gift to President Washington; it has been at Mount Vernon since.

Long before his 1792 arrival in France, Paine had met Benjamin Franklin in London. This meeting precipitated Paine's first trip to America in 1774 which resulted in many years of valuable service there, including fighting in the Continental Army and service to the Congress.[73] Between 1777 and early 1779 Paine was employed as a secretary for foreign affairs in the "Foreign Department" of the US Congress. Resigning that post after he imprudently (but honestly) involved himself in a diplomatic and financial controversy, Paine wrote that he had been "the victim of my integrity."[74]

The loss of this position was another in a string of financial and professional disappointments that followed earlier failures in business, marriage, and government service in England. Paine's wealth of literary skill and the fullness of his love for justice were never rewarded by any personal attainment of financial success; his life was lived in poverty, or on the edges of it. His desire to assist in assuring liberty for mankind had always been far larger than the contents of his pocket. Indeed, his enthusiasm for improving the condition of humanity in general consistently superseded prudence.

One exchange in particular between Franklin and Paine illustrates Paine's expansive revolutionary horizons. "Where liberty is, there is my home," Franklin declared. Paine's response: "where liberty is not, there is my home."[75] Paine was much more than an American nationalist; he was a republican revolutionary with a global, humanity-wide horizon. Jefferson's defenses of and apologies for the excesses of the French Revolution (seen most particularly in his letter to William Short) characterized the blood and horror of that upheaval as a small price to pay when weighed against the long-term benefits that republican democracy would bring to humanity. For similar reasons, Paine felt drawn to take part personally and directly in the French

Revolution; that he barely spoke the language of the country was, to him, entirely irrelevent.

In a toast given in England to the "Revolution Society" of like-minded anti-monarchists, Paine had declared, "Gentlemen, I give you the revolution of the world."[76] Jefferson, like Paine, associated democratic revolution with the advancement of humanity. One biographer linked Paine's Quaker childhood with his expansive view of the struggle for the freedom of man from tyranny; for Paine the Revolution did not end at the borders of France or the United States. "Since his Quaker childhood, humanity had been a mainspring of his actions; and, as he grew older, it became in his mind indissolubly connected with liberty."[77] Paine's revolutionary political vision, like Jefferson's, was not limited to the eradication of monarchism in America or France. Both Paine and Jefferson saw republicanism as inevitable and desirable, and hoped that revolutions on the American model would occur wherever monarchism and tyranny ruled.

With the success of the Revolution in America, the battleground of republicanism shifted to France. (Washington delivered his First Inaugural Address three months before the fall of the Bastille.) Paine believed that he should involve himself directly in the French Revolution because it had become the "ground zero" of the humanity-wide war against tyranny. Unfortunately for Paine and many others, the same radicalism and absolutism that brought down the Bastille, and led to the execution of the king and queen, were eventually turned against those who had unleashed and supported the Revolution.

Paine's unhappy life in France after his hasty departure from England paralleled the implosion of the Revolution itself. An opponent of the execution of the king on both humanitarian and political grounds, Paine spoke out unsuccessfully in the Convention to spare Louis XVI's life.[78] Soon after the execution of the king on January 21, 1793, Paine, then aligned with the more centrist Girondins, was rebuked by the Jacobins, sentenced to prison, and barely escaped the guillotine during the Terror.[79] Finally released from jail in November 1794, with significant help from James Monroe, then serving as American minister to France, Paine withdrew from active involvement in politics.[80] During his many months in prison, Paine became embittered by what he considered lack of action by the American government to secure his freedom. He directed his rage and frustration toward his former commander and friend, George Washington.

Paine injudiciously published a harshly worded open letter to Washington. In this vitriolic 1796 assault, Paine attacked Washington's military and political record, as well as his personal character. "In what a fraudulent light must Mr. Washington's character appear in the world, when his declarations and his conduct are compared together," Paine publicly exclaimed from Paris.[81] This bitter, acerbic, and excessive diatribe against Washington, described by one Paine biographer as "the vials of his gall and wrath" and a "monument of grief and shame," would have a catastrophic effect on Paine's reputation in the United States.[82] Paine's *Age of Reason* was published in the same year. Its harsh attacks on organized religion did not receive a favorable reception in America.

Samuel Adams, then in declining health, wrote his last known letter to Thomas Paine to challenge this assault against religion. In his letter to Paine of November 30, 1802, Adams acknowledged the importance of Paine's writings to the success of the American Revolution. Paine's earlier work, Adams wrote appreciatively, had "unquestionably awakened the public mind, and led the people loudly to call for a declaration of our national independence." A devout Puritan, Adams was widely known for his strong belief in the value of religion and the morality that it encouraged in the minds and hearts of believers. Adams further told Paine that his work for American liberty had made him a friend of humanity. "I therefore esteemed you as a warm friend to the liberty and lasting welfare of the human race," Adams wrote. However, Paine's newest project had, for Adams, put those old views about Paine into doubt. "I am told that some of our newspapers have announced your intention to publish an additional pamphlet upon the principles of the Age of Reason," Adams wrote. "Do you think that your pen, or the pen of any other man, can unchristianize the mass of our citizens, or have you hopes of converting a few of them to assist you in so bad a cause?" Adams asked.

Closing his letter to Paine with a warning, and advising caution to his old friend, Adams wrote, "Neither religion nor liberty can long subsist in the tumult of altercation, and amidst the noise and violence of faction. *Felix qui cautus*. Adieu."[83] Paine's thoughtful though highly argumentative response was written in January 1803, months before Adams's death in October of the same year. Though he likely read Paine's letter, there is no record of Adams having written a reply.

With unfortunate timing, Paine in his response had told the dying and devout Samuel Adams, "you, my friend, will find even in your last moments, more consolation in the silence of resignation than in the murmuring wish of prayer."[84] Adams, a man devoted to his religion, would not likely have thought well of Paine's recommendation to abandon religion and prayer in his last moments. Paine alienated most of his greatest American supporters and friends with his harsh public criticism of their religion and of their great hero/leader, Washington. However, during those unpleasant years that he remained in France after his miserable stay in prison, there remained at least one man in the United States who had not abandoned him.

After Paine's release from jail in late 1794, he remained in Paris declining along with the Revolution, which his writings had been so influential in fomenting. By 1802, the second year of Jefferson's presidency, the republican Revolution in France had finally devoured itself. The revolutionary government had itself been overthrown and replaced by the first consul, Napoleon Bonaparte. By then, Paine's situation in Paris had deteriorated significantly, though his tiny, dirty apartment at a bookshop on the Rue de Théatre Français was certainly an improvement from the months he had spent waiting to be guillotined in prison.[85] If Paine reviewed all of his experiences since his celebrated arrival in Calais, he was likely more than a little disappointed that his not-insignificant contributions and sacrifices for the revolutions in the United States and France had ultimately led him first to prison, then deeper into penury and obscurity. The influence of Paine's writings on the course of the American Revolution including *Common Sense* and *The American Crisis,* a series of essays written during the lowest period of the war—particularly when Paine wrote essays "for weeks on a drumhead in General Greene's tent as the American army retreated across New Jersey"—is difficult to exaggerate.[86] As the Continental Army prepared for its attack on Trenton on Christmas night, 1776, Washington ordered copies of Paine's *The American Crisis* distributed around the camps and read by commanders to the men.

> These are the times that try men's souls. The summer soldier and the sunshine patriot will, in this crisis, shrink from the service of their country; but he that stands it *now*, deserves the love and thanks of man and woman. Tyranny, like hell, is not easily conquered; yet we have this consolation with us, that the harder the conflict, the more glorious the triumph.[87]

The morale boost that this reading provided to the Continental soldiers played a critical role, as the following morning Washington surprised the Hessian forces at Trenton and won an important and desperately needed victory with few losses. By 1802, with Thomas Jefferson the third president, democracy in America was established and the new country thriving. The situation, however, in formerly revolutionary France where Paine, much to his chagrin, remained, was entirely different.

Throughout his life as an author and activist up to that point, Paine had "attacked all who differed from him in the two most sensitive spots in human nature," one biographer explained, and had consequently "paid the penalty."[88] Paine had had enough of France, and its failed Revolution. He was ready to return to the United States, which he considered his adopted homeland. A fellow Republican and old friend from England travelling in France at the time, Henry Redhead Yorke, searched for Paine and found him in his small room in a bookshop in Paris. "Nearly ten years had elapsed since we were last together, and I felt deeply interested in learning his opinions concerning the French revolution, after all the experience, which so long a period of uninterrupted storms and convulsion, must necessarily have afforded him," Yorke wrote in his memoirs of the trip, *Letters from France in 1802*.[89] "It was not without considerable difficulty that I discovered his residence, for the name of Thomas Paine is now as odious in France as it is in England, perhaps more so," he reported.[90] Mr. Yorke's troubles were well-rewarded as Paine, outspoken as usual, did not hesitate to share his views about the failed Revolution in France with his old friend.

Yorke described Paine's home as "a little dirty room, containing a small wooden table, and two chairs." In the brief moment that was required to survey Paine's residence, Yorke concluded that he had "never sat down in such a filthy apartment in the whole course of my life."[91] Horrified by the conditions, Yorke sadly observed that "such was the wretched habitation of Thomas Paine, one of the founders of American Independence . . . How different the humble dwelling of this Apostle of Freedom, from those gorgeous mansions tenanted by the founders of the French Republic!"[92] Yorke and Paine had then not seen one another for a decade; after several awkward minutes of explanation and reminiscence, Paine finally recognized him as an old friend.

"They have shed blood enough for liberty, and now they have it in perfection. This is not a country for an honest man to live in; they do not understand anything at all of the principles of free government, and the best way is, to leave them to themselves," Paine exclaimed. "You see they have conquered all Europe, only to make it more miserable than it was before."[93] Yorke was surprised that Paine spoke in such "desponding language" as he (Yorke) thought that "much might yet be done for the Republic." This comment from Yorke elicited a strong reaction from Paine.

> Republic! Do you call this a Republic? why, they are worse off than the slaves at Constantinople; for there, they expect to be bashaws in heaven, by submitting to be slaves below, but here, they believe neither in heaven nor hell, and yet are slaves by choice. I know of no Republic in the world, except America, which is the only country for such men as you and I. It is my intention to get away from this place as soon as possible, and I hope to be off in autumn; you are a young man, and may see better times, but I have done with Europe, and its slavish politics.[94]

So many who had helped to spawn and support the Revolution in France had been devoured by it; Paine was fully aware of his good fortune in having escaped the Revolution with his life. Some time prior to Yorke's visit, Paine had sent a letter to then Vice President Jefferson, requesting that he be allowed to return to the United States in a "public manner." Yorke believed that this request related to Paine's concerns for his "personal security," though a more likely explanation is that Paine hoped the transatlantic crossing to America would be paid for by the US government.[95] Jefferson replied favorably to Paine's request, March 18, 1801, during the first month of his presidency. "You expressed a wish to get a passage to this country in a public vessel," Jefferson wrote to Paine. The "sloop of war" *Maryland*, which was carrying Robert Livingston to France as the new American minister, would be available to "receive and accommodate you back if you can be ready to depart at such short warning," Jefferson instructed. Jefferson also expressed hopes that Paine would be happy being back in the United States, and that he would "find us returned generally to sentiments worthy of former times."[96]

The quiet return of Paine to the United States on a government ship caused Jefferson some small political discomfort, as some opponents made it appear that Jefferson had invited and brought back, at public expense, the now-reviled Thomas Paine. Such political repercussions were of little moment to Jefferson because, as one of Paine's few remaining friends and supporters, the president believed that Paine's government-sponsored return to the United States was simply the reasonable and decent thing to do in light of Paine's many previous services to the country. Because of the significant contributions he had made to the success of American independence, Paine could certainly find a place for himself in America once again—if President Jefferson had any say in the matter.

Paine had been instrumental in supporting and influencing two of the greatest revolutions in history. Finally, he was abandoned and condemned by one (France), and had alienated himself from the other (America).

Owing much to his own irascibility, bitter criticism, and attacks against people and ideas that were held in high regard in the United States, Paine was entirely responsible for the collapse of his reputation. When Thomas Paine died in New York City in 1809, five people attended his funeral.[97] One of them was Madame Bonneville, whom Paine had brought to America from Paris, with her son, at his own expense. At his graveside she said, "Oh, Mr. Paine, my son stands here as testimony of the gratitude of America, and I for France!"[98]

There were few in America who had much gratitude left for Paine. His attacks on religion, Washington, and others had soured most Americans who, in the main, once had revered and loved him. Chief among these later detractors was John Adams. In an 1805 letter, Adams wrote, "I know not whether any man in the world has had more influence on its inhabitants or affairs than Tom Paine. There can be no severer satire on the age."[99] Adams's ire against Paine wasn't based solely on the pamphleteer's many attacks on religion, Burke, Washington, or simply well-meaning people who weren't as radical as he, but also the fact that Adams himself had been publicly targeted. Paine had repeatedly attacked Adams in a series of letters which appeared in the *National Intelligencer*.[100] Years later, in an 1823 letter to Jefferson, Adams toned down his bitter attacks on Paine from previous decades, leaving only classic New England sarcasm. "I could have enumerated Alexander Hamilton and Thomas Paine, the two most extraordinary Men that this Country, this Age or this World, ever produced. 'Ridendo dicere verum quid vetat.'"[101]

Adams had certainly mellowed over the years and, while his pen continued to record some of his less-than-positive opinions of particular individuals, he was less bitter in the delivery of the later criticism of Paine than he had been years before. Adams's 1805 comment on Paine is a case in point. "For such a mongrel between pig and puppy," Adams then wrote of Paine, "begot by a wild boar on a bitch wolf, never before in any age of the world was suffered by the poltroonery of mankind, to run through such a career of mischief." Finally, Adams derisively suggested that the then-current era should be called "the Age of Paine."[102]

Paine's astounding fall had been almost entirely self-orchestrated, and parallels the implosion of the French Revolution. Adams had abandoned the French revolution as lost long before Paine had finally accepted that the dream of republicanism in France had failed. Paine's abandonment of the Revolution in France came only after years of agitation for and direct involvement with the Revolution itself. For Burke and Adams, the Jacobin Terror had been the final signal that republicanism in France could not succeed. Saint-Just, Robespierre's friend and colleague on the Committee of Public Safety, declared quite rightly but without irony or apparent introspection in October 1793 that "a people has only one dangerous enemy: its government."[103] Less than a year following this prescient statement, Saint-Just met his end along with Robespierre and other senior Jacobin leaders at the very same guillotine to which they had sent countless political enemies, and the "apathetic."[104]

Sharing the same rigid and unforgiving perspective of the likes of Saint-Just and his mentor Robespierre was Joseph Fouché, a leading Jacobin police official in revolutionary France and an extraordinarily coldhearted political partisan. Described by one historian of the Revolution as "one of the most sadistic and versatile political actors and opportunists in French history,"[105] Fouché's viewpoint justified the most appalling acts of violence and cruelty. His particular political spin on them was one that any extremist radical could appreciate. "Terror, salutary terror, is now the order of the day here . . . We are causing much impure blood to flow but it is our duty to do so, it is for humanity's sake."[106] With the heavy responsibility of "humanity's sake" upon their shoulders, a revolutionary could justify and defend and explain most any action, no matter how heinous it might appear to those not so similarly burdened. Many years later Jefferson conceded to Adams that his negative predictions of the outcome of the Revolution in France had been correct, and that he (Jefferson) hadn't expected it to be so violent and costly.

Revolutionary change requires first a personal one—which Paine had already long before done. Jefferson never did embrace the kind of universal revolution so favored by Paine. The limits of Jefferson's revolutionary imagination would later have catastrophic consequences.

Paine had consistently opposed slavery and viewed it as an evil injustice to be eradicated; Jefferson's lack of significant action to hasten the end of slavery during his presidency and afterward was more a failure of moral courage than a simple lack of desire on his part to effect revolutionary change. Jefferson's failure to actively work for abolition as Paine had long done has been excused by some scholars by placing him in the context of the elite, wealthy, and landed Southern slaveholding planter culture into which he had been born, was raised, and lived his life. Jefferson's descriptions of the damage done by slavery to both masters and slaves in his *Notes on the State of Virginia* tend to support this contention. Though an early draft of his Declaration of Independence had criticized slavery, the section was struck out so as not to offend (and alienate) Southern slaveholders; consequently, he was unwilling to take a significant public stand against slavery thereafter—even when personally pressed on the matter to do so.

In his only book, *Notes on the State of Virginia*, Jefferson wrote that blacks and whites could not live together peacefully in a democracy because of the anger and bitterness on both sides wrought by slavery. Jefferson added, "the real distinctions which nature has made" as well as differences "which are physical and moral" were further reasons why the two races could not live together.[107] Jefferson described slavery as "this great political and moral evil," though he hoped that "the minds of our citizens may be ripening for a complete emancipation of human nature."[108]

For Jefferson, the separation of the races was a consequence of the condition of humanity itself, and therefore only human evolution could contend against it. With such a belief underlying his justifications for slavery, there is little wonder that during his retirement, when faced with a direct challenge to take a strong public position against the institution he refused. Jefferson's condemnation of slavery in his only published book seems strong and heartfelt, though mixed and tempered by his own feelings of enslavement to human nature, seemed to offer him no alternative to the "great political and moral evil" of slavery. Jefferson wrote of slavery in *Notes on the State of Virginia*:

Indeed I tremble for my country when I reflect that God is just:
That his justice cannot sleep for ever: that considering numbers,

nature and natural means only, a revolution of the wheel of fortune, an exchange of situation, is among possible events: that it
may become probable by supernatural interference! The Almighty
has no attribute which can take side with us in such a contest. —But
it is impossible to be temperate and to pursue this subject through
the various considerations of policy, of morals, of history natural
and civil. We must be contented to hope they will force their way
into every one's mind. I think a change already perceptible, since
the origin of the present revolution.[109]

Jefferson and his fellow revolutionaries had put in place a political
system and philosophy of republicanism that made the end of slavery inevitable. Its existence was contrary to the ideas of liberty upon
which the new republic had been founded, and was in opposition to
Jefferson's own stated hostile views toward it. Jefferson believed that
a cultural shift must also occur, that legislation alone would not suffice, before slavery could or *should be* ended.

The spirit of the master is abating, that of the slave rising from the
dust, his condition mollifying, the way I hope preparing, under the
auspices of heaven, for a total emancipation, and that this is disposed, in the order of events, to be with the consent of the masters,
rather than by their extirpation.[110]

Jefferson's expectation that the ongoing development of a democracy
in American would itself (eventually) bring about the end of slavery
was a utopian view that removed the responsibility of action from
him, and his generation. "The man must be a prodigy who can retain
his manners and morals undepraved by such circumstances," Jefferson wrote of slavery.[111] Many in the South quietly concurred with
Jefferson's view that slavery corrupted the master just as it kept
the slaves in bondage, though unfortunately not enough of them
believed that such corruption of the masters, and injustice to the
enslaved, should therefore necessarily result in the eradication of
the institution itself.

The failure of the revolutionary generation—particularly those
of the South—and one of its greatest leaders, Thomas Jefferson, to

directly challenge this stain of injustice and hypocrisy upon the Revolution, and the country would only be resolved by civil war in 1861.

Though Jefferson had attempted to make a strong statement against slavery in 1776, it was clear to him from its rejection that it was not then the right time for challenging, and attempting to dismantle, what he then had attempted to publicly identify as an injustice. His highly charged anti-slavery comments in *Notes on the State of Virginia* five years after the *Declaration* were clearer and stronger and would seem to have been the perfect launching platform for a public agitation against the abysmal and, self-admittedly, destructive status quo. Though he took no action during his presidency to demolish that institution which he himself had identified as a corrupter of master and slave alike, he was, in 1814, provided with another opportunity to effect radical and beneficial change based upon his powerful anti-slavery sentiments from years before.

Then out of office and living in retirement as a renowned private citizen, Jefferson was contacted by longtime friend and fellow Virginian Edward Coles, an ardent abolitionist. At the time Coles was secretary to Jefferson's successor, President James Madison, and would later serve as the second governor of Illinois. Jefferson's unfavorable response to Coles's request for assistance to fight for emancipation showed that—just as it had been in 1776 with the stricken anti-slavery statement of the draft *Declaration*—1814, too, for Jefferson, was not the "right time" to publicly oppose slavery.

Jefferson had made it clear on numerous occasions that he thought slavery an injustice that should be ended; he had written on the subject, and had ensured that language of freedom and equality was included in the Declaration of Independence which, by its very existence, was a direct challenge to slavery in America. However, when an opportunity came through his friend Edward Coles, to take a public stand on the matter, he demurred.

Even with the familiarity of their friendship, and their shared antagonism toward slavery, Coles was nevertheless nervous when he began writing his letter to Jefferson. Coles wrote that he had "never took up my pen with more hesitation, or felt more embarrassment than I do now in addressing you on the subject of this letter."[112]

His hesitations however were reasonable ones as few in the South addressed anyone, let alone a former president (and current slave-holder), on the subject of "a general emancipation of the slaves of Virginia."

Coles asked Jefferson for his "knowledge and influence in devising and getting into operation some plan for the gradual emancipation of slavery." He hoped that Jefferson would help because "this difficult task could be less exceptionally and more successfully performed by the revered fathers of all our political and social blessings than by any succeeding statesmen."[113] For such an ardent abolitionist as was Coles, who better to take up the mantle of abolition than one of the greatest of those great men who had founded the republic?

Unrelenting in his polite and respectful pressure on his friend Jefferson, Coles wrote, "it is a duty, as I conceive, that devolves particularly on you, from your known philosophical and enlarged view of subjects . . ." Showing full well how deeply he understood Jefferson's heart and mind, particularly his general dislike of the British, Coles described slavery as "this most degrading feature of British Colonial policy, which is still permitted to exist," and that it was repugnant "to the principles of our revolution." To demonstrate his seriousness about emancipation, Coles informed Jefferson that because of his hatred of slavery he planned to leave Virginia, "and with it all my relations and friends."[114] (He would later be good to his word and leave the state, and then free all of his slaves.) Coles's heartfelt honesty and passion evoked from Jefferson a spirited and sympathetic, but ultimately disappointing response.

In his reply to Coles, Jefferson professed that his friend's anti–slavery "sentiments" had done "honor to both the head and heart of the writer."[115] Coles could not have known of the significance of Jefferson's use of the term "head and heart." This was the very same juxtaposition Jefferson had used almost thirty years before in his evocative and emotional letter to his adored though finally unattainable Maria Cosway. Perhaps it was a quiet self-admission on Jefferson's part that showed that he believed, much like his unsuccessful pursuit of Maria Cosway in Paris thirty years before, that though he'd prefer otherwise, abolition was not then attainable. It seems that his heart was with emancipation, but his head was not.

Jefferson also mentioned an honored colleague (Colonel Theodorick Bland) who had long before in the Congress "undertook to move for certain moderate extensions of the protection of the laws to these people" and, because of this, had been "denounced as an enemy to his country, and was treated with the grossest indecorum." Jefferson explained that he had later gone to France and then returned, and from his return in 1789 through his tenure as vice president and president he had had "little opportunity of knowing the progress of public sentiment here on this subject," and that Coles's "solitary but welcome voice is the first which has brought this sound to my ear, and I have considered the general silence which prevails on this subject as indicating an apathy unfavorable to every hope, yet the hour of emancipation is advancing in the march of time."[116]

Though Coles's letter had clearly impressed Jefferson with its honesty and moral authority regarding an issue about which he had long ago proclaimed his support, he was not swayed enough by it to take action. Citing his advanced age (he would live another active and productive twelve years) Jefferson encouraged Coles to continue his abolition work but told him, unconvincingly, that he would not himself be involved because "this enterprise is for the young, for those who can follow it up and bear it through to its consummation."

In a late September 1814 reply to Jefferson's polite refusal to assist him, Coles addressed Jefferson's age-related objection by reminding him of another founder who had been active and engaged on public matters at a far more advanced age than his. "Doctor Franklin, to whom, by the way, Pennsylvania owes her early riddance of the evils of slavery, was as actively and as usefully employed on as arduous duties after he had past your age as he had ever been at any period of his life."[117] Coles's appeal to Jefferson to ignore his advancing age and follow the path of Franklin fell on deaf ears, as there is no record that Jefferson responded to Coles's September letter.

If Jefferson had informed Coles that his attentions and interests lay elsewhere, Coles's attempts to parry Jefferson's complaints of advancing age would have been unnecessary. Though Jefferson had supportively informed Coles that his abolition efforts "shall have all my prayers, and these are the only weapons of an old man," Jefferson assuredly had more strength of head and heart than he was willing to admit.[118] Perhaps Jefferson was reluctant to take on such a daunting challenge as abolition because he did not believe he would see it through to its conclusion and, more importantly, he had already determined to undertake another project.

The creation of the University of Virginia would take up the bulk of Jefferson's public efforts for the rest of his life. Had he lent his sizable reputation, intellectual gifts, and leadership skills to the eradication of slavery only speculation can answer as to what the outcome might have been. When Coles sent his letter, Jefferson had already made his choice to focus his not insignificant energies on the "Virginia Academical Village" project that was so close to his heart. Had Jefferson partnered instead with Coles in 1814, perhaps the upheaval of the Civil War may not have been necessary; perhaps the difficult groundwork for the eradication of the institution of slavery could have been laid by these two brave men so that slavery could have been expunged, as Jefferson had said, without the eradication of the masters. Unfortunately, Jefferson chose to leave the slavery issue to the young and to succeeding generations, and thus allow it to continue to percolate and fester over time. Like an over-pressurized furnace the issue finally exploded decades later. For slavery to finally be eradicated in the United States, the cost would be a devastating civil war and the deaths of almost a million Americans.

Jefferson's refusal to begin the lengthy work with Coles to advance abolition in 1814, and the consequences of that decision, demonstrated a folly of Jefferson's radical generational political theory. Jefferson had suggested to Madison that the earth belongs in usufruct to the living, and that the living owe no debts to the dead; every generation must suffer for the mistakes (and benefit from the wise decisions) of those who preceded, as we are all prisoners of the forward march of time.

Adams understood that the present is surely indebted to and linked with decisions that were made by previous generations. That humanity is undeniably trapped in its linear existence, such that decisions made by previous generations, that is, the dead, have direct impacts on the lives of the living is perhaps the greatest challenge to Jefferson's utopian (and not altogether possible) desires for freedom from obligations to the past. Because Jefferson and his generation were unwilling or unable to resolve the problem of slavery it was therefore left to later generations to resolve. The continuing existence of slavery then would be one of the most challenging inheritances left to future generations, and from which no American by 1861 could escape.

Americans of 1861 had no choice but to confront and resolve the issue that previous generations had passed down to them. Jefferson was confident that future generations could resolve whatever problems were left to them. "Our children will be as wise as we are and will establish in the fullness of time those things not yet ripe for establishment," Jefferson wrote to John Tyler, Sr., governor of Virginia, several years before Coles asked for Jefferson's support to fight slavery.[119] Long before his letter to Tyler, he had written in a similar optimistic vein that "whenever our affairs go obviously wrong, the good sense of the people will interpose, and set them to rights."[120] After all, Jefferson believed, future Americans would have all the intellectual tools they would need, and the wisdom of hindsight to guide them, to resolve once and for all this most divisive and unfortunate issue. Jefferson's positive view of the capabilities and intelligence of the people (of his own time and into the future), an idea that was essential to republican political thought, allowed him to easily justify refusing Coles's requests for aid and to delay action on the issue of slavery—leaving it for later generations, for good or ill.

In a later letter to Adams, Jefferson proclaimed, "I like the dreams of the future better than the history of the past."[121] To have a positive predilection for the capabilities of future generations is well and good, but it is quite another matter to be a seer, something which Jefferson never claimed to be. Jefferson believed that all the tools necessary to resolve the issue of slavery, and most any other, would be available for use by future Americans *when the time was right*. Though he expressed deep concern in *Notes on the State of Virginia* for the future of the country due to the existence of the slavery institution, he himself was neither prepared, nor sufficiently interested, to take action himself when the opportunity to do so was presented to him by Edward Coles. None can see what the future will bring, although insightful and brilliant people such as Jefferson are perhaps best positioned for that kind of guesswork. Jefferson had made his negative views on slavery publicly clear numerous times, though he continued to possess slaves at Monticello. Questions and doubts about the nature of his relationship with one of these slaves in particular would haunt his retirement years, and cast a troubling pall over his historical reputation.

Allegations of an intimate relationship between Jefferson and his Monticello slave Sally Hemings originally appeared publicly during Jefferson's first term in office. James Callender's disturbing accusations were renewed most recently due to a late 1990s DNA test, which definitively linked a male in the Jefferson family (though not to any particular individual, specifically Thomas Jefferson) to the descendents of Sally Hemings. The Jefferson-Hemings controversy adds another layer of complexity to understanding Jefferson's refusal to support the abolition efforts of his friend Edward Coles in 1814.

If the DNA evidence of the late 1990s, combined with the circumstantial evidence surrounding the likely sexual relationship between Jefferson and Hemings, which includes the six children of Sally Hemings, whom many historians and some contemporaries believed were fathered by Jefferson, then any modern assessment of the character of Jefferson must be significantly affected. Although the 1998 DNA test results have been, in conjunction with circumstantial evidence, widely accepted as sufficiently convincing to support the view that Jefferson most likely *did* have a long-term physical (in the least) relationship with Sally Hemings (and that their relationship resulted in children), the issue nevertheless remains open for debate and may never be definitively resolved.[122]

If the allegations of Jefferson's lengthy liaison with Sally Hemings are even partly accurate, then his refusal to aid Coles must then be considered an act of a deeply conflicted man. Jefferson had condemned the slavery system on a number of occasions yet continued to participate in it and benefit by it. His decision to construct a university, an otherwise worthy undertaking, and thus leave the great issue of the abolition of slavery for resolution by future Americans, provides an almost unresolvable conundrum which has caused many students, admirers, and critics of Jefferson to take one side or the other on the issue, and on him. Because the available evidence is not conclusive, the taking of a strong position on either side of the Sally Hemings relationship matter seems a mistaken approach. There are many disturbing questions that surround Jefferson's refusal to assist Edward Coles in 1814, one of which relates to priorities.

There were then more than several schools of higher learning in the new republic; Harvard College in Cambridge, for example, Adams's alma mater; and The College of William and Mary in Williamsburg, where Jefferson had attended, were two of the leading colleges in the country. The College of New Jersey, later Princeton, and Columbia in New York were also available to often well-connected students. Jefferson's refusal of Edward Coles's request to partner with him to challenge the existence of slavery, in combination with Jefferson's desire to implement his own ideal concept of a republic in which all men were free and equal under the laws, is an uncomfortable riddle without an attractive solution.

The new University of Virginia in Charlottesville became a reality within Jefferson's lifetime, adding justifiable glory to Jefferson's reputation. The school would provide the youth of the South with a republican-influenced education in buildings, and using curricula, based on its founder's own designs. The evils of the slave system however continued unabated and undermined the foundations of both the young republic and Jefferson's new school, where the education provided to students was meant to solidify American democracy through its graduates. The contradiction of Jefferson's slaveholding and republican idealism, a paradoxical view embraced by many across the United States, could not stand for long. Perhaps it is a sad and bitter irony that Great Britain, a country that Jefferson loathed for its monarchism and tyranny, successfully ended slavery without internecine war, while the new American Republic—built upon radical concepts of human equality, individual liberty, and freedom from tyranny—would almost destroy itself to reach the same out-come. Generations of Americans now far removed from Jefferson and Coles and their unhappy correspondence of 1814 can but wonder at the great opportunity that was then lost.

The Jefferson-designed rotunda of the University of Virginia stands as a monument to him and to the concepts of freethinking that he espoused throughout his life. But it is also a silent and bit-ter reminder of an opportunity squandered. That Jefferson could have made a significant contribution to the eradication of slavery, as Coles had suggested, is undeniable. In the bloody light of what came decades later, Jefferson's decision to not act must be seen as a failure of moral imagination, and a terrible mistake.

It seems unlikely that his reluctance to assist Coles was based on an aversion to possible insults or accusations of treason such as his old colleague Colonel Bland had had to suffer; Jefferson had been excoriated time and again in the press over the course of his pub-lic career. Other than his self-admittedly failed attempt to bring the American press back to "credibility," he rarely responded to attacks made against him. Jefferson had shown again and again that he was more than ready to take extraordinary action and labor long and hard for those issues that were close to his heart. His refusal to aid Coles and focus his still powerful energies instead on university building must unavoidably be seen by later generations as a sad decision and symptomatic of a certain unfortunate ambivalence.

American democracy is a radical departure from the monarchist political system from which it sprang. The freedoms that were prom-ised to all, but were denied to black slaves, were eventually deliv-ered to all Americans (but not yet women) after a horrific civil war. Women would have to wait until the twentieth century to see equality under the law granted to them. Jefferson, in 1814, told Edward Coles that he did not believe that the country was ready for emancipation, so he instead focused his efforts and his attentions elsewhere. But Jeffer-son knew from experience that the role of leadership was to bring the people forward to democracy and human progress, just as it would be required to prepare the people and society for emancipation. Though Jefferson had expressed support for emancipation, and had described it as necessary and inevitable, he had also expressed negativity and ambivalence about black slaves.

In his letter to Coles, Jefferson described the black slaves in America as "pests in society by their idleness, and the depredations to which this leads them. Their amalgamation with the other color produces a degradation to which no lover of his country, no lover of excellence in the human character, can innocently consent."[123] Jefferson certainly does not sound the ardent abolitionist or emancipationist in this part of his letter to Coles. Much like his revolutionary experiments in governing, and in foreign policy, Jefferson was not always capable of reconciling the requirements of necessity and desire, and revolutionary republican social or political change.

By the beginning of his second term, Jefferson was prepared to admit that his experiment in taming the press had been unsuccessful. That he would admit defeat in the press matter was admirable and comprehensible, his excessive adherence to the Embargo Act during his second term, even to the point of abandoning key constitutional principles, is more difficult to countenance. The failure of these initiatives is evidence that revolutionary change has limits, as do the leaders who pursue it, and that a wise leader enamored with political experimentation must know when the time has come to stop.

13

"This Is Impossible: How Can a Man Repent of His Virtues?"

JEFFERSON'S SECOND INAUGURAL Address, delivered March 5, 1805, both acknowledged the past and declared that he and the nation were prepared to meet the challenges of the future. It was a positive opening to Jefferson's second term as president. By addressing taxation, Jefferson returned to the matter of the freedom of the present generation from debts to the past. This homage to the "usufruct of the living" concept, which he had some years previously discussed with Madison, was noted perhaps only by those who had closely read Paine's ten-year-old controversial pamphlet, *Age of Reason,* which espoused similar concepts. Jefferson positively declared,

> *In time of war*, if injustice, by ourselves or others, must sometimes produce war, increased as the same revenue will be increased by population and consumption, and aided by other resources reserved for that crisis, it may meet within the year all the expenses of the year, without encroaching on the rights of future generations, by burdening them with the debts of the past.[1]

264

Jefferson's linkage of this radical, though clearly favored desire to prevent current debts being passed to future generations (at least monetarily, in this case) with the challenges of war was likely more prophetic than the president had intended. This idea of shielding future generations of citizens from the mistakes and debts of the present generation remains a popular theme in American politics today.

Though Jefferson had couched his revolutionary language in the context of preventing a tax burden being passed down to later generations, the theme must have been unmistakable for those Republicans who were listening closely. While hints of a difficult immediate future were unintentionally linked with references to the revolutionary recent past, Jefferson also acknowledged the failure of his efforts to eliminate what he considered to be falsehoods from the American press. Jefferson declared,

> During this course of administration, and in order to disturb it, the artillery of the press has been leveled against us, charged with whatsoever its licentiousness could devise or dare . . .These abuses of an institution so important to freedom and science, are deeply to be regretted, inasmuch as they tend to lessen its usefulness, and to sap its safety; they might, indeed, have been corrected by the wholesome punishments reserved and provided by the laws of the several States against falsehood and defamation; but public duties more urgent press on the time of public servants, and the offenders have therefore been left to find their punishment in the public indignation.

The important task of correcting the press would be left to "he who has time . . . in reforming these abuses by the salutary coercions of the law." Jefferson reminded those of the press who might be listening, "since truth and reason have maintained their ground against false opinions in league with false facts, the press, confined to truth, needs no other legal restraint." Jefferson asserted also that "the public judgment will correct false reasonings and opinions, on a full hearing of all parties" and if licentiousness and falsehoods should continue in the press, the issue would be dealt with "by the censorship of public opinion."

With the president's abiding faith in the wisdom of the American people as his bulwark against the abuses of the press, and a not-too-subtle warning of future legal action at the state level by those who "have the time," Jefferson turned his attentions to other matters. Soon enough, the war between England and the failed revolutionary French Republic, now the Empire of France under Napoleon Bonaparte, would require much more of his official time.

The end of the Quasi-War period that Adams had circumnavigated so adroitly to avoid outright war with France did not signify a conclusion to the ongoing conflict between that once-important (and formerly loved) ally and England. Just as had been the case during the latter part of Adams's single term, the hostile acts of both England and France necessarily became the focus of Jefferson's second term. The issue became once again the national *cause célèbre* when in late June 1807, the US Navy frigate *USS Chesapeake* was attacked off the Virginia coast by a British warship. After a brief cannonade during which the unprepared American ship ignominiously fired only one shot, the *Chesapeake* surrendered and was boarded. Several sailors were removed from the American ship in this egregious demonstration of the British asserting their self-proclaimed "right" to impress American seamen or anyone onboard an American vessel who they deemed to be a British subject. While the Jay Treaty gave the United States "most favored nation" trading status with Great Britain, it did not resolve the matter of British seizure of American ships and their personnel. Such matters were to be handled "by arbitration."[2] The English, however, were not the only challenge that Jefferson faced.

The French were also seizing American vessels and impounding their cargoes as contraband of war. (Napoleon apparently did not consider the Treaty of Mortefontaine worth honoring.) As a young country with limited naval capabilities, the United States was an easy target for the two great land and sea powers of the "old world." In the wake of the attack on the *Chesapeake,* and British intransigence that followed, talk of war exploded in the United States much as had war fever against France after the publication of the XYZ dispatches. Jefferson's response was identical to that of his predecessor—prevent, if at all possible, war between the United States and France, and

England. The United States could not then respond effectively, that is decisively, to either British or French naval power. Jefferson determined that one option only was available to him.

Jefferson believed that the United States could not mount a decisive military (i.e., naval) response, and that the only offensive weapon he could deploy, that had the possibility of success, was economic. England and France therefore would be denied access to American exports. Though this alternative to military engagement was specifically targeted against France and England, Jefferson's horizons were much broader. Jefferson's plan for economic coercion as a substitute for international war became the Embargo Act.

Though Britain and France were the targets of the new punitive legislation, American economic pressure was not to be limited to them alone. Jefferson hoped to use the global economy as leverage against America's enemies. The economy of the entire world would be brought to bear to create overwhelming pressure—*every* country would be denied American exports *until* British and French attacks ceased.

The embargo would be Jefferson's application of revolutionary concepts to the realm of foreign affairs and war; all the old concepts of international economic relations and conflict would be challenged. Jefferson truly believed in the ideas of generational freedom from the past that he had elucidated to Madison in his 1789 "usufruct of the living" letter; as president, he had not forgotten them. If the domestic politics and society of a country could be radically remade, and improved, why not also the manner in which countries interact and resolve their differences? The conflict with France and England presented Jefferson with an extraordinary opportunity, built on the harsh foundations of necessity, to attempt to remake the world. Jefferson would hold tight to his belief in the rightness of the embargo policy despite intense opposition. The consequences would be dire.

American merchantmen would thus be required to dock their ships and walk away from them as landsmen, until such time as American ships could travel unmolested on the oceans of the world. This ambitious and ultimately devastating policy became the central issue of the latter part of Jefferson's second term. There were cata-

strophic economic consequences for many Americans, but little if any
for French and Englishmen, or anybody else.

Faced with an almost impossible choice between war and submission, so commonly experienced by neutral nations that found
themselves caught between two powerful warring states, Jefferson
believed that an embargo was the only viable third option. "You will
see that we have to choose between the alternatives of embargo and
war," Jefferson wrote to Thomas Lehré in November 1808. "There
is indeed one and only one other, that is submission and tribute."[3]
One of the leading historians of the embargo, however, saw it as a
component of a dual policy of diplomacy and preparations for war,
similar in many ways to Adams's approach to the French Directory
ten years previously. "By itself, the embargo could not and was never
intended to solve the nation's dilemma. Only through creative and
forceful diplomacy might the nation find redress."[4]

When Jefferson wrote to Lehré, the Embargo Act had already
been in place almost a year. It was passed in Congress in late December
1807, with little debate or public fanfare. Seeing no viable national
American military response to the hostile actions of the British and
French available, and willing to accept neither submission nor sur-
render, Jefferson chose instead almost total economic isolation and
noninvolvement as the cornerstone of American foreign policy for
the remainder of his second term. This extraordinary measure, which
some historians consider to be indicative of a strain of pacifism within
Jefferson, was rather instead a revolutionary experiment at international relations. The truth of the matter was that President Jefferson
had few, if any, attractive alternatives. In his seventh Annual Message
to Congress on October 27, 1807, delivered two months prior to the
enactment of the embargo, Jefferson said,

> I have called on the States for quotas of militia, to be in readiness
> for present defense, and have, moreover, encouraged the accep-
> tance of volunteers; and I am happy to inform you that these have
> offered themselves with great alacrity in every part of the Union.
> They are ordered to be organized and ready at a moment's warning
> to proceed on any service to which they may be called.[5]

Dumas Malone, one of Jefferson's most respected modern biographers, quite rightly wrote, "the designation of him as a prophet of pacifism is unwarranted."[6] Jefferson and his supporters believed that though the United States was not then strong enough to wage a successful military/naval war against England and France, the embargo would provide time to prepare for war (if it should become unavoidable). It was also hoped that a successful outcome of the embargo would make such war preparations, though reasonable and prudent, finally unnecessary.

Jefferson's dual approach to French and English anti-American policies and attacks on American shipping was strikingly similar to Adams's carrot-and-stick handling of the French Republic. That Jefferson would employ an even costlier method in responding to European aggression than that employed by Adams is perhaps ironic. At the time, Vice President Jefferson had been strident in his view that Adams had been warmongering, and that his diplomatic efforts and preparations for war were accomplishing little other than to move the country closer toward war with France. Jefferson opened his eighth and final Annual Message to Congress, delivered at the height of the embargo, November 8, 1808, with an unhappy announcement.[7]

> It would have been a source, fellow citizens, of much gratification if our last communications from Europe had enabled me to inform you that the belligerent nations, whose disregard of neutral rights has been so destructive to our commerce, had become awakened to the duty and true policy of revoking their unrighteous edicts.

Not only had the belligerents not revoked their policies; they had also ignored an offer to suspend the embargo. The offer of suspension was predicated upon "a compliance with our just demands by one belligerent and a refusal by the other in the relations between the other and the United States," Jefferson explained. The president had hoped to use the offer of suspension of the embargo to encourage one or both of the belligerents to normalize relations, or at least to discontinue their offensive policies. If one accepted the suspension but the other refused, the recalcitrant belligerent would alone face the economic wrath of the United States. The president admitted that though "this candid and liberal experiment having thus failed," the embargo would remain in place, at least for the time being, since neither the British nor the French had yet responded to (nor accepted) his offer of suspension. In the meantime, preparations for war continued. Much like Adams ten years previously, Jefferson mentioned both naval and land preparations in his speech.

> Of the gun boats authorized by the act of December last, it has been thought necessary to build only 103 in the present year . . . Under the act of the last session for raising an additional military force so many officers were immediately appointed as were necessary for carrying on the business of recruiting, and in proportion as it advanced others have been added. We have reason to believe their success has been satisfactory.

Jefferson advanced a dual military and diplomatic approach to resolving the conflict with bellicose and hostile European powers just as Adams had done. What had been unacceptable to Vice President Jefferson in the Adams federalist administration was embraced and surpassed by Jefferson as president.

Jefferson was aware that the embargo would cause economic hardship in the United States, particularly in New England where the economy was founded in large part on shipping and access to international markets. Despite the great financial losses faced by Americans, Jefferson remained willing to pursue the embargo as the only alternative to submission to France and England, an alternative he was not prepared to accept.

American economic losses that were directly related to the embargo were not inconsequential, and were likely higher than Jefferson and the Republicans had expected. One historian calculated the losses as follows: "During 1808 American exports declined nearly eighty percent (from $103,343,000 to $22,431,000) and imports declined nearly sixty percent (from $144,740,000 to $58,101,000). Most of the decline in exports took place in the last three-quarters of 1808, as stricter enforcement of the embargo steadily took effect."[8] As the domestic economic impact of the embargo grew more painful and widespread, smuggling and evasion of the law increased dramatically. Jefferson responded by increasing enforcement efforts.

There were time constraints, too, on the policy—economic hardships that were a direct consequence of the embargo would eventually make the policy untenable. Jefferson believed that "for a certain length of time I think the embargo is a less evil than war. But after a time it will not be so."[9] Jefferson used the embargo as an economic alternative to military action to bring weighty direct and indirect nonmilitary pressure on the two combatants, and to buy time. "Till they return to some sense of moral duty therefore, we keep within ourselves. This gives time, time may produce peace in Europe," Jefferson explained to John Taylor in early 1808.[10] In a letter to Madison two months later, Jefferson was more specific in explaining how he hoped the embargo would play out and the results that he hoped to achieve. Jefferson ordered Madison to

> instruct our ministers at Paris and London, by the next packet, to propose . . . but without assuming the air of menace, to let them both perceive that if they do not withdraw these orders and decrees there will arrive a time when our interests will render war preferable to a continuance of the embargo, and then when this time arrives, if one has withdrawn and the other not, we must declare war against that other [and] if neither shall have withdrawn, we must take our choice of enemies between them.[11]

As Congress had not debated the Embargo Act, and Jefferson had said little publicly on the matter prior to its passage, public understanding of the policy was limited mainly to observations of enforcement and the economic damage that it wrought at home. Therefore, soon after the Act was passed, four anonymous articles/editorials were published in the *National Intelligencer* with the apparent purpose of educating the American people about the purposes and goals of the embargo.

These authoritative articles were widely reprinted. One of Jefferson's biographers wrote that they were "most likely" written by Secretary of State James Madison.[12] The embargo was necessary, according to the editorialist, because "the ocean presents a field only where no harvest is to be reaped but that of danger, of spoliation and of disgrace."[13] The administration saw much more in the embargo than simply a way in which to keep American merchantmen safe from French and British attacks. "It is singularly fortunate that an embargo, whilst it guards our essential resources, will have the collateral effect of making it to the interest of all nations to change the system which has driven our commerce from the ocean," the author of the *National Intelligencer* pieces ambitiously proclaimed.[14] Jefferson and Madison viewed the embargo as (hopefully) a new method, without resorting to war, to influence and change the actions and policies of hostile countries. Madison's editorials did not convince the American people to acquiesce quietly to the heavy economic costs (to some a bitter financial disaster) of the president's experiment in international relations.

One historian of the era declared that "the embargo dominated Jefferson's last year in office like no other issue of his presidency . . . and led him to adopt policies of government control inconsistent with his basic philosophy of government . . . As he became more and more committed to the policy, it became less a measure of precaution and more a system of coercion."[15] Albert Gallatin, secretary of the treasury, had cautioned Jefferson early on that "governmental prohibitions do always more mischief than had been calculated; and it is not without much hesitation that a statesman should hazard to regulate the concerns of individuals as if he could do it better than themselves."[16] Gallatin's cautionary statement is expressive of a fundamental republican ideal of individual freedom from government intrusiveness, which Jefferson temporarily abandoned in order to avoid war with England and/or France.

The not-insignificant economic hardships caused by the embargo produced a growing opposition movement, which included active obstructionism. Most disturbingly, there was no indication of any diminishment of French or British hostility toward the United States as a consequence of the embargo. The combination of economic hardship at home, the apparent ineffectiveness of the policy to change British or French behavior, and growing widespread anger at Jefferson's sometimes heavy-handed enforcement of the policy, brought louder calls for repeal.

An Enforcement Act was passed in April 1808, which authorized US Navy ships "to stop vessels suspected of being engaged in unlawful trade, and customs officials were empowered to detain them in suspicious cases until a presidential decision had been reached."[17] The day before the House passed the Enforcement Act, Jefferson ominously wrote to Treasury Secretary Gallatin that he believed "it important to crush every example of forcible opposition to the law."[18]

Less than a year later, by January 1809, Jefferson increased the pressure with a second Enforcement Act described by one historian as "extremely draconian."[19] The new Act did little to make the embargo more effective, though it did increase popular anger toward both Jefferson and the embargo. Most importantly however was that Jefferson's obduracy reinvigorated the Federalist Party, and brought the New England states to open discussions of nullification and secession. Overt and covert acts of defiance against the embargo increased in every state of the Union. "The United States government was virtually at war with its own people," one modern historian wrote, "especially those in Massachusetts, whose opposition to the embargo, said Jefferson, 'amounted almost to rebellion and treason.'"[20]

The Embargo and the Enforcement acts also did significant damage to Republican Party unity as some New England Republicans openly criticized the policy. There was little left to do as Jefferson's second term came to its conclusion but to repeal the unpopular and failed revolutionary experiment at economic warfare. Jefferson had by then already declared that he would not seek a third term. The failed Embargo Act would be the unpleasant legacy of his second term.

Jefferson had been prepared to make sacrifices for the sake of an experiment in international relations, which necessity and circumstances had thrust upon him. He saw no other alternative but to put on an embargo, both to buy time and to influence the policies of two warring countries while avoiding war with one or both. Jefferson's challenges, similar to those his predecessor had faced, were founded on his belief that the United States would be defeated if drawn into a war with England and/or France. Jefferson's noble but ultimately costly and self-destructive experiment at economic coercion through embargo produced catastrophic economic and political consequences at home but no discernible effect on either England or France. The Embargo Act was repealed in the last days of Jefferson's presidency and replaced by a Non-Intercourse Act, allowing American merchants to trade with any nation except England and France.

Though the pressure to repeal the Embargo Act had often been intense, Jefferson and Madison opposed its cancellation. They both believed that just a little more time would be sufficient and that England and France, in the end, would succumb. In a letter written in mid-1815, some months after the conclusion of the War of 1812, Jefferson declared to Thomas Leiper that he had "constantly maintained" that "a continuance of the embargo for two months longer would have prevented our war."[21] In an early 1809 letter to James Monroe, written as the repeal of the Embargo Act was swiftly approaching, Jefferson explained that he was still, even then, completely dedicated to the embargo, and barred other options from consideration. Monroe recommended a special diplomatic mission to France or England to alleviate the present difficulties with those countries, much as Adams had done by sending three diplomats to France in the aftermath of the publication of the XYZ documents, the mission that had finally secured peace between republican France and the United States in 1800.

Despite his awareness of Adams's previous success with diplomacy, Jefferson informed Monroe that "the idea of sending a special mission to France or England is not entertained here at all . . . Such a mark of respect as an extraordinary mission, would be a degradation against which all minds revolt here."[22] Apparently referring to the embargo, which was soon to be repealed, Jefferson reasserted its importance and his confidence that it could have and *should have* worked. "There has never been a situation of the world before," Jefferson declared to Monroe, "in which such endeavors as we have made would not have secured our peace."[23]

By the end of his second term, Jefferson seemed exhausted. "Five weeks more will relieve me from a drudgery to which I am no longer equal, and restore me to a scene of tranquility, amidst my family and friends, more congenial to my age and natural inclinations," the soon-to-retire president confided to Monroe.[24] The embargo was officially repealed on March 4, 1809; the very day that Madison became the fourth president.

As the embargo was approaching its repeal, John Adams felt a great sympathy for the difficulties faced by his old friend. The impossibility of the choices available to Jefferson later became clear to Adams; his opinion underwent a significant shift from total opposition to a begrudging acceptance of the necessity of it. When the Embargo Act was first passed Adams quickly understood the domestic economic damage that would likely result. The former president saw his successor's economic warfare policy as the mutually exclusive confluence of pragmatic statecraft and republican idealism. "Hail Massachusetts, New York, and Pennsylvania!" Adams declared in a letter to Benjamin Rush written at the close of 1807. "Sacrifice loyally your commerce and clank your chains in harmonious concert with Virginia! She tells you commerce produces money, money luxury, and all three are incompatible with republicanism!" Then, venting his bitterness and frustration at the destructiveness of the embargo, Adams sarcastically declared, "virtuous, simple, frugal Virginia hates money and wants it only for Napoleon, who desires it only to establish freedom throughout the world!"[25] By the end of 1808, however, Adams plainly saw the almost impossible difficulty of Jefferson's situation.

In an April 1808 letter to Dr. Rush, Adams presciently wrote, "we may depend upon it that every device that human wit can conceive will be employed to evade the embargo."[26] Though he continued to quietly oppose the embargo, and complained of the economic damage that it caused domestically, he acknowledged in a letter to Josiah Quincy, a federalist congressman from Massachusetts, and grandson of friend and neighbor Colonel Josiah Quincy, that there was no easy solution. Adams warned,

> If you continue the Embargo, the times will be hard. If you institute a total non-intercourse, the times will not be more cheerful. If you repeal the Embargo, circumstances will occur of more animation, but perhaps not more profit or more comfort . . . If you arm our merchantmen, there will be war. The blood will not stagnate, it is true; but it may run too freely for our health and comfort. If you declare war against France and England at once, this will be sublime, to be sure . . . that is, we might obtain by it much wealth and a good peace.

Adams informed Congressman Quincy, "I have made up my mind for hard, dull times, in all events."[27] With his studies of politics and history ongoing much in the same way that Jefferson's pursuit of knowledge and insight also never ceased, Adams found some small solace in world history. "I have another resource, too, for reconciling myself to our fate, and that is by running over again the history of the world . . ." Adams continued to Quincy. "When I find that this globe has been a vast theatre, on which the same tragedies and comedies have been acted over and over again in all ages and countries, how can I hope that this country should escape the universal calamity?" Adams sadly asked. "Despair itself hardens, if it does not comfort."[28] Josiah Quincy's response to Adams reiterated the difficulties that the embargo had caused, particularly to the New England states, and that the policy was being vigorously opposed. Quincy wrote to Adams,

> That the country cannot remain in the condition in which it is, I was certain . . . That it was the determination of the Administration to adhere pertinaciously to the Embargo, I was also certain. That they and their majority were in good measure ignorant of the real temper and sufferings of our people, I knew. My object has been, as far as possible, to shake their confidence in that system, which, whatever they believed or intended, I was conscious was ruining the hopes of New England.[29]

Quincy was not exaggerating when he told Adams that he would do what he could to "shake their confidence" in the Embargo. Less than three weeks before replying to Adams, Quincy had delivered his first address on foreign relations before the House. In the midst of decrying American retreat before English and French attacks and harassments, Quincy dramatically proclaimed, "Mr. Chairman, other gentlemen must take their responsibilities,—I shall take mine. This Embargo must be repealed."[30]

As the months of 1808 passed, Adams's minimal support for the embargo and his sensitivity to the difficult decisions that Jefferson was forced to make all faded away. Perhaps Josiah Quincy's strong-hearted and reasoned public opposition to the policy had inspired Adams to harden his views. "The embargo is a cowardly measure,"

Adams wrote to Rush in July. "We are taught to be cowards both by Federalists and Republicans. Our gazettes and pamphlets tell us that Bonaparte is omnipotent by land, and Britain is omnipotent at sea," Adams wrote. "The American people are not cowards nor traitors."[31] Adams's disillusionment at the international ineffectiveness and domestic destructiveness of the embargo was plain, though he made certain to demonstrate to Rush (a friend to both he and Jefferson) that his opposition to the embargo was not indicative of any bitterness toward Jefferson personally. Adams was not entirely successful in communicating this message, however.

In his letter to Rush of mid-April 1808, Adams wrote, "I have no resentment against him, though he had honoured and salaried almost every villain he could find who had been an enemy to me."[32] It became clear to Adams that the embargo was perceived by the Jefferson Administration as the only means of responding to the attacks of France and England, specifically because the United States did not have a strong navy. The United States did not have a sizable navy because the president did not desire one. At the outset of his presidency Jefferson had assured one of his many correspondents that, by the end of May 1801, "The navy will be reduced to the legal establishment."[33] He had also proclaimed, in a January, 26, 1799, letter to Elbridge Gerry, that he supported a navy only in so far as it "may protect our coasts and harbors from such depredations as we have experienced . . . not for a navy, which by its own expenses and the eternal wars in which it will implicate us, will grind us with public burthens, and sink us under them."[34] Several months after Josiah Quincy's speech to the House and only two months prior to the repeal of the onerous law itself, Adams wrote again to Rush.

The creation of a powerful navy had long been a key issue for Adams, and once again he found the wisdom of that earlier course validated. "The embargo must be removed . . . If it is kept on till Doomsday it will not bend France or England," Adams wrote. "We are in a shocking delusion not only in our opinion of the efficacy of the embargo, but in our unaccountable aversion to Naval Preparations." Complaining at length to Rush about French and British influence in American politics, Adams declared that the only way the

United States could free itself of the influence and intrigues of France and England was through naval power. "A Navy is the only object that can form an independent American party. France and England are both sensible of this tho we are not, and accordingly both Powers set their faces against a Navy in this Country and do all they can to discourage it." Adams also noted that, as a result of the significant economic damage caused by the embargo, federalism was rising again, and republicanism was becoming "more and more unpopular." Adams predicted that "nothing will check this career but a repeal of the Embargo Laws, Non Importation Laws, Non Intercourse laws, and beginning in earnest a Naval force."[35]

In a letter to Jefferson, then several years into his retirement, written one month before a declaration of war against England was voted in Congress in 1812, Adams told Jefferson much the same things he had Rush. "In the Measures of Administration I have neither agreed with you or Mr. Madison. Whether you or I were right Posterity must judge. I have never approved of Non Importations, Non Intercourses, or Embargoes for more than Six Weeks," Adams wrote. "I never have approved and never can approve of the Repeal of the Taxes, the Repeal of the Judiciary System, or the Neglect of the Navy. You and Mr. Madison had as good a right to your Opinions as I had to mine, and I must acknowledge the Nation was with you. But neither your Authority nor that of the Nation has convinced me. Nor, I am bold to pronounce will convince Posterity."[36] Adams's use of hot and provocative language was an attempt to draw Jefferson into a discussion of controversial issues. Jefferson replied with silence.

With the repeal of the Embargo Act, Jefferson's forty years of public service were coming to a close. He was described by one attendee at Madison's inaugural as neither sad nor regretful. Jefferson's obvious delight at his upcoming departure from Washington, from politics, and from public life was in stark contrast to the bitterness and disappointment of Adams's exit from the capital. Upon seeing the outgoing president there, nineteen-year-old Francis Few, niece of Mrs. Albert Gallatin, later wrote, "Mr. Jefferson appeared one of the most happy among this concourse of people."[37] On the day following the repeal of the embargo, and several days before Madison's (first) inauguration, Jefferson wrote a particularly illuminating letter to his old republican friend Pierre Samuel du Pont de Nemours who had emigrated from France to the United States in 1799.

The two had met at the start of the French Revolution while Jefferson was serving as American minister in Paris. Their friendship lasted until du Pont de Nemours's death in 1817. Arrested and condemned by the Jacobins during the Great Terror, du Pont de Nemours had been a moderate during the Revolution and a supporter of the king. He survived the guillotine only by chance and the fall of Robespierre.[38] Apparently reconciled to the idea that the embargo had failed and that the expense and suffering, as well the danger of ruptures to the Union it had caused could no longer be defended, Jefferson wrote, "We have now taken off the embargo, except as to France and England and their territories, because fifty millions of exports, annually sacrificed, are the treble of what war would cost us. Besides that by war we should take something, & lose less than at present."[39] The experiment in revolutionary international economic pressure had been pressed as far as possible (and almost too far) and had failed; and now, war seemed, at least economically, a less expensive option. Jefferson's later recollections of the demise of the embargo include a different and far weightier layer of import, however.

In a letter written seven months before his death, Jefferson's reminiscences about the losses that would have occurred had the embargo not been repealed were much more serious than those he had described to du Pont de Nemours years previously. "Far advanced in my eighty-third year, worn down with infirmities which have confined me almost entirely to the house for seven or eight months past, it afflicts me much to receive appeals to my memory for transactions so far back," Jefferson sadly declared in the opening to his letter of December 25, 1825, to William Giles. Stating that his "memory is indeed become almost a blank," the recollection of a visit by John Quincy Adams was still very much fresh in his mind. Adams had then recently resigned his Senate seat in preparation to take on the role of Minister to Russia. He had been the only federalist senator who supported the embargo. Adams's meeting with Jefferson would have considerable impact.

That interview I remember well; not indeed in the very words which passed between us, but in their substance, which was of a character too awful, too deeply engraved in my mind, and influencing too materially the course I had to pursue, ever to be forgotten. Mr. Adams called on me pending the embargo, and while endeavors were making to obtain its repeal. ... He spoke then of the dissatisfaction of the eastern portion of our confederacy with the restraints of the embargo then existing, and their restlessness under it. That there was nothing which might not be attempted, to rid themselves of it. That he had information of the most unquestionable certainty, that certain citizens of the eastern States (I think he named Massachusetts particularly) were in negotiation with agents of the British government, the object of which was an agreement that the New England States should take no further part in the war then going on; that, without formally declaring their separation from the Union of the States, they should withdraw from all aid and obedience to them... He assured me that there was eminent danger that the convention would take place; that the temptations were such as might debauch many from their fidelity to the Union; and that, to enable its friends to make head against it, the repeal of the embargo was absolutely necessary. ... and however reluctant I was to abandon the measure, (a measure which persevered in a little longer, we had subsequent and satisfactory assurance would have effected its object completely,) [sic] from that moment, and influenced by that information, I saw the necessity of abandoning it, and instead of effecting our purpose by this peaceful weapon, we must fight it out, or break the Union. I then recommended to yield to the necessity of a repeal of the embargo, and to endeavor to supply its place by the best substitute, in which they could procure a general concurrence.[40]

Jefferson had not likely been agreeable, the day after signing the repeal, to the idea of sharing the entire truth with du Pont de Nemours. Certainly there had been a convergence of opposition and lack of real results from the embargo policy which would have seen the eventual end of the embargo. However, it was John Quincy Adams's dire warning that had firmly signaled the failure of Jefferson's experiment, and the price that would be paid if he did not desist. As his presidency closed, and the threat to the Union that had resulted from his experiment in international relations was removed, Jefferson had clearly learned a key lesson of revolutionary change; there comes a time to listen, reassess, and most importantly, to stop.

As his presidency concluded, Jefferson was more than ready to put politics and the frustrations of governing behind him. "Never did a prisoner, released from his chains, feel such relief as I shall on shaking off the shackles of power," Jefferson proclaimed to du Pont de Nemours. He also declared that nature's intent for him had never been politics but an intellectual's life instead. "Nature intended me for the tranquil pursuits of science, by rendering them my supreme delight." With forty years having been spent not in the pursuits of his passion but rather propelled by moral necessity to "resisting" the "enormities of the times in which I have lived," Jefferson was ready to return to his books, learning, and his self-designed home at Monticello.[41] Jefferson welcomed his approaching life of retirement out of the halls of power in a way that Adams, at the end of his presidency, could not then conceive—he was excited about the future.

Jefferson was able to leave Washington and the presidency without a second thought because, should there be further crises, or even war (both he knew were inevitable), he was confident that he had left the country and the ship of state sound and in good hands. "I leave everything in the hands of men so able to take care of them, that if we are destined to meet misfortunes, it will be because no human wisdom could avert them," he wrote to du Pont de Nemours.[42] Jefferson, with his former friend Adams's help, had participated in the successful creation of a new country, and institutions to support and protect it; all that remained was for its leaders to make the right decisions.

Though Jefferson had been preparing for his return to Monticello for several months, his departure from Washington was a far more relaxed affair than the precipitous exit of his predecessor eight years before.[43] Two weeks passed from Madison's inauguration to Jefferson's departure home to Charlottesville. His return took four days of travel in difficult weather over bad roads.

Jefferson filled the remaining years of his private life with study as he said that he would do, and with building. The now-retired president finished his architecturally grand second home in Virginia (Poplar Forest) that rivaled Monticello in its beauty (though not in size) for which he had laid the foundation in 1806.[44] He also worked tirelessly on the University of Virginia project which included designing the school's buildings and its republican educational foundations. But there was something else, too, that remained to be built, or rebuilt, in this case—his old and ruined friendship with John Adams.

Dr. Benjamin Rush of Philadelphia, a fellow signer of the Declaration of Independence and a renowned physician and educator, was perhaps the only man in the country who could rightly state that he was on close and friendly terms with both Adams and Jefferson.[45] Though Rush's "political loyalties lay with Jefferson," he was "bound at the same time by the strongest personal ties to John Adams,"[46] and with good reason.

During the epidemic of yellow fever of 1793 which "claimed the lives of between 4,000 and 5,000 residents of Philadelphia, or about one-tenth of the population," Rush bravely remained in the city, treating patients during the course of the one hundred–day epidemic when many other physicians had fled.[47] His self-sacrifice and demonstration of courage and duty in remaining in the stricken city, and his considerable efforts to help as many as he could, at great risk to himself, made him a "popular hero." However, his reliance on "bloodletting" (as well as the inducement of vomiting) was thought ineffective and dangerous (i.e., excessive) by many both within and without the Philadelphia medical community.[48]

One enterprising medical historian "made an effort to identify by name as many of Rush's patients as possible and to track outcomes of his management. He estimated that 46 percent of Rush's patients died."[49] Described by another historian as "unshakable in his convictions, as well as self-righteous, caustic, satirical, humorless, and polemical," Rush responded to another epidemic of yellow fever the following year, and again in 1797, with the same questionable and controversial "depletion therapy."[50] In 1797 criticism against Rush personally, and his controversial, aggressive treatment methods, grew into a firestorm of criticism stoked in large part by bitter condemnatory articles by pamphleteer William Cobbett and newspaper editor John Ward Fenno. Rush sued both for libel.

Rush had become convinced that the origin of the epidemic was local rather than imported sources. This controversial belief (later disproved), which he spoke and wrote about publicly and fearlessly, made him highly unpopular with city leaders and other partisans of Philadelphia. Being the stubborn and profoundly humanitarian person that he was, Rush pressed ahead and argued heavily for his theory regarding the local origins of yellow fever, knowing full well that attacks against him were inevitable.[51] Consequentially, Rush's medical reputation was ruined and, as a result, "his income was so reduced that he felt he must abandon either the practice of medicine or the city of Philadelphia."[52]

Criticism of Rush and his treatment methods did not only come from trenchant journalists, Philadelphia city leaders, and medical rivals. Even Jefferson, a longtime friend, confidentially concurred with Rush's detractors. "For classical learning I have ever been a zealous advocate," Jefferson wrote to Dr. Thomas Cooper the year following Rush's death. "And in this, as in his theory of bleeding and mercury, I was ever opposed to my friend Rush, whom I greatly loved; but who has done much harm, in the sincerest persuasion that he was preserving life and happiness to all around him."[53] The consequences to Rush of his widely unpopular and later disproven epidemic origin theory, which he stridently and very publicly espoused, and his controversial treatments during those horrible and tragic events, were not insignificant. Rush's personality unfortunately did not help to soothe matters.

Though it appears that Rush had been pressured to resign from the Philadelphia College of Physicians in 1793, an organization that he had helped to create, one Rush biographer suggested alternatively that Rush voluntarily left the organization out of frustration and pique.

The attacks on his opinions of origin and treatment so embittered him that, on November 5, he resigned from the College of Physicians, the organization which he had helped to found.[54] Rush's personal offense and annoyance at the widespread criticism heaped upon him in the wake of his extraordinary service to the citizens of Philadelphia is perfectly understandable. These attacks must have come as a cruel reward particularly as Rush's motives in risking his life to treat epidemic victims had been entirely humanitarian. "I was favored," he wrote in his own account of the first epidemic, "with an exemption from the fear of death in proportion as I subdued every selfish feeling, and labored exclusively for the benefit of others.[55]

The horrors he had seen and experienced while working tirelessly to ameliorate the suffering of the afflicted had a deep impact on Rush. "Never can I forget the awful site of mothers wringing their hands,—fathers dumb for a while with fear & apprehension—and children weeping aloud before me, all calling me to hasten to the relief of their sick relations."[56] A sensitive and religious man, Rush was anguished by the suffering of his many patients. He wrote to his wife, Julia, in August 1793:

> While I depend upon divine protection, and feel that at present I live, move, and have my being in a more especial manner in God alone, I do not neglect to use every precaution that experience has discovered, to prevent taking the infection . . . I even strive to subdue my sympathy for my patients, otherwise I should sink under the accumulated loads of misery I am obliged to contemplate. You can recollect how much the loss of a single patient once in a month used to affect me. Judge then how I must feel, in hearing every morning of the death of three or four![57]

Though Rush had taken as much care as he could to avoid becoming a victim of the fever himself, those close to him succumbed quickly. Weeks after Rush wrote to his wife in August, three of his students died, and two more contracted the fever but survived. Closer to home, Rush's sister died on the first of October. Rush himself became ill in mid-September. In early October, Rush collapsed while on a patient visit and was carried home. It is impossible to know what roles Rush's self-treatment (including bleedings), his strong constitution, luck, and/or divine intercession played in his recovery by the end of October.[58]

Rush had bravely and tirelessly fought against the scourge of the yellow fever in Philadelphia when so many residents and medical people had left the city. One of Rush's few biographers, Nathan G. Goodman, wrote, "his lot seemed doubly bitter when he was met with the enmity and wrath of fellow physicians for his wide and general use of the lancet upon which he pinned his faith for his success in combating the scourge."[59] The resulting harsh and sometimes personal criticism of his medical approach to treating patients during the epidemics was, to Rush, extremely irksome and painful. The sometimes bitter retorts that Rush used to defend himself resulted in unpleasant consequences.

Rush's defense of his treatment methods was so strident, and the consequences of his obstinate adherence to his views (very much in the Adams vein) so professionally damaging that, by 1797, his financial and professional options had all but disappeared from Philadelphia. Finally convinced that no opportunities remained open to him in that city, Rush made ready to leave. However, regardless of the controversies swirling around him in Philadelphia, he was still one of the most highly trained physicians in the country, and remained an impressive and even heroic figure to many.

An offer to join the faculty of the Medical School at Columbia University in New York City arrived, which Rush quickly and prudently accepted. A formal resolution of the medical faculty dated October 20, 1797, unanimously invited Rush to join the staff there. The next step in the hiring process was approval by the Columbia Board of Trustees. The university medical faculty, all of whom supported Rush, apparently believed that this would be little more than a formality. Unfortunately for Rush and his allies on the medical faculty, one of the university trustees was Alexander Hamilton.

When the Columbia Board of Trustees took up the issue of Rush's appointment, Hamilton informed his colleagues that there was no need for additional medical faculty at Columbia. This challenge by Hamilton caused Rush's appointment to be tabled until the next meeting of the Board. Though the medical faculty enthusiastically supported Rush and was appalled at Hamilton's opposition, Rush asked his medical colleagues to drop the offer, and immediately withdrew himself from consideration. Knowing full well that the motives behind Hamilton's opposition to his appointment was likely both personal (Rush's friendship with both Adams and Jefferson perhaps played a part) and political, and that the challenge to his appointment had not been a rejection by his fellow physicians at Columbia Medical, Rush wrote to his sponsor there, "It is peculiarly gratifying to me to know that the opposition to my appointment came from that gentleman."[60] If John Adams was aware of Hamilton's obstruction of Rush's appointment at Columbia, his strong desire to assist his old friend Rush, then in serious financial difficulty, must only have increased.

In 1797, the position of Treasurer of the United States Mint became available. Passing over forty applicants, President Adams offered it to his old friend Rush, then in dire need, though he had not applied for the job.[61] Grateful for the desperately needed income that came with the post, Rush wrote to Adams, "had it not been for the emoluments of the office you gave me (for which I hope gratitude will descend to further generations in my family), I must have retired from the city and ended my days upon a farm upon the little capital I had saved from the labors of former years."[62] Adams's affections for Rush had never waivered despite his anti-federalist, republican views. Rush retained the US Mint position until his death in 1813.

Despite the numerous controversies that swirled around his treatment of Philadelphia yellow fever victims and his strident responses to criticism during and after the epidemics, Rush continued to practice medicine, and worked tirelessly in the field of education as well. His work to develop new and more humane treatments for the insane is just one of the many accomplishments for which he will be long remembered. One historian, a graduate of Dickinson College, a school founded by Rush, wrote:

> The combative, disputatious, idealistic Benjamin Rush is virtually unknown today, except by physicians. His obscurity is in stark contrast to his staggering array of accomplishments achieved by his mid forties. Two hundred years ago this crusading doctor initiated

social movements that flourish today: civil rights, feminism, prison reform, free medical care for the poor, and humane treatment for the mentally ill. He is considered the founder of both psychiatry and the temperance movement and was a pioneer in the study of dentistry and veterinary medicine.[63]

Rush had been brought low in large part because of his tireless adherence to his beliefs—regardless of their popularity. John Adams understood all too well the high price that sometimes had to be paid for being true to one's convictions. When Rush learned that he had been awarded the highly competitive Treasury post, he went to Adams to thank him personally. "He took me by the hand," Rush wrote later, "and with great kindness said, 'You have not more pleasure in receiving the office, than I have in conferring it upon an old Whig.'"[64]

Rush's deep affection for Adams was of a more personal nature than that of his friendship with Jefferson, whose political views he more closely shared. Adams was more effusively open and engaging with his friends, though sometimes sharing too much and, detrimentally to himself, too often bitingly critical or harsh in his comments. Adams's bitter criticisms, with which he was occasionally overly generous, had almost brought about catastrophic consequences in 1810 when William Cunningham, whom Adams had mistakenly trusted, threatened to publish their highly charged series of letters. Harsh letters from Adams (and sometimes too strong words in conversation), like those to Cunningham, were unfortunately all too common in the years following his defeat to Jefferson. A genuinely kind and gentle man, Adams was aware of this character defect, as was Abigail who acted as a calming voice of reason, her own rather savage epistolary handling of Jefferson during his grief at his daughter Polly's death notwithstanding. Jefferson was expert at keeping his more strident emotions in check.

Jefferson adopted a stylized and formal aloofness from his friends. He employed the elevated written language of his era to a consistently extreme degree, which made him appear more distant than he perhaps truly was. With his daughters he was the very picture of loving affection. Jefferson's doting on his grandchildren is the stuff of legend within the family. His obvious affection for Maria Cosway was, as expressed in his letters to her, tempered by this self-distancing. There is a sense in reading Jefferson's letters that his emotional aloofness was neither an affectation nor indicative of a lack of personal warmth on his part, but rather the actions of a man who deeply desired, yet insulated himself from, what he perceived as potentially dangerous emotional relationships. Jefferson's analytical and amorous "head and heart" letter to Mrs. Cosway appears to support this view.[65]

Jefferson's intense and debilitating bereavement at the death of his wife of ten years, Martha Wayles Skelton Jefferson, in 1782, particularly his apparent destruction of their correspondence, seems to support the contention that her loss caused deep emotional scarring from which he never quite fully recovered.[66] Martha Jefferson Randolph, the couple's eldest daughter, described her father's inconsolability: "For four months that she lingered, he was never out of calling; when not at her bedside, he was writing in a small room which opened immediately at the head of her bed. A moment before the closing scene, he was led from the room almost in a state of insensibility by his sister, Mrs. Carr, who with great difficulty got him into his library, where he fainted and remained so long insensible that we thought he would never revive. The scene that followed I did not witness, but the violence of his emotion, when almost by stealth I entered his room at night, to this day I dare not trust myself to describe."[67]

Soon after his wife's death Jefferson wrote, "A single event wiped away all my plans and left me a blank which I had not the spirits to fill up."[68] Afterward, Jefferson retained a greater emotional distance between himself and his friends than Adams did, by comparison. As for Rush, Jefferson "admired" him, and "had trusted him with his most confidential thoughts on religion."[69] Though his manner was often formal and distant there was no want of trust from Jefferson for those he considered friends.

Jefferson certainly respected and trusted Dr. Benjamin Rush, in much the same deep way that Rush was trusted and appreciated by Adams. Rush's friendships with Jefferson and Adams, and his easy access to both, made him perhaps the only person who could successfully bring about reconciliation between the two former presidents. Rush was not ignorant of the opportunity that his special relationship to both men presented. He determined to bring them back to each other, seeing this as his duty to them and to the country. By 1808, there was little reason for Rush to believe that a renewal of the Adams-Jefferson friendship could be easily, or even successfully, arranged. In a letter to Rush early in that year, Adams had written,

> Mr Jefferson has reason to reflect upon himself. How he will get rid of his remorse in his Retirement I know not. He must know that he leaves the Government infinitely worse than he found it and that from his own error or Ignorance. I wish his Telescopes and Mathematical Instruments, however, may secure his Felicity. But if I have not mismeasured his ambition, he will be uneasy and the sword will cutt away the scabbard. As he has however a good Taste for Letters and an ardent curiosity for Science, he may and I hope will find amusement and consolation from them.[70]

Upon his retirement, much in line with Adams's hopes for him, Jefferson did find amusement and consolation at Monticello, as well as in his books and scientific experiments; Adams had indeed "mismeasured." Jefferson left Washington (and national politics) greatly excited to be returning to his beloved home, family, and his books. He felt a solid confidence in the knowledge that he had been instrumental in creating institutions through which qualified men of good character could lead the country into the future, and that his friend and associate Madison had followed him to the president's chair. Jefferson's comfort in knowing that he had left a stable government in capable hands allowed him to exit public life without looking back, as Adams had suggested to Rush that he should. After his unfortunate exit from public life, Adams never stopped looking back.

If Jefferson had chosen to "reflect upon himself" as Adams had suggested to Rush that he ought to do, he may have felt satisfied with his efforts in 1804, though ultimately unsuccessful, to renew his friendship with Abigail and, through their correspondence, with his former friend John Adams. Then, Abigail's anger at Jefferson's partisanship, combined with Jefferson's emotionally distant and overly analytical responses, doomed that opportunity for reconciliation to failure.

The death of Jefferson's daughter Polly in 1804 was the sad event which caused Abigail to break the several years of silence. The correspondence, which had been opened by Abigail to express her deep sympathies to Jefferson, quickly devolved to recriminations, justifications, and harsh words. After several letters back and forth the correspondence was concluded with neither party gaining any sense of fulfillment or satisfaction. The purposeful silence that filled the space between Monticello and Montezillo, interrupted only by Abigail's 1804 expression of sympathy to Jefferson (sent without John's knowledge), was similar to the silence of circumstance that grew between John Adams and Benjamin Rush after the former's relocation from Philadelphia in 1800 when the national capital moved to Washington. There was no purpose in this silence however; Adams and Rush had simply lost touch.

"It seemeth unto me that you and I ought not to die without saying Goodby or bidding each other Adieu," Adams wrote to Rush in 1805. Demonstrating to Rush that he still retained a sense of humor, Adams identified his return address as "Mount Wollaston, alias Quincy."[71] In this first letter after several years of silence between the two old friends, Adams inquired about Rush's family. Not surprisingly, he also wrote of politics.

In his oft-employed inflammatory style (which some modern readers might consider politically incorrect) Adams compared the spread of democracy with the virulence of the plague and yellow fever. With this comparison Adams introduced a series of questions meant as a criticism of Jeffersonian-Republicanism. "I cannot help thinking that Democracy is a Distemper of this kind and when it is once set in motion and obtains a Majority it converts every Thing good bad and indifferent into the dominant epidemic."[72] Adams's observation that the popularity of democracy and its rapid spread was comparable to a plague was a challenge to Rush's republicanism, and an incitement/invitation to further intellectual engagement on the subject. The mention of "epidemics" and "plague" also could not help but remind Rush of his own sad and frustrating experiences in the Philadelphia yellow fever horrors, from which Adams, like most government officials and wealthy citizens, had prudently fled.

Adams's love of debate, discourse, intellectual discovery, and desire for challenging conversation with highly intelligent friends (sometimes, as in the case of Cunningham, poorly chosen) was often built upon rhetorical controversies of his own creation. This was Adams's way of getting his correspondents' attention, as it were, and to determine if they would take up the gauntlet and participate in discussions on controversial subjects or opinions; Rush did not disappoint.

Adams was adamant (obstinate, too) as well as honest. The several years of silence that predated his letter to Rush was, as he tried to revive their correspondence, of little concern to Adams. What did matter to him was that there had been a long-standing and firm foundation of friendship and mutual respect between them. With his opening letter to Rush in 1805, after years of silence, Adams simply "picked up where he had left off."

The retired president had good reason to trust that Rush would be amenable to a direct and challenging reestablishment of their correspondence as intellectual honesty had always been a theme between them. Depth, honesty, and openness were the cornerstones of their friendship until Rush's death in 1813. In an 1808 letter to Adams, Rush complained bitterly against what he viewed as a decline in American morals due mainly to an excessive popular interest in the acquisition of money. Describing America as a "bedollared nation," Rush observed, "even at our convivial dinners 'Dollars' are a standing dish upon which all feed with rapacity and gluttony."[73] Emboldened by the openness of their correspondence and friendship, Rush reminisced darkly about his involvement in the Revolution. Rush was well aware of Adams's numerous negative comments about democracy, which likely made Adams, at least in Rush's mind, the perfect recipient of these disturbing comments. If Rush had somehow convinced himself that Adams would be sensitive to, or empathize with, his self-castigations over his revolutionary activities and accomplishments, he quickly learned that he was sorely mistaken.

"I feel pain when I am reminded of my exertions in the cause of what we called liberty, and sometimes wish I could erase my name from the Declaration of Independence," Rush wrote to Adams in mid–1808. "In case of a rupture with Britain or France, which shall we fight for? For our Constitution? I cannot meet with a man who loves it. It is considered as too weak by one half of our citizens and too strong by the other half."[74] Adams wasted little time in replying to his troubled old friend, and in equally strong language. "My dear Physical and Medical Philosopher," Adams addressed Rush, "I give you this Title for the present only. I shall scarcely allow you to be a political, moral or Christian Philosopher till you retract some of the Complaints, Lamentations, Regrets and Penitences in your letter of the 13th. But more of this presently."[75] Adams would be true to his promise, there would be much more on these matters in the letter. First, however, Rush would have to read of Massachusetts politics and how federalism had recently made a surprising resurgence. Adams's choice of words was not unusual for him, nor for their correspondence in general. Rush had "tweaked" Adams with his regrets about signing the Declaration and the implied criticism of the revolutionaries of '76 that came with such regret; it was Adams's turn to tweak back.

"Just so our good old Massachusetts, for a few years past has been declining into the rankest democratical Debauchery; but the embargo, like a Plague, Pestilence or Famine, has awakened her from her vicious dream and turned her into a furious persecuting enthusiast for hyperfederalism." Rush could not have missed Adams's numerous references to Rush's political views and professional experience (and failures), but there was a very personal remonstrance to follow.

> Now sir, for your Groans. You and I in the Revolution acted from Principle; we did our Duty, as we then believed, according to our best Information, Judgment and Consciences. Shall we now repent of this? God forbid! No! If a banishment to Cayenne, or to Bottany Bay or even the Guillotine were to be the necessary Consequences of it to us, we ought not to repent. Repent? This is impossible: how can a Man repent of his virtues? [76]

Adams continued on at length complaining of the condition of the country, and the overemphasis of parties in American politics—which he believed was encouraged by the Constitution. He also added a further complaint against the failed embargo.

"You ask, in case of a Rupture with Britain or France, what shall we fight for? I know of no better answer to give than this, to get rid of the embargo. This object as I understand the Politicks of the times is worth a war with all the World. But where are we to trade, when we are at war with all the world?"[77] The honesty and stridency of these letters show clearly the similar characters of Adams and Rush, both unafraid to carry the banner of their views wherever it might lead them, and accept whatever negative reactions they might garner even from their most cherished friends. Rush's dark introspections and self-doubts of 1808 were not the first indications to Adams of this disturbing side of his old friend.

"In looking back upon the years of our Revolution, I often wish for those ten thousand hours that I wasted in public pursuits and that I now see did no *permanent* work for my family nor my country," Rush wrote in late April 1807.[78] This theme of personal regret is a common one in many of Rush's later letters. Adams, also a deeply introspective man, was a perfect foil and audience for this kind of negative review of the past. Rush likely knew that Adams would not look kindly on such regrets and retroactive criticisms of their great revolutionary achievements. Perhaps he hoped that by Adams's counterarguments, Rush himself might be set on a path of more positively remembering those great events of '76 and his own not-insignificant role.

"Do you not sometimes imprecate the same evils upon the day on which you became a politician that Job did upon the day of his birth?" Rush provocatively asked Adams.[79] Adams reacted very seriously to Rush's negativity about the Revolution and their personal involvement in national politics. He was just the friend that Rush needed to provide a reasoned and self-justified viewpoint that, from Adams's perspective, was meant to both free Rush from unnecessary and unjustified self-doubts but also to unburden and explain Adams to himself. In his response written several days after receiving Rush's

April twenty-second letter, Adams spent several pages teasing his old friend with sly banter about having been the first to suggest American independence in 1755, beating Jefferson on the issue by decades. Finally, he got to the point.

> Now sir, to be serious: I do not curse the day, when I engaged in public affairs. I do not say when I became a Politician, for that I never was. I cannot repent of any Thing I ever did, conscientiously from a sense of Duty. I never engaged in public affairs, for my own Interest, Pleasure, Envy, Jealousy, Avarice or Ambition or even the desire of Fame . . . If any of these had been my Motives, my Conduct would have been very different. In every considerable Transaction of my public Life, I have invariably acted according to my best judgment for the public good, and I can look up to God for the sincerity of my Intentions. How then is it possible I can repent. Notwithstanding this I have an immense Load of Errors, Weaknesses, follies and sins to mourn over and repent of, and these are the only affliction of my present Life.[80]

Adams had consistently been a vocal proponent of the "be true to yourself" school of politics, philosophy, and personal comportment. Rush adopted this approach as well. His strict adherence to and later defense of his widely unpopular course of medical treatments during and after the 1793 yellow fever epidemic in Philadelphia was a path built on the Adams model. His strident public arguments for his controversial local origin theory of the disease brought Rush few supporters. The friendship between Rush and Adams was of a deep and long-standing character; Rush's stubborn and strident defense of his treatments and origin theory may have, in a sense, originated with Adams himself.

Adams's *Discourses on Davila* appeared in serial form in the *Pennsylvania Gazette* in 1790. Though he considered the *Davila* essays his greatest effort at political analysis, Adams was shocked and deeply disappointed at the generally unfavorable response it received. Jefferson's comments about "political heresies" published as the foreword to the first American version of Thomas Paine's pamphlet *Rights of Man*, which appeared soon after *Davila*, did little to alleviate Adams's discomfiture. Many of the accusations about Adams's "monarchism" resulted from the criticisms of republicanism and democracy, and his strong support for a powerful executive found in *Davila*, as well as his earlier work, *Defence of the Constitutions of Government of the United States*. Adams's honest, though unpopular views as expressed in the *Davila* essays, and elsewhere,[81] were not only the results of his analyses of history and politics but also simply the consequence of Adams's direct and fearless approach to politics and life in general. Dr. Rush had always appreciated Adams's self-assuredness and bravery in the face of adversity, and had thanked Adams for teaching him "to despise public opinion when set in competition with the dictates of my judgment and conscience."[82] In matters of asserting unpopular views, Rush would have been hard-pressed to find a better guide than his friend John Adams.

During the Philadelphia yellow fever epidemic, Rush had become an expert at "despising" public and private opinions that were in opposition to his views. His vocal and argumentative support for a local cause of the epidemic, as opposed to some contagion brought in to Philadelphia by ship, alienated him from his medical colleagues and from the city's leaders. Rush's very public and often strident adherence to these politically charged and unpopular views in the face of the harshest criticism and threats to his livelihood were in the best tradition of the Adams "be true to yourself" school of public and private behavior. When Adams reopened their correspondence in 1805 all the years of non-communication seemed to melt away with the flow of the retired president's pen.

> Let me put a few Questions to your Conscience, for I know you have one. Is the present state of the Nation Republican enough? Is Virtue the Principle of our Government? Is honour? Or is Ambition and avarice, adulation, Baseness, Covetousness, the thirst of Riches, indifference concerning the Means of rising and enriching, the contempt of Principle, the spirit of Party and of Faction the Motive and the Principle that governs? These are serious and dangerous Questions: but Serious Men ought not to flinch from dangerous questions.[83]

Fully aware that Rush's politics were strongly republican, Adams's leading "serious and dangerous" questions might have been ill-received by Rush, had Adams not known his friend so very well. Rush replied positively and swiftly to this challenging yet friendly opening from Adams. In his excitement with finding that his old friend was willing and ready to intellectually engage through the mails and renew their old friendship, Adams declared simply in his response of February 27, 1805, "I have just now received your friendly Letter of the 19th."[84] Their association had been and would be again a source of comfort, enjoyment, and intellectual pleasure for both men until the death of Rush eight years later. Rush was not unaware that the rekindled association between himself and Adams could readily serve as a model for a renewal of the moribund bond that had once existed so strongly between Adams and Jefferson. The opportunity for Rush to press this point would not be long delayed and came, quite unintentionally, from Adams himself.

Rush sometimes shared his dreams with Adams.[85] "If I could dream as much wit as you," Adams wrote on the day of Madison's inauguration in 1809, "I think I should wish to go to sleep for the rest of my Life, retaining however one of Swifts Flappers to awake me once in 24 hours to dinner, for you know without a dinner one can neither dream nor sleep. Your Dreams descend from Jove according to Homer." Then, sardonically describing the celebrations of local Quincy Republicans on the inauguration of Madison as marking "the Accession of the new Monarch to the Throne," Adams challenged Rush to dream a specific dream for him. "Jefferson expired and Madison came to Life, last night at twelve o'clock," Adams wrote. "Will you be so good as to take a Nap, and dream for my Instruction and edification a Character of Jefferson and his Administration?"[86]

Adams's early March 1809 request for a dream-to-order waited almost till the end of the year before it generated a response. Dreams are tightly focused or expansive, though they are sometimes both. The dream that Rush reported to Adams in a letter of October 17, 1809, was expansive *and* highly focused, though its subject was not Jefferson's character and administration as per Adams's request. Instead, Rush used Adams's request for a dream about Jefferson as the opening act in what would become a long drama of reconciliation. Upon reading Rush's superb "dream report" Adams was delighted to find that the long delay had been well worth the wait. Rush's report opened with a dream conversation he'd had with his son Richard about American history. This brief exchange between father and son would serve as the introduction to one of the most extraordinary letters Adams ever received.

> "What book is that in your hands?" said I to my son Richard a few nights ago in a dream. "It is the history of the United States," said he. "Shall I read a page of it to you?" "No, no," said I. "I believe in the truth of no history but in that which is contained in the Old and New Testaments." "But, sir," said my son, "this page relates to your friend Mr. Adams." "Let me see it then," said I. I read it with great pleasure and herewith send you a copy of it.[87]

Adams had requested that Rush dream for him a dream, and then tell him all about it. Though the subject was not exactly the same as that requested by Adams, Rush had no intention of disappointing his friend nor of sparing any subtleties.

> 1809–Among the most extraordinary events of this year was the renewal of the friendship and intercourse between Mr. John Adams and Mr. Jefferson, the two ex-Presidents of the United States. They met for the first time in the Congress of 1775. Their principles of liberty, their ardent attachment to their country, and their views of the importance and probable issue of the struggle with Great Britain in which they were engaged being exactly the same, they were strongly attracted to each other and became personal as well as political friends. They met in England during the war while each of them held commissions of honor and trust at two of the first courts of Europe, and spent many happy hours together in reviewing the difficulties and success of their respective negotiations. A difference of opinion upon the objects and issue of the French Revolution separated them during the years in which that great event interested and divided the American people. The predominance of the party which favored the French cause threw Mr. Adams out

of the Chair of the United States in the year 1800 and placed Mr.
Jefferson there in his stead. The former retired with resignation and
dignity to his seat at Quincy, where he spent the evening of his
life in literary and philosophical pursuits surrounded by an amiable
family and a few old and affectionate friends. The latter resigned
the Chair of the United States in the year 1808, sick of the cares and
disgusted with the intrigues of public life, and retired to his seat at
Monticello in Virginia, where he spent the remainder of his days
in the cultivation of a large farm agreeably to the new system of
husbandry. In the month of November 1809, Mr. Adams addressed
a short letter to his friend Mr. Jefferson in which he congratulated
him upon his escape to the shades of retirement and domestic happiness, and concluded it with assurances of his regard and good
wishes for his welfare. This letter did great honor to Mr. Adams.
It discovered a magnanimity known only to great minds. Mr. Jefferson replied to this letter and reciprocated expressions of regard
and esteem. These letters were followed by a correspondence of
several years, in which they mutually reviewed the scenes of business in which they had been engaged, and candidly acknowledged
to each other all the errors of opinion and conduct into which they
had fallen during the time they filled the same station in the service
of their country. Many precious aphorisms, the result of observation, experience, and profound reflection, it is said, are contained in
these letters. It is to be hoped the world will be favored with a sight
of them when they can neither injure nor displease any persons
or families whose ancestors' follies or crimes were mentioned in
them. These gentlemen sunk into the grave nearly at the same time,
full of years and rich in the gratitude and praises of their country
(for they outlived the heterogeneous parties that were opposed to
them), and to their numerous merits and honors posterity has added
that they were rival friends. With affectionate regard to your fire-
side, in which all my family join, I am, dear sir, your sincere old
friend, Benjn: Rush.[88]

In his response to Rush's dream report, Adams playfully kept Rush in
suspense for several pages, talking of family matters and, of course,

sharing his views on politics. Then, finally, he got to the point. "A dream again! I wish you would dream all day and all Night, for one of your Dreams puts me in spirits for a Month. I have no other objection to your Dream, but that it is not history. It may be Prophecy," Adams wrote. Adams then asserted, "there has never been the smallest Interruption of the Personal Friendship between me and Mr. Jefferson that I know of." Proceeding on to a general review of his professional associations with Jefferson, Adams concluded the letter with some bitter and clearly pained reminiscences.

> I have a Bushell of Letters from him. If I were disposed to be captious I might complain of his open Patronage of Callender, Paine, Brown[89] and twenty others my most abandoned and unprincipled enemies. But I have seen Ambition and Party in so many Men of the best Character of all Parties that I must renounce almost all Mankind if I renounce any for such Causes. Fare them all well. Heaven is their Judge and mine. I am not conscious that I ever injured any of them in thought word or deed to promote my own Interest or Reputation or to lessen theirs. Let them one and all say the same if they can.[90]

Though Adams in his October letter seemed ambivalent about his old friend Jefferson, his next letter to Rush (written in December) presented a more forgiving, if not slightly melancholy, tone.

> Your Prophecy my dear Friend has not become History as yet. I have no Resentment or Animosity against the Gentleman and abhor the Idea of blackening his Character or transmitting him in odious Colours to Posterity. But I write with difficulty and am afraid of diffusing myself in too many Correspondences. If I should receive a Letter from him however I should not fail to acknowledge and answer it.[91]

Rush's views about reconciliation between Jefferson and Adams were made quite clear to the latter by the end of 1809. Rush's deep friendship with Adams allowed him to broach and press this subject without concern of causing alienation. Adams's responses to Rush on the matter showed that he was amenable to a renewal of some kind of a friendship with Jefferson, but that he would take no definitive action himself to bring it about. That is, if Jefferson were to write him a letter he'd be pleased to receive it, though he'd not make the first approach.

Among the many fine qualities of Dr. Rush's complex character, patience was there in abundance. Since Adams had clearly communicated his guardedly positive views on reconciliation, the time had come for Rush to approach Jefferson. Ascertaining Jefferson's feelings about a reconciliation with Adams, however, presented Rush with a serious challenge. His friendship with the third president was of a less personal and emotional nature than his relationship with Adams and, most importantly, Jefferson's reserve made him more difficult to approach on private and personal matters. Rush believed that he had no option but to patiently wait for an opportune moment. A year passed before it arrived.

The year 1810 concluded for Rush with a letter from Adams. This was the very letter of opportunity for which Rush had been waiting. "I sent my wife to the Post Office this morning with a Letter to you . . . and as she brought me back yours of the 21 [sic] you will receive this by the same mail," Adams wrote on December twenty-seventh. Writing at length of the comparative evils of monarchy and aristocracy, Adams proceeded to expound on "the Banking Infatuation [that] pervades America."[92] Soon after receipt of this letter from Adams, Rush wrote to Jefferson. Well aware that Jefferson's views on the American banking system were closely in line with those expressed by Adams, Rush included Adams's comments on the subject and, slyly minimizing the extent of their considerable correspondence, wrote, "your and my old friend Mr. Adams now and then drops me a line from his seat at Quincy."[93] Having introduced the subject of Adams to Jefferson, it was high time for Rush to get to the crux of the matter.

> When I consider your early attachment to Mr. Adams, and his to you; when I consider how much the liberties and independence of the United States owes to the concert of your principles and labors; and when I reflect upon the sameness of your opinions at present upon most of the subjects of government and all the subjects of legislation, I have ardently wished a friendly and epistolary inter-

course might be revived between you before you take a final leave of the common object of your affections. Such an intercourse will be honorable to your talents and patriotism and highly useful to the course of republicanism not only in the United States but all over the world. Posterity will revere the friendship of two ex-presidents that were once opposed to each other. Human nature will be a gainer by it. I am sure an advance on your side will be cordial to the heart of Mr. Adams. Tottering over the grave, he now leans wholly upon the shoulders of his old Revolutionary friends . . . Adieu! My dear friend, and believe me to be yours truly and affectionately, Benjamin Rush.[94]

This solicitous and heartfelt letter brought a comprehensive response from Jefferson only two weeks later. Replying in a vein similar to Adams's letter to Rush in which he had included a review of his friendship with Jefferson, Jefferson did much the same, even including copies of his 1804 correspondence with Abigail Adams for Rush's review. Regarding his communications to Abigail, Jefferson informed Rush that he had "never communicated it to any mortal breathing." The inclusion of the Abigail letters was further reiteration of Jefferson's trust and faith in Rush, already established when Rush had kept Jefferson's confidence about his Bible commentary and revisions some years previously. Of his onetime political mentor and close friend John Adams, Jefferson wrote,

I have the same good opinion of Mr. Adams which I ever had. I know him to be an honest man, an able one with his pen, and he was a powerful advocate on the floor of Congress. He has been alienated from me, by belief in the lying suggestions contrived for electioneering purposes, that I perhaps mixed in the activity and intrigues of the occasion. My most intimate friends can testify that I was perfectly passive. They would sometimes, indeed, tell me what was going on; but no man ever heard me take part in such conversations; and none ever misrepresented Mr. Adams in my presence, without my asserting his just character . . . And I am satisfied Mr. Adams's conduct was equally honourable towards me.[95]

In opening this lengthy letter Jefferson acknowledged Rush's desire to see a reconciliation between himself and Adams, and affirmed similar feelings. "I receive with sensibility your observations on the discontinuance of friendly correspondence between Mr. Adams and myself, and the concern you take in its restoration. This discontinuance has not proceeded from me, nor from the want of sincere desire and of effort on my part, to renew our intercourse." The inclusion of his 1804 correspondence with Abigail was likely meant simply to validate and reiterate this point to Rush. Jefferson also listed at length those aggravations, particularly the judgeship appointments of Adams's last day in office, which had rankled him then, but that "a little time and reflection effaced in my mind this temporary dissatisfaction with Mr. Adams, and restored me to that just estimate of his virtues and passions, which a long acquaintance had enabled me to fix." Demonstrating to Rush that he had been solicitous of Adams's comfort, Jefferson explained that, after his election to his first term, he had

> suggested to some republican members of the delegation from his State, the giving him, either directly or indirectly, an office the most lucrative in that State, and then offered to be resigned, if they thought he would not deem it affrontive. They were of opinion he would take great offence at the offer; and moreover, that the body of Republicans would consider such a step in the outset, as auguring very ill of the course I meant to pursue. I dropped the idea, therefore, but did not cease to wish for some opportunity of renewing our friendly understanding.[96]

In communication with both Adams and Jefferson on his great personal and patriotic mission of reconciliation, Rush could see that his two old friends of '76 were equally desirous of reestablishing their friendship. However, neither man seemed quite ready to take the next step. In closing his very agreeable letter to Rush, Jefferson wrote,

> I have gone, my dear friend, into these details, that you might know every thing which had passed between us, might be fully possessed of the state of facts and dispositions, and judge for yourself whether

they admit a revival of that friendly intercourse for which you are so kindly solicitous. I shall certainly not be wanting in any thing on my part which may second your efforts; which will be the easier with me inasmuch as I do not entertain a sentiment of Mr. Adams, the expression of which could give him reasonable offence. And I submit the whole to yourself, with the assurance, that whatever be the issue, my friendship and respect for yourself will remain unaltered and unalterable.[97]

Rush thanked Jefferson for sending along the correspondence between he and Abigail Adams. He told Jefferson that he

was delighted with the kindness, benevolence, and even friendship discovered in your answers to Mrs. Adams' letter. I believe they were the genuine effusions of your heart, for they exactly accord with the expressions of regard and the opinion of the integrity of Mr. Adams which I have heard you utter a hundred times in our familiar intercourse with each other during the last four winters you passed in Philadelphia.[98]

Rush had masterfully set the stage for a renewal of the friendship between the second and third presidents. It is unlikely that anyone else could have accomplished what Rush had so far been able to do. More work however was needed to finally bring the two together. Though Rush's work was not yet done, other players would soon enter the drama. Edward Coles, President Madison's private secretary, and a friend of Jefferson, would soon be travelling from Virginia to New England with his brother John; a visit to Adams at Peace field was planned.

In the summer of 1811, while secretary to President Madison, I, accompanied by my brother John, made a tour through the Northern States, and took letters of introduction from the President to many of the most distinguished men of that section of the Union— among others, to ex-President John Adams, with whom we spent the greater part of two days, and were treated by him and his wife with great civility and kindness.[99]

So begins Edward Coles's recollections of the part he played in the rapprochement between the two former presidents. During the course of his two-day visit to Adams at Peace field, Coles recounted for his host Jefferson's version of his first visit to Adams in the aftermath of the contentious election of 1800. When Coles told Adams his story, describing for him the events of that day as Jefferson had described them to him, Adams expressed astonishment at the accuracy of Coles's narration. According to Coles, Adams then proceeded to express friendly and positive views of Jefferson. "I always loved Jefferson, and still love him," Adams had said.[100]

By the winter of 1811, Edward Coles had returned to Virginia, and Jefferson was soon thereafter enthusiastically composing a letter at his correspondence desk. Writing to Rush from his second home, Poplar Forest, some 90 miles from Charlottesville, which he had both designed and constructed, Jefferson once again mentioned his correspondence with Abigail Adams. Recollecting that Mrs. Adams's harsh tone and recriminations had for him precluded any return to friendship without a "total renunciation" of those negative "sentiments . . . avowed and maintained in her letters," Jefferson related to Rush that he realized, upon hearing Edward Coles report of his visit to Adams, that he had made a terrible mistake.

"In these jaundiced sentiments of hers I had associated Mr. Adams, knowing the weight her opinions had with him, and notwithstanding she declared in her letters that they were not communicated to him," Jefferson admitted to Rush.[101] With Coles's report of his visit to Adams at Quincy fresh in his mind, Jefferson announced to Rush, "a late incident has satisfied me that I wronged him as well as her, in not yielding entire confidence to this assurance on her part."[102]

Jefferson's "late incident" was Edward Coles's report of his visit to John Adams in Quincy. "Among many other topics," Jefferson wrote to Rush of Adams's conversations with Coles, "he adverted to the unprincipled licentiousness of the press against myself, adding, 'I always loved Jefferson, and still love him.'"[103] Jefferson's next sentence was proof enough to Rush that his years of patience and effort to bring his two friends back together had, finally, been successful; "This is enough for me. I only needed this knowledge to revive towards him all the affections of the most cordial moments of our lives," Jefferson wrote.[104]

> Changing a single word only in Dr Franklin's character of him,[105] I knew him to be always an honest man, often a great one, but sometimes incorrect and precipitate in his judgments: and it is known to those who have ever heard me speak of Mr. Adams, that I have ever done him justice myself, and defended him when assailed by others, with the single exception as to his political opinions. But with a man possessing so many other estimable qualities, why should we be dissocialised by mere differences of opinion in politics, in religion, in philosophy, or any thing else? His opinions are as honestly formed as my own. Our different views of the same subject are the result of a difference in our organization and experience. I never withdrew from the society of any man on this account, although many have done it from me; much less should I do it from one with whom I had gone through, with hand and heart, so many trying scenes. I wish, therefore, but for an apposite occasion to express to Mr. Adams my unchanged affections for him.[106]

Jefferson was both an idealist and a pragmatist, and thus likely tempered his enthusiasm for a renewal of his old friendship with John Adams with concern about the "awkwardness which hangs over the resuming a correspondence so long discontinued, unless something could arise which should call for a letter. Time and chance may perhaps generate such an occasion, of which I shall not be wanting in promptitude to avail myself."[107] Jefferson suggested, "perhaps I may open the way in some letter to my old friend Gerry, who I know is in the habits of the greatest intimacy with him."[108]

Jefferson apparently underestimated the impact, authority, and persistence of Rush, and of the good doctor's deep friendship and extensive correspondence with Adams. Rush's mission was by then almost complete and he had no intention of relying upon the (unnecessary) involvement of another mutual friend—nor certainly of accepting any further delay that adding another player to the drama would likely cause. There is no record that Jefferson wrote to Gerry on the matter, nor was such a communication necessary. Rush wasted little time upon receipt of Jefferson's enthusiastic letter; less than two weeks later a letter from Rush was on its way to Adams. The next act of this now swiftly moving drama would soon be played.

In his letter of December 16, 1811, to Adams, Rush quoted extensively from Jefferson's letter to him in which Jefferson had declared, "this is enough for me." "And now, my dear friend," Rush dramatically announced to Adams, "permit me again to suggest to you to receive the olive branch which has thus been offered to you by the hand of a man who still loves you."[109] In his enthusiasm Rush also included an example of the kind of letter that Adams might wish to send to Jefferson. "Were I near to you," Rush offered up to Adams by way of recommended prose, "I would put a pen into your hand and guide it while it composed the following short address to Mr. Jefferson: 'Friend and fellow laborer in the cause of the liberty and independence of our common country, I salute you with the most cordial good wishes for your health and happiness. – John Adams.'"[110] Fully aware that he was pressing the matter hard, Rush included a polite, concise postscript in which he asked Adams to "excuse the liberty I have taken."[111]

The following day Rush wrote to Jefferson informing him that he had "selected such passages from your letter as contained the kindest expressions of regard for Mr. Adams and transmitted them to him."[112] Reiterating his earnest desire to bring the two men together, Rush, appealing to Jefferson's patriotism and humanism told him, "I sincerely hope this my second effort to revive a friendly intercourse between you by letters will be successful. Patriotism, liberty, science, and religion will all gain a triumph by it."[113]

By Christmas 1811, Adams had received Rush's imploring and excited letter. "I never was so much at a loss how to answer a letter as yours of the 16th," Adams wrote.[114] It was clear to Adams that Rush's dream-as-future-history project had advanced to such a stage of finality that the years of silence between him and his old friend Jefferson could now readily melt away; but Adams was not quite sure how to proceed. "Shall I assume a sober face and write a grave essay on religion, philosophy, laws, or government? Shall I laugh like Bacchus, among his grapes, wine vats, and bottles?" Adams rhetorically asked, perhaps alluding to Jefferson's famous expertise in wines. Confirming Jefferson's realization to Rush that no negative feelings had ever been in his heart toward his old friend, Adams wrote, "I perceive plainly enough, Rush, that you have been teasing Jefferson to write to me, as you did me some time ago to write to him. You gravely advise me 'to receive the olive branch,' as if there had been war; but there has never been any hostility on my part, nor that I know, on his. When there has been no war, there can be no room for negotiations of peace." Then, revisiting their political differences which Adams explained were only matters of administration, Adams wrote the following: "Mr. Jefferson speaks of my political opinions; but I know of no difference between him and myself relative to the Constitution, or to forms of government in general. In measures of administration, we have differed in opinion." Adams made a point to describe the specific issues upon which they had differed including the embargo, the army and navy, and other matters of national importance.

Adams reminded Rush that he had always supported the processes and foundational concepts of the new democracy, that is, he always had acquiesced to the will of the country even when popular decisions were not to his liking. "But I have raised no clamors nor made any opposition to any of these measures. The nation approved them; and what is my judgment against that of the nation?"[115] Adams asked. In contrast, Adams cited Jefferson's active opposition to laws enacted during Adams's administration. "On the contrary, he disapproved of the alien and sedition law, which I believe to have been constitutional and salutary, if not necessary." Sharing his old frustrations, Adams provided several additional instances of Jefferson's "disapproval" for Rush's consideration. Then, with great insight into the essential foundation of a sustainable democracy, that political differences should not shatter personal relationships, Adams recalled his prescient views of the French Revolution upon which Jefferson and Rush, both ardent Republicans, had not concurred.

> We differed in opinion about the French revolution. He thought it
> wise and good, and that it would end in the establishment of a free

republic. I saw through it, to the end of it, before it broke out, and
was sure it could end only in a restoration of the Bourbons, or a
military despotism, after deluging France and Europe in blood . . .
In this opinion I differed from you as much as from Jefferson; but
all this made me no more of an enemy to you than to him, nor to
him than to you. I believe you both to mean well to mankind and
your country.

Having made his point that the lack of communication between him
and Jefferson had not been the result of political differences or personal hostility, Adams then humorously and sarcastically reviewed
(and minimized) the political differences between himself and
Republicans.

In point of republicanism, all the difference I ever knew or could
discover between you and me, or between Jefferson and me, consisted,

In the difference between speeches and messages. I was a monarchist because I thought a speech more manly, more respectful to
Congress and the nation. Jefferson and Rush preferred messages.

I held levees once a week, that all my time might not be wasted
by idle visits. Jefferson's whole eight years was a levee.

I dined a large company once or twice a week. Jefferson dined
a dozen every day.

Jefferson and Rush were for liberty and straight hair. I thought
curled hair was as republican as straight.

In these, and a few other points of equal importance, all miserable frivolities, that Jefferson and Rush ought to blush that they
ever laid any stress upon them, I might differ; but I never knew
any points of more consequence, on which there was any variation
between us.[116]

Adams's lighthearted yet serious retort to Rush's intense and emotional exhortations appeared to confirm that if Adams had ever had
any negative feelings toward Jefferson, they had long ago melted
away. "You exhort me to 'forgiveness and love of enemies,' as if I
considered, or had ever considered, Jefferson as my enemy," Adams

wrote. "This is not so; I have always loved him as a friend. If I ever received or suspected any injury from him, I have forgiven it long and long ago, and have no more resentment against him than against you."[117]

Then, wielding his pen like a sledgehammer, Adams smashed the entirety of all of Rush's reconciliation efforts.

> But why do you make so much ado about nothing? Of what use can it be for Jefferson and me to exchange letters? I have nothing to say to him, but to wish him an easy journey to heaven, when he goes, which I wish may be delayed, as long as life shall be agreeable to him. And he can have nothing to say to me, but to bid me make haste and be ready.[118]

With this apparent failed denouement to all of Rush's hard work, Adams was playing a cruel trick on his friend Rush. While Adams's conclusion appeared to be an abandonment of the entire reconciliation enterprise, his final line in the letter, in which he used the very same phrasing that Jefferson had used days before, suggested something else entirely. "Time and chance, however, or possibly design, may produce ere long a letter between us."[119] Adams was having some small fun at his friend Rush's expense by responding with sardonic mystery to Rush's dire seriousness. In actuality, there was no need for time nor chance to play a role in the next step as Adams likely then already had his plan in mind; a letter was on its way from Quincy to Monticello less than a week later.

14

"Liberty, Friendship, Faith, Thou Wilt Hold Fast"

IN 1783, JOHN Adams and other American officials representing the United States signed the Treaty of Paris, which formally ended the Revolutionary War with Great Britain. In affixing his signature to the formal Treaty document, Adams had impressed the seal of his mother's family, the Boylstons, into hot red wax at the bottom of the parchment sheet. Impressions of Benjamin Franklin's and John Jay's seals can also be clearly seen in photographs of this historic treaty. Such family seals, though clearly of an era of monarchism and aristocracy, which the American Revolution was meant to eradicate, at least in the United States, were *de rigueur* for formal European diplomatic functions of the time.

Late in that same year Adams paid a London artisan to engrave a plate for him. A seal engraver was engaged two years later to "cut a seal with identical imagery," most likely of the plate that was cut two years before.[1] The image on the 1783 plate was a redesign and customization by Adams of the Boylston family crest which became the image used on his personal bookplate. This "family crest" of Adams's own design, was later a foundational design element in John Quincy Adams's version of his own crest. John Adams rarely used his bookplate however, preferring to signify ownership of his books simply by signing his name.[2] Perhaps the association of a family crest with monarchism and aristocracy prompted him to abandon it.

In his bookplate design Adams had placed a strap and buckle encircling the crest,[3] with a paraphrasing of Tacitus: "Libertatem Amicitiam Retinebis Et Fidem." One nineteenth-century Adams biographer translated this motto as: "Liberty, friendship, faith, thou wilt hold fast."[4] Adams had always held liberty close, and his faith, too. He had also held fast to his friendships except, perhaps, for one. Due to Rush's dogged efforts and strategic prodding, the moment had finally come to revive that friendship which, but for his marriage to Abigail, had been the most important and fulfilling relationship of his life. On the first day of the year 1812, Adams wrote to his old friend Thomas Jefferson.

"As you are a Friend to American Manufactures under proper restrictions, especially Manufactures of the domestic kind, I take the Liberty of sending you by Post a Packett containing two pieces of Homespun lately produced in this quarter by One who was honored in his youth with some of your Attention and much of your kindness," Adams wrote.[5] Adams's opening letter was short and familiar, with news of his daughter Abigail Smith's precarious health (known as Nabby), and of her unlucky husband included.

What Adams had purposefully and playfully failed to do, was to inform Jefferson that the term "homespun" was not a reference to clothing or textiles. Adams cleverly and truthfully hinted to Jefferson that the producer of the "homespun" was someone whom Jefferson had known during that person's youth. This was a little game with which Adams shined a light into the darkness that had long separated him from his old friend Jefferson. Adams's letter arrived before the "packett" of "homespun," but that did not prevent Jefferson from enthusiastically responding at length without waiting for the arrival of the "homespun." This was the first letter that Jefferson had received from Adams since March 24, 1801; he was keen to reply.

On January 21, Jefferson wrote, "I thank you before hand (for they are not yet arrived) for the specimens of homespun you have been so kind as to forward me by post."[6] Regarding the package of "homespun" which he assumed was clothing, Jefferson wrote, "I doubt not their excellence, knowing how far you are advanced in these things in your quarter."[7] After discoursing at length on local clothing manufacturing in Virginia, quality of cloth, and tools used in homes for the production of clothing, Jefferson wrote:

> A letter from you calls up recollections very dear to my mind. It carries me back to the times when, beset with difficulties and dangers, we were fellow laborers in the same cause, struggling for what is most valuable to man, his right of self-government. Laboring always at the same oar, with some wave ever ahead threatening to overwhelm us, and yet passing harmless under our bark, we knew not how, we rode through the storm with heart and hand, and made a happy port.[8]

Jefferson also briefly mentioned the international challenges that they had both faced, "in your day, French depredations, in mine, English . . ." Regardless of past challenges and the growing threat from England, which would soon lead to war, Jefferson confidently wrote, "and so we have gone on, and so shall we go on, puzzled and prospering beyond example in the history of man."[9]

The retired third president then informed the second that he had abandoned politics and newspapers "in exchange for Tacitus and Thucydides, for Newton and Euclid, and I find myself much the happier." Jefferson observed also that few signers of the Declaration of Independence remained alive, with himself as the sole survivor south of the Potomac. Noting their mutual good health Jefferson described his daily regime of "three or four hours" on horseback, and his quarterly visits to "a possession I have ninety miles distant, performing the winter journey on horseback."[10] In closing, Jefferson reasserted his deep friendship for Adams. "No circumstances have lessened the interest I feel in these particulars respecting yourself; none have suspended for one moment my sincere esteem for you; I now salute you with unchanged affection and respect."[11] Two days later Adams's packet of "homespun" arrived at Monticello; Jefferson immediately wrote another letter.

"A little more sagacity of conjecture in me, as to their appellation, would have saved you the trouble of reading a long dissertation on the state of real homespun in our quarter." Though he'd only been in possession of the "homespun" from Quincy for less than two days, Jefferson wrote that he had "already penetrated so far into them as to see that they are a mine of learning and taste . . ."[12] Adams's "homespun" had not been clothing at all, but a two-volume set of lectures on rhetoric and oratory delivered by John Quincy Adams during his two-year tenure (1806–1808) as the first Boylston Professor of Rhetoric and Oratory at Harvard College. John Quincy had accepted the position with the proviso that his government service (he was then a US Senator from Massachusetts) would take precedence over his academic duties. By 1809, Adams had resigned his Senate seat and his professorship, and been appointed American Ambassador to Russia. It is likely that both Adams and Jefferson found Professor Adams's Lecture 16, "Excitation and Management of the Passions," of particular interest.

In this lecture John Quincy discussed the differences between passions and habits. He explained that the ancient Greek thinkers considered habits "the mild and orderly emotions . . . quiet and peaceable impulses." In contrast, the passions "were tumultuous agitations." The younger Adams also analyzed the two terms by the consistency and continuity which both represented. "Generally speaking the words marked a difference in duration, as well as in degree. The passions were momentary, the habits constant; the former an occasional, the latter a permanent influence."[13] John Quincy chose friendship as the example through which he would illustrate the differences between passions and habits.

> Although the distinction between these two powers, which divide between them the control of the human will, is obvious and important, they are sometimes of precisely the same nature, and differ only in degree . . . Thus for instance love is included among the passions, but friendship among the habits. Still more common is to find them in opposition to each other, and the most vehement appeals to the passions are counteracted by addresses to the calmer influence of the habits.[14]

Certainly, the renewal of his father's great friendship with Jefferson, someone who John Quincy Adams, as a young man, had respected and revered, illustrated the accuracy of Professor Adams's analysis of the calming influence of habit in conquering the often excessive impulses of passion. Rush had implored his friends Adams and Jefferson for several years to conquer their passions and return to their habit of friendship for one another; finally, they had done so. Neither forgot Rush's patient and tireless efforts for them. Jefferson was the first to communicate his appreciation.

When Jefferson responded to Adams's first letter he retained a copy of his reply, as he did with much of his outgoing correspondence. On the same day that Jefferson mailed his first letter to Adams in over ten years, he mailed a copy of it to Rush. "As it is through your kind interposition that two old friends are brought together, you have a right to know how the first approaches are made. I send you, therefore a copy of Mr. Adams' letter to me & my answer."[15] Jefferson, in a brief introduction to Rush, explained how he had avoided discussion of Adams's family, and that his letter to Adams was "a rambling, gossiping epistle which gave openings for the expression of sincere feelings, & may furnish him ground of reciprocation . . ." In desiring to keep his distance from the subject of Adams's family, an approach he previously had told Rush that he would take, Jefferson missed the mark slightly in his reply to Adams's first letter. Rush made note of this in his response to Jefferson, written several weeks later. Jefferson's letter to him was Rush's first confirmation that his efforts to reunite his two old revolutionary friends had been successful.

"Few of the acts of my life have given me more pleasure than the one you are pleased to acknowledge in your last letter," Rush wrote to Jefferson. Rush kindly chided Jefferson for not having acknowledged Adams's comments about his daughter and her husband. "I wish in your reply to Mr. Adams' letter you had given him the echo of his communications to you respecting his daughter, Mrs. Smith and her husband. The former has been saved from certain death by a painful operation, and the honor and interest of the latter lie near his heart."[16]

Jefferson took Rush's admonishment to heart, apparently, as later letters to Adams were increasingly less reserved. "It will give me pleasure to hear of a frequent exchange of letters between you and Mr. Adams," Rush continued. "I associate the idea of your early friendship for each other, founded upon a sympathy of just opinions and feelings, with every retrospect I take of the great political, moral, and intellectual achievements of the Congress of 1775 and 1776."[17] It became clear later that Rush was not alone in associating the friendship of Adams and Jefferson with the events of American independence. By early February 1812, Adams had received Jefferson's gracious and friendly response to his "homespun" letter. He, too, wrote effusively to Rush in thanks and appreciation. His letter to Rush is nothing short of exuberant.

> Mr Dreamer,—Your dream is out, and the Passage you read in the History that Richard was reading is come to pass, notwithstanding you said you believed no History but the Bible.
>
> Mr Mediator,—You have wrought wonders! You have made Peace between Powers that never were at War! You have reconciled Friends that never were at enmity! You have brought again Babylon and Carthage long since annihilated, into fresh existence! Like the Pythoness of Endor you have called up Spirits from the vasty deep of obscurity and oblivion, to a new acquaintance with each other!
>
> Mr Conjuror,—In short the mighty defunct Potentates of Mount Wollaston and Monticello by your Sorceries and Necromances, are again in being. Intercourse and Commerce have been restored by your Magic, between Neutrals, whose Interests and Reputation has been long sacrificed by the Systems of Retalliation adopted by two hostile and enraged and infuriated Factions.
>
> Huzza! You will say, but what does all this Rhapsody mean? Nothing more nor less than that a Correspondence of thirty five or thirty six years standing interrupted by various causes for some time, has been renewed in 1812 and no less than four letters have already passed between the Parties; Those from Jefferson written with all the elegance, purity and sweetness, I would rather say Mellifluity or Mellifluidity, of his youth and middle age, and what I envy still more with a firmness of Finger and a steadiness of Chirography, that to me is lost, forever.[18]

One week later an ecstatic Rush replied, "I rejoice in the correspondence which has taken place between you and your old friend Mr. Jefferson. I consider you and him as the North and South Poles of the American Revolution. Some talked, some wrote, and some fought to promote and establish it," Rush wrote, "but you and Mr. Jefferson *thought* for us all."[19] Rush poured out his love, respect, and affection to Adams, in a way that he could not so readily have done with Jefferson. "I admire, as do all my family, the wonderful vivacity and imagery of your letters. Some men's minds wear well, but yours don't appear to wear at all. O! king, live forever, said the Eastern nations to their monarchs! Live-Live, my venerable friend (to use a less extravagant Spanish salutation), a thousand years, to make your family and friends around you happy and to instruct and delight with your letters."[20] Adams must have chuckled at Rush's complimentary association of him with the terms "king" and "monarch."

Rush continued to correspond with both Adams and Jefferson until his death the following year. Several weeks after his "king" and "monarch" letter to Adams, completely satisfied that his efforts had been crowned with success, Rush wrote to Jefferson.

> In a letter which I received a few days ago from Mr. Adams, he informs me, with a kind of exultation, that after a correspondence of five or six and thirty years had been interrupted by various causes, it had been renewed, and that four letters had passed between you and him. In speaking of your letters, he says, 'They are written with all the elegance, purity, and sweetness of style of his youth and middle age . . .' It will give me pleasure as long as I live to reflect that I have been in any degree instrumental in effecting this reunion of two souls destined to be dear to each other and animated with the same dispositions to serve their country (though in different ways) at the expense of innumerable sacrifices of domestic ease, personal interest, and private friendships.

Closing his letter to Jefferson with an appreciation of Adams, Rush declared unnecessarily, "I am sure you will be delighted with his correspondence. Some of his thoughts electrify me. I view him as a mountain with its head clear and reflecting the beams of the sun, while all below it is frost and snow."[21]

In the months remaining to him, Rush sent two more letters to Monticello, though twenty-two made their way to Quincy.[22] The friendship of Rush and Adams was a deep, emotional, and lengthy one. Upon Rush's death in April 1813, Adams reacted with profound grief and a staggering sense of personal loss. Jefferson's reaction in contrast appears consciously self-controlled, though he too was deeply affected. Adams's response to the death of Rush was in perfect keeping with his fearless, emotionally demonstrative character. Jefferson's more self-conscious and controlled reaction is consistent with his emotional distance, and a chilliness that prompted friends like Rush and others to pause, and likely restrain themselves as best they could from sharing too much depth of feeling, or expecting similar in return.

Since Rush's joyful note to Jefferson of early March 1812, nine letters had gone back and forth between Adams and Jefferson through April 1813. On April 10, 1813, Rush wrote Adams the penultimate letter of his life. The aging doctor had a clear sense that the end was approaching when he wrote, "time is short and that the night of imbecility of mind or of death is fast approaching."[23] Little over a week later, Rush's worthy, extraordinary, and sometimes difficult life ended. He was sixty-eight years old. Adams was horrified and overwhelmed with grief at Rush's unexpected death. Soon after learning of it, he sent a letter to Rush's son, Richard.

> In what terms can I address you? There are none that can express my sympathy with you and your family, or my own personal feelings on the loss of your excellent father . . . There is not another person, out of my own family, who can die, in whom my personal happiness can be so deeply affected. The world would pronounce me extravagant and no man would apologize for me if I should say that in the estimation of unprejudiced philosophy, he has done more good in this world than Franklin or Washington.[24]

Prior to sending this condolence to Rush's son, Adams had written to Elbridge Gerry—the very same mutual friend that Jefferson had recommended to Rush as a potential (though unnecessary) catalyst to move Rush's reconciliation plans forward. In his letter to Gerry,

Adams remembered those few signers of the Declaration of Independence who then remained alive.

> A few facts I wish to put upon paper, & an awful warning to do it soon has been given me by the sudden death of our Friend Rush .
> . . Livingston & Clymer had preceeded him in the same year, the same spring. How few remain. Three in Massachusetts I believe are a majority of the surviving signers of a Declaration, which has had much credit in the World. As a man of Science, Letters, Taste, Sense, Philosophy, Patriotism, Religion, Morality, Merit, Usefulness, taken all together, Rush has not left his equal in America; nor that I know in the World. In him is taken away, & in a manner most sudden & unexpected, a main prop of my Life. Why should I grieve, when grieving I must bear.[25]

Gerry then wrote to Richard Rush, and included Adams's grief-stricken appreciation of Rush's father with the declaration that Adams's emotional outpouring of friendship, love, and loss "expresses an opinion in unison with my own."[26] Several weeks later, on May 31, 1813, Jefferson wrote in sadness and concern to Richard Rush.

> No one has taken a more sincere part than myself in the affliction which has lately befallen your family, by the loss of your inestimable and ever to be lamented father . . . His virtues rendered him dear to all who knew him, and his benevolence led him to do all men every good in his power. Much he was able to do, and much therefore will be missed.

Jefferson also informed the young man that he had written two letters to his father whose existence, in the context of his father's sudden death, now caused him "anxiety." The friendship of Jefferson and Benjamin Rush had been one of mutual trust and respect; while Rush lived, Jefferson had been completely confident that the two letters would "be kept from the public eye."[27] The first letter was dated April 21, 1803, and concerned Jefferson's views on Jesus and Christianity. Then, Jefferson had informed Benjamin Rush, "To the corruptions of Christianity I am indeed opposed; but not to the genuine precepts of Jesus himself." A comparison between "the merit of the doctrines of

Jesus, compared with those of others" had been included for Rush's review.[28] The second letter that caused Jefferson concern was dated January 16, 1811, and was written a year before the renewal of his friendship with Adams. Jefferson had then told Rush that, during his first term, he had considered arranging, "either directly or indirectly," a sinecure for Adams but had been dissuaded.[29]

Jefferson explained to Richard Rush that during his father's lifetime Jefferson had had complete confidence that neither of these letters would be exposed to the public eye. Now that Rush was gone, Jefferson wanted to be certain that they would not see the light of day. "I have too many enemies disposed to make a lacerating use of them, not to feel anxieties inspired by a love of tranquility, now become the *summum bonum* of life," Jefferson explained to Rush's son.[30] There was legitimate cause for Jefferson's apprehension about the two letters; the publication of one would likely have catastrophic consequences to the quietude of his retirement, and the other could do damage to his renewed friendship with Adams. Several days before writing to Richard Rush about these letters, Jefferson had written to Adams on the subject of Rush's death.

"Another of our friends of 76 is gone, my dear Sir, another of the Co-signers of the independence of our country," Jefferson wrote to Adams.[31] "And a better man, than Rush, could not have left us, more benevolent, more learned, of finer genius, or more honest. We too must go; and that ere long." Adams received this letter on June 11, 1813, and replied the following day. "I lament with you the loss of Rush, I know of no Character living or dead, who has done more real good in America," Adams declared.[32]

After his retirement in 1809, Jefferson never left Virginia; Adams did much the same, staying close to Peace field to the end. Though they never saw each other again, their correspondence kept them close, and the renewed friendship that arose thanks to Rush's tireless patience became a profoundly comforting element in their lives, for Adams in particular. The letters they wrote to each other over the following decade and more became one of the crowning achievements in American literature. Renowned for their historical importance and literary beauty, they provide an intimate and deeply honest record of a friendship between two of the most important men in American history—a lost friendship rescued through the tireless love and care of a mutual friend.

Though their correspondence became known by the observance of their letters at the various post offices through which their letters passed, both men at first expressed indifference about seeing their letters published. "I have no thought, in this correspondence, but to satisfy you and myself," Adams wrote in 1813. "If our Letters should be shewn to a friend or two, in confidence; and if that confidence should be betrayed; your Letters will do you no dishonour. As to mine I care not a farthing. My Reputation has been so much the Sport of the public for fifty Years, and will be with Posterity, that I hold it, a bubble, a Gossameur that idles in the wanton Summers Air."[33] Several days later however, Adams contradicted himself when, in his letter to Jefferson of June thirtieth, he tacitly acknowledged that their letters would one day be published, "I beg leave to correct an Idea that some readers may infer from an expression in one of your Letters."[34] He clarified his position during the following week by asserting that he had no objection to the publication of the letters in a national newspaper. Adams closed his letter of July 3, 1813, with, "I am, and shall be for Life, Your Friend."[35] Years later, Jefferson would see the wisdom of Adams's openness to the idea of their correspondence being placed before the public, with a specific caveat, however, that "some device should be thought of for their getting before the public otherwise than by our own publication."[36]

Noted historian L. H. Butterfield, editor of the only collection of Benjamin Rush's letters, wrote of the Adams-Jefferson correspondence that it was "shrewd, humorous, and philosophical by turns and often concurrently, their letters form a commentary on man and his works that has never been surpassed in either range or readableness in America. Perhaps it has not been surpassed anywhere."[37]

Adams represented his political viewpoint for posterity as did Jefferson, but what they did even more was to sustain each other with their active minds and total intellectual engagement on a wide range of subjects. Their quest for learning and insight, their mutual respect and affection, and the extraordinary history that bound them together provided each, through their letters, with a profound comfort. Yet more important still than the pleasure they took in the life of the mind that both men so vigorously lived was their mutual contentment in the simple fact that the other was alive.

They were both keenly aware that their friendship was as important to them as their own political views, which were often in marked contrast. Among the many areas of mutual interest, there were two unifying themes that forever bound them together: love of country and a deep appreciation for their friendships. Only Benjamin Rush was able to remind them that love of country and love of friend were not mutually exclusive "passions," as Professor John Quincy Adams might have said, but rather were important "habits" of a lifetime.

Among the many great services that Adams and Jefferson performed during their long and extraordinary lives, years that were full of self-sacrifice and public service, was to model for future generations this idea—that friendship should be immune to political differences. Similarly, they both set a standard for forgiveness and understanding and, finally, of acceptance.

Adams and Jefferson faithfully continued their correspondence through the joys, sorrows, and challenges of the years that remained to them. Upon Abigail's death in 1818, Adams joined Jefferson in widowhood.[38] But as they aged, their minds remained vigorous, active, and unfettered by the physical ravages of time. Jefferson's University of Virginia was founded in 1819 for example, with the first classes sitting in 1825.[39] Though Jefferson was particularly distracted with his farm, buildings, and numerous projects, he made time as best he could to reply to Adams's many often challenging, though always friendly and compassionate letters. Adams was not offended or dissuaded when he noted that often his three or four (or more) letters to Jefferson would result in a single reply from Monticello. Adams had so much to say, overflowing as he was with memories, ideas, and insights; he therefore took advantage enthusiastically of the one remaining great friend of his life to whom he could truly speak, and be entirely heard and understood. As more of the revolutionary generation departed, their friendship became all the more important.

The undeniable march of time was taking its toll on the health, though not intellectual acuity, of both men. By 1823, Adams was eighty-eight, still with vigorous mind, though his physical condition had deteriorated considerably. Barely able to write, and reading with great difficulty, one of Adams's grandchildren would read Jefferson's letters aloud to him, and write Adams's dictated replies. Jefferson was then eighty, and in physical though not mental decline. Two years before Adams had declared that since he was the oldest remaining member of Congress from 1776, and likely the next to depart, Jefferson was the youngest and probably would be the last to go to his reward.[40] Perhaps believing that each letter to Jefferson might be his last, Adams was unrestrained in sharing his fond feelings to his friend. Adams closed his letter of September, 24, 1821, with this promise: "Whether in the body or out of the body I shall always be your friend."[41]

By October 12, 1823, Jefferson was finding it difficult to write. "Against this *tedium vitae* however I am fortunately mounted on a Hobby, which indeed I should have better managed some thirty or forty years ago, but whose easy amble is still sufficient to give exercise and amusement to an Octogenary rider. This is the establishment of an University . . ." It was in this same letter—described by Adams as "the best letter that ever was written"—that Jefferson wrote of his having seen "extracts" of Adams's unfortunate and inflammatory correspondence with William Cunningham.

When Adams replied to Jefferson's letter of forgiveness, less than three years remained to the retired presidents; sixteen more letters passed between them. The final letter in their correspondence was a short one, dated April 17, 1826, sent from Quincy to Monticello. Jefferson's grandsons had visited Adams and carried with them what would be Jefferson's last letter to Adams. In this hand-delivered letter to Adams, Jefferson introduced his grandson Thomas Jefferson Randolph. Jefferson wrote,

> Like other young people, he wishes to be able, in the winter nights
> of old age, to recount to those around him what he has heard and
> learnt of the Heroic age preceding his birth, and which of the Argo-

nauts particularly he was in time to have seen. It was the lot of our early years to witness nothing but the dull monotony of colonial subservience, and of our riper ones to breast the labors and perils of working out of it. Theirs are the Halcyon calms succeeding the storm which our Argosy had so stoutly weathered.[42]

In his short reply, Adams humorously wondered why Virginians seemed so much taller in comparison to New Englanders and observed that when young Mr. Randolph stood beside someone, his height made them seem as but a "Pygmie." "Your letter," Adams declared to Jefferson, "is one of the most beautiful and delightful I have ever received."[43]

The fiftieth anniversary of the United States was swiftly approaching when Adams wrote this final letter. Both retired chief executives likely assumed that President John Quincy Adams would see to it that July 4, 1826, would be a day to remember.

Ten years previously Adams had written to Jefferson about his reading habits. Both men were book lovers. In December 1816, Adams told Jefferson that he had been

a Lover and a Reader of Romances all my Life. From Don Quixotte and Gill Blass to the Scottish Chiefs and an hundred others. For the last Year or two I have devoted my self to this kind of Study: and have read 15 Volumes of Grim, Seven Volumes of Tuckers Neddy Search and 12 Volumes of Dupuis besides a 13th of plates and Traceys Analysis, and 4 Volumes of Jesuitical History! Romances all! I have learned nothing of importance to me, for they have made no Change in my moral or religious Creed, which has for 50 or 60 Years been contained in four short Words "Be just and good."[44]

His "creed" was a simple paraphrase of the motto on his rarely used customized family crest bookplate. Though he did not prepare his own epitaph (as Jefferson had done), the memorial stone of his ancestor Henry Adams, for which he had written the inscription, is enlightening as to the traits of character that Adams most revered.[45] "This stone and several others have been placed in this yard by a great, great, grandson from a veneration of the piety, humility, simplicity, prudence, frugality, industry and perseverance of his ancestors in hopes of recommending an affirmation of their virtues to their posterity."[46]

Though it is not known if Jefferson had a personal motto,[47] he did write his own epitaph, and designed the burial monument upon which it would be chiseled. What Jefferson chose to include and, more importantly, exclude is as important and illuminating as Adams's choice of personal maxim.

> Among his papers there were found written on the torn back of an old letter the following directions for his monument and its inscription ". . . on the faces of the Obelisk the following inscription, & not a word more:
> HERE WAS BURIED
> Thomas Jefferson
> Author of the Declaration of American Independence,
> Of the Statute of Virginia for Religious Freedom,
> And Father of the University of Virginia;
> because by these, as testimonials that I have lived, I wish most to be remembered."[48]

Jefferson did not include any elected political office, or diplomatic post that he had held. That he had been the president of the United States for two terms, and the vice president for one, minister to France, governor of Virginia, and the first secretary of state is significantly unmentioned. There are a great many accomplishments that Jefferson could have listed; their absence from the stone illuminates Jefferson's nature, in a sense, which seems likely to have been his purpose.

The three accomplishments that Jefferson selected for his epitaph are not related to party, partisanship, or power; they are gifts that Jefferson left for future generations of his countrymen. Always a forward-thinking man, Jefferson was clear about how he wanted to be remembered—concisely inscribing his most treasured successes in the definitiveness and finality of stone. In the silent cemetery at Monticello Jefferson's epitaph is forever unequivocal in communicating to present and future Americans those accomplishments he believed had defined his life.

As celebrations, orations, and patriotic military marches were being finalized for the fiftieth anniversary of the United States, July 4, 1826, in Quincy, Massachusetts, and far to the south in Charlottesville, Virginia, the second and third presidents of the United States were passing their final hours. At one point several days prior, Jefferson had said to his doctor, "A few hours more, doctor, and it will all be over."[49] He had also told his daughter Martha Randolph, that after his death which was soon sure to come, she would find something special from him "in a certain drawer, in an old pocket book."[50] Late in the evening of the third, Jefferson, slowly and quietly taking leave of his extraordinary life, apparently thinking that it was the early morning of the next day, declared; "This is the fourth of July."[51] Jefferson lingered until noon of the fourth, and then was gone.[52] At Peace field a similar sad, but inevitable, scene was played out.

In Boston, celebrations of the great day were under way. On Boston Common, Josiah Quincy Sr. delivered a lengthy address to the joyful citizens of the city on the fiftieth anniversary of the nation's founding. At one point in his oration, Quincy specifically mentioned John Adams. His comments were as applicable to Jefferson as they were to Adams. "He, indeed . . . hears not our public song or voice of praise, or ascending prayer. But the sounds of a nation's joy, rushing from our cities, ringing from our valleys, echoing from our hills, shall break the silence of his ancient ear."[53] Adams was then at home at Peace field attended by his family and friends, all of whom knew that the end was swiftly approaching.

Several days previously a representative of the Quincy July fourth commemoration committee paid a visit to Adams, hoping that the former president would provide a few words that could be shared during the upcoming celebrations. "Spent a few minutes with him in conversation, and took from him a toast, to be presented on the Fourth of July as coming from him," the man reported later. "I should have liked a longer one; but as it is, this will be acceptable. 'I will give you,' said he, 'Independence forever!'" When asked if he had anything at all to add, Adams replied, "Not a word."[54] At around noon, Adams spoke for the last time, "Thomas Jefferson survives." By six o'clock Adams was gone.[55]

Soon after Jefferson's death, Martha Jefferson Randolph found something in the drawer just as her father had promised.[56] This is what she found, in Jefferson's own hand.[57]

> A Death-bed Adieu from Th. J. to M.R.
>
> Life's visions are vanished, its dreams are no more;
>
> Dear friends of my bosom, why bathed in tears?
>
> I to my fathers, I welcome the shore
>
> Which crowns all my hopes or which buries my cares.
>
> Then farewell, my dear, my lov'd daughter, adieu!
>
> The last pang of life is in parting from you!
>
> Two seraphs await me long shrouded in death;
>
> I will bear them your love on my last parting breath.

The almost simultaneous deaths of Jefferson and Adams on July fourth were widely acknowledged across the country as a profound event, and an unlikely coincidence. In an August oration delivered at Boston's Faneuil Hall, Daniel Webster, the great lawyer and politician, famous for his lengthy and insightful speeches, characterized their deaths on July fourth as divine confirmation. "Neither of these great men, fellow-citizens, could have died, at any time, without leaving an immense void in our American society . . . But the concurrence of their death on the anniversary of Independence has naturally awakened stronger emotions . . ." Webster observed. "As their lives themselves were the gifts of Providence, who is not willing to recognize in their happy termination, as well as in their long continuance, proofs that our country and its benefactors are objects of His care?"[58] For Webster, and many others, the deaths of Adams and Jefferson on July fourth seemed heavy with suggestion.

> No two men now live, fellow-citizens, perhaps it may be doubted whether any two men have ever lived in one age, who, more than those we now commemorate, have impressed on mankind their own sentiments in regard to politics and government, infused their own opinions more deeply into the opinions of others, or given a more lasting direction to the current of human thought. Their work doth not perish with them . . . May not such events raise the

suggestion that they are not undesigned, and that Heaven does so order things, as sometimes to attract strongly the attention and excite the thoughts of men? The occurrence has added new interest to our anniversary, and will be remembered in all time to come.[59]

One month after their deaths, Webster had observed, "The tears which flow, and the honors that are paid, when the founders of the republic die, give hope that the republic itself may be immortal."[60]

Adams had consistently noted that without the Union itself, the American experiment in representative democracy would not succeed. Jefferson came to share this view completely. Long aware of the dangers that partisanship presented to the survival of the nation, Adams explained in an 1808 letter to Rush,

> When public virtue is gone, when the national spirit is fled, when a party is substituted for the nation and faction for a party, when venality lurks and skulks in secret, and, much more, when it imprudently braves the public censure, whether it be sent in the form of emissaries from foreign powers, or is employed by ambitious and intriguing domestic citizens, the republic is lost in essence, though it may still exist in form.[61]

When Adams wrote that letter, he was then not in contact with Jefferson. In an 1813 letter to Adams, Jefferson referenced two private letters (written to other correspondents) that had been published without his knowledge. "Whether the character of the times is justly portrayed or not, posterity will decide. But on one feature of them they can never decide, the sensations excited in free yet firm minds, by the terrorism of the day. None can conceive who did not witness them, and they were felt by one party only."[62] Upon receipt of this letter from Jefferson, Adams was irate at the assertion that only "one party" had been victimized. In his reply Adams provided a lengthy list of examples of the "terrorism of the day" that he had experienced.

> I believe You never felt the Terrorism of Gallatin's Insurrection in Pensilvania [sic]: You certainly never reallized the Terror of Fries's, most outragious Riot and Rescue, as I call it, Treason, Rebellion, as the World and great Judges and two Juries pronounced it. You

certainly never felt the Terrorism, excited by Genet, in 1793, when Ten thousand People in the streets of Philadelphia, day after day, threatened to drag Washington out of his House, and effect a Revolution in the Government, or compell it to declare War in favour of the French Revolution, and against England.

Adams was determined that Jefferson should have the full list so that he would realize that his assertion of one-sided political extremism had been wrong.

The coolest and the firmest Minds, even among the Quakers in Philadelphia, have given their Opinions to me, that nothing but the Yellow Fever, which removed Dr. Hutchinson[63] and Jonathan Dickinson Sargent[64] from this World, could have saved the United States from a total Revolution of Government. I have no doubt you was fast asleep in philosophical Tranquility, when ten thousand People, and perhaps many more, were parading the Streets of Philadelphia, on the Evening of my Fast Day;[65] When even Governor Mifflin himself, thought it his Duty to order a Patrol of Horse and Foot to preserve the peace; when Markett Street was as full as Men could stand by one another, and even before my Door; when some of my Domesticks in Phrenzy, determined to sacrifice their Lives in my defence; when all were ready to make a desperate Salley among the multitude, and others were with difficulty and danger dragged back by the others; when I myself judged it prudent and necessary to order Chests of Arms from the War Office to be brought through bye Lanes and back Doors: determined to defend my House at the Expence of my Life, and the Lives of the few, very few Domesticks and Friends within it. What think you of Terrorism, Mr. Jefferson?[66]

Clearly dismayed and upset that Jefferson would suggest that only Federalists were guilty of excesses against Republicans, Adams wanted him and anyone who might later read their correspondence to understand that extreme partisanship was not the shame of one party alone. "Upon this Subject I despair of making myself understood by Posterity, by the present Age, and even by you. To collect and arrange the documents illustrative of it, would require as many Lives as those of a cat." [67]

To assure that there would be no misunderstanding by any reader of his letter, Jefferson or otherwise, Adams concluded his lengthy list of the terrorism of partisanship that he had faced with an unmistakable assertion that both parties were equally to blame.

> The real terrors of both Parties have allways [sic] been, and now are, The fear that they shall loose the Elections and consequently the Loaves and Fishes; and their Antagonists will obtain them. Both parties have excited artificial Terrors and if I were summoned as a Witness to say upon Oath, which Party had excited, Machiavillialy, the most terror, and which had really felt the most, I could not give a more sincere Answer, than in the vulgar Style "Put Them in a bagg and shake them, and then see which comes out first."[68]

* * *

Adams would write to Jefferson in the summer of 1813, soon after the renewal of their friendship:

> The first time, that you and I differed in Opinion on any material Question; was after your Arrival from Europe; and that point was the French Revolution, You was [sic] well persuaded in your own mind that the Nation would succeed in establishing a free Republican Government: I was as well persuaded, in mine, that a project of such a Government, over five and twenty millions people, when four and twenty millions and five hundred thousands of them could neither write nor read: was as unnatural irrational and impracticable; as it would be over the Elephants Lions Tigers Panthers Wolves and Bears in the Royal Menagerie, at Versailles.[69]

Adams reminded Jefferson of an evening at Jefferson's residence in Paris when Lafayette had "harangued You and me, and John Quincy Adams . . . and developed the plans then in Operation to reform France." According to Adams's reminiscence of the event, both Adams and Jefferson kept their silence during Lafayette's "harangue," though he was shocked at what Lafayette, then one of the leading voices during the Revolution's early period, was saying. "In plain Truth I was astonished at the Grossness of his Ignorance of Gover[n] ment and History, as I had been for Years before at that of Turgot, Rochefaucault, Condercet and Franklin."

Adams doubted the outcome of the Revolution in France from the moment he first learned of its foundational concepts. He found "Turgots 'Government in one Centre and that Center the Nation,'" entirely nonsensical and when he realized that French revolutionary concepts were making their way to America, he wanted no part of them. "Sympathies in America had caught the French flame: I was determined to wash my own hands as clean as I could of all this foulness." Adams suspected that his rejection of the Revolution in France would not be without personal cost.

"I had then strong forebodings that I was sacrificing all the honours and Emoluments of this Life; and so it has happened, but," Adams noted in hindsight, "not in so great a degree as I apprehended." Adams also observed, with perhaps a smattering of pique, that Jefferson's enthusiastic support for the Revolution in France had had the opposite consequence. "Your steady defence of democratical Principles, and your invariable favourable Opinion of the french Revolution laid the foundation of your Unbounded Popularity."[70]

Ten years later, Adams wrote to Jefferson of a private discussion he had had as vice president with their mutual friend Dr. Priestley about the French Revolution.[71] Respectful of his friend Priestley's pro–French Revolution, republican views, Adams engaged the great scientist and theologian in a kind of Socratic discourse. Though Adams does not provide the date of this meeting, Priestley had dedicated the first volume of a two-volume work on "revealed religion" to Adams in 1796, and Adams's reference to the execution of Louis XVI likely puts the meeting sometime in 1793.[72]

"Not long after the denouement of the tragedy of Louis 16th. [sic] when I was vice-President, my friend the Dr. came to breakfast with me alone. He was very sociable, very learned and eloquent on the subject of the French revolution." According to Adams, Dr. Priestley believed that the Revolution in France "was opening a new era in the world and presenting a near view of the millennium."[73] After listening to Priestley's views, Adams responded with questions. "At last I asked the Doctor, do you really believe the French will establish a free democratical government in France? He answered; I do firmly believe it. Will you give me leave to ask you upon what grounds you entertain this opinion? Is it from anything you ever read in history—is there any instance of a Roman Catholic Monarchy of five and twenty millions at once converted into a free and rational people? No, I know of no instance like it," Priestley responded.[74]

Jefferson's response to Adams's letter was unusually swift. "Your letter of Aug. 15. was received in due time, and with the welcome of every thing which comes from you. With it's [sic] opinions on the difficulties of revolutions, from despotism to freedom, I very much concur," Jefferson wrote to Adams on September 4, 1823. Jefferson proceeded to explain his generational perspective on republican revolution which was essentially that of a visionary's. A visionary's perspective however is not necessarily a mistaken one.

As they lived out their twilight years at Montezillo and Monticello, Adams was more open to radical concepts, particularly when presented to him by Jefferson. No one, however, could convince Adams that the lessons of history were valueless in judging the validity or likely success of a political movement of the present day. Jefferson deeply appreciated the importance of history and did not make such a case.

That controversial argument, which Jefferson had shared in detail with Madison but never with Adams, was founded on the idea that historical precedent should not be considered an unbreakable binding blueprint for the present or the future. Though Jefferson clearly appreciated the importance of history and its unavoidable influence on the present and the future, his "usufruct of the living" contention was essentially a total rejection of the authority of precedent. These radical concepts were foundational to the development of American democracy.

Jefferson's 1823 reply to Adams shows a maturation of his views on the rejection of the power of the past, and of the place of revolution in the course of human affairs. This was the lesson of the French Revolution for Jefferson: A new political order entirely opposed to the existing order(s) requires, much like a great wine, many years and, generally, much longer. The overturning of tyranny by revolutionary means and its replacement by governments founded on popular representation could not likely be accomplished in only one generation or even two.

Jefferson made a persuasive argument that explained, and gave a new context to, the violence and horrors of the French Revolution. (In fact, any revolution against oppression that had the rights of the individual at its core was included in Jefferson's interpretation.) Adams, finally, came to understand and appreciate Jefferson's position. What had formerly for Adams been unacceptable and appalling, suddenly was now viewed, after reading Jefferson's letter, as an unfortunate fact of political and human development. This extraordinary and late shift in Adams's political views was apparently due entirely to Jefferson's eloquence, passion, and logic.

> The generation which commences a revolution can rarely compleat it . . . Habituated from their infancy to passive submission of body and mind to their king and priests, they are not qualified, when called on, to think and provide for themselves and their inexperience, their ignorance and bigotry make them instruments often, in the hands of the Bonapartes and Iturbides to defeat their own rights and purposes. This is the present situation of Europe and Spanish America. But it is not desperate. The light which has been shed on mankind by the art of printing has eminently changed the condition of the world. As yet that light has dawned on the middling classes only of the men of Europe. The kings and the rabble of equal ignorance, have not yet received it's [sic] rays; but it continues to spread. And, while printing is preserved, it can no more recede than the sun return on his course. A first attempt to recover the right of self-government may fail; so may a 2d, a 3d, etc., but as a younger, and more instructed race comes on, the sentiment becomes more and more intuitive, and a 4th. a 5th. or some subsequent one of the ever renewed attempts will ultimately succeed . . . To attain all this however rivers of blood must yet flow, and years of desolation pass over . . . Yet the object is worth rivers of blood,

and years of desolation for what inheritance so valuable can man leave to his posterity?

Jefferson's confidence in the transformation of the world from one of tyranny and injustice to one of representative government and individual rights was absolute. "You and I," he assured Adams, "shall look down from another world on these glorious achievements to man, which will add to the joys even of heaven."[75] Adams's response was swift. His eyes failing, Jefferson's letter was read aloud to him. "With much pleasure I have heard read the sure words of prophecy in your letter of Sep. 4th," Adams proclaimed.[76] He was a man convinced.

> It is melancholy to contemplate the cruel wars, dessolutions of Countries, and ocians [sic] of blood which must occure, before rational principles, and rational systems of Government can prevail and be established . . . But as these are inevitable we must content ourselves with the consolations which you from sound and sure reasons so clearly suggest. Thes[e] hopes are as well founded as our fears of the contrary evils; on the whole, the prospect is cheering . . .[77]

Brought together by revolution, then separated by it, and finally reunited through Benjamin Rush's tireless efforts, Adams and Jefferson left their correspondence to posterity as a message. Their letters are a record of one of their most revolutionary achievements—the victory of friendship over partisanship.

Jefferson and Adams understood that political conflict could too readily ruin friendships, associations, and finally the country; they and their revolutionary colleagues transferred their understanding of this essential truth to the structure of the new government. The checks and balances system is designed to both facilitate and (to a certain extent) control the continuous conflict of views as expressed among the people and then, through their representatives, within the government itself. With this systemic and institutional acceptance of perpetual conflicts of opinions, the founders demonstrated their recognition that the new democracy signaled the end of political simplicity, rigidity, and enforced unity that had been so characteristic of monarchical and tyrannical rule.

The open, unhindered discussion of politics—that is, clashing views—and even criticism of presidents in the press that sometimes drove both Adams and Jefferson to distraction would be the new American standard. Political parties funneled these discussions, brought like-minded people together under their banners, and came to represent particular viewpoints. The difficulty of striking a balance between political debate, whether organized or not, and the ongoing harmonious existence of the Union was then, and continues to be, a central challenge for all Americans.

The creators of the republic encouraged open and vigorous political discourse, and built its protection into the foundational structure of the government. The founders believed that public involvement in politics provides the necessary vigor that is essential to sustain the health of the democracy and preserve a perpetual link between citizens and government. At the end of the nineteenth century, one Adams biographer wrote, "In the contest of the present day, republican should not call democrat an enemy of his country, nor democrat accuse republican of lack of patriotism, so long as each deems the other honest, but mistaken. The demagogue, the political boss and the dishonorable officeseeker are the only enemies of the commonwealth."[78]

The work of the revolution started by Adams and Jefferson will never be done. The revolution itself is an ongoing process, not a static condition; perhaps this is one of the lessons that Adams and Jefferson wanted to leave for future generations. As the republic that they worked so hard to create and sustain continues to mature, all the citizens must fight the deepest internal struggle of all and contemplate this central challenge—If I am right, then what of those who disagree? The correspondence of Adams and Jefferson is an illustration for posterity that meaningful associations and political opinions must not be mutually exclusive.

* * *

Dr. Priestley had once told Vice President Adams that the French Revolution was "a near view of the millennium." It has become over time a kind of archetype of the injustices and catastrophes that arise when toleration and clemency have died.

It is true that the human desire for individual freedom remains very much alive. Many contemporary observers have expressed frustration and cynicism at the slow and bloody march of human progress. Thomas Jefferson's optimistic view of the revolutionary process should restore even the most skeptical observer's heart.

Let the timeless friendship of John Adams and Thomas Jefferson forever stand as a model of learning, acceptance, and forgiveness. Let us hope that the lessons of these men find their way to the core of our democracy so that the habits of personal relationships are not overturned by the passions of political differences; such are the challenges faced by every generation.

Acknowledgments

At the head of the extensive list of people who assisted and supported me during the years that passed while this book was being written is my friend Eric Wittenberg. I would not have undertaken this project nor likely seen it through without his encouragement. Eric kindly read early drafts of the manuscript and offered his insights on corrections and rewrites long afterward. His thoughtful support and consideration throughout, and particularly for his patience with my many late-night email "requests for review," were all very much appreciated.

My wife Kendra has shown extraordinary patience, thoughtfulness, and support through these many years of research, writing, learning, etc. Her consideration and care were foundational to this project.

My children Madeline, Graeme, and Ilana have all been superbly patient and considerate. I am very proud of each of them as they are all people of fine character. Perhaps this book will be an inspiration to them to study history—to learn why things happen and understand why people do what they do. These, after all, are the essential questions of human civilization.

My longtime friend Tony Kawas provided too many thoughtful and spot-on critiques to count, his support and fine eye for logic and flow were invaluable. Professor Satoshi Masamune (Yamaguchi University), my dear and long-time friend, also read early drafts and gave of his extensive expertise and kind support. My friends Malik

Sagarad and Shaun Kelly also gave freely of their time and valuable opinions. Shaun also kindly assisted during several challenging periods of research frustrations.

A number of patient professionals at museums, libraries, historical sites, universities, and elsewhere helped me significantly in tracking down difficult-to-find details, locating obscure sources and references, and also with encouragement. Anne Berkes (Research Librarian, Monticello) and Jack Robertson (Foundation Librarian, Monticello) helped me to understand the physical layout and architectural history of Monticello. William Durden (President, Dickinson College, retired), Christine Bombaro (Associate Director for Information Literacy & Research Services, Dickinson College Library), and Roy Goodman (Assistant Librarian and Curator of Printed Materials, American Philosophical Society) kindly helped me with details of eighteenth-century Philadelphia and particularly with matters of the good Dr. Benjamin Rush.

Michael Scullin (Honorary Consul of France in Philadelphia) and Edouard de Limairac helped me with a particularly troublesome translation challenge and with matters of French Consul Létombe in Philadelphia.

David Andress (Associate Dean, Research and Professor of Modern History, Univ. of Portsmouth, UK), Philip Barnard (Professor of English, Univ. of Kansas), Robert Rhodes Crout (Adjunct Professor, College of Charleston), and Siân Reynolds (Professor, University of Stirling, Scotland, UK) all kindly communicated with me and shared their knowledge of select details of the Revolution in France, and of the Early Republic period. Mary Claffey (Associate Editor, Administration, Adams Papers, Massachusetts Historical Society) kindly assisted with some matters of John Adams.

I am indebted to the Nashville-Davidson County Public Library and the InterLibrary Loan system for their superior collections, helpful and knowledgeable staff, and the access to books and other important resources that they provide. The collection of online scanned books stored on Google's servers also was an invaluable resource. Locating and accessing often little-known histories and memoirs would have been much more difficult but for this invaluable service provided by Google and all of its associated university and library partners.

My mother and father, Melvin and Judith Mallock, have been unwavering supporters of me personally, and of this project from the very first mention of it. I will always be grateful that my father was able to see an early draft a year before his death and was fully aware and supportive of me and this book. I will always cherish their lifelong lessons of diligence, thoughtfulness, personal honor, ethics, faith, and perseverance.

Sheldon and Tybee Zuckerman have been supportive and helpful in many ways over the years.

My agent, Roger Williams, has been a tireless champion for me and for this book, for which I am very grateful. I appreciate the excellent work of the editorial staff at Skyhorse.

As a lifelong student of history there were important teachers and guides who helped, prodded, challenged, and inspired. I can't thank these brilliant people enough for sharing their knowledge with me, and for inspiring me with their love of learning and of history. Mr. Arthur Svenson, Central Junior High School, Mr. Lawrence Osborne, Central Junior High, Mrs. Janice Gillespie, Central Junior High, Mrs. Linda Day, Quincy High School, Mr. Bruce McDonald, Quincy High, Mr. Edgar Tatro, Quincy High, Prof. Paul Axelrod, Ripon College, Prof. Seale Doss, Ripon College; Mr. Clifford Boatner, Quincy High, my teacher and friend in J. S. Bach, a brilliant and thoughtful man who demonstrated through his mastery of the piano and of mathematics that extraordinary effort can result in the most sublime beauty; and my friend Daniel "Moley" Feigenbaum who personified *joie-de-vivre*.

For my brother Alan and sister Audrey: Though the winds of time and circumstance may carry us in thought or in truth far away—even to other sides of the planet—we are always family.

Friends, like family, are a blessing. To my friends Derek and Carol Stearns, Sam Hood, Greg Biggs, Bo Warburton, Lillian Hamilton, Deb Holmes, Bob MacFarland, Caroline Hughes, Carissa Parker, Adrian Hall, Dyann Dorgan, Quennel Kappenman, Anilkumar Gopalakrishnan, Cynthia Sepulveda, Joel Norton, John Summers, Steve

Dooner, Tom and Mary Montag, Thomas Siegworth, Arthur Mallock, Satoshi, Tony, Shaun, Malik, and Eric, I say, thank you.

Had I not undertaken this project I would now be a different person; lesser, I think. Thank you to John Adams and Thomas Jefferson for their example of forgiveness and patience, love, and respect. Thank you to Dr. Rush for his great care for people, and for his love for his friends.

I needed all of them then, and now.

Endnotes

Chapter One: "The Best Letter That Ever Was Written"

[1] Please see John Adams to Thomas Jefferson, November 23, 1819, in *The Adams-Jefferson Letters: The Complete Correspondence between Thomas Jefferson and Abigail and John Adams,* edited by Lester J. Cappon, 2 vols., Chapel Hill: University of North Carolina Press for the Institute of Early American History and Culture, Williamsburg, Virginia, 1959, v.2, p.547; hereafter cited as *Correspondence.*

[2] *John Adams,* by Page Smith, (Doubleday & Co., New York), 1962, v.2, p.1028.

[3] Jefferson to James Madison, January 30, 1787; *Memoirs, Correspondence, and Private Papers of Thomas Jefferson,* edited by Thomas Jefferson Randolph, Volume 2, (Colburn and Bentley, London), 1829, p.86.

[4] Adams to Rush, August 17, 1812; *John Adams* by Page Smith, (Doubleday & Co., New York), 1962, v.2, p.1102.

[5] *Passionate Sage: The Character and Legacy of John Adams,* by Joseph J. Ellis, (Norton, New York), 1993, p.75.

[6] Their relationship is described by Adams in a letter to Cunningham, November 25, 1808; "The great regard I had for your grandfather, and for your grandmother, who was a beloved sister of my mother . . ." in *Correspondence Between the Hon. John Adams (Late President of the United States) and the Late Wm. Cunningham, Esq. (Beginning in 1803 and ending in 1812),* (E.M. Cunningham, Boston), 1823, p.54.

[7] John Adams to William Cunningham, January 16, 1804, *Ibid.,* pp.10–11.

[8] Letter 17, June 8, 1809, *Correspondence of the Late President Adams, Originally published in the Boston Patriot, In a Series of Letters, Number 1,* (Everett and Munroe, Boston), 1809, p.81.

[9] John Adams to William Cunningham, July 31, 1809, *Correspondence Between the Hon. John Adams (Late President of the United States)*

and the Late Wm. Cunningham, Esq. (Beginning in 1803 and ending in 1812), op. cit., p.151.

[10] There are numerous criticisms of Hamilton and Jefferson written by Adams in his unfortunate correspondence with Cunningham; the following should suffice: "Hamilton's ambition, intrigues, and caucusses [sic] have ruined the cause of federalism . . ." (p.28); "I found Hamilton at Trenton. He came to visit me. I said nothing to him upon politics. He began to give his advice unasked. I heard him with perfect good humour, though, never in my life, did I hear a man talk more like a fool." (p.48) Cunningham, in replying to Adams's letter of August 22, 1809, wrote, "Of all the qualities of a virtuous soul, pure integrity is the brightest–it takes no counsel from human law, nor from even the common propensities of our nature; the perfection from which it emanated, is its sole example and security–of this divine virtue, you have shewn [sic] me that Hamilton was totally destitute." (p.164) Regarding Jefferson, Adams wrote on January 16, 1804, "He always professed great friendship for me, even when, as it now appears, he was countenancing Freneau, Bache, Duane, and Callender." (p.10) Concluding the same letter, Adams wrote, "I wish him no ill. I envy him not. I shudder at the calamities, which I fear his conduct is preparing for his country: From a mean thirst of popularity, an inordinate ambition, and a want of sincerity." (pp.10–11). Cunningham's extraordinarily personal and negative reaction to Adams's criticisms was fundamental to the demise of their correspondence and perhaps played a part in the former's suicide.

[11] William Cunningham to John Adams, June 14, 1809, *Ibid.*, pp.126–27.

[12] John Adams to William Cunningham, June 22, 1809, *Ibid.*, pp.133–35.

[13] "I received, by the last mail, your esteemed favour of the 22nd inst. The united testimony of your most amiable family in repulsion of the calumny which was said to have originated with Mr. Whitney has not disappointed me. Should it become again a topic of your social board, I pray that my affectionate respects may go along with it to the company." William Cunningham to John Adams, June 30, 1809, *Ibid.*, pp.135–36.

[14] John Adams to William Cunningham, January 16, 1810, *Ibid.*, pp.216–17.

[15] *Ibid.*, pp. 216–17.

[16] William Cunningham to John Adams, January 21, 1812, *Ibid.*, p.219.

[17] Diary of Charles Francis Adams, Volume 1, Monday, May 17, 1824, *fn.;* please see *Founding Families: Digital Editions of the Papers of the Winthrops and the Adamses,* ed., C. James Taylor. Boston: Massachusetts Historical Society, 2007, www.masshist.org/ff/.

[18] Original grammar and syntax, and occasional odd spellings and sentence constructions, in the Adams-Jefferson correspondence have been retained. Letters of Rush and others are also not edited for grammar and syntax. Later letters of Adams were dictated to family members with unusual spelling errors occasionally resulting. These idiosyncratic spellings and language usage are all retained so that no modern prism of language might alter the meanings and character of the original materials. Where necessary [sic] has been parenthetically added.

[19] Jefferson to Adams, October 12, 1823, in *Correspondence*, v.2, p.599.

[20] *Ibid.*, v.2, p.600.

[21] *Ibid.*, v.2, p.600.

[22] *Ibid.*, v.2, p.600.

[23] Jefferson to Adams, October 12, 1823, *Correspondence*, v.2, p.601.

[24] Adams to Jefferson, November 10, 1823, in *Ibid.*, v.2, p.601.

[25] *Ibid.*, v.2, p.602.

[26] Adams to Jefferson, September 24, 1821, *Ibid.*, v.2, p.576.

Chapter Two: "An Affection That Can Never Die"

[1] "Daniel Webster visited Jefferson at Monticello toward the close of 1824. He quoted Jefferson as having said in conversation: 'John Adams was our Colossus on the floor. He was not graceful, nor elegant, nor remarkably fluent; but he came out, occasionally, with a power of thought and expression that moved us from our seats.'" *The Jeffersonian Cyclopedia,* edited by John P. Foley, (Funk & Wagnalls, New York), 1900; p.7, *fn.* Foley cites "A Discourse in Commemoration of the Lives and Services of John Adams and Thomas Jefferson, Delivered in Faneuil Hall, Boston, on the 2d of August, 1826," *The Great Speeches and Orations of Daniel Webster* by Edwin P. Whipple, (Little, Brown, & Co., Boston), 1886, p.166.

[2] *The Founding Fathers Reconsidered*, by R.B. Bernstein, (Oxford University Press), 2009, p.123.

[3] *Twilight at Monticello: The Final Years of Thomas Jefferson,* by Alan Pell Crawford, (Random House), 2008, p.86.

[4] Adams to Jefferson, July 3, 1813; *Correspondence*, v.2. p.350.

[5] Jefferson to Adams, August 10, 1815; *Ibid.*, v.2, p.453.

[6] Adams to Jefferson, July 12, 1822; *Ibid.*, v.2 p.582.

[7] *Passionate Sage: The Character and Legacy of John Adams*, by Joseph J. Ellis; (Norton, New York), 1993, p.114.

[8] Smith, *John Adams*, v.2, op. cit., p.1106.

[9] *Jefferson and His Time, Biography in Six Volumes, The Sage of Monticello*: Volume 6 by Dumas Malone; (Little, Brown), 1970, p.95.

[10] Adams to Jefferson, July 15, 1813, *Correspondence*, v.2, p.357.

[11] Jefferson to Adams, August 22, 1813, *Ibid.*, p.370.

[12] Smith, *John Adams*, op. cit., v.2, p.675.

[13] *Ibid.*, p.675.

[14] *Ibid.*, p.675.

[15] Bernstein, *The Founding Fathers Reconsidered*, op. cit., p.104.

[16] According to the Thomas Jefferson Foundation, "Jefferson himself made neither a public response nor any explicit reference to this issue, but a 1998 DNA study genetically linked her male descendants with male descendants of the Jefferson family. Based on documentary, scientific, statistical, and oral history evidence, the Thomas Jefferson Foundation and most historians believe that, years after his wife's death, Thomas Jefferson was the father of the six children of Sally Hemings mentioned in Jefferson's records." Cited in www.monticello.org/site/plantation-and-slavery/sally-hemings (accessed July 3, 2012; Sept. 25, 2015); For the *Report of the Research Committee on Thomas Jefferson and Sally Hemings*, see: www.monticello.org/site/plantation-and-slavery/report-research-committee-thomas-jefferson-and-sally-hemings (accessed July 3, 2012). For an erudite discussion of the Jefferson-Hemings relationship and associated allegations please also see Crawford, *Twilight at Monticello*, op. cit.

[17] "Presidential Difference in the Early Republic: The Highly Disparate Leadership Styles of Washington, Adams, and Jefferson" by Fred I. Greenstein, in *Presidential Studies Quarterly*, v.36, no.3 (September, 2006).

[18] David McCullough, *John Adams*, 2001; Joseph Ellis, *Passionate Sage*, 2001.

[19] Greenstein, p.379, quoting Alan Taylor, "John Adams" in *The Reader's Companion to the American Presidency*, edited by Alan Brinkley and Davis Dyer, (Houghton Mifflin, Boston), 2000.

[20] Adams to Jefferson, July 15, 1813; *Correspondence*, v.2, p.358.

[21] In an April 2, 1790, letter to his friend and fellow republican revolutionary the Marquis de Lafayette, Jefferson wrote that he had been informed of his appointment to the office "in the newspapers on the day of my arrival in Virginia." He added that he "had indeed been asked while in France, whether I would accept of any appointment at home, and I had answered that, not meaning to remain long where I was, I meant it to be the last office I should ever act in. Unfortunately," Jefferson dramatically concluded, "this letter had not arrived at the time of arranging the new Government." *The Writings of Thomas Jefferson*, v.8, Monticello Edition, Albert Bergh, Managing Editor, (Thomas Jefferson Memorial Association, Washington, DC), 1904, p.12.

[22] Adams to Jefferson, March 1, 1787; *Correspondence*, v.1, p.177.

[23] Jefferson to Adams, February 20, 1787, *Ibid.*, v.1, p.172.

[24] Jefferson to Abigail Adams, February 2, 1788, *Ibid.*, v.1, p.222.

[25] Adams to Jefferson, December 10, 1787; *Ibid.*, v.1, p.215.

[26] Adams to Jefferson, December 10, 1787; *Ibid.*, v.1, p.215.

[27] Adams to Jefferson, January 2, 1789; *Ibid.*, v.1, p 234.

[28] Nabby (Abigail) Adams Smith, Adams's daughter and eldest child. Married Colonel William Smith, June, 1786.

[29] Jefferson expected that his trip to the United States late in 1789 would be a leave only and that he'd be returning to Europe to continue his diplomatic mission. Washington appointed him first Secretary of State on September 29, 1789, instead. Please see: Cappon in *Correspondence*; v.1, p.239; and US Department of State: future.state.gov/when/timeline/1784_timeline/jefferson_first_secretary.html, (accessed July 8, 2012).

[30] Jefferson to Adams, May 10, 1789; *Correspondence*; v.1, pp.237–38.

[31] Jefferson to Adams, December 5, 1788; *Ibid.*, v.1, p.231.

[32] While it is acknowledged that Jefferson was at the head of the new party called "Democratic-Republicans," later known as "Republicans" and finally "Democrats," Adams was not considered the key "leader" of the Federalist Party. This role was played by Alexander Hamilton, former secretary of the treasury, major general in the Revolution, and aide-de-camp to Washington. Hamilton's behind-the-scenes party machinations and personal ambition would result in major impacts for several of Adams's cabinet officers and forever alienate him from Adams. Adams's position as president made him however the public face of the Federalist Party. In the years following Hamilton's 1804 death in a duel with then Vice President Aaron Burr at Weehawken, New Jersey, Adams's anger at Hamilton was undiminished, as clearly seen in his later bitter denunciations of Hamilton to Cunningham. Jefferson's view of Hamilton was also decidedly negative.

[33] John Adams to Benjamin Rush, October 10, 1808, *Old Family Letters copied From the Originals for Alexander Biddle,* edited by Alexander Biddle, Series A, (J.P. Lippincott Co., Philadelphia), 1892, p.204.

[34] *Ibid.*, p.204.

[35] This body of representatives of the three "estates" of France, nobility, church, and the "third estate" the common people, was convened by the King in 1788 as both a risky and desperate response to a critical financial crisis, and as a way to acknowledge the growing popular dissatisfaction with his rule. From the agitation of representatives of the third estate for a voice in national life, a revolu-

tionary concept in monarchical France, the National Assembly was born which was a direct challenge to the authority of the monarch. Once such an independent and powerful body had arisen the fiery undercurrents of revolution soon overtook both the king and the Estates-General.

36 For an excellent discussion of Jefferson's travels through the wine regions of France, Italy, etc., and his role as America's first wine connoisseur, please see *Passions: The Wines and Travels of Thomas Jefferson*, by James M. Gabler, (Bacchus Press: Baltimore), 1995.

37 Jefferson here is referring to King Louis XVI.

38 Jefferson to Abigail Adams, August, 9, 1786; *Correspondence*; v.1, p.149.

39 Gabler, *Passions: The Wines and Travels of Thomas Jefferson*, op. cit., p.28.

40 Jefferson to George Washington, May 2, 1788; *Ibid.*, p.157.

41 Jefferson to Adams, December 5, 1788; *Correspondence*, v.1, p.231.

42 *The French Revolution: A Very Short Introduction,* by William Doyle, (Oxford University Press: New York), 2001, p.33.

43 Jefferson to Count Diodati, March 29, 1807, in Foley, ed., *The Jeffersonian Cyclopedia*, op. cit., section 7518; for full text of letter please see: *Memoirs, Correspondence, and Private Papers of Thomas Jefferson*, edited by Thomas Jefferson Randolph, v.4, (Henry Colburn and Richard Bentley, London), 1829, p.69.

44 Jefferson to George Washington, December, 1788. p.770 in *The Jeffersonian Cyclopedia*, section: 7501.

45 "John Adams and the Coming of the French Revolution" by C. Bradley Thompson, *Journal of the Early Republic*, v.16, No. 3 (Autumn, 1996), pp.361–87 referencing Adams to Richard Rush, May 14, 1821, in Adams, ed., *Works of Adams*, v.10, p.397; Adams to Benjamin Rush, Aug. 28, 1811, in *The Spur of Fame: Dialogues of John Adams and Benjamin Rush*, 1805–1813 (San Marino, CA, 1966), p.134.

46 Adams and Jefferson were not alone in attributing the French Revolution to American antecedents. Georges Lefebvre, a noted French historian and authority of the Revolution, wrote just prior to WW2 that "the government crisis went back to the American war. The revolt of the English colonies may in fact be considered the principal direct cause of the French Revolution, both because in invoking the rights of man it stirred up great excitement in France, and because Louis XVI in supporting it got his finances into very bad condition." Georges Lefebvre, *The Coming of the French Revolution*, (Princeton University Press, New Jersey), 1947, 1979, p.21.

Chapter Three: "I Would Have Seen Half the Earth Desolated"

[1] Jefferson to Abigail Adams, February, 22, 1787; *Correspondence*, v.1, p.173.

[2] John Adams to Jefferson, December 6, 1787; *Ibid.*, p.213.

[3] *Jefferson and His Time, Biography in Six Volumes, Jefferson and the Ordeal of Liberty,* by Dumas Malone, v.3, (Little, Brown, Boston), 1962, pp.47–48. (Later citations of this multi-volume biography by Malone will include only cited volume number.)

[4] *Citizens* by Simon Schama, (Vintage, New York), 1990, quoted in *The Terror in the French Revolution,* by Hugh Gough, (Palgrave, UK and New York), 1998, p.4.

[5] Jefferson to William Smith, November 13, 1787. For a full transcript of the "Tree of Liberty" letter please see www.theatlantic.com/past/docs/issues/96oct/obrien/blood.htm (accessed July 15, 2012); or, for a sizable extract please see Thomas Jefferson Foundation, www.monticello.org/site/jefferson/tree-liberty-quotation (accessed October 6, 2013).

[6] "Governments are instituted among men, deriving their just powers from the consent of the governed. That whenever any form of government becomes destructive of these ends, it is the right of the people to alter or abolish it . . ." Preamble, Declaration of Independence, July 4, 1776.

[7] "He put himself under my guidance at nineteen or twenty years of age; he is to me therefore as an adopted son." Thomas Jefferson to John Trumbull, June 1, 1789; *Autobiography, Reminiscences and Letters of John Trumbull from 1756 to 1841*, (Wiley and Putman, New York), 1841, p.156.

[8] Please see Library of Congress website "The Early Republic" for more on William Short and Jefferson at: memory.loc.gov/ammem/collections/jefferson_papers/mtjtime3b.html, (accessed July 15, 2012); see Thomas Jefferson Foundation for a discussion of William Short and Jefferson at: www.monticello.org/site/research-and-collections/william-short, (accessed July 15, 2012).

[9] According to insightful nineteenth-century English historian and professor of modern history at Cambridge University, William Smyth, the leaders of the revolutionary government applauded the horrors and encouraged their repetition across the country. An official document from the Committee of Public Safety dated September third (as cited by Smyth), and signed by Danton then Executive Minister of Justice, as well as six members of the Committee, was sent to all the departments of France. This official communication supported the massacres and upped the ante considerably. "Aware that hordes of barbarians

are advancing against us," declared the signatories, "the commune of Paris hasten to inform their brothers of all the departments, that a number of the ferocious conspirators confined in the prisons have been put to death by the people, -an act of justice, which appeared to them indispensible, -to restrain by terror those legions of traitors lurking within the walls, at the moment that the citizens were going to march against the enemy; and no doubt the whole nation, after the long series of treasons which have led them to the brink of the abyss, will be eager to adopt these means, so useful and so necessary, and all the French will cry, like the Parisians, Let us march against the enemy, but do not let us leave behind us these brigands to cut the throats of our wives and children." (Smyth, pp.381–82.) Furthermore, in his extensive lectures on the Revolution, Smyth cites an unnamed memoir stating that "those who were working to preserve the salubrity of the air of the 3rd, 4th, and 5th of September . . ." [i.e., those killers who participated in the massacres] were afterwards paid by the Commune of Paris (Smyth, p.384). *Lectures on History: The French Revolution*, by William Smyth, v. 2, (William Pickering, J. & J.J. Deighton, Cambridge), 1842. French historian and Danton biographer Louis Madeline corroborates Smyth regarding the communication by Danton and members of the Committee (known as *An Account Rendered to the Sovereign People*) but with a caveat that since an associate of Danton "held the Minister's official stamp: in this case he probably affixed it without his master's leave. But even if we grant that Danton knew nothing about the matter, we must feel that his henchman was very sure his action would never be disavowed: and this fact, again, is not devoid of gravity. The best we can say, on the whole, is that Danton allowed the 'royalist' prisoners to be murdered without feeling any sense of indignation or making any attempt to put a stop to the bloodshed." *Danton,* by Louis Madelin, (Translated by Lady Mary Loyd), (Alfred A. Knopf, New York), 1921, p.198.

10 Schama, *Citizens,* op. cit., p.637.
11 *Men and Women of the French Revolution*, by Philip Gibbs, (Kegan Paul, Trench, Trubner, London), 1906, p.209.
12 For a thorough discussion of the destructive influence and pervasiveness of rumors in Paris during the Revolution, please see *The Coming of the Terror in the French Revolution*, by Timothy Tackett, (Belknap Press of Harvard University Press, Cambridge), 2015.
13 Barbaroux reported these comments of Marat: "Give me two hundred Neapolitans, armed with daggers and I will raise the revolution through France. Anarchy cannot cease until two hundred thousand heads have fallen . . . Let all the moderatists, constitutionalists, and partisans of the foreigner

be collected in the streets, and then slaughtered." Please see: "Marat: 'The Delirium of the Revolution,'" (author anonymous: possibly George Henry Calvert) *Temple Bar: A London Magazine for Town and Country Readers,* v.32, July, 1871, (Richard Bentley & Son: London), p.360. Note: George Henry Calvert was the author of "Mirabeau: An Historical Drama," (Riverside Press, Cambridge), 1873.

[14] *Ibid.,* p. 210.

[15] *Camille Desmoulins: A Biography,* by Violet Methley, (Martin Secker, London), 1914, p.46.

[16] *Among the Great Masters of Oratory: Scenes in the Lives of Famous Orators,* by Walter Rowlands, (Dana Estes & Co., Boston), 1901, p.187.

[17] *Ibid.,* p.189.

[18] *A History of the French Revolution,* by Henry Morse Stephens, v.1, (Charles Scribner's Sons, New York), 1905, p.130.

[19] Review of 'Etude Revolutionnaires' in *The Westminster Review,* Volume 55, July 1851, American Edition, Leonard Scott, and Co., New York, p.127.

[20] Gibbs, *Men and Women of the French Revolution,* op. cit., p.214.

[21] Methley, *Camille Desmoulins,* op. cit., p.88.

[22] *Ibid.,* p.122.

[23] *Danton: A Study,* by Hilaire Beloc, (Charles Scribner's Sons, New York), 1911, pp.250–51.

[24] "Friends, Enemies, and the Role of the Individual" by Marisa Linton, *A Companion of the French Revolution,* edited by Peter McPhee, (Wiley-Blackwell, West Sussex, UK), 2013, p.274.

[25] *Biographical Memoirs of The French Revolution,* by John Adolphus, F.S.A., v.1., (T. Cadell, Jun., and W. Davies, in the Strand:London), 1799, p.344.

[26] Several years before her marriage to Camille, Lucille Duplessis wrote in her Journal for June 1788 of a short discussion with her mother. "I came back, I filled in a bobbin. Before unwinding it, I asked Mother if she wanted to write something on the sheet of paper on which I was going to unwind. Mother wrote: 'Time flies as this thread between your fingers.'" Please see: "Writing and Measuring Time: Nineteenth-Century French Teenagers' Diaries," by Marilyn Himmesoete, in *Controlling Time and Shaping the Self: Developments in Autobiographical Writing Since the Sixteenth Century,* edited by Arianne Baggerman, Rudolf Dekker, & Michael Mascuch, (Brill, Leiden, The Netherlands), 2011, p.159.

[27] *Surviving the French Revolution: A Bridge Across Time,* by Bette W. Oliver, (Lexington Books, Plymouth, UK), 2013, p.28; See also, *Marriage and Revolution: Monsieur and Madame Roland,* by Siân Reynolds, (Oxford University Press, Oxford), 2012, p.145.

28 Gibbs, *Men and Women of the French Revolution*, op. cit., p.227.
29 Methley, *Camille Desmoulins*, op. cit., p.203.
30 Gibbs, *Men and Women of the French Revolution*, op. cit., p.369.
31 Gough, *The Terror in the French Revolution*, op. cit., p.56.
32 Speech of Saint-Just to the Convention, March 13, 1793; in *Twelve Who Ruled: The Year of the Terror in the French Revolution*, by R. R. Palmer, Bicentennial Edition, (Princeton University Press, Princeton, NJ), 1941, 1989, p.291.
33 *Camille Desmoulins and his Wife: Passages from the History of the Dantonists*, by Jules Claretie, (Translated by Mrs. Cashel Hoey), (Smith, Elder & Co., London), 1876, p.246.
34 Linton, "Friends, Enemies, and the Role of the Individual," *A Companion of the French Revolution*, op. cit., p.270.
35 *Brissot de Warville: A Study in the History of the French Revolution*, by Eloise Ellery, Ph.D. (Houghton Mifflin Company, Boston), 1915, p.243.
36 "Camille Desmoulins," by George Spencer Bower, *The Westminster and Foreign Quarterly Review*, July and October, 1882, New Series; v.62, (Trubner & Co., Ludgate Hill, Great Britain), 1882, p.53.
37 *Ibid.*, p.52.
38 Linton, "Friends, Enemies, and the Role of the Individual," op. cit., p.271.
39 "Danton and Camille Desmoulins," *Temple Bar: A London Magazine for Town and Country Readers*, v.32, July, 1871, op. cit., p.490.
40 *Ibid.*, p.487.
41 Violet Methley, a Desmoulins' biographer, identified Vilate as a "juror" of the tribunal, Claretie provides no title, and Carlyle describes him as "juryman Vilate." A recent historian however describes him as "a former judge on the revolutionary tribunal." *A Natural History of Revolution: Violence and Nature in the French Revolutionary Imagination, 1789–1794*, by Mary Ashburn Miller, (Cornell University, Ithaca), 2011, p.15; also, *The French Revolution: A History*, v.3, by Thomas Carlyle, (James Fraser, London), 1837, p.369. Vilate, in the introduction of his book, *Causes Secretes de la Revolution du 9 au 10   Thermidor, v.1*, (Paris), ("L'An III De La Republique") {9–1794/9–1795}, describes himself thusly: "J'ai ete jure au tribunal revolutionnnaire de paris, et je suis entre dans l'intimite des hommes, qui depuis le 31 mai 1793, ont joue les premiers roles sur le theatre sanglant de la revolution."
42 Methley, *Camille Desmoulins: A Biography,* op. cit., p.220.
43 Gibbs, *Men and Women of the French Revolution*, op. cit., p.233. (Gibbs cites Claretie as his source.)
44 *Ibid.*, p.233.

[45] "At what hour does your friend die?" (Robespierre) "Citizen, at nine o'clock precisely." (M. Legrand) "At nine o'clock! That is unfortunate! for you know I work late; and as I go to bed late, I rise late. I am much afraid I shall not be up in time to save your friend . . . but we shall see, we shall see!" Please see *Book of Days: A Miscellany of Popular Antiquities*, edited by R. Chambers, (W. & R. Chamber, London), 1864, p.134.

[46] Methley, op. cit., pp.259–60.

[47] *Ibid.*, p.261.

[48] Bower, "Camille Desmoulins," *The Westminster and Foreign Quarterly Review*, 62, op. cit., p.57.

[49] *Ibid., fn*, p.57. (Bower cites Fleury, v.2, p.157.)

[50] *Ibid.*, p.58.

[51] Methley, *Camille Desmoulins*, op. cit., p.273.

[52] Methley, *Ibid.*, p.314.

[53] Methley, *Ibid.*, p.314.

[54] Methley, *Ibid.*, p.314.

[55] Methley, *Ibid.*, p.314. Her rejected comforter was General Arthur Dillon, father of Lucie de la Tour du Pin Gouvernet.

[56] Smyth, *Lectures on History: The French Revolution*, 2, op. cit., pp.212–13. (Smyth cites the *Memoir* of Barbaroux as his source.)

[57] Jefferson to William Short, January 3, 1793; for full text: www.theatlantic.com/past/docs/issues/96oct/obrien/adam.htm (accessed July 15, 2012).

[58] Thomas Jefferson to William Short, January 3, 1793, *The Writings of Thomas Jefferson*, Definitive Edition, edited by Albert Ellery Bergh, v.9, (The Thomas Jefferson Memorial Association, Washington, DC), 1907, p.10.

[59] Barbaroux's *Memoir* was not published until 1822. It is unlikely that Jefferson was aware in early 1793 of Roland's comments. Please see: Encyclopaedia Brittanica, 1911, Vol 3, *Barbaroux, Charles Jean Marie*.

[60] *Ibid.*, p.10.

[61] *The True Believer*, by Eric Hoffer, (HarperCollins, New York), 1951:2002, p.32.

[62] Thomas Jefferson to William Short, January 3, 1793, *The Writings of Thomas Jefferson*, Definitive Edition, edited by Albert Ellery Bergh, v.9, op. cit., p.10.

[63] "Jefferson's proneness to express himself more vehemently in private letters and memoranda than in public papers and official communications does not make him unique among human beings." Malone, *Jefferson and the Ordeal of Liberty*, op. cit., p.45.

[64] Thomas Jefferson to William Short, January 3, 1793, *The Writings of Thomas Jefferson*, Definitive Edition, edited by Albert Ellery Bergh, op. cit., p.10.

65 "Thomas Jefferson: Radical and Racist," by Conor Cruise O'Brien, in *The Atlantic Monthly*, October, 1996; Volume 278, No. 4, pp.53–74. See: www.theatlantic.com/past/docs/issues/96oct/obrien/obrien.htm (accessed July 15, 2012; October 12, 2014).

66 *Ibid.*

67 Hoffer, *The True Believer*, op. cit., p.8.

68 *Jefferson and His Time*, volumes 1–6 by Dumas Malone, 1975 Pulitzer Prize for history.

69 Malone, *Jefferson and the Ordeal of Liberty*, op. cit., p.49.

70 *Ibid.*, p.45.

71 *The Long Affair: Thomas Jefferson and The French Revolution, 1785–1800*, by Conor Cruise O'Brien, (University of Chicago Press, 1996), p.322.

72 Adams to Jefferson, January 28, 1786; *Correspondence*, v.1, p.117.

73 Adams to Jefferson, May 1, 1812; *Ibid.*, v.2, p.301.

74 Adams to Jefferson, July 3, 1813; *Ibid.*, v.2, p.350.

75 *John Adams: A Character Sketch*, by Samuel Willard, M.D., LL.D., (HG Campbell, Milwaukee), 1898, 1903, p.56.

76 Jefferson to William Short, January 3, 1793, *The Writings of Thomas Jefferson*, Library Edition, edited by Albert Ellery Bergh, v.9, (Thomas Jefferson Memorial Association, Washington, DC), 1903, p.12.

77 Adams to Jefferson, January 31, 1796; *Correspondence*, v.1, p.259.

78 Jefferson to Adams, February 28, 1796; *Ibid.*, v.1, p.259.

79 Jefferson to Benjamin Stoddert, February 18, 1809, *The Writings of Thomas Jefferson*, edited by H. A. Washington, v.5, (Derby and Jackson, New York), 1859, p.427.

80 To a Mrs. Church, Jefferson wrote on November 27, 1793, "I shall be liberated from the hated occupations of politics, and remain in the bosom of my family, my farm, and my books." *The Jeffersonian Cyclopedia*, section: 6738. Please see also *Dutiful Correspondent: Philosophical Essays on Thomas Jefferson*, by M. Andrew Holowchak, (Rowan & Littlefield, Plymouth, UK), 2013, p.88.

81 In a May 1798 letter to his daughter Martha Jefferson Randolph, Jefferson wrote, "Politics and party hatreds destroy the happiness of every being here." *The Jeffersonian Cyclopedia*, op. cit., section: 6727.

82 *A review of the correspondence between the Hon. John Adams, and the late William Cunningham, ESQ., Beginning in 1803 and Ending in 1812*, by Timothy Pickering, (Cushing and Appleton, Salem), 1824.

83 Jefferson to Timothy Pickering, February, 27, 1821, in *The Life of Timothy Pickering*, by Charles Upham, v.4, (Little, Brown, & Co., Boston), 1873, p.327.

[84] Jefferson to Lafayette, April 2, 1790; *The Writings of Thomas Jefferson*, v.8, Monticello Edition, Albert Bergh, Managing Editor, (Thomas Jefferson Memorial Association, Washington, DC), 1904, p.13.

Chapter Four: "The Universal Destroyer"

[1] John Adams to Abigail Adams, March 9, 1797; Smith, *John Adams*, v.2, op. cit., p.917.

[2] "Under the new constitution (Year III) there were to be five Directors acting collectively as executive heads of state, one being replaced every year. Lots would be drawn each year to decide which one would leave." *A New Dictionary of the French Revolution*, by Richard Ballard, (I.B. Tauris & Co., Ltd., London), 2011, p.114.

[3] Jefferson to Adams, July 11, 1786; *Correspondence*, v.1, p.143.

[4] *The Old Regime and the Revolution* by Alexis De Tocqueville (translated by John Bonner), (Harper & Brothers, New York), 1856, p.24.

[5] *Ibid.*, p.24.

[6] *Ibid.*, p.24.

[7] *Ibid.*, p.21.

[8] *Ibid.*, pp.21–22.

[9] *Ibid.*, pp.26–27.

[10] *Ibid.*, p.27.

[11] *Ibid.*, p.36.

[12] "The Origins, Causes, and Extension of the Wars of the French Revolution and Napoleon," by Gunther E. Rothenberg in *The Journal of Interdisciplinary History*, v.18, No. 4, "The Origin and Prevention of Major Wars," (Spring, 1988), pp.771–93; p.778.

[13] *Ibid.*, p.781.

[14] "Improvising a Government in Paris in July, 1789," by Henry E. Bourne, in *American Historical Review*, Volume X, No. 2, January, 1905; pp.280–308; p.287.

[15] Jefferson to Jean Pierre Brissot de Warville, May 8, 1793, in *The Works of Thomas Jefferson in Twelve Volumes*, Federal Edition, edited by Paul Leicester Ford, v.7, (G.P. Putnam's Sons, New York), 1904, p.322.

[16] Bourne, *Improvising a Government in Paris in July, 1789*, op. cit., p.298.

[17] Bourne, *Ibid.*, pp.298–99.

[18] De Tocqueville, *Old Regime and the Revolution,* op. cit., p.14.

[19] *A Critical Dictionary of the French Revolution* by François Furet, Mona Ozouf, (Harvard University Press, Cambridge), 1989, p.226.

[20] Lafayette to George Washington, March 17, 1790, National Archives; Founders Online: founders.archives.gov/documents/Washington/05-05-02-0159, (accessed October 6, 2013); Source: *The Papers of George Wash-*

ington, Presidential Series, *16 January 1790–30 June 1790,* v.5; ed. Dorothy Twohig, Mark A. Mastromarino, and Jack D. Warren. Charlottesville: University Press of Virginia, 1996, pp.241–43. Please also see www.monticello.org/site/jefferson/marquis-de-lafayette, (accessed October 19, 2014).

21 Lafayette to Washington, January 22, 1792, in *Lafayette in Two Worlds,* by Lloyd Kramer, (University of North Carolina Press, Chapel Hill), 1996; p.42; and, National Archives; Founders Online: founders.archives.gov/documents/Washington/05–09-02–0289, (accessed October 6, 2013); Source: *The Papers of George Washington,* Presidential Series, *23 September 1791–1729 February 1792,* v.9, ed. Mark A. Mastromarino. Charlottesville: University Press of Virginia, 2000, pp.493–95.

22 For a general introduction to Battle of Barren Hill, May 18, 1778, please see "About General Lafayette, The Man and His Times. From Valley Forge to Barren Hill and Back," by Rudy Cusumano at American Friends of Lafayette: www.friendsoflafayette.org/barren_hill.html, (accessed October 6, 2013).

23 De Tocqueville, *Old Regime and the Revolution,* op. cit., p.16.

24 *Ibid.,* p.16.

25 Rothenberg, "The Origins, Causes, and Extension of the Wars of the French Revolution and Napoleon," op. cit., p.789.

26 *Ibid.,* p.790.

Chapter Five: "Their Virtuous Enterprise"

1 *Diary of Charles Francis Adams,* August 29, 1824, v.1, p.304; *Founding Families: Digital Editions of the Papers of the Winthrops and the Adamses,* ed.C. James Taylor. Boston: Massachusetts Historical Society, 2007. Online at: www.masshist.org/publications/apde/portia.php?-mode=p&id=DCA01p305, (accessed May 26, 2013).

2 *Ibid.,* p.304.

3 *Ibid.,* p.305.

4 Smith, *John Adams,* v.2, op. cit., p.1133.

5 Crawford, *Twilight at Monticello: The Final Years of Thomas Jefferson,* op. cit., p.202.

6 Please see: www.monticello.org/site/research-and-collections/paris-residences, (accessed October 19, 2014).

7 Malone, *Jefferson and the Rights of Man,* p.223.

8 Crawford, *Twilight at Monticello: The Final Years of Thomas Jefferson,* op. cit., p.202.

[9] Jefferson to James Madison, January 30, 1787, in *The Works of Thomas Jefferson*, Federal Edition, v.5, edited by Paul Leicester Ford, (G.P. Putnam's Sons, New York), 1904, p.258.

[10] This injury occurred in the midst of Jefferson's likely unconsummated Parisian courtship with the married Maria Cosway.

[11] "In a former letter, I mentioned to you the dislocation of my wrist. I can make not the least use of it, except for the single article of writing, though it is going on five months since the accident happened . . . I have great anxieties, lest I should never recover any considerable use of it." See, Jefferson to James Madison, January 30, 1787, *The Works of Thomas Jefferson*, Federal Edition, v.5, ed., Ford., (1904), op. cit., p.260.

[12] Jefferson to Madison, January 30, 1787, *Ibid.*, p.255.

[13] *Ibid.*, p.256.

[14] Jefferson to Madison, January 30, 1787, *Ibid.*, p.256.

[15] *Ibid.*, p.258.

[16] Jefferson's January, 30, 1787 letter to Madison, also quoted on page 3 of this book.

[17] Jefferson to Madison, January 30, 1787, *The Works of Thomas Jefferson*, Federal Edition, v.5, Ford, ed., (1904), op. cit., p.259.

[18] *Ibid.*, p.260.

[19] Adams to Jefferson, December 6, 1787; *Correspondence*, v.1, p.213.

[20] *Ibid.*, p.213.

[21] *Ibid.*, p.213.

[22] "As often as elections happen, the danger of foreign influence recurs. The less frequently they happen the less danger. . . . Elections, my dear sir, Elections to offices which are great objects of Ambition, I look at with terror." Adams to Jefferson, December 6, 1787; *Correspondence*, v.1, p.214.

[23] For perhaps reasons too obvious to enunciate, Adams no longer feared elections by the time of his inaugural, viz., "There may be little solidity in an ancient idea that congregations of men into cities and nations are the most pleasing objects in the sight of superior intelligences, but this is very certain, that to a benevolent human mind there can be no spectacle presented by any nation more pleasing, more noble, majestic, or august, than an assembly like that which has so often been seen in this and the other Chamber of Congress, of a Government in which the Executive authority, as well as that of all the branches of the Legislature, are exercised by citizens selected at regular periods by their neighbors to make and execute laws for the general good. Can anything essential, anything more than mere ornament and decoration, be added to this by robes and diamonds?" Inaugural address of President John Adams,

March 4, 1797, Philadelphia. For full text please see: avalon.law.yale. edu/18th_century/adams.asp.

24 "The Jefferson-Adams Rupture and the First French Translation of John Adams 'Defence,'" by Joyce Appleby, in *The American Historical Review*, v.73, No. 4, (Apr., 1968), pp.1084–91; see p.1090.

25 *Ibid.*

26 Thompson, "John Adams and the Coming of the French Revolution," op. cit., p.379.

27 "The Dream of Benjamin Rush: The Reconciliation John Adams and Thomas Jefferson" by L.H. Butterfield; *The Yale Review*, Volume XL, December, 1950, No. 2, p.302.

28 "Returning to the bosom of my country after a painful separation from it for ten years, I had the honor to be elected to a station under the new order of things, and I have repeatedly laid myself under the most serious obligations to support the Constitution. The operation of it has equaled the most sanguine expectations of its friends, and from an habitual attention to it, satisfaction in its administration, and delight in its effects upon the peace, order, prosperity, and happiness of the nation I have acquired an habitual attachment to it and veneration for it. What other form of government, indeed, can so well deserve our esteem and love?" Inaugural address of President John Adams, March 4, 1797, Philadelphia. For full text please see: avalon.law.yale.edu/18th_century/adams. asp, (accessed September 26, 2015).

29 First French edition published 1792; *Correspondence*, v.1, p.175, *fn.*

30 Appleby, "The Jefferson-Adams Rupture and the First French Translation of John Adams' Defence," op. cit., p.1090.

31 Jefferson to Adams, February 23, 1787; *Correspondence*, v.1, p.174.

32 Jefferson to Adams, July 7, 1785; *Ibid.*, v.1, p.38.

33 Jefferson to Adams, February 23, 1787; *Ibid.*, v.1, p.174.

34 Appleby, op. cit., p.1090.

35 Ellis, *Passionate Sage: The Character and Legacy of John Adams,* op. cit., p.131.

36 Jefferson to Adams, December 31, 1787; *Correspondence*, v.1, p.219.

37 Jefferson to Mr. Lehré, November 8, 1808; *The Jeffersonian Cyclopedia*, section: 2517, op. cit., p.287.

38 "President Jefferson signs the Embargo Act, putting a halt to all trading with any country in the entire world." Presidential Key Events, Thomas Jefferson; Miller Center, University of Virginia; millercenter.org/president/jefferson/key-events, (accessed September 1, 2013).

39 " . . .The question was simply between that (Embargo) and war." Jefferson to Charles Pinckney, March 1808, *The Jeffersonian Cyclopedia*, op. cit., section: 2528, p.288.

[40] Jefferson to Mr. Lehré, November 1808; *The Jeffersonian Cyclopedia*, *Ibid.*, section: 2517, p.287.

[41] For a thorough discussion of the failure of Confederate trade policy and the frustrated attempt to pressure European powers to intercede in the American Civil War by withholding Southern cotton exports, please see: Frank Owsley, *King Cotton Diplomacy: Foreign Relations of the Confederate States of America* (originally published 1931).

[42] *George Washington, First in Peace*, by John Alexander Carroll and Mary Wells Ashworth, v.7, (Charles Scribner's Sons, New York), 1957; pp.33–34.

Chapter Six: "I Know You Too Well to Fear"

[1] "Adams wrote the Defence and the Davila essays, in large measure, to counter the a priori, hyper-rationalist tradition of political science that had begun with Descartes and was now reaching its logical conclusion in Condorcet. Adams was suspicious, if not overtly contemptuous, of all theories, hypotheses, or conjectures that could not be demonstrated empirically or inferred from observation and the experimental laboratory of history." "John Adams and the Coming of the French Revolution," C. Bradley Thompson, *Journal of the Early Republic*, v.16, No. 3, (Autumn, 1996), pp.361–87; pp.374–75.

[2] Smith, *John Adams*, v.2, op. cit., p.801.

[3] *Ibid.*, v.2, p.801.

[4] *Ibid.*, v.2, p.802.

[5] *The Age of Federalism-The Early American Republic, 1788–1800,* by Stanley Elkins & Eric McKitrick, (Oxford University Press, 1993), p.237.

[6] *George Washington: A Life,* by Willard Sterne Randall, (Henry Holt and Company, New York), 1997, p.470.

[7] Jefferson to Washington, May 8, 1791; *The Writings of Thomas Jefferson*, edited by H. A. Washington, v.3, (H.W. Derby, New York), 1861, p.257; also at National Archives: Founders Online, source: *The Papers of Thomas Jefferson*, v.20, *1 April–4 August 1791*, ed. Julian P. Boyd. Princeton: Princeton University Press, 1982, pp.291–92; founders.archives.gov/documents/Jefferson/01–20–02–0076-0003, (accessed October 6, 2013).

[8] *Ibid.*, p.257, and National Archives: Founders Online, *Ibid.*

[9] *Ibid.*, p.258; and National Archives: Founders Online. *Ibid.*

[10] Tobias Lear to George Washington, May 8, 1791; *The Writings of George Washington*, v.12, edited by Worthington Chauncey Ford, (Putnam-Knickerbocker Press, New York), 1891, pp.38–39; and *The Writ-*

ings of George Washington by Jared Sparks, v.10, (Russell, Shattuck and Williams, et al., Boston), 1836, p.162 *fn.*

11 Jefferson to Adams, July 17, 1791; *Correspondence*, v.1, p.246.

12 *Ibid.*, p.246.

13 Adams to Jefferson, July 29, 1791, *Ibid.*, p.247.

14 *Ibid.*, pp.247–48.

15 Adams to Jefferson, July 29, 1791, *Correspondence*, v.1, p.250.

16 *Ibid.*, pp.248–49.

17 *Ibid.*, p.249.

18 Thomas Jefferson to Thomas Paine, July 29, 1791, *The Writings of Thomas Jefferson*, v.5, 1788–1792, Letter Press Edition, edited by Paul Leicester Ford, (G.P. Putnam's Sons, New York), 1895, p.367. Please see also O'Brien, *The Long Affair: Thomas Jefferson and the French Revolution, 1785–1800*, (University of Chicago Press, 1996), p.109.

19 "Like Burr, Thomas Jefferson found strength in secrecy, in silence. Shy and aloof, he seldom made eye contact with listeners yet could be a warmly engaging presence among small groups of like-minded intimates . . . The plain dress, mild manners, and unassuming air were the perfect costume for a crafty man intent upon presenting himself as the spokesman for the common people." *Alexander Hamilton,* by Ron Chernow, (The Penguin Press, New York), 2004, p.311.

20 Jefferson is referring to his unintentionally published preface to the "Rights of Man" pamphlet.

21 Jefferson to Adams, August 30, 1791; *Correspondence*, v.1, p.250.

22 *Ibid.*, p.250.

23 *Ibid.*, p.251.

24 Emphasis in original.

25 Jefferson to Adams, August 30, 1791; *Correspondence*, v.1. p.251.

26 Jefferson to Adams, April 25, 1794; *Ibid.*, p.253.

27 Adams to Jefferson, May 11, 1794; *Ibid.*, p.255.

28 *Ibid.*, p.255.

29 "George Washington, First in Peace," v.7, by Douglas Southall Freeman (completed by J. A. Carroll and M. W. Ashworth), (1957), p.418.

30 *Ibid.*, p.32.

31 Jefferson to James Sullivan, February 9, 1797, *The Works of Thomas Jefferson,* Federal Edition (G.P. Putnam's Sons, New York), 1904–1905, v.8, p.195. Note: Carroll and Ashworth in *Washington*, v.7, (1957), erroneously cite the date of this letter as February 8, 1796; see p.425, *fn* 99.

32 Jefferson to Adams, December 28, 1796; letter never sent to Adams; *Correspondence*, v.1, p.262.

33 *Ibid.*, v.1, p.262.

34 *Ibid.*, v.1, p.263.

35 "Indeed it is possible that you may be cheated out of your succession by a trick worthy the subtlety of your arch-friend of New York, who has been able to make of your real friends tools to defeat their and your just wishes." *Ibid.*, v.1, p.263.

36 *Ibid.*, v.1, p.263.

37 *Ibid.*, v.1, p.263.

38 "Jefferson, Man of Ideas," by Louis B. Wright, *The Yale Review*, Volume XL, September 1950, No. 1; p.160.

39 Jefferson to Madison, January 1, 1797; *Correspondence*, v.1, p.262, *fn* 54.

40 Madison to Jefferson, January 15, 1797; *The Writings of James Madison, comprising his Public Papers and his Private Correspondence, including his numerous letters and documents now for the first time printed,* Gaillard Hunt, ed., v.6, (G.P. Putnam's Sons, New York), 1900. Chapter: *1797: TO THOMAS JEFFERSON. mad. mss.* oll.libertyfund. org/title/1941/124440, (accessed September 9, 2012).

41 Elkins & McKitrick, *The Age of Federalism*, op. cit., p.540.

42 John Adams to Abigail Adams, January 3, 1797, *Ibid.*, p.540; and Smith, *John Adams*, v.2, op. cit., p.910.

Chapter Seven: "We Came to Fifth Street, Where Our Road Separated"

1 The George Washington Papers at the Library of Congress; Time Line: The Early Republic, memory.loc.gov/ammem/gwhtml/gwtimeer.html, (accessed September 2, 2013).

2 Washington's *Farewell Address*, September 19, 1796; for the full text please see: www.gpo.gov/fdsys/pkg/GPO-CDOC-106sdoc21/pdf/GPO-CDOC-106sdoc21.pdf, or here: avalon.law.yale.edu/18th_century/washing.asp.

3 Smith, *John Adams*, v.2, op. cit., p.1030.

4 "French Opinion as a Factor in Preventing War Between France and the United States, 1795–1800," by James Alton James, *The American Historical Review*, v.30, No. 1 (Oct., 1924), pp.44–55, Published by: The University of Chicago Press on behalf of the American Historical Association, p.46.

5 John Adams to John Quincy Adams, March 31, 1797; quoted in Elkins & McKitrick, *Age of Federalism*, op. cit., p.558; capitalization in original.

6 Malone, *Ordeal of Liberty*, v.3, op. cit., p.297.

7 *Ibid.*, p.296.

8 *Ibid.*, p.297.

9   Bernstein, *The Founding Fathers Reconsidered*, op. cit., p.83.

10 Abigail Adams to John Adams, May 23, 1797. *Adams Family Papers: An Electronic Archive.* Massachusetts Historical Society; www.masshist.org/digitaladams/, (accessed October 1, 2012).

11 John Adams to Abigail Adams, March 5, 1797, *Letters of John Adams Addressed to His Wife,* edited by Charles Francis Adams, v.2, (Charles C. Little and James Brown, Boston), 1841; p.244. Please see p.52, *fn* 1 of this book.

12 *Our Political Drama, Conventions, Campaigns, Candidates,* by Joseph Bucklin Bishop (Scott-Thaw, New York), 1904, p.176.

13 John Adams to Abigail Adams, March 9, 1797; *Ibid.*, p.247.

14 *Ibid.*, p.247.

15 *Ibid.*, p.247.

16 Abigail Adams to John Adams, March 25, 1797; *Adams Family Papers: An Electronic Archive.* Massachusetts Historical Society. www.masshist.org/digitaladams/, (accessed October 1, 2012).

17 *Ibid.*

18 Inaugural Address of John Adams, March 4, 1797; available online at avalon.law.yale.edu/18th_century/adams.asp, (accessed September 22, 2012).

19 Elkins & McKitrick, *Age of Federalism*, op. cit., pp.541–42.

20 William Paterson to James Iredell, March 7, 1797; *The Presidency of John Adams – The Collapse of Federalism, 1795–1800*, (University of Pennsylvania Press, 1957), p.222*; Party of the People—A History of the Democrats*, by Jules Witcover, (Random House, New York), 2003, includes an inexact version of this quote on p.51.

21 Willard, *John Adams: A Character Sketch*, op. cit., p.105.

22 Letter XIII, John Adams, May 29, 1809, published in the *Boston Patriot* cited in *The Works of John Adams, Second President of the United States with a Life of the Author*, by Charles Francis Adams, v.9, (Little, Brown and Company, Boston), 1854, pp.284–85.

23 *Ibid.*, p.282.

24 *Ibid.*, p.285.

25 Adams here is referring to bitter partisan rhetoric.

26 Letter XIII, John Adams, May 29, 1809, *Boston Patriot* cited in *The Works of John Adams, Second President of the Unite States with a Life of the Author*, by Charles Francis Adams, v.9, op. cit., p.285.

27 *The Writings of Thomas Jefferson: Memoir, Correspondence, and Miscellanies,* edited by Thomas Jefferson Randolph, v.4, (F. Carr and Co., Charlottesville), 1829, p.501.

28 *Ibid.*, p.501.

29 *Ibid.*, p.502.

30 *Ibid.*, p.502.

[31] *American Creation* by Joseph J. Ellis, (Vintage, New York), 2008, p.206. The author states that the night walk occurred on the "evening before the Adams inauguration," which does not match Jefferson's date for the event, "Monday the 6th of March."

[32] *The Writings of Thomas Jefferson: Memoir, Correspondence, and Miscellanies,* edited by Thomas Jefferson Randolph, v.4, op. cit., p.502.

[33] Thomas Jefferson to James Madison, January 27, 1797, *Memoirs, Correspondence and Private Papers of Thomas Jefferson,* edited by Thomas Jefferson Randolph, v.3, (Henry Colburn and Richard Bentley, London), 1829, p.353.

[34] Malone, *Jefferson and the Ordeal of Liberty,* v.3, op. cit., p.334.

[35] Thomas Jefferson to James Madison, January 27, 1797; *Memoirs, Correspondence and Private Papers of Thomas Jefferson,* edited by Thomas Jefferson Randolph, v.3, op. cit., p.353.

[36] United States Senate biography of Thomas Jefferson, 2nd Vice President (1797–1801); www.senate.gov/artandhistory/history/common/generic/VP_Thomas_Jefferson.htm, (accessed September 29, 2012).

[37] John Adams to Abigail Adams, March 13, 1797, *Adams Family Papers: An Electronic Archive.* Massachusetts Historical Society. www.masshist.org/digitaladams/, (accessed October 1, 2012).

[38] John Adams was then Minister to the Court of St. James in London. Polly arrived on the English coast on her way to meet her father in Paris. John and Abigail took Polly and Sally Hemings in and cared for them for several weeks, during which time a great bond of love grew between Abigail and Polly. Abigail was devastated when Polly died at the young age of twenty-five, in 1804. The death of Polly evinced a letter of sympathy from her to Jefferson and prompted a correspondence for a short time between the two. It must be also noted that Sally Hemings accompanied Polly on the voyage to France and stayed with her throughout her time in Europe as servant and minder. Hemings would have been approximately fourteen years old when she arrived in England. Abigail, for her part, found little of note in Sally Hemings and was concerned that she was not qualified by temperament to care for the younger Polly. Genealogist Helen F. M. Leary, author of an influential 2001 article on the Jefferson-Hemings relationship, believes that Jefferson's sexual involvement with Miss Hemings began in France ("Sally Hemings's Children: A Genealogical Analysis of the Evidence" in The National Genealogical Society Quarterly, September, 2001). Pulitzer Prize-winning historian, Jon Meacham, in *Thomas Jefferson: The Art of Power* (Random House, 2012), wrote of the arrival of Polly and Sally Hemings in Paris during the summer of 1797, that "in this tempestuous time, Jefferson apparently began a sexual relationship with his late wife's enslaved half sister," (Meacham, p.216).

[39] Abigail Adams to John Adams, March 25, 1797, *Adams Family Papers: An Electronic Archive.* Massachusetts Historical Society. www.massh-ist.org/digitaladams/, (accessed October 1, 2012).

[40] Malone, *Jefferson and the Ordeal of Liberty*, v.3, op. cit., p.296.

[41] Smith, John Adams, v.2, op. cit., p.924.

[42] Jefferson to Edmund Randolph, June 27, 1797; quoted in *John Marshall: Definer of a Nation*, by Jean Edward Smith, (Henry Holt, 1996), p.190.

Chapter Eight: "Conceal the Lever"

[1] "Washington's Farewell Address: A Foreign Policy of Independence," by Samuel Flagg Bemis, *The American Historical Review*, v.39, No. 2 (Jan., 1934), pp.250–68; p.263.

[2] Diplomatic correspondence of Ambassador Adet, quoted in Bemis, *Ibid.*, p.263.

[3] Bemis, *Ibid.*, pp.257–58.

[4] *The Moniteur*, quoted in "Early French Policy Toward the United States," by Donald H. Nicholson, *Bulletin of the Chicago Historical Society*, January, 1926, v.3, n.7, p.57. As a preface to this quote, Nicholson wrote, "France expected a profound gratitude from Americans for the aid which she gave them during the Revolution."

[5] "Jefferson's fear of war was nothing if not genuine. Indeed, it was so profound that he was not only unwilling but quite unable to grasp the prudential side of Adams's policy; to him, negotiation could not be coupled with measures of defense; the two were simply incompatible." Elkins & McKitrick, *The Age of Federalism*, op. cit., p.555.

[6] *The Diplomacy of the United States, Being an Account of the Foreign Relations of the Country, from the first treaty with France, in 1778, to the treaty of Ghent, in 1814, with Great Britain*, by Theodore Lyman, (Wells and Lilly, Boston), 1826, p.77. (Hereafter "The Diplomacy of the United States.")

[7] Bemis, "Washington's Farewell Address: A Foreign Policy of Independence," op. cit., p.254.

[8] Bemis, *Ibid.*, p.255.

[9] Bemis, *Ibid.*, p.255., (cit. #12-Arch. Aff. ttr., ttats-Unis, v.42, f. 445).

[10] Bemis, *Ibid*, p.256.

[11] Monroe to Secretary of State, April 14, 1795; Bemis, *Ibid.*, p.256.

[12] Bemis, *Ibid.*, p.256. Bemis's citation for this allegation is as follows: Monroe to the minister of foreign affairs, Paris, Feb. 17, 1796 (28 pluviose, an IV.), Arch. Af. ttr., Etats-Unis, v.45, f. I46.

[13] *The New American Cyclopedia*, v.1, "John Adams," edited by George Ripley and Charles Dana, (D. Appleton and Co., 1868), p.95.

[14] Letter of Otto to Monroe and others, March 20, 1797; in "The Directory and the United States," by E. Wilson Lyon, *American Historical Review*, v.43, No. 13; (April, 1938), pp.514–32; p.517.

[15] Delacroix to Adet, January 3, 1797; Lyon, *Ibid.*, p.517.

[16] Lyon, *Ibid.*, p.524. (The author cites the following French source: *Considerations sur la conduite du Gouvernement des Etats-Unis envers la France depuis 1789 jusqu'en 1797*, messidor, an 5 [June 19–July 18, 1797], par M. Otto, A.A.E., Ettats-Unis, v.47, f. 414.)

[17] "French Opinion as a Factor in Preventing War Between France and the United States, 1795–1800," by James Alton James, *The American Historical Review*, v.30, No. 1 (Oct., 1924), pp.44–55; Published by: The University of Chicago Press on behalf of the American Historical Association, p.44.

[18] Lyon, "The Directory and the United States," op. cit., p.515.

[19] Adet to Delacroix, October 3, 1796, in Lyon, *Ibid.*, p.517.

[20] Lyon, *Ibid.*, p.517.

[21] Bemis, "Washington's Farewell Address: A Foreign Policy of Independence," op. cit., p.267.

[22] Lyon, "The Directory and the United States," op. cit., p.516.

[23] "Jay's Treaty at last having gone into effect, the French Directory prepared its denunciation of the treachery of Washington's government. As a warning to the American people of worse things to follow if President Washington were continued in office it decided to suspend Adet's functions, and with them formal diplomatic relations with the United States." Please see Bemis, "Washington's Farewell Address: A Foreign Policy of Independence," op. cit., p.264.

[24] A previous Treaty that existed between France and the United States since 1778 is a case in point. "The 16th article of the Treaty was alternately violated and respected in the course of the year '93 no less than five times." See Lyman, *The Diplomacy of the United States, Being an Account of the Foreign Relations of the Country, from the first treaty with France, in 1778, to the treaty of Ghent, in 1814, with Great Britain*, op. cit., p.80.

[25] Both Britain and France had participated in attacks on American ships and confiscation of goods, with the British engaging in the heinous practice of forced impressments of American sailors since the onset of hostilities in 1793. The American government therefore was forced to choose between two hostile parties. The French had successfully made themselves obnoxious to Washington, thus driving the United States into the camp of the British. Please see, *The Age of Federalism*, p.538.

[26] Crawford, *Twilight at Monticello – The Final Years of Thomas Jefferson*, op. cit., p.30.

27 Lyon, "The Directory and the United States," op. cit., p.518.

28 Lyman, *The Diplomacy of the United States*, op. cit., p.85.

29 "Munitions of war were on the request of the American government to be furnished by Great Britain, and a portion of her fleet, manned by American seamen and with British officers, was tendered for the protection of American commerce." See James, "French Opinion as a Factor in Preventing War Between France and the United States, 1795–1800," op. cit., p.49.

30 Otto, "Considerations on the Conduct of the Government of the United States toward France, 1789–1797," June, 1797; cited in James, *Ibid.*, p.47.

31 Adams speech to Joint House of Congress, May 16, 1797.

32 Adams's speech to the Congress of May 16, 1797, is available in its entirety at Yale University Law School, online: avalon.law.yale.edu/18th_century/ja97–03.asp, (accessed October 14, 2012).

33 Jefferson to Peregrine Fitzhugh, June 4, 1797; in Malone, *Ordeal of Liberty*, v.3, op. cit., p.321.

34 Malone, *Ibid.*, p.321

35 Smith, *John Adams*, v.2, op. cit., p.940.

36 John Adams to Uriah Forrest, June 20, 1797, in Smith, *Ibid.*, v.2, p.940.

37 Malone, *Ordeal of Liberty*, v.3, op. cit., p.322.

38 John Adams to John Quincy Adams, November 3, 1797; in Smith, *John Adams,* v.2, op. cit., p.940.

39 Lyon, "The Directory and the United States," op. cit., p.518.

40 "The American Mission of Citizen Pierre-August Adet: Revolutionary Chemistry and Diplomacy in the Early Republic," by Michael F. Conlin, *The Pennsylvania Magazine of History and Biography*, v.124, No.4 (Oct., 2000), pp.489–520; p.519.

41 Conlin, *Ibid.*, p.519.

42 Lyon, "The Directory and the United States," op. cit., p.518.

43 Gerry's list of accomplishments is impressive: signer of the Declaration of Independence, signer of the Articles of Confederation, member of the Continental Congress, delegate to the Constitutional Convention, member of the House of Representatives, and later, two-term governor of Massachusetts. See Elkins & McKitrick, *Age of Federalism*, op. cit., p.566.

44 "Whereas the phrase in the Declaration of Independence 'All men are created equal,' was suggested by the Italian patriot and immigrant Philip Mazzei;" in *Joint Resolution of the House #175 of the 103rd Congress, 2nd Session*, "Designating October 1993 and October 1994 as 'Italian-American Heritage Month;'" John F. Kennedy also cited Mazzei in his book, *A Nation of Immigrants,* (Harper Perennial, New York), 1964,

2008; pp.15–16; "The great doctrine 'All men are created equal,' incorporated in the Declaration of Independence by Thomas Jefferson, was paraphrased from the writing of Phillip Mazzei, an Italian-born patriot and pamphleteer, who was a close friend of Jefferson."

45 "We gave in its chronological place a letter of Mr Jefferson to Philip Mazzei, dated April 24th 1796. The latter, having no permission so to do, published an Italian translation of it in Florence on the first of January 1797. From thence it appeared . . .", *The Life of Thomas Jefferson*, by Henry Stephens Randall, (Derby and Jackson, New York), 1858; v.2, p.361. Randall's statement that a translation first appeared in Italian in Florence is contradicted by the editors of the Thomas Jefferson Papers.

46 *The Papers of Thomas Jefferson, Volume 29: 1 March 1796 to 31 December 1797* (Princeton University Press, 2002), pp.73–88; online at www.princeton.edu/~tjpapers/mazzei/index.html#notes, (accessed October 20, 2012).

47 James Madison to N.P. Trist, May, 1832, in Malone, *Ordeal of Liberty*, v.3, op. cit., p.268.

48 *Party of the People-A History of the Democrats,* by Jules Witcover, op. cit., p.55.

49 *The Papers of Thomas Jefferson, Volume 29: 1 March 1796 to 31 December 1797*, op. cit., pp.86–87, online at http://jeffersonpapers.princeton. edu/selected-documents/extract-and-commentary-printed-new-york-minerva, (accessed September 8, 2015). Parenthetical comments are from the *Minerva* version of Jefferson's letter, and are supplied because this is the version of the letter that was placed by Webster before the American people.

50 Thomas Jefferson to General Washington, November 14, 1786, *The Writings of Thomas Jefferson*, edited by H. A. Washington, v.2, (Derby and Jackson, New York), 1859, p.62.

51 Thomas Jefferson to Martin Van Buren, June 29, 1824, *Works of Thomas Jefferson*, edited by Paul Leicester Ford, v.12, (G.P. Putnam's Sons, New York), 1905, p.368.

52 Thomas Jefferson to Martin Van Buren, June 29, 1824, *Ibid.*, v.12, p.366.

53 *Ibid.*, p.369.

54 *The Life of Thomas Jefferson*, Randall, v.2, op. cit., p.364.

55 *Jefferson and The American Democracy*, by Cornelius Henri de Witt, (Longman, London), 1862, p.213.

56 *The Life and Times of Noah Webster: An American Patriot,* by Harlow Giles Unger, (John Wiley & Sons, 1998), p.218.

57 Thomas Jefferson to James Madison, August 12, 1801, *Works of Jefferson,* edited by Paul Leicester Ford, v.9 (of 12), Federal Edition, (G.P. Putnam's Sons, New York), 1905, p.285.

58 *The Pirate Coast: Thomas Jefferson, the First Marines, and the Secret Mission of 1805*, by Richard Zacks, (Hyperion, New York), 2005, p.219. The author does not provide a source for these quotes from the overseer at Mount Vernon. In addition, there appears to be some confusion as to the identity of Mr. Albin Rawlins, described by Mr. Zacks as "an overseer at Mount Vernon." The website of Mount Vernon Ladies' Association of the Union (caretakers of Mount Vernon) describes Albin Rawlins as "George Washington's Secretary" while Mr. George Rawlins is described as an "overseer." (Mount Vernon Estate Museum and Gardens website; "Mourning Washington by Laborers at Mount Vernon," www.mountvernon.org/educational-resources/encyclopedia/mourning-mountvernon, accessed October 21, 2012.)

59 Please see Randall, *The Life of Thomas Jefferson*, v.2, op. cit., p.367, for a discussion of Lear's character.

60 Jefferson, quoting Pickering, in a letter to Martin Van Buren, June 29, 1824, *The Writings of Thomas Jefferson*, Library Edition, v.16, edited by Albert Ellery Bergh, (Thomas Jefferson Memorial Association, Washington, DC), 1904., p.56. Jefferson cites *Pickering*, p.34, in his letter to Van Buren.

61 "Again, Mr Jefferson has affirmed that no correspondence took place between him and Washington, during the interval in which none has been found among the papers of the latter . . ." *The Writings of George Washington*, by Jared Sparks, v.1, (American Stationers' Company, Boston), 1837, p.521.

62 Jared Sparks to Henry Randall, May 3, 1856; in Randall, *The Life of Thomas Jefferson*, v.2, op. cit., p.370.

63 *The History of the United States; John Adams and Thomas Jefferson*, v.2 (of 3), by Richard Hildreth, (Harper & Brothers, New York,) 1863, p.54.

64 There is some small historical irony in that Mr. Ford, the great historian and defender of Jefferson, was the great-grandson of Noah Webster, who had played such a significant role in the controversy by re-publishing Jefferson's letter to Mazzei in his newspaper, *Minerva*. Noted historian Worthington C. Ford was the brother of Paul Leicester Ford. Please see *American Naturalistic and Realistic Novelists: A Bibliographic Dictionary* by E. C. Applegate, Greenwood Press, Westport, CT, 2002, p.142.

65 "The Washington-Jefferson Letters," by Worthington C. Ford., July 24, 1902, Letter, *The Nation*, v.75, No. 1936, p.112.

66 *Ibid.*, p.112.

67 One of Ford's accomplishments was the editing of *The Writings of George Washington* in fourteen volumes. Ford's brother Paul Leicester Ford, also a noted biographer and historian, was the editor of the

renowned *The Writings of Thomas Jefferson* which remains a valuable resource to many historians, including the author of this book.

[68] "Born amid the great events of the Revolution, by the death of his father, (Col. Custis, of the army, and a son of Mrs. Washington by a former marriage,) which occurred near the close of the war, he found his home during childhood and youth at Mount Vernon, where his manners were formed after the noblest models . . ." Death Notice of George Washington Parke Custis, by the Editors of *The National Intelligencer*, as printed in Custis's posthumously published book, "*Recollections and Private Memoirs of Washington*," 1859.

[69] Ford letter to *The Nation*, op. cit., p.112.

[70] *Ibid.*, p.113.

[71] Italics in Ford's transcription of Custis letter.

[72] Ford letter to *The Nation*, op. cit., p.113.

[73] *Ibid.*, p.113.

[74] Italics in original Ford transcription; *Ibid.*, p.113.

[75] *Ibid.*, p.112.

[76] Worthington C. Ford letter to *The Nation*, op. cit., pp.112–113.

[77] Jefferson to Martin Van Buren, June 29, 1824, *The Writings of Thomas Jefferson*, Library Edition, v.16, edited by Albert Ellery Bergh, op. cit., p.56.

[78] *The Works of Thomas Jefferson*, edited by Paul Leicester Ford, v.12, (G.P. Putnam's Sons, New York), 1905, p.361.

[79] *The Checkered Career of Tobias Lear*, by Ray Brighton, (Portsmouth Marine Society), 1985, p.173.

[80] *Ibid.*, p.175.

[81] *Ibid.*, p.171.

[82] *Ibid.*, p.175.

[83] *Ibid.*, p.172.

[84] Zacks, *The Pirate Coast*, op. cit., p.218.

[85] *Ibid.*, p.221.

[86] *Jefferson's War: America's First War on Terror 1801–1805*, by Joseph Wheelan, (Carroll & Graf, New York), 2003, p.276.

[87] Jefferson to Martin Van Buren, June 29, 1824, *The Writings of Thomas Jefferson*, Library Edition, v.16, edited by Albert Ellery Bergh, op. cit., p.65.

[88] Chief Justice John Marshall, a strong Federalist and opponent of Jefferson, wrote in a letter to Alexander Hamilton, "The morals of the author of the letter to Mazzei cannot be pure." Marshall to Hamilton, January 1, 1801, in *The Life of John Marshall*, v.2, by Albert Jeremiah Beveridge, (Houghton, Mifflin Company, Boston), 1916, 1919, p.537.

[89] Thomas Jefferson to Benjamin Rush, April 21, 1803, *The Works of Thomas Jefferson*, Federal Edition, edited by Paul Leicester Ford, v.9, (G.P. Putman's Sons, New York), 1905, p.457; also *Proceedings of the Massachusetts Historical Society*, v.12, (1897–1899), p.267.

[90] Please see Smithsonian Institution, National Museum of American History for more information on the "Jefferson Bible," americanhistory.si.edu/JeffersonBible/history/, (accessed October 27, 2012).

[91] Benjamin Rush to John Adams, April 5, 1808; *Letters of Benjamin Rush*, edited by L.H. Butterfield, 2 vols., (Princeton University Press for the American Philosophical Society, Princeton, New Jersey), 1951, v.2, p.963.

Chapter Nine: "All Doors Wide Open"

[1] Jefferson to Gerry, May 13, 1797; Malone, *Jefferson and the Ordeal of Liberty*, v.3, op. cit., p.313.

[2] Elbridge Gerry to Abigail Adams, January, 7, 1797, *Ibid.*, p.317.

[3] Jefferson to Edward Rutledge, June 24, 1797, *Ibid.*, pp.313–14.

[4] "The excitement throughout the United States became more intense during the summer of 1798 because of the prevailing belief that the French were preparing to invade America." Please see "French Opinion as a Factor in Preventing War Between France and the United States, 1795–1800," by James Alton James, *The American Historical Review*, v.30, No. 1 (Oct 1924), op. cit., p.50.

[5] Adams speech to joint session of Congress, May 16, 1797.

[6] *Philadelphia Directory for 1797*, by Cornelius William Stafford, (William Woodward, Philadelphia), 1797, p.112.

[7] *Historic Hotels: Past and Present,* by Robert B. Ludy, M.D., (David McKay Company, Philadelphia), 1927, p.118.

[8] To Adams's request in March that he return to France on a diplomatic mission Jefferson had demurred. While Jefferson's lack of desire to return to Europe was likely his overriding reason in refusing the offer, he was not entirely averse to skirting the laws if necessity required. During his own presidency Jefferson wrote, "Should we have ever gained our Revolution if we had bound our hands by manacles of the law, not only in the beginning, but in any part of the revolutionary conflict?" (Quoted in Crawford, *Twilight at Monticello: The Final Years of Thomas Jefferson*, op. cit., p.47.)

[9] John Adams, Message to the Senate, May 31, 1797; online at Yale University, Lillian Goldman School of Law, avalon.law.yale.edu/18th_century/ja97-04.asp, (accessed October 30, 2012).

[10] That is, "peace and tranquility."

11   John Adams, Address to the House of Representatives, June 2, 1797; in *Ibid.*, Yale online, avalon.law.yale.edu/18th_century/hotoja01.asp, (accessed October 30, 2012).

12   The Reply was an official letter to the House which would have been read aloud to that body though not by Adams himself.

13   John Adams Reply to the House of Representatives, June 3, 1797, in *Ibid.*, Yale online, avalon.law.yale.edu/18th_century/ja97–07.asp, (accessed October 30, 2012).

14   The three diplomats did not assemble in Paris until October.

15   Smith, *John Marshall: Definer of a Nation*, op. cit., p.190.

16   "The bachelor President accepted the social leadership expected of him, turning his home into the most interesting social center in the city. With the help of Phillipe Létombe, the French envoy in Philadelphia, Jefferson assembled a staff of eight with the most important slots going to two Frenchmen." Gabler, *Passions–The Wines and Travels of Thomas Jefferson*, op. cit., p.197.

17   Chernow, *Alexander Hamilton*, op. cit., p.547.

18   *First Family-Abigail and John Adams*, by Joseph Ellis, (Vintage, New York), 2010, p.177.

19   Chernow, *Alexander Hamilton,* op, cit., p.547.

20   Elkins & McKitrick, *The Age of Federalism*, op. cit., p.566.

21   *Ibid.*, p.566.

22   Smith, *John Marshall: Definer of a Nation*, op. cit., p.190. Note: Smith is referring to France's war against Great Britain.

23   Malone is referring to Jefferson's view of the vice president's role.

24   Malone, *Ordeal of Liberty*, v.3, op. cit., p.317.

25   *John Adams*, by David McCollough, (Simon and Schuster, New York), 2001, p.489.

26   "Annual Report of the American Historical Association for the Year 1903," v.2, "Correspondence of the French Ministers to the United States, 1791–1797," edited by Frederick J. Turner, (Washington, Government Printing Office), 1904. The Introduction to this important resource, written by Dr. Turner, begins thusly: "The following transcripts from the dispatches of the ministers of France to the United States from 1791 to 1797 were procured by Worthington C. Ford and the late Paul Leicester Ford, and by them presented to the New York Public Library. By the liberality of Worthington C. Ford and Dr. J. S. Billings, the director of the library, the Historical Manuscripts Commission is permitted to publish them in this report of the American Historical Association." Létombe's verbatim quotes of Jefferson appear in his dispatch to Delacroix of June 7, 1797, on page 1030.

27 Jay Winik in *The Great Upheaval: America and the Birth of the Modern World, 1788–1800,* (Harper, New York), 2007, p.521, wrote that Jefferson had met with Létombe "on his own initiative." Mr. Winik provides no footnotes in the cited edition of his book, nor endnotes, but does provide a "Bibliographic Notes" section which is of little value to determine the sources that Mr. Winik consulted relative to specific statements. It is important to note that there is no historical evidence from which to make an absolute determination as to the origins, or the official or unofficial nature, of Jefferson's meetings with Létombe.

28 "President Adams determined to make a treaty with fractious France, and consulted with Jefferson, whom he would have sent as minister, had they not both agreed that such function was unsuitable for a Vice President." Willard, *John Adams: A Character Sketch,* op. cit., p.107.

29 John Adams, Essay #18, June 10, 1809, in *Boston Patriot;* cited in *The Works of John Adams, Second President of the United States with a Life of the Author,* by Charles Francis Adams, v.9, (Little, Brown and Company, Boston), 1854, p.308.

30 Letombé to Delacroix, July 25, 1797, in Smith, *John Marshall: Definer of a Nation,* op. cit., p.190.

31 Nicholson, "Early French Policy Toward the United States," op. cit., p.58.

32 Elkins & McKitrick, *The Age of Federalism,* op. cit., p.539.

33 Bemis, **"Washington's Farewell Address: A Foreign Policy of Independence,"** op. cit., p.263.

34 "In replacing her husband, Talleyrand had the courtesy to appoint him minister to The Hague, a small gesture of thanks to a poor fellow whose job and wife he had stolen." *Talleyrand, The Art of Survival,* by Jean Orieux, (Alfred A. Knopf), 1974, p.175; Jean Smith in *John Marshal: Definer of a Nation* (p.587, *fn* 19) wrote: "It would appear that Talleyrand replaced Charles Delacroix not only in the foreign ministry but also in the matrimonial bedroom. Upon assuming office, Talleyrand appointed Delacroix ambassador to Holland. While Delacroix was in The Hague, the new foreign minister took up with Madame Delacroix, and their son, Eugene Delacroix, the famous painter, was born in April 1798. Charles Delacroix assumed paternity, but there was little doubt that Talleyrand was the actual father. Eugene Delacroix looked like Talleyrand, exhibited many of his behavioral traits, and was anonymously supported by the foreign minister during his early years." (Smith cites Bernard, *Talleyrand*, p.210.)

35 Talleyrand hoped that being in possession of an official passport from the French government would prevent later accusations that he had fled France as an émigré aristocrat. Without the passport, and the official

status that his travel to England thus appeared to have, he would have likely been barred from government service if and when he returned to France, and possibly arrested.

36 The binding nature (or lack thereof) of this promise of allegiance, for Talleyrand, can best be understood by the following: Then Bishop of Autun, Talleyrand had, at the express desire of King Louis XVI, celebrated Mass at the Ceremony of Federation which commemorated the first anniversary of the fall of the Bastille. Several months later the Bishop wrote, in a letter to his mistress the Countess de Flahaut, "After all the vows we have made and broken, after having so often sworn fidelity to a constitution, to nature, to the law, to the king, to all sorts of things existing only in name, what can one oath more matter?" Please see *Memoirs of a Contemporary*, by Ida Saint-Elme, (translated by Lionel Strachey), (Doubleday, Page, and Co., New York), 1902, p.62. It should be noted here also that Talleyrand, colorful, opportunistic, and conniving, had a vigorous sense of humor and of the absurd. At this very same festival, "Talleyrand, going up to the altar with two priests in attendance, bent over to Lafayette and whispered to him, 'Now, please, don't make me laugh.'" (*Ibid.*)

37 "Talleyrand's Oath of Allegiance," by William Otis Sawtelle, *Sprague's Journal of Maine History,* v.12, No.3, (July, August, September, 1924), pp.147–48, p.148.

38 La Tour du Pain's father, General Arthur Dillon, and her father-in-law were both guillotined during the Terror of the Jacobins. Lucille Desmoulins, General Arthur Dillon, and sixteen others were absurdly accused of "having conspired against the safety of the people, and of having wished to destroy the National Convention, further, of being in the pay of the foreigner and of having aimed at replacing on the throne of France the son of Louis XVI." All were tried together, convicted, and guillotined, including Jacques Hebert's widow. (Methley, p.313.) Previously, Camille Desmoulins had created doubts over his republican credentials by successfully defending General Dillon against accusations of royalism. (Methley, p.213.)

39 *Recollections of the Revolution and the Empire* (from the French "*Journal D'Une Femme De Cinquante Ans*"), by La Marquise De La Tour du Pain (edited and translated by Walter Geer), (Brentano's, New York), 1920, p.203. Please also see, *Dancing to the Precipice: The Life of Lucie de La Tour du Pin: Eyewitness to an Era*, by Caroline Moorehead, (Harper Perennial, New York), 2010, p.210.

40 Lyon, "The Directory and the United States," op. cit., p.519.

41 "A Neglected Memoir by Talleyrand on French-American Relations, 1793–1797," by William Stinchcombe, *Proceedings of the American*

Philosophical Society, v.121, No. 3, (June 15, 1977), pp.195–208, p.196.

[42] Stinchcombe, *Ibid.*, p.196; "Historically speaking, Asylum Township has one of the most interesting backgrounds in Bradford County. French refugees who fled from the French Revolution settled the village of Azilum. Nearly forty families erected the village, where they remained until around 1800, when a large portion of them returned to France." Please see "Asylum Township" at: www.bradfordcountypa.org/Our-Towns/Asylum-Township.asp, (accessed November 14, 2014).

[43] James, "French Opinion as a Factor in Preventing War Between France and the United States, 1795–1800," op. cit., p.45.

[44] *Ibid.*, p.46.

[45] "In 1797 the American government could do nothing to stop the French raids. It had no navy. Except for a few small revenue cutters, each manned by crews of six men, it did not have a single national vessel in commission . . . Not until after the publication of the XYZ dispatches and the enactment of the war measures, did the government hasten to equip and send a naval force to sea." *The Quasi War,* by Alexander De Conde, (Charles Scribner's Sons, New York), 1966, p.125.

[46] Stinchcombe, "A Neglected Memoir by Talleyrand on French-American Relations, 1793–1797," op. cit., p.204.

[47] Elkins & McKitrick, *The Age of Federalism*, op. cit., p.562. The original French of Talleyrand's astounding statement is found in Louis Madelin, *Talleyrand*, p.56: "Il faut y faire une fortune immense, une immense fortune, une immense fortune, une fortune immense."

[48] Nicholson, "Early French Policy Toward the United States," op. cit., p.58.

[49] Elkins & McKitrick, *The Age of Federalism*, op. cit., p.565. (Talleyrand to Létombe, August 4, and September 1, 1797.)

[50] In her controversial biography, *Thomas Jefferson: An Intimate History* (W.W. Norton, New York, 1974), Fawn Brodie suggests that Talleyrand was motivated to abuse the American Ministers due to "social ostracism" that he had experienced when he lived in Philadelphia in 1794 (p.307). Brodie believed that because Talleyrand had caused a scandal by "openly escorting a handsome mulatto woman about the streets" of the capital, the "doors of fashionable Philadelphia closed tight against him" (pp.288–89). There is no historical evidence however to support Brodie's speculative theory linking Talleyrand's earlier frustrations in Philadelphia with his unfriendly behavior to the three American diplomats four years later. Talleyrand's (French) patriotic and self-aggrandizing goals would certainly have been more than enough impetus to drive both his monetary demands and disrespectful behavior toward the

American delegation, not to mention Jefferson's recommendations to obstruct them. Petty revenge against three men, none of whom had ever personally aggrieved him, for actions done by their countrymen that had occurred four years previously does not seem a reasonable motivator. In the absence of any way to disprove Ms. Brodie's theory, when coupled with Talleyrand's sometimes outrageous actions and unscrupulous personality, the possibility that the French Foreign Minister was motivated in some fashion by resentment against American society cannot be entirely dismissed.

51 Orieux, *Talleyrand*, p.134; Talleyrand to Lord Landsdowne, February 1, 1795.

52 John Marshall to George Washington, September 15, 1797, in "Letters of John Marshall When Envoy to France," *The American Historical Review*, v.2, No. 2, (Jan 1897), pp.294–306.

53 John Marshall to George Washington, September 15, 1797, *Ibid.*

54 Marshall to Washington, October 24, 1797, *Ibid.*

55 *History of the United States of America*, by Richard Hildreth, Revised Edition, v.5. (of 6), (The Bradley Company, New York), 1879, p.130.

56 *Ibid.*, p.132.

57 *Ibid.*, p.135.

58 *Ibid.*, p.140.

59 "The exact date of the dinner has been the subject of some controversy. Marshall recorded it in his journal as 'ca, [circa] December 2, 1797,' although Gerry, in a letter to his wife, listed it prospectively on November 26." Smith, *John Marshall: Definer on a Nation*, op. cit., p.593.

60 Lyon, "The Directory and the United States," op, cit., p.523.

61 *Ibid.*, p.523.

62 John Marshall to George Washington, from Paris, March 8, 1798, in "Letters of John Marshall When Envoy to France," op. cit., p.303.

63 Lyon, "The Directory and the United States," op, cit., p.523.

64 "Mr. Gerry stated to the American government, that he did not leave Paris with his colleague, because the Minister of Foreign Relations had assured him, that event would be followed by an immediate declaration of war on the part of France." Willard, *John Adams Character Sketch*, op. cit., p.108; also, Lyman, *The Diplomacy of the United States*, op. cit., p.94.

65 Hildreth, *History of the United States*, v.5, op cit., p.159.

66 Lyon, "The Directory and the United States," op. cit., p.524.

67 Elbridge Gerry to Thomas Jefferson, January 15, 1801; *Some Letters of Elbridge Gerry of Massachusetts, 1784–1804*, edited by Worthington Chauncey Ford, (Historical Printing Club, Brooklyn), 1896, p.15.

68 Lyon, op. cit., p.524.

69 *Ibid.*, p.527.

70 "John Adams, Message to the Senate and House, Regarding Dispatches from the Envoys to France, March 5, 1798," *A Compilation of the Messages and Papers of the Presidents, Prepared under the direction of the Joint Committee on printing, of the House and Senate, Pursuant to an Act of the Fifty-Second Congress of the United States.* New York: Bureau of National Literature, Inc., 1897, at Yale University, online, op. cit., avalon.law.yale.edu/18th_century/ja98–02.asp, (accessed November 10, 2012).

71 John Adams, Message to the Senate and House of March 19, 1798, Regarding Reports of the Envoys to France; A Compilation of the Messages and Papers of the Presidents, op. cit., online at avalon.law.yale.edu/18th_century/ja98–01.asp, (accessed November 10, 2012). Please see also *The Addresses and Messages of the Presidents of the United States*, (McLean & Taylor, New York), 1839, p.78.

72 John Adams, Message to the Senate and House of March 19, 1798, *Ibid.*

73 Jefferson to Madison, March 21, 1798, *The Writings of Thomas Jefferson*, edited by Albert Ellery Burgh, v.10, (The Thomas Jefferson Memorial Association, 1905), pp.9–10.

74 Abigail Adams to Mary Cranch, March 20, 1798, Smith, *John Adams*, v.2, op. cit., p.956.

75 Abigail Adams to William Smith, March 28, 1798, in *Ibid.*, v.2, p.958.

76 John Adams, Message to the Senate and House of April 3, 1798, Yale University, online, op. cit., avalon.law.yale.edu/18th_century/ja98–03.asp, (accessed November 10, 2012).

77 *Ibid.*

78 Smith, *John Adams*, v.2, op. cit., p.959.

Chapter Ten: "A Civil War Was Expected"

1 Jefferson to Madison, April 6, 1798, quoted in Beveridge, *The Life of John Marshall*, v.2, op. cit., p.340.

2 *Ibid.*, referring to letter of Jefferson to Madison, April 26, 1798, p.340.

3 George Washington to Alexander Hamilton, May 27, 1798, quoted in *Ibid.*, p.341.

4 Lyon, "The Directory and the United States," op. cit., p.524.

5 Talleyrand to Barras, May 29, 1798, quoted in Lyon, *Ibid.*, p.524.

6 " 'Not One Cent for Tribute': The Public Addresses and American Popular Reaction to the XYZ Affair, 1798–1799," by Thomas M. Ray, *Journal of the Early Republic*, v.3, No. 4 (Winter, 1983), pp.389–412; p.411.

7 *Ibid.*, p.391.

8 "No sentiment or expression in any of my Answers to Addresses were obtruded or insinuated by any Person about me. Every one of them was written with my own hand. I alone am responsable [sic] for all the Mistakes and Errors in them." John Adams to Thomas Jefferson, June 30, 1813, *Correspondence*, v.2, p.346.

9 "Having thoroughly scoured these sources, the total number of addresses I have discovered is 296. Undoubtedly, many more existed but are no longer extant." "Not One Cent for Tribute": The Public Addresses and American Popular Reaction to the XYZ Affair, 1798–1799," op. cit., p.400, *fn.*

10 *Ibid.*, p.397.

11 *Ibid.*, p.397.

12 *Ibid.*, p.395.

13 Jefferson to James Madison, April 6, 1798, *The Works of Thomas Jefferson*, edited by H. A. Washington, v.4, (New York, Derby & Jackson), 1859, p.233.

14 Jefferson to Madison, April 12, 1796, *Ibid.*, v.4, p.234.

15 "'Oh That I Was a Soldier': John Adams and the Anguish of War," by John E. Ferling, in *American Quarterly*, v.36, No. 2, (Summer, 1984), pp.258–275; p.272.

16 James, "French Opinion as a Factor in Preventing War Between France and the United States, 1795–1800," op. cit., pp.52–53.

17 *Correspondence Between Thomas Jefferson and Pierre Samuel Du Pont de Nemours, 1798–1817*, edited by Dumas Malone, (Houghton, Mifflin, Boston), 1930; p.xiii.

18 James, op. cit., p.53.

19 Historian James Alton James uses the term "conversations" rather than the singular "meeting." He also describes these meetings as "confidential conversations." Though he did not cite the source of the term "confidential conversations," which he quotes, one can reasonably speculate that the source was Victor Du Pont. Please see, James, *Ibid.*, p.53.

20 *Ibid.*, p.53.

21 Malone, ed., Jefferson to Pierre Du Pont de Nemours, April 25, 1802; *Correspondence Between Thomas Jefferson and Pierre Samuel Du Pont De Nemours, 1798–1817*, op. cit., pp.48–49.

22 "An Act to Suspend the Commercial Intercourse between the United States and France, and the Dependencies Thereof," *United States Statutes at Large, 1 U.S. Stat 565;* at Yale University online, op. cit., avalon.law.yale.edu/18th_century/qw01.asp, (accessed November 15, 2012).

23 *Ibid.*

24 "The Reestablishment of the Navy, 1787–1801, Historical Overview and Select Bibliography," *Naval History Bibliographies, No. 4,* "Histor-

ical Overview of the Federalist Navy, 1787–1801"; Department of The Navy—Naval Historical Center, by Michael J. Crawford, and Christine F. Hughes (no date of authorship provided), www.history.navy.mil/biblio/biblio4/biblio4a.htm, (accessed November 15, 2012).

25 "An Act to Authorize the Defense of the Merchant Vessels of the United States against French Depredations, Approved June 25, 1798," *United States Statutes at Large, 1 Stat 572;* at Yale University, op. cit., avalon. law.yale.edu/18th_century/qw02.asp, (accessed November 15, 2012).

26 "Nothing now remained to be done but to prepare for war. Congress authorized the President to enlist ten thousand men, as a provisional army, and to call them into actual service, if war should be declared against the United States, or whenever in his opinion there should be danger of an invasion." *The Writings of George Washington,* by Jared Sparks, v.1, (American Stationers' Company, Boston), 1837, p.524.

27 "He never seriously believed, that the French would go to the extremity of invading the United States. But it had always been a maxim with him, that a timely preparation for war afforded the surest means of preserving peace; and on this occasion he acted with as much promptitude and energy, as if the invaders had been actually on the coast." *Ibid.,* p.528.

28 "In 1798, when a provisional army was raised, in consequence of the injuries and demands of France, Washington suspended his acceptance of the command of it, on the condition that Hamilton should be his associate and second in command. This arrangement was made." *Annals of the American Revolution,* by Jedidiah Morse, (Hartford, 1824), Appendix, p.16.

29 Crawford, and Hughes, "The Reestablishment of the Navy, 1787–1801, Historical Overview and Select Bibliography," op. cit., www.history. navy.mil/biblio/biblio4/biblio4a.htm, (accessed November 15, 2012).

30 "Message from the President of the United States to Congress, June 21, 1798," *State Papers and Publick Documents of the United States, 1797–1801,* v.3, (T.B. Wait and Sons, Boston), 1815, p.305.

31 "John Adams Message to the Senate and House, June 21, 1798, Regarding Envoys to France," *A Compilation of the Messages and Papers of the Presidents, 1789–1902,* v.1, by James B. Richardson, (Bureau of National Literature and Art, Inc., New York), 1907, p.266; online at Lillian Goldman Law Library, Yale University, avalon.law.yale.edu/18th_century/ja98–04.asp, (accessed November 17, 2012).

32 *"The Presidents of the United States of America,"* by Frank Freidel and Hugh Sidey. Copyright 2006 by the White House Historical Association. https://www.whitehouse.gov/1600/presidents/johnadams (accessed October 11, 2015).

33 *James Madison,* by Garry Wills, (Times Books, New York), 2002, p.48.

[34] Kentucky Resolutions, 1798, Foley, ed., *The Jeffersonian Cyclopedia*, section #286, op. cit., p.31.

[35] Wills, op. cit., p.49.

[36] John Adams to Thomas Jefferson, June 14, 1813, *Correspondence*, v.2. p.329.

[37] Lyon, "The Directory and the United States," op. cit., p.530.

[38] *Ibid.*, p.530.

[39] "The Murray-Pichon interviews, which began on June 26 and lasted until mid-September, were kept secret from the French minister at The Hague." *Ibid.*, p.530.

[40] Talleyrand to Pichon, August 15, 1798, *Ibid.*, p.530.

[41] Talleyrand to Pichon, August 28, 1798, *Ibid.*, p.530.

[42] Lyman, *The Diplomacy of the United States*, op. cit., p.99.

[43] *Ibid.*, p.99.

[44] *Ibid.*, p.100.

[45] "John Adams: Message to the Senate of February 18, 1799, Transmitting a Letter from Talleyrand," *A Compilation of the Messages and Papers of the Presidents, Prepared under the direction of the Joint Committee on printing, of the House and Senate, Pursuant to an Act of the Fifty-Second Congress of the United States.* op. cit., Lillian Goldman Law Library at Yale University, avalon.law.yale.edu/18th_century/ja99–02.asp, (accessed November 15, 2012).

[46] "John Adams: Message to the Senate of February 25, 1799, Regarding New Envoys to France," *Ibid.*, Lillian Goldman Law Library at Yale University, avalon.law.yale.edu/18th_century/ja99–03.asp, (accessed November 15, 2012).

[47] *Ibid.*

[48] See Lyman, *The Diplomacy of the United States*, op. cit., p.80.

[49] *Ibid.*, p.102.

[50] "The time was very auspicious for negotiation. Napoleon, at his first accession to the Consulate, sought for peace with all the world. France truly needed it. She was exhausted by the bloody wars of Germany, Italy, and the low countries, and by the internal commotions of the Vendeans and Chouans. He proposed peace to England and to the enemies of France on the continent. But America was the only country with whom a treaty was at that time concluded." Lyman, *The Diplomacy of the United States*, op. cit., pp.105–06.

[51] *Convention of 1800, Treaties and Other International Acts of the United States of America*, edited by Hunter Miller, v.2, Documents 1–40: 1776–1818, (Government Printing Office, Washington), 1931; online at Yale Law School, avalon.law.yale.edu/19th_century/fr1800.asp, (accessed November 20, 2012).

52 John Adams to James Lloyd, March 31, 1815, *The Works of John Adams, Second President of the United States with a Life of the Author*, by Charles Francis Adams, v.10, (Little, Brown, and Company, Boston), 1856, p.152.
53 John Adams to James Lloyd, January, 1815; *Ibid.,* pp.108–09.
54 *Ibid.,* p.113.
55 *Ibid.,* p.113.
56 *Ibid.,* p.113.
57 *Ibid.,* p.113.
58 John Adams to James Lloyd, February 6, 1815, *Ibid.,* p.115.
59 Adams to Lloyd, January 1815, *Ibid.,* p.112.
60 Adams to Lloyd, February 6, 1815, *Ibid.,* p.115.
61 Adams to Lloyd, February 17, 1815, *Ibid.,* p.126.
62 Adams to Lloyd, March 30, 1815, *Ibid.,* p.152.
63 *Ibid.,* p.152.
64 *Ibid.,* p.153.
65 *Ibid.,* p.155.
66 Thomas Jefferson to Edmund Pendleton, February 19, 1799, *The Works of Thomas Jefferson*, v.9, edited by Paul Leicester Ford, (G.P. Putnam's Sons, New York), 1905, pp.54–55.
67 *Ibid.,* pp.54–55.
68 Jefferson to Adams, June 15, 1813, *Correspondence*, v.2, p.333.
69 Jefferson to Adams, January 11, 1816; *Ibid.,* p.459.

Chapter Eleven: "Mr. Jefferson Said I Was Sensitive, Did He!"

1 Smith, *John Adams*, v.2, op. cit., p.1052.
2 For more please see: "The Presidential Election of 1800," by James Parton, *The Atlantic Monthly,* July, 1873.
3 John Adams to Thomas Adams, December 17, 1800, in Smith, op. cit., v.2, p.1053.
4 *Abigail Adams,* by Woody Holton, (Free Press, New York), 2009, p.251.
5 *The Intimate Lives of the Founding Fathers*, by Thomas Fleming, (HarperCollins, New York), 2009, 2010, p.166.
6 *John Adams: A Life,* by John Ferling, (Oxford University Press), 1992, p.386.
7 *Descent from Glory: Four Generations of the Adams Family,* by Paul C. Nagel, (Harvard University Press), 1983, p.79.
8 John Adams to Abigail Adams, October 12, 1799, *Adams Family Papers: An Electronic Archive.* Massachusetts Historical Society. www.masshist.org/digitaladams/, (accessed October 15, 2015).
9 Nagel, *Descent from Glory: Four Generations of the Adams Family,* op. cit., p.80.

[10] *Old New York: a journal relating to the history and antiquities of New York City,* by W.W. Pasko, (W.W. Pasko, New York), 1890; Mr. Peter Talbot, writing of Charles Adams's burial site on the "Find a Grave" website, states, "The church was destroyed in the Great Fire of 1835, and remains were re-interred at other locations, many being moved to Green-Wood Cemetery. His present burial site is unknown, though we continue to search so that he may be properly remembered." Rachel, a visitor on the same site wrote, "Your family will find you. Rest In Peace Cousin." www.findagrave.com/cgi-bin/fg.cgi?page=gr&GRid=20772235, (accessed December 22, 2012).

[11] Letter to Henry S. Randall from Edward Coles, May 11, 1857, in Randall, *The Life of Thomas Jefferson,* v.3, op. cit., pp.639–40.

[12] *Ibid.*

[13] *Ibid.*

[14] Jefferson to Benjamin Rush, January 16, 1811, in Randolph, ed., *Memoirs, Correspondence, and Private Papers of Thomas Jefferson*, v.4, op. cit., p.157.

[15] Smith, *John Adams*, v.2, op. cit., p.1065.

[16] John Adams to John Marshall, August 17, 1825, quoted in Robert J. Lukens, "Jared Ingersoll's Rejection of Appointment as One of the 'Midnight Judges' of 1801: Foolhardy or Farsighted," *Temple Law Review*, 70, (1997): 229; cited in "The Midnight Appointments," by Richard Samuelson, *White House History*, #7, p.21.

[17] Thomas Jefferson to Pierrepont Edwards, March, 1801, in *The Jeffersonian Cyclopedia*, section # 6109, op. cit., p.649.

[18] For more information on the Judiciary Act of 1801 please see "The Judiciary Act of 1801: 'An Act to provide for the more convenient organization of the Courts of the United States.'" 2 Stat. 89, February 13, 1801, in *History of the Federal Judiciary*, at Federal Judicial Center online at www.fjc.gov/history/home.nsf/page/landmark_03.html, (accessed December 29, 2012).

[19] *Sketches of the Life, Writings, and Opinions of Thomas Jefferson*, by B. L. Rayner, (Francis and Boardman, New York), 1832, p.307.

[20] Beveridge, *The Life of John Marshall*, v.2, op. cit., pp.561–62.

[21] Rayner, *Sketches of the Life, Writings, and Opinions of Thomas Jefferson*, op. cit., p.308.

[22] *Ibid.*, p.308.

[23] Holton, *Abigail Adams*, op. cit., pp.335–36.

[24] John Adams's note in letter of Abigail to Thomas Jefferson, November 19, 1804, *Correspondence*, v.1, p.282.

[25] Thomas Jefferson to Abigail Adams, June 13, 1804, *Ibid.*, p.270.

[26] *Ibid.*, pp.270–71.

27 Thomas Jefferson to Benjamin Rush, January 16, 1811, in Randolph ed., *Memoirs, Correspondence, and Private Papers of Thomas Jefferson*, v.4, op. cit., p.161.

28 *Ibid.*, p.161.

29 *Ibid.*, p.161; emphasis in original.

30 *Ibid.*, p.161.

31 Abigail Adams to Thomas Jefferson, July 1, 1804, *Correspondence*, v.1, p.274.

32 Abigail Adams to Thomas Jefferson, October 25, 1804, *Ibid.*, p.281.

33 *Ibid.*, p.281.

34 Willard, *John Adams: A Character Sketch*, op. cit., p.112.

35 Parton, "The Presidential Election of 1800," *Atlantic Monthly*, July 1873, op. cit.

36 Hildreth, *History of the United States*, v.2, op. cit., p.412.

37 Thomas Jefferson to John Adams, March 8, 1801, *Correspondence*, v.1, p.264.

38 John Adams to Thomas Jefferson, March 24, 1801, *Ibid.*, v.1, p.264.

Chapter Twelve: "We Are All Republicans, We Are All Federalists"

1 Thomas Jefferson to Spencer Roane, September 6, 1819, *The Jeffersonian Cyclopedia*, section #7340, op. cit., p.754; and *The Portable Thomas Jefferson,* edited by Merrill D. Peterson, (Penguin, New York), 1975.

2 Thomas Jefferson to Edward Livingston, April 30, 1800, *Ibid.*, #7345, p.755; and Randall, *The Life of Thomas Jefferson*, v.2, op. cit., p.526.

3 Joint Congressional Committee on Inaugural Ceremonies, Swearing-In Ceremony for President Thomas Jefferson, Fourth Inaugural Ceremonies, March 4, 1801, www.inaugural.senate.gov/swearing-in/event/thomas-jefferson-1801, (accessed June 21, 2013).

4 Thomas Jefferson to James Madison, September 1795, *Jefferson Cyclopedia*, #3616, op. cit., p.396.

5 *The Republican; or, a Series of Essays on the Principles and Policy of Free States. Having a Particular Reference to the United States of America and the Individual States*, by William C. Jarvis, Esq., (Phinehas Allen, Pittsfield), 1820.

6 Thomas Jefferson to William Charles Jarvis, September 28, 1820, *The Writings of Thomas Jefferson*, v.10., edited by Paul Leicester Ford, Letter Press Edition, (G.P. Putnam's Sons, New York), 1899, p.160.

7 *Ibid.*, all quotes in this paragraph from letter cited above in *en* 6.

8 Jefferson here is referring to the three branches of government: executive, legislative, and judicial.

9 Thomas Jefferson to William Charles Jarvis, September 28, 1820, *The Writings of Thomas Jefferson*, v.10., Ford, ed., op. cit., p.160.

[10] Thomas Jefferson to John Adams, June 27, 1813, *Correspondence*, v.2, p.337.

[11] Thomas Jefferson to Francis Hopkinson, March 13, 1789; *The Jeffersonian Cyclopedia*, #6424, op. cit., p.677, and, *The Republic; or A History of the United States of America in the Administrations, from the Monarchic Colonial Days to the Present Times,* by John Robert Irelan, v.3, (Fairbanks and Palmer, Chicago), 1886, p.522.

[12] *The Jeffersonian Cyclopedia*, section #6434, op. cit., p.677, and *The Works of Thomas Jefferson,* edited by Paul L. Ford, Federal Edition, v.9, (G.P. Putnam's Sons, New York), 1905, p.193. Dr. Ford in his footnote to Jefferson's First Inaugural Address writes that this sentence was part of an original draft of that speech, "but for some reason [was] not included."

[13] *George Washington: The Indispensable Man,* by James Thomas Flexner, (Little, Brown, and Co., Boston), 1969, 1973, 1974.

[14] Thomas Jefferson to Archibald Stuart, January 4, 1797, *The Jeffersonian Cyclopedia*, section #9027, op. cit., p.931, and *The Writings of Thomas Jefferson*, v.3, edited by Paul Leicester Ford, Letter Press Edition, (G.P. Putnam's Sons, New York), 1896, p.101.

[15] *The Life of Thomas Jefferson,* v.3, Henry S. Randall, (Derby and Jackson, New York), 1858, p.70.

[16] *Ibid.*, p.70.

[17] Thomas Jefferson to William C. Claiborne, May 24, 1803, *The Jeffersonian Cyclopedia*, section #2946, op. cit., p.328, and, Randall, *The Life of Thomas Jefferson*, v.3, *Ibid.,* p.69.

[18] Jefferson's First Inaugural Address.

[19] First Inaugural Address of Thomas Jefferson, March 4, 1801, Lillian Goldman Law Library, Yale University, online at avalon.law.yale.edu/19th_century/jefinau1.asp, (accessed January 6, 2013).

[20] *In Pursuit of Reason: The Life of Thomas Jefferson*, by Noble E. Cunningham, Jr., (Louisiana State University Press), 1987, p.218.

[21] Thomas Jefferson's draft version of the Kentucky Resolution, October 1798, available online at Yale Law School, Lillian Goldman Law Library, avalon.law.yale.edu/18th_century/jeffken.asp, (accessed January 9, 2013).

[22] Thomas Jefferson to James Madison, May, 1798, *The Jeffersonian Cyclopedia,* section #289, op. cit., p.32.

[23] Thomas Jefferson to James Madison, August 23, 1799, Cunningham, *In Pursuit of Reason: The Life of Thomas Jefferson*, op. cit., p.219.

[24] Thomas Jefferson to Wilson C. Nicholas, September 5, 1799, in Ford, ed., *The Works of Thomas Jefferson*, v.9, op. cit., p.80.

[25] *Ibid.*, p.80.

26 Thomas Jefferson to James Madison, August 23, 1799, *The Papers of James Madison Digital Edition,* J. C. A. Stagg, editor. Charlottesville: University of Virginia Press, Rotunda, 2010, rotunda.upress.virginia. edu/founders/JSMN-01–17-02–0167, (accessed January 10, 2013).

27 "Jefferson, Man of Ideas," by Louis B. Wright, *The Yale Review*, Vol XL, #1, September, 1950, (Yale University Press), p.160.

28 Jefferson here is referring to the prosecution of federalist editors.

29 Thomas Jefferson to Thomas McKean, February 19, 1803, *The Writings of Thomas Jefferson*, Letter Press Edition, edited by Paul Leicester Ford, v.8, (G.P. Putnam's Sons, New York), 1897, p.218.

30 Thomas Jefferson to Thomas McKean, February 19, 1803, *Ibid.*, p.219.

31 *The Founders' Constitution,* v.5, Amendment 1 (Speech and Press), Document 28, People v. Croswell; 3 Johns. Cas. 337 N.Y. 1804, The University of Chicago Press, press-pubs.uchicago.edu/founders/documents/amendI_speechs28.html, (accessed January 20, 2013).

32 *Ibid.*

33 Chernow, *Alexander Hamilton*, op. cit., p.669.

34 *Ibid.*, p.670.

35 *Ibid.*, p.669.

36 *Ibid.*, p.670.

37 *Ibid.*, p.670.

38 Thomas Jefferson to Thomas Seymour, February 11, 1807, *The Works of Thomas Jefferson,* edited by Paul Leicester Ford, Federal Edition, v.10, (G.P. Putnam's Sons, New York), 1905, p.366; emphasis in original. Please also see: "Jefferson and the Newspaper," by Worthington Chauncey Ford, *Records of the Columbia Historical Society* (Washington, DC), v.8, (Columbia Historical Society, Washington), 1905, p.106.

39 *Ibid.*, v.10, p.368.

40 *Ibid.*, v.10, p.368.

41 Thomas Jefferson to Thomas Seymour, February 11, 1807, *The Works of Thomas Jefferson*, edited by Paul Leicester Ford, Federal Edition, v.10, (G.P. Putnam's Sons, New York), 1905, p.368.

42 "It was by Mr. Jefferson's advice that he removed to Washington and established the *National Intelligencer.*" From manuscript "Reminiscences" of Mrs. Samuel Harrison Smith regarding her husband Samuel Harrison Smith's move from Philadelphia to Washington and the establishment of that newspaper, as quoted in Ford, W.C., "Jefferson and the Newspaper," op. cit., p.111.

43 Thomas Jefferson to Abigail Adams, July 22, 1804, *Correspondence*, v.1, p.275.

44 "I affirm that act to be no law, because in opposition to the Constitution; and I shall treat it as a nullity, wherever it comes in the way of my func-

tions." Thomas Jefferson to Edward Livingston, November 1801; *The Jeffersonian Cyclopedia*, section #7762, op. cit., p.796.

45   *The United States Statutes at Large, Fifth Congress, Session 2,* "Chapter 54, 1798," The Library of Congress, p.566. Available online at The Library of Congress: memory.loc.gov/cgi-bin/ampage?collId=llsl&fileName=001/llsl001.db&recNum=689, (accessed January 12, 2013).

46   "John Marshall and the Enemy Alien: A Case Missing from the Canon," by Gerald L. Neuman and Charles F. Hobson; Columbia Law School, *Report*, Winter 2006 – "Academia Meets Free Agency"; online at www.law.columbia.edu/law_school/communications/reports/winter06/facforum2, (accessed January 12, 2013).

47   Please see Pennsylvania Historical and Museum Commission: "Joseph Priestley"; online at www.portal.state.pa.us/portal/server.pt/community/people/4277/priestley,_joseph_(ph)/443569, (accessed August 4, 2013).

48   Thomas Jefferson to Dr. Joseph Priestley, March 21, 1801, *The Writings of Thomas Jefferson,* Letter Press Edition, edited by Paul Leicester Ford, v.8, (G.P. Putnam's Sons, New York), 1897, pp.21–23; also, see *Memoir, Correspondence, and Miscellanies from the Papers of Thomas Jefferson*, edited by Thomas Jefferson Randolph, v.3, second edition, (Gray and Bowen, Boston), 1830, pp.461–62.

49   Draft version of *Declaration of the Rights of Man and of the Citizen,* August 1789, in Malone, *Jefferson and the Rights of Man,* v.2, (1951), p.224.

50   Thomas Jefferson to James Madison, September 6, 1789, *The Works of Thomas Jefferson,* edited by Paul Leicester Ford, Federal Edition, v.6, (G.P. Putnam's Sons, New York), 1904, pp.3–11.

51   "My first thoughts though coinciding with many of yours, lead me to view the doctrine as not in *all* respects compatible with the course of human affairs." Madison closed the letter with, "our hemisphere must be still more enlightened before many of the sublime truths which are seen thro' the medium of Philosophy, become visible to the naked eye of the ordinary Politician." James Madison to Thomas Jefferson, February 4, 1790, *The Founders' Constitution*, v.1, Chapter 2, Document 24, op. cit., press-pubs.uchicago.edu/founders/documents/v1ch2s24.html, The University of Chicago Press; (accessed January 13, 2013).

52   Thomas Jefferson to James Madison, September 6, 1789, Ford, ed., *The Works of Thomas Jefferson*, Federal Edition, v.6, op. cit., pp.3–11.

53   *Rights of Man: Being an Answer to Mr. Burke's Attack on the French Revolution,* by Thomas Paine, (J.S. Jordan, London), 1791, p.9.

54   *Ibid.*, p.9.

55 Please see: *The Road to Monticello: The Life and Mind of Thomas Jefferson,* by Kevin J. Hayes, (Oxford University Press, 2008), p.463.

56 "Joseph Priestley," by Sharon Hernes Silverman, Pennsylvania Historical and Museum Commission, www.portal.state.pa.us/portal/server.pt/community/people/4277/priestley,_joseph_(ph)/443569, (accessed January 19, 2013).

57 Mrs. Hart of Exeter, writing in 1822, quoted in *Life and Correspondence of Joseph Priestley, LLD, FRS, etc.*, by John Towill Rutt, v.2, (George Smallfield, Hackney, London), 1832, p.333 (*note*).

58 Joseph Priestley to Rev. T. Lindsey, January 13, 1797, *Ibid.*, pp.370–71.

59 As Priestley identified with the Jeffersonians, he is referring to the Federalist Party here.

60 Joseph Priestley to Rev. T. Belsham, March 2, 1801; in *Ibid.*, p.455; Please see also *Jefferson's Secrets: Death and Desire at Monticello*, by Andrew Burstein, (Basic Books, New York), 2005, p.242.

61 Thomas Jefferson to Dr. Joseph Priestley, March 21, 1801, *The Writings of Thomas Jefferson,* Letter Press Edition, edited by Paul Leicester Ford, v.8, (G.P. Putnam's Sons, New York), 1897, pp.21–23.

62 Hayes, *The Road to Monticello: The Life and Mind of Thomas Jefferson,* op. cit., p.463.

63 *World's Best Orations from the Earliest Period to the Present Time,* edited by David Josiah Brewer, Official Edition, v.1, (Ferd. P. Kaiser, St. Louis), 1899, p.94.

64 "The written Declaration of Independence was dated July 4 but wasn't actually signed until August 2. Fifty-six delegates eventually signed the document, although all were not present on that day in August." National Archives, Press Release, June 1, 2005, "Did You Know . . . Independence Day Should Actually Be July 2? And Other Little Known Facts About The Declaration Of Independence." www.archives.gov/press/press-releases/2005/nr05–83.html, (accessed January 26, 2013).

65 Speech of Samuel Adams to Congress, August 1, 1776, in Brewer, ed., *World's Best Orations,* op. cit., p.108.

66 *Ibid.*, p.97.

67 Thomas Jefferson to Samuel Adams, March 29, 1801, *The Writings of Thomas Jefferson*, edited by Paul Leicester Ford, Letter Press Edition, v.8, (G.P. Putnam's Sons, New York), 1897, pp.38–40.

68 Thomas Jefferson to Elbridge Gerry, March 29, 1801, in *Ibid.*, p.41.

69 *Thomas Paine*, by Ellery Sedgwick, (Small, Maynard, & Company, Boston), 1899, p.71.

70 *Ibid.*, p.80.

71 *Ibid.*, p.69.

72 *Ibid.*, p.80.

[73] In his letter of introduction, which Paine carried with him to America, Franklin described Paine as an "ingenious worthy young man." Please see Sedgwick, *Thomas Paine,* op. cit., p.11. Please see also, Franklin to Richard Bache, September 30, 1774, online at, http://founders.archives. gov/documents/Franklin/01-21-02-0170, (accessed October 22, 2015).

[74] *Life and Writings of Thomas Paine,* edited by Daniel Edwin Wheeler, Independence Edition, (Vincent Parke and Company, New York), 1908, p.26. The controversy referenced was the Silas Deane Affair.

[75] *Ibid.,* p.333.

[76] Sedgwick, *Thomas Paine*, op. cit., p.63.

[77] *Ibid.,* p.81.

[78] "I endangered my own life . . . by opposing in the Convention the executing of the king, and laboring to show they were trying the monarch and not the man, and that the crimes imputed to him were the crimes of the monarchical system . . . ." Thomas Paine to Samuel Adams, January 1, 1803, in *The Theological Works of Thomas Paine*, (Belfords, Clarke, & Co., Chicago), 1879, p.317.

[79] "Up to half a million people were imprisoned for political 'crimes,' and revolutionary courts sent more than 16,000 of them to the guillotine. A further 20,000 died in prison before trial, and over 200,000 perished in a brutal civil war in the Vendée in the west of France." *The Terror in the French Revolution,* by Hugh Gough, (Palgrave, 1998), p.2.

[80] Please see Sedgwick, *Thomas Paine,* op. cit.

[81] *The Writings of Thomas Paine*, v.3, edited by Moncure Daniel Conway, (G.P. Putnam's Sons, New York), 1895, p.243. Please see also "Thomas Paine," by Kevin Grimm at Mount Vernon, Estate, Museum and Gardens, www.mountvernon.org/educational-resources/encyclopedia/thomas-paine, (accessed February 3, 2013).

[82] Sedgwick, op. cit, p.112.

[83] Samuel Adams to Thomas Paine, November 30, 1802; *The Writings of Samuel Adams 1778–1802*, edited by Harry Alonzo Cushing, v.4, Letter Press Edition, (G.P. Putnam's Sons, New York), 1908, pp.412–13; Please see also *Samuel Adams: A Life,* by Ira Stoll, (Free Press, New York), 2008, p.258.

[84] Thomas Paine to Samuel Adams, January 1, 1803, in Blanchard, *The Theological Works of Thomas Paine*, op. cit., p.319.

[85] *The Life of Thomas Paine,* by W.T. Sherwin, (Muir, Gowans, and Co., Glasgow), 1833, p.31.

[86] Randall, *George Washington: A Life*, op. cit., p.323.

[87] Thomas Paine, "The American Crisis, December, 1776," in Randall, *Ibid.,* p.323.

[88] Sedgwick, op. cit, p.vii (preface).

89   *Letters from France in 1802,* by Henry Redhead Yorke, Esq., v.2, (H.D. Symonds, London), 1804, p.337.

90   *Ibid.,* p.337.

91   *Ibid.,* p.339.

92   *Ibid.,* p.340.

93   *Ibid.,* p.341.

94   *Ibid.,* pp.341–42.

95   *Ibid.,* p.344.

96   Thomas Jefferson to Thomas Paine, March 18, 1801, in Ford, ed., *The Writings of Thomas Jefferson*, v.8, op. cit., pp.18–19.

97   Sedgwick, *Thomas Paine,* op. cit, p.140.

98   *The Life of Thomas Paine,* by Moncure Daniel Conway, v.2, (G.P. Putnam's Sons, New York), 1892, 1908, p.418. Madame Bonneville's seven-year-old son became Brigadier General Benjamin Bonneville, USA.

99   John Adams to Benjamin Waterhouse, 1805; *The Conservative Mind, From Burke to Eliot,* by Russell Kirk, (Regnery, Washington, DC; 1953, 1960, 1972, 1985), 2001, p.86.

100 "To the Citizens of the United States and Particularly to the Leaders of the Federal Faction," by Thomas Paine, in *National Intelligencer*, Washington, 1802; cited in *Correspondence,* v.2, p.587, *fn.*

101 Latin translation is "What forbids me to speak the truth by joking?" John Adams to Thomas Jefferson, February 10, 1823, *Correspondence*, v.2, pp.587–88.

102 *Thomas Paine, Enlightenment, Revolution, and the Birth of Modern Nations,* by Craig Nelson, (Penguin Books, New York), 2006, p.9; Please see also, Kirk, op. cit., pp.86–87.

103 *Men of Ideas,* by Lewis A. Coser (Free Press Paperbacks, New York), 1965, 1970, 1997, p.155.

104 "In his speech to the Convention introducing the 10 October decree, Saint-Just had mapped out the survival path for the revolution, which reflected a new and draconian approach to all forms of opposition: 'You have no longer have [sic] any reason for restraint against enemies of the new order . . . You must punish not only traitors but the apathetic as well; you must punish whoever is passive in the Republic . . . We must rule by iron those who cannot be ruled by justice.'" in Gough, *The Terror in the French Revolution*, op. cit., p.43.

105 *Napoleon Bonaparte,* by Alan Schom, (Harper Perennial, New York), 1997, p.251.

106 *Ibid.,* p.253.

107 *Notes on the State of Virginia,* by Thomas Jefferson, (John Stockdale, London), 1781–1782, 1787, p.229.

[108] *Notes on the State of Virginia*, by Thomas Jefferson, (Lilly and Wait, Boston), 1781–1782, 1832, p.93.

[109] *Ibid.*, pp.170–71.

[110] *Ibid.*, p.171.

[111] *Ibid.*, p.170.

[112] Edward Coles to Thomas Jefferson, July 31, 1814, *Sketch of Edward Coles, Second Governor of Illinois, and the Slavery Struggle of 1823–1824,* by Elihu Benjamin Washburne, Collections of the Illinois State Historical Library, v.15, Biographical Series 1, (Illinois Printing Company, Danville), 1882, 1920; p.22.

[113] *Ibid.*, p.23.

[114] *Ibid.*, p.24.

[115] *Ibid.*, Jefferson to Coles, August 25, 1814, p.24.

[116] *Ibid.*, Jefferson to Coles, p.26.

[117] Edward Coles to Thomas Jefferson, September 26, 1814, *Ibid.,* p.29.

[118] Jefferson to Coles, August 25, 1814, *Ibid.,* p.26–27.

[119] Thomas Jefferson to John Tyler, Sr., May 26, 1810, *The Writings of Thomas Jefferson,* Library Edition, v.12, edited by Lipscomb and Bergh, (Thomas Jefferson Memorial Association, Washington, DC), 1904, p.394.

[120] Thomas Jefferson to David Humphreys, 1789; *The Jeffersonian Cyclopedia,* section #7832, op. cit., p.802.

[121] Thomas Jefferson to John Adams, August 1, 1816, *Correspondence,* v.2, p.485.

[122] There are numerous sources, some already referenced, for a pro or con view. For a good criticism of this theory please see William G. Hyland, Jr., *In Defense of Thomas Jefferson: The Sally Hemings Sex Scandal,* (Thomas Dunne Books/St. Martin's Press, New York), 2009; for a strongly supportive view of the theory, please see this interview with genealogist Helen F. M. Leary, an important researcher into this controversy, and author of the influential article "Sally Hemings's Children: A Genealogical Analysis of the Evidence" which appeared in the September 2001 issue of *The National Genealogical Society Quarterly.* This interview is available on the Internet at: www.youtube.com/watch?v=eOf3VJYdW4k&feature=related, (accessed September 4, 2013). The interview is also available on the National Genealogical Society's website: www.ngsgenealogy.org/cs/publications/videos/helen_leary/jefferson_hemings_research, (accessed September 26, 2015).

[123] Thomas Jefferson to Edward Coles, August 25, 1814, Washburne, *Sketch of Edward Coles, Second Governor of Illinois, and the Slavery Struggle of 1823–1824*, op. cit., p.26.

Chapter Thirteen: "This Is Impossible: How Can a Man Repent of His Virtues?"

1   Jefferson's Second Inaugural Address, Yale University Law School, op. cit., online at avalon.law.yale.edu/19th_century/jefinau2.asp, (accessed March 2, 2013).

2   US Department of State: Office of the Historian, "Milestones: 1784–1800, John Jay's Treaty, 1794–95," online at: https://history.state.gov/milestones/1784–1800/jay-treaty, (accessed September 15, 2015).

3   Thomas Jefferson to Mr. Lehré, November 8, 1808, *The Writings of Thomas Jefferson,* edited by H.A. Washington, v.5, (Derby & Jackson, New York), 1859, p.384.

4   *Jefferson's English Crisis: Commerce, Embargo, and the Republican Revolution,* by Burton Spivak, (University Press of Virginia, Charlottesville), 1979, p.120.

5   Thomas Jefferson: "Seventh Annual Message," October 27, 1807. Online by Gerhard Peters and John T. Woolley, *The American Presidency Project.* www.presidency.ucsb.edu/ws/?pid=29449, (accessed March 4, 2013).

6   Malone, *Jefferson the President, Second Term,* v.5, (Little, Brown, and Company, Boston), 1974, p.473.

7   It is understood that Jefferson rarely delivered speeches, but instead had them read aloud by others.

8   *Empire of Liberty: A History of the Early Republic,* by Gordon S. Wood, (Oxford University Press, 2009), p.655.

9   Thomas Jefferson to Major Joseph Eggleston, March 7, 1808, in Malone, v.5, op. cit, p.483.

10 Thomas Jefferson to John Taylor, January 6, 1808, in Malone, *Ibid.,* p.483.

11 Thomas Jefferson to James Madison, March 11, 1808, quoted in Spivak, op. cit., p.120.

12 Malone, *Jefferson the President, Second Term,* v.5, op. cit, p.487.

13 *National Intelligencer* editorial, December 1807, quoted in Malone, *Ibid.,* p.488.

14 *Ibid.,* p.488.

15 Cunningham, *In Pursuit of Reason: The Life of Thomas Jefferson,* op. cit., p.315.

16 Gallatin to Thomas Jefferson, December 18, 1807, quoted in Malone, v.5, op. cit, p.482.

17 *Ibid.,* p.580.

18 Thomas Jefferson to Albert Gallatin, April 19, 1808, *The Writings of Thomas Jefferson*, Definitive Edition, edited by Albert Ellery Bergh,

v.11, (Thomas Jefferson Memorial Association, Washington, DC), 1907; p.29.

19 Wood, *Empire of Liberty*, op. cit., p.656.

20 *Ibid.*, p.656; Wood cites Jefferson's letter to Mr. Thomas Lehré of November 8, 1808. Please see also *Jeffersonian Cyclopedia*, op. cit., section: 2525, p.288. Note: The editor of the *Jeffersonian Cyclopedia* misidentified "Mr. Lehré" as "Mr. Letue." This confusion of "Letue" for "Lehré" appears in several older collections of Jefferson scholarship including Bergh's *The Writings of Thomas Jefferson*, 1904, (v.12, p.190), and Washington's *The Writings of Thomas Jefferson*, 1859, (v.5, p.384). As the letter is available for viewing on the Internet (Library of Congress) there is no mistaking "Mr. Lehré" in Jefferson's own hand. http://memory.loc.gov/master/mss/mtj/mtj1/042/0900/0929.jpg, (accessed November 30, 2014).

21 Thomas Jefferson to Thomas Leiper, June 12, 1815, *The Writings of Thomas Jefferson,* Definitive Edition, edited by Albert Ellery Bergh, v.13, (Thomas Jefferson Memorial Association, Washington, DC, 1907), p.309; and Malone, v.5, op. cit., p.656.

22 Thomas Jefferson to James Monroe, January 28, 1809, *Memoir, Correspondence, and Miscellanies from the Papers of Thomas Jefferson*, edited by Thomas Jefferson Randolph, v.3, (F. Carr, and Co., Virginia), 1829, p.122.

23 *Ibid.*, p.122.

24 *Ibid.*, p.123.

25 John Adams to Benjamin Rush, December 28, 1807, Smith, *John Adams*, v.2, op. cit., p.1092.

26 John Adams to Benjamin Rush, April 18, 1808, Biddle, ed., *Old Family Letters*, op. cit, p.180.

27 John Adams to Josiah Quincy, November 25, 1808, *Life of Josiah Quincy of Massachusetts,* by Edmund Quincy, (Fields, Osgood, and Co., Boston), 1869, p.145; and Malone, v.5, op. cit, p.630.

28 John Adams to Josiah Quincy, November 25, 1808, *Ibid.*, p.145.

29 Josiah Quincy to John Adams, December 15, 1808, in Quincy, *Ibid.*, p.146.

30 Speech on Foreign Relations to the House of Representatives by Congressman Josiah Quincy of Massachusetts, November 28, 1808, *Ibid.*, p.151.

31 John Adams to Benjamin Rush, July 25, 1808, Biddle, ed., *Old Family Letters,* op. cit., pp.191–92.

32 John Adams to Benjamin Rush, April 18, 1808, *Ibid.*, p.181.

33 Thomas Jefferson to Nathaniel Macon, May 14, 1801, Foley, ed., *The Jeffersonian Cyclopedia*, section #5787, op. cit., p.619.

34 Thomas Jefferson to Elbridge Gerry, January 26, 1799, Foley, ed., *The Jeffersonian Cyclopedia*, section #5791, op. cit., p.620.

35 John Adams to Benjamin Rush, January 23, 1809, *Ibid.*, p.214, pp.216–17, and, Smith, John Adams, v.2, op. cit., p.1092.

36 John Adams to Thomas Jefferson, May 1, 1812, *Correspondence*, v.2, p301.

37 Cunningham, *In Pursuit of Reason,* op. cit., p.319.

38 Du Pont de Nemours biographical details from Malone, ed., *Correspondence Between Thomas Jefferson and Pierre Samuel du Pont de Nemours, 1798–1817*, op. cit., p.*xv*.

39 Thomas Jefferson to du Pont de Nemours, March 2, 1809; *Ibid.*, pp.121–22.

40 Thomas Jefferson to William B. Giles, December 25, 1825, *The Works of Thomas Jefferson,* edited by H.A. Washington, v.7, (Townsend Mac Coun, New York), 1859, pp.424–26.

41 Thomas Jefferson to du Pont de Nemours, March 2, 1809; *Ibid.*, pp.121–22.

42 *Ibid.*, pp.121–22.

43 *Jefferson and His Time: The Sage of Monticello*, by Dumas Malone, v.6, (Little, Brown and Company, Boston), 1970, p.3.

44 The Corporation for Jefferson's Poplar Forrest, History, www.poplar-forest.org/retreat/history, (accessed March 26, 2013).

45 "A man who could remain on intimate terms with men of such diverse character and political views as Adams, Jefferson, Pickering, Dickinson, Gates, Greene, Madison, Peters, Wayne, and Rittenhouse did not stand alone against the world. And to this company of his friends and admirers in public life must be added others from the learned world: Price, Priestley, Belknap, Lettsom, Ramsay, Waterhouse, Samuel Miller, Samuel Stanhope Smith, and Noah Webster." *Letters of Benjamin Rush*, edited by L.H. Butterfield, op. cit., p.*lxxi*.

46 Butterfield, "The Dream of Benjamin Rush: The Reconciliation of John Adams and Thomas Jefferson," op. cit., p.298.

47 "Benjamin Rush (1746–1813)," Penn Biographies, University of Pennsylvania Archives and Record Center, www.archives.upenn.edu/people/1700s/rush_benj.html, (accessed March 24, 2013).

48 *Ibid.*

49 "The Medical Reputation Of Benjamin Rush: Contrasts Over Two Centuries," by R.H. Shyrock, *Bulletin of Historical Medicine*, Nov-Dec, 1971; 45(6):507–52, cited in "Benjamin Rush, MD: assassin or beloved healer?" by Robert L. North, MD, *Proceedings* (Baylor University Medical Center), January 2000; 13(1): 45–49; www.ncbi.nlm.nih.gov/pmc/articles/PMC1312212/, (accessed March 24, 2013).

Note: Without knowledge of the mortality rates of any other physicians who treated victims during the 1793 epidemic these statistics should be understood in the context of such a crisis. That is, without a valid comparison between the mortality rate of Rush's patients versus those of other physicians, and those victims who received no treatment, the statistic can only be referential. However, many of the people of the time, including many of Rush's physician-colleagues, believed that the death rates of Rush's patients during the 1793 yellow fever epidemic was excessive and a direct consequence of Rush's aggressive and enthusiastic application of the lancet.

50 "Benjamin Rush, MD: assassin or beloved healer?" *Ibid.*

51 "Having laboured nearly six years to no purpose, to persuade the citizens of Philadelphia that the yellow fever is of domestic origin, I had concluded to desist from all further attempts to produce conviction upon this subject; but a retrospect of the scenes of distress which I have witnessed from that terrible disease, and the dread of seeing them speedily renewed, with aggravated circumstances, have induced me to make one more effort to prevent them, by pointing out their causes, and remedies. I anticipate from it, a renewal of the calumnies to which my opinion of the origin of our annual calamity has exposed me . . ." *Observations upon the origin of the malignant bilious, or yellow fever in Philadelphia, and upon the means of preventing it: addressed to the citizens of Philadelphia* (by Benjamin Rush), Philadelphia: Printed by Budd and Bartram, for Thomas Dobson, at the stone house, no 41, South Second Street., 1799, p.3.

52 Butterfield, "The Dream of Benjamin Rush," op. cit., p.298.

53 Thomas Jefferson to Dr. Thomas Cooper, October 7, 1814, *The Writings of Thomas Jefferson,* Definitive Edition, edited by Albert Ellery Bergh, v.13., (Thomas Jefferson Memorial Association, Washington, DC), 1907, p.200.

54 *Benjamin Rush, Physician and Citizen,* by Nathan G. Goodman, (University of Pennsylvania Press, 1934), pp. 194–95; Binger also concurs with this view, please see: *Revolutionary Doctor, Benjamin Rush, 1746–1813,* by Carl Binger, MD., (W.W. Norton and Company, New York), 1966, p.228.

55 Goodman, *Ibid.,* p.183.

56 Benjamin Rush to Elias Boudinot, September 25, 1793, quoted in *Ibid.,* p.184.

57 Benjamin Rush to Julia Rush, August 25, 1793, *Old Family Letters Relating to the Yellow Fever,* Series B, (J. Lippincott, Philadelphia), 1892, p.6.

58 Please see, Goodman, *Benjamin Rush,* op. cit., p.186.

59 *Ibid.,* p.345.

60 Benjamin Rush to Dr. John R. B. Rodgers, November 6, 1797, quoted in Goodman, *Ibid.*, p.212; Please also see Binger, op. cit., p.236.

61 *Benjamin Rush: Patriot and Physician,* by Alyn Brodsky, (Truman Talley Books, New York), 2004, p.336.

62 Benjamin Rush to John Adams, *Ibid.*, p.337. Date of this letter is not cited in Brodsky's text. Please see Butterfield, ed., *Letters of Benjamin Rush*, v.2, op. cit., p.975; Rush to John Adams, August 24, 1808.

63 "The Remarkable Dr. Benjamin Rush," by Eric Cox, *The Human Quest*, March/April, 1999, re-published in *Dickinson Magazine*, April 1, 2010, online at www.dickinson.edu/news-and-events/publications/dickinson-magazine/2010-spring/The-Remarkable-Dr--Benjamin-Rush/, (accessed March 30, 2013).

64 *A Memorial containing Travels Through Life or Sundry Incidents in the Life of Dr. Benjamin Rush written by Himself also Extracts from His Commonplace Book as well as A Short History of the Rush Family in Pennsylvania,* private publication, by Louis Alexander Biddle, (Philadelphia, 1905), p.74.

65 For the full text of Jefferson's "head and heart" letter to Maria Cosway please see, online: www.pbs.org/jefferson/archives/documents/ih195811.htm, (accessed September 17, 2015).

66 There is no definitive proof that Jefferson destroyed the correspondence between him and his wife. The absence of such a correspondence in the historical record—a correspondence that certainly must have once existed, and the extreme impact that his wife's early death had upon him suggests no other explanation.

67 Randall, *The Life of Thomas Jefferson,* v.1, op. cit., p.382.

68 Thomas Jefferson to the Chevalier De Chattellux, November 26, 1782, Washington, ed., *The Writings of Thomas Jefferson*, v.1, op. cit., p.322.

69 Butterfield, "The Dream of Benjamin Rush," op. cit., p.309.

70 John Adams to Benjamin Rush, April 18, 1808, Biddle, ed., *Old Family Letters*, op. cit., p.181.

71 The Adams's land holdings in Quincy were extensive, and included the area then, and still, known as Mount Wollaston. In 1792, the "north precinct of Braintree" was incorporated into a new town called "Quincy." Adams's fascination with (and fun in knowing) that Mount Wollaston was included in "Adams land" related to the activities of one Thomas Morton in 1626, "an adventurer in both the ancient and modern sense of the word and a jovial sort of roisterer too. He soon won control and crowned himself 'Lord of Misrule' although he only ruled a short time. The Mount became in name and fact Merry Mount. The records of Quincy prove that there was

'no law or order' at Mount Wollaston or Merry Mount." *Quincy 350 Years,* edited by H. Hobart Holly, Quincy Heritage Inc., Quincy, MA, 1974, pp.33–34.

[72] John Adams to Benjamin Rush, February 6, 1805, Biddle, ed., *Old Family Letters,* op. cit, p.62.

[73] Benjamin Rush to John Adams, June 13, 1808, *Our Sacred Honor: Words of Advice from the Founders in Stories, Letters, Poems, and Speeches,* edited by William J. Bennett, (Simon & Schuster, New York), 1997, p.88.

[74] Rush to Adams, *Ibid.,* p.88.

[75] John Adams to Benjamin Rush, June 20, 1808, Biddle, ed., *Old Family Letters,* op. cit., p.183.

[76] *Ibid.,* p.184.

[77] *Ibid.,* pp. 184–85.

[78] Benjamin Rush to John Adams, April 22, 1807, Butterfield, ed., *Letters of Benjamin Rush,* v.2, op. cit., p.941.

[79] *Ibid.,* p.941.

[80] John Adams to Benjamin Rush, May 1, 1807, Biddle, ed., *Old Family Letters,* op. cit., p.137.

[81] Adams's earlier scholarly work on political theory, "Defence of the Constitutions of the United States of America," published in three volumes in 1787 had also caused unintended negative consequences. Adams' affection for the British Constitution and his advocacy of a form of government in which an American aristocracy "and popular elements were held in balance by a strong executive" resulted in strong negative reactions from the Republicans, and from his friend Jefferson in particular. (Please see: Butterfield, "The Dream of Benjamin Rush," op. cit., pp.302–03.)

[82] Benjamin Rush to John Adams, February 12, 1790, Butterfield, ed., *Letters of Benjamin Rush,* v.1, op. cit., p.531; please also see Binger, *Revolutionary Doctor: Benjamin Rush, 1746–1813,* op. cit., p.289.

[83] John Adams to Benjamin Rush, February 6, 1805, Biddle, ed., *Old Family Letters,* op. cit., p.62.

[84] John Adams to Benjamin Rush, February 27, 1805, *Ibid.,* p.63.

[85] Rush's influence on the development of psychiatry was significant; his portrait had been included in the logo of the American Psychiatric Association (APA) from 1921 until May 2015. "1812- Benjamin Rush, M.D. (1745–1813), signer of the Declaration of Independence and the Father of American Psychiatry, published the first psychiatric textbook in the United States, *Inquiries and Observations on Diseases of the Mind,*" "History of the APA," www.psychiatry.org/about-apa-psychiatry/more-about-apa/history-of-the-apa, (accessed April 6, 2013); for

APA's new logo, please see online: http://www.apadailybulletin.com/apa-kicks-off-new-branding-campaign/, (accessed September 18, 2015).

86 John Adams to Benjamin Rush, March 4, 1809, Biddle, ed., *Old Family Letters,* op. cit., pp.219–20.

87 Benjamin Rush to John Adams, October 17, 1809, Butterfield, ed., *Letters of Benjamin Rush,* v.2, op. cit., pp.1021–22. In a draft of the same letter written the previous day, Rush described a different introduction to his dream, which he struck out: "What would you think of some future historian of the United States concluding one of his chapters with the following paragraph?" (*Ibid.,* p.1023, *fn.*3.)

88 Benjamin Rush to John Adams, October 17, 1809, Butterfield, ed., *Letters of Benjamin Rush,* v.2, op cit., pp.1021–22.

89 Adams is most likely referring to Andrew Brown, a one-time British Army officer who fought on the American side during the Revolution, and later the republican editor of the Philadelphia Gazette. Please see *Compendium of Irish Biography,* 1878; www.libraryireland.com/biography/AndrewBrown.php, (accessed, July 6, 2013).

90 John Adams to Benjamin Rush, October 25, 1809, Biddle, ed., *Old Family Letters,* op. cit., pp.246–47.

91 John Adams to Benjamin Rush, December 21, 1809, *Ibid.,* p.249.

92 John Adams to Benjamin Rush, December 27, 1810, *Ibid.,* p.272.

93 Benjamin Rush to Thomas Jefferson, January 2, 1811, Butterfield, "The Dream of Benjamin Rush," op. cit., p.309.

94 Benjamin Rush to Thomas Jefferson, January 2, 1811, *Ibid.,* pp.309–10.

95 Thomas Jefferson to Benjamin Rush, January 16, 1811, Randolph, ed., *Memoirs, Correspondence and Private Papers,* v.4, (1829), op. cit., pp.158–62.

96 Thomas Jefferson to Benjamin Rush, January 16, 1811, *Ibid.,* pp.157–58.

97 Thomas Jefferson to Benjamin Rush, January 16, 1811, *Ibid.,* p.159.

98 Benjamin Rush to Thomas Jefferson, February 1, 1811, Butterfield, ed., *Letters of Benjamin Rush,* v.2, op. cit., p.1078.

99 Letter of Edward Coles to Henry S. Randall, May 11, 1857, Randall, *The Life of Thomas Jefferson,* v.3, op. cit., pp.639–40.

100 *Ibid.,* p.640.

101 Thomas Jefferson to Benjamin Rush, December 5, 1811, Randolph, ed., *The Writings of Thomas Jefferson, Memoirs, Correspondence, and Miscellanies,* v.4, op. cit., p.167.

102 *Ibid.,* p.167.

103 *Ibid.,* p.167.

[104] Rush was noted by many as a compassionate, sensitive and caring man. One friend, Jeremy Belknap, wrote, "Dear Doctor I can compare you to nothing better than *Mr. Great Heart* in Bunyan who attacks without mercy all the Giants, Hydras, Hobgoblins etc. which stand in the way of his Pilgrims & conducts them thro' all opposition to the celestial City." Jeremy Belknap to Benjamin Rush, October 7, 1790; in Butterfield, ed., *Letters of Benjamin Rush*, v.1, op. cit., p.*lxix*.

[105] Jefferson is referencing Benjamin Franklin's description of John Adams which Jefferson had included in a letter to James Madison, written from Paris, July 29, 1789. "Always an honest one (?) often a great one but sometimes absolutely mad." (Question mark in Ford; common transcription is "Always an honest man.") Please see *The Works of Thomas Jefferson,* Federal Edition, edited by Paul Leicester Ford., v.5, (1904), p.485.

[106] Thomas Jefferson to Benjamin Rush, December 5, 1811, in Randolph, ed., *The Writings of Thomas Jefferson, Memoirs, Correspondence, and Miscellanies*, op. cit., p.167.

[107] *Ibid.*, pp.167–68.

[108] *Ibid.*, p.168.

[109] Benjamin Rush to John Adams, December 16, 1811, quoted in Butterfield, "The Dream of Benjamin Rush," op. cit., p.313.

[110] *Ibid.*

[111] Benjamin Rush to John Adams, December 16, 1811, in Butterfield, ed., *Letters of Benjamin Rush*, v.2, op. cit., p.1111.

[112] Benjamin Rush to Thomas Jefferson, December 17, 1811, *Ibid.*, p.1111.

[113] *Ibid.*

[114] John Adams to Benjamin Rush, December 25, 1811, C.F. Adams, ed., *The Works of John Adams, Second President of the United States, with a Life of the Author*, op. cit., p.10.

[115] *Ibid.*, p.10.

[116] *Ibid.*, p.11.

[117] *Ibid.*, p.12.

[118] *Ibid.*, p.12.

[119] *Ibid.*, p.12.

Chapter Fourteen: "Liberty, Friendship, Faith, Thou Wilt Hold Fast"

[1] *The Adams Papers: Papers of John Adams,* edited by Lint, Taylor, et al., v.15., (The Belknap Press of Harvard University Press, 2010), p.*xii*.

[2] *Ibid.*

3 "John Adams and John Quincy Adams, 2nd and 6th Presidents of the United States," By Joseph McMillan, (*The American Herald,* No. 2; 2007), American Heraldry Society, www.americanheraldry.org/pages/index.php?n=president.adams, (accessed May 8, 2013).

4 Willard, *John Adams: A Character Sketch,* op. cit., p.114. Other translations include "Keep liberty, friendship, and fidelity," (*The Adams Papers,* op. cit. p.*xii*); and "Hold fast to liberty, friendship, and faith," (McMillan, *The American Herald,* op. cit.).

5 John Adams to Thomas Jefferson, January 1, 1812, *Correspondence,* v.2, p.290.

6 Thomas Jefferson to John Adams, January 21, 1812, *Ibid.,* p.290.

7 Thomas Jefferson to John Adams, January 11, 1812, *Ibid.,* p.290.

8 Thomas Jefferson to John Adams, January 11, 1812, Randolph, ed., *Memoirs, Correspondence, and Private Papers of Thomas Jefferson,* v.4, op. cit., p.173.

9 *Ibid.,* p.173.

10 Poplar Forrest.

11 Thomas Jefferson to John Adams, January 11, 1812, Randolph, ed., *Memoirs, Correspondence, and Private Papers of Thomas Jefferson,* v.4, op. cit., p.174.

12 Thomas Jefferson to John Adams, January 23, 1812, *Correspondence,* v.2, op. cit., pp.292–93.

13 *Lectures on Rhetoric and Oratory,* Lecture 16, "Excitation and Management of the Passions," by John Quincy Adams, v.1, (Hilliard and Metcalf, Cambridge), 1810, p.377.

14 *Ibid.,* p.378.

15 Thomas Jefferson to Benjamin Rush, January 21, 1812, *The Writings of Thomas Jefferson, 1807–1815,* edited by Paul Leicester Ford, Letter Press Edition, v.9, (G.P. Putnam's Sons, New York), 1898, p.332.

16 Abigail Adams was then recovering from breast cancer surgery. She died little more than a year later.

17 Benjamin Rush to Thomas Jefferson, February 11, 1812, Butterfield, ed., *Letters of Benjamin Rush,* v.2, op. cit., pp.1118–19.

18 John Adams to Benjamin Rush, February 10, 1812, Biddle, ed., *Old Family Letters,* op. cit., pp.453–54.

19 Benjamin Rush to John Adams, February 17, 1812, Butterfield, ed., *Letters of Benjamin Rush,* op. cit., v.2, p.1127.

20 *Ibid.,* p.1127.

21 Benjamin Rush to Thomas Jefferson, March 3, 1812, *Ibid.,* pp.1127–28.

22 Locals pronounce Quincy, Massachusetts "Qwin-zee," as opposed to "Qwin-see" which is the local pronunciation for Quincy, Illinois, and

eighteen other cities by that name in the United States. It is believed that "Qwin-zee" is the pronunciation of the family name of Colonel John Quincy for whom the city of Quincy, Massachusetts, was named (the other "Quincy" cities having been named for John Quincy Adams). Please see "Why Do We Pronounce it 'Quin-zee'" at City of Quincy, online, www.quincyma.gov/Utilities/faq.cfm, (accessed November 14, 2014; September 26, 2015).

23 Benjamin Rush to John Adams, April 10, 1813, Butterfield, ed., *Letters of Benjamin Rush*, v.2, op. cit., p.1192.

24 John Adams to Richard Rush, May 5, 1813, in Goodman, *Benjamin Rush*, op. cit., pp.348–49.

25 John Adams to Elbridge Gerry, April 26, 1813, Biddle, ed., *Old Family Letters,* op. cit., "Prefatory" page.

26 Elbridge Gerry to Richard Rush, April 8, 1814, *Ibid.*

27 Thomas Jefferson to Richard Rush, May 31, 1813, Ford, ed., *The Writings of Thomas Jefferson*, v.9, op. cit*.*, p.385.

28 Thomas Jefferson to Benjamin Rush, April 21, 1803, Randall, *The Life of Thomas Jefferson*, op. cit., v.3, (1858), op. cit*.*, p.556.

29 Thomas Jefferson to Benjamin Rush, January 16, 1811, Randolph, ed., *Memoirs, Correspondence, and Private Papers of Thomas Jefferson*, v.4, op. cit., p.158.

30 Thomas Jefferson to Richard Rush, May 31, 1813, Ford, ed., *The Writings of Thomas Jefferson*, v.9, op. cit., p.385.

31 Thomas Jefferson to John Adams, May 27, 1813, *Correspondence,* v.2, op. cit., p.323.

32 John Adams to Thomas Jefferson, June 11, 1813, *Ibid.*, p.328.

33 John Adams to Thomas Jefferson, June 25, 1813, *Ibid.*, p.333.

34 John Adams to Thomas Jefferson, June 30, 1813, *Ibid.*, p.346.

35 John Adams to Thomas Jefferson, July 3, 1813, *Ibid.*, p.350.

36 Thomas Jefferson to John Adams, June 27, 1822, *Ibid.*, p.581.

37 Butterfield, "The Dream of Benjamin Rush," op. cit., p.317.

38 Several years before her death, Abigail added a postscript to one of John's letters to Jefferson. These few sentences overturned the unfortunate rift of 1804, and renewed good feeling between Abigail and Jefferson, once close friends. "I have been looking for some time for a space in my good Husbands Letters to add the regards of an old Friend, which are still cherished and preserved through all the changes and vicissitudes which have taken place since we first became acquainted, and will I trust remain as long as [signed] A. Adams." Postscript by Abigail Adams in letter from John Adams to Thomas Jefferson, July 15, 1813, *Correspondence,* v.2, p.358.

39 *Short History of U.Va.,* "Founding of the University," University of Virginia; www.virginia.edu/uvatours/shorthistory/, (accessed July 10, 2013).

40 John Adams to Thomas Jefferson, September 24, 1821, *Correspondence,* v.2, p.576.

41 *Ibid.,* p.576.

42 Thomas Jefferson to John Adams, March 25, 1826, *Correspondence,* v.2, p.614.

43 John Adams to Thomas Jefferson, April 17, 1826, *Ibid.,* p.614.

44 John Adams to Thomas Jefferson, December 12, 1816, *Ibid.,* p.499.

45 "Unlike Jefferson, Adams had not composed his own epitaph." McCullough, *John Adams,* op. cit., p.649.

46 *Ibid.,* p.649.

47 A seal which Jefferson rarely used, and whose design is also depicted on one of the gates of the cemetery at Monticello, contains the phrase "Rebellion to tyrants is obedience to God." This phrase was included in Jefferson's submission for his design for the Great Seal of the United States, which was rejected. Please see: www.monticello.org/site/jefferson/personal-seal and www.americanheraldry.org/pages/index.php?n= president.jefferson, (accessed July 10, 2013).

48 *The Domestic Life of Thomas Jefferson,* by Sarah N. Randolph, (Harper & Brothers, New York), 1871, p.431.

49 *Ibid.,* p.427.

50 *Ibid.,* p.429.

51 Statement of Dr. Dunglison, quoted in *Ibid.,* p.428.

52 An early biographer of Jefferson, B. L. Rayner, asserted that Jefferson's last coherent words were, "I have done for my country, and for all mankind, all that I could do, and I now resign my soul, without fear, to my God, my daughter to my country." Rayner also asserted, "all that was heard from him afterwards, was a hurried repetition, in indistinct and scarcely audible accents, of his favorite ejaculation, *Nunc Dimittas, Domine--Nunc Dimittas, Domine.*" As the several eyewitnesses who left a record of Jefferson's death did not report that Jefferson had uttered these words, and Rayner provides no source for these supposed final utterances, most Jefferson biographers, and other historians, have ignored Rayner's description of the event. Please see *Life, Writings, and Opinions of Thomas Jefferson,* by B.L. Rayner, (A. Francis and W. Boardman, New York), 1832, p.554. Please also see "Jefferson's Last Words" online at Thomas Jefferson Foundation, www.monticello.org/site/research-and-collections/jeffersons-last-words, (accessed July 15, 2013).

53 Smith, *John Adams,* v.2, op. cit., p.1136.

[54] *The Life of John Adams, begun by John Quincy Adams, completed by Charles Francis Adams*, v.2, (J.B. Lippincott & Co., Philadelphia), 1871, p.403.

[55] Smith, *John Adams*, v.2, op. cit., p.1137.

[56] An alternative description of this event is provided in Rayner, *Life, Writings, and Opinions of Thomas Jefferson*, op. cit., p.553; "To his daughter he presented a small morocco case which he requested her to open immediately after his decease. On opening the case it was found to contain an elegant and affectionate strain of poetry 'on the virtues of his dutiful and incomparable daughter.'"

[57] S.N. Randolph, *Domestic life of Thomas Jefferson*, op. cit., p.429.

[58] "A Discourse in Commemoration of the Lives and Services of John Adams and Thomas Jefferson, Delivered in Faneuil Hall, Boston, on the 2d of August, 1826," *The Great Speeches and Orations of Daniel Webster*, by Edwin P. Whipple, (Little, Brown, & Co., Boston), 1886, p.156.

[59] *Ibid.*, pp.158–59.

[60] Daniel Webster, *A Discourse in Commemoration of the Lives and Services of John Adams and Thomas Jefferson*, op. cit., p.156.

[61] John Adams to Benjamin Rush, September 27, 1808, Biddle, ed., *Old Family Letters, op cit.*, p.201.

[62] Thomas Jefferson to John Adams, June 15, 1813, *Correspondence*, v.2, p.331.

[63] Please see American Philosophical Society for a concise biography, and description of the papers of Dr. James Hutchinson, anti-federalist and supporter of Thomas Jefferson, victim of the Yellow Fever in Philadelphia of 1793, www.amphilsoc.org/mole/view?docId=ead/Mss.B.H97p-ead.xml, (accessed August 10, 2013).

[64] Please see University of Pennsylvania Archives for a concise biography of John Dickinson Sargent, anti-federalist and supporter of Jefferson, victim of the Yellow Fever in Philadelphia of 1793, www.archives.upenn.edu/people/1700s/sergeant_jd.html, (accessed August 10, 2013).

[65] "President John Adams proclaimed April 25, 1799, as a fast day, that God 'would withhold us from unreasonable discontent, from disunion, faction, sedition, and insurrection . . .'" See *Correspondence*, v.2, p.347, *fn.*

[66] John Adams to Thomas Jefferson, June 30, 1813, *Correspondence*, v.2, pp. 346–47.

[67] *Ibid.*, p.346.

[68] *Ibid.*, p.347.

[69] John Adams to Thomas Jefferson, July 13, 1813, *Ibid.*, pp.354–55.

[70] John Adams to Thomas Jefferson, July 13, 1813, *Ibid.*, p.356.

71 Adams had previously described his meeting with Dr. Priestley in a letter to Dr. Rush of December 22, 1808. Adams's recollection of the meeting to Rush and to Jefferson are very similar. Please see, Biddle, ed., *Old Family Letters*, op. cit., pp.209–10.

72 "The first volume of these Discourses is dedicated to John Adams, Vice-President of the United States of America, betwixt whom and our Author a sincere friendship at that time subsisted, and who had been one of his constant hearers." *Memoirs of Dr. Joseph Priestley to the Year 1795,* by Dr. Joseph Priestley and his son Joseph Priestley, (J. Johnson, London), 1807, p.760.

73 John Adams to Thomas Jefferson, August 15, 1823, *Correspondence,* v.2, op. cit., pp.594–95.

74 John Adams to Thomas Jefferson, August 15, 1823, *Ibid.*, p.595.

75 Thomas Jefferson to John Adams, September 4, 1823, *Correspondence*, v.2, op. cit., pp. 596–97.

76 John Adams to Thomas Jefferson, September 18, 1823, *Ibid.*, p.598.

77 *Ibid.* Author's Note: The numerous spelling errors in Adams's later letters are likely due to his having dictated them to someone not as careful a speller as he. His failing eyesight prevented him from comfortably writing during the later years of his retirement.

78 Willard, *John Adams: A Character Sketch*, op. cit., p.10.

Bibliography

Adams, Abigail. Abigail Adams to John Adams, May 23, 1797. *Adams Family Papers: An Electronic Archive.* Massachusetts Historical Society. <http://www.masshist.org/digitaladams/>, accessed 11 October, 2013.

———. to John Adams, March 25, 1797, *Adams Family Papers: An Electronic Archive.* Massachusetts Historical Society. <http://www.masshist.org/digitaladams/>, accessed 13 October, 2013.

Adams, Charles Francis. *Letters of John Adams Addressed to His Wife,* Vol. 2. Boston: Charles C. Little and James Brown, 1841.

———. *The Works of John Adams, Second President of the United States with a Life of the Author,* Vol. 9. Boston: Little, Brown and Company, 1854.

———. *The Works of John Adams, Second President of the United States with a Life of the Author,* Vol. 10. Boston: Little, Brown and Company, 1856.

Adams, John. *Correspondence of the Late President Adams, Originally published in the Boston Patriot, In a Series of Letters,* Number 1. Boston: Everett and Munroe, 1809.

———. *Inaugural Address, March 4, 1797,* Philadelphia, PA. Yale Law School: Lillian Goldman Law Library: The Avalon Project-Documents in Law, History, and Diplomacy. <http://avalon.law.yale.edu/18th_century/adams.asp>, accessed 11 October, 2013.

———. "Message to the Senate and House, Regarding Dispatches from the Envoys to France, March 5, 1798." *A Compilation of the Messages and Papers of the Presidents, Prepared under the direction of the Joint Committee on printing, of the House and Senate, Pursuant to an Act of the Fifty-Second Congress of the United States.* New York: Bureau of National Literature, Inc., 1897. Yale University, Avalon Project. <http://avalon.law.yale.edu/18th_century/ja98-02.asp>, accessed 12 October, 2013.

————. *Special Message to the Senate and House,* May 16, 1797, Philadelphia. Yale University Law School, Avalon Project. <http://avalon.law.yale.edu/18th_century/ja97-03.asp>, accessed 11 October, 2013.

————. to Abigail Adams, March 13, 1797, *Adams Family Papers: An Electronic Archive.* Massachusetts Historical Society. <http://www.masshist.org/digitaladams/>, accessed 11 October, 2013.

Adams, John, and William Cunningham. *Correspondence Between the Hon. John Adams (Late President of the United States) and the Late Wm. Cunningham, Esq. (Beginning in 1803 and ending in 1812).* Boston: E.M. Cunningham, 1823.

Adams, John Quincy. *Lectures on Rhetoric and Oratory,* Vol. 1. Cambridge: Hilliard and Metcalf, 1810.

————. and Charles Francis Adams. *The Life of John Adams, begun by John Quincy Adams, completed by Charles Francis Adams,* Vol. 2. Philadelphia: J.B. Lippincott & Co., 1871.

The Addresses and Messages of the Presidents of the United States. New York: McLean & Taylor, 1839.

Adolphus, John, F.S.A. *Biographical Memoirs of The French Revolution,* Vol. 1., London: T. Cadell, Jun., and W. Davies, 1799.

Appleby, Joyce. "The Jefferson-Adams Rupture and the First French Translation of John Adams' Defence." *The American Historical Review*, 73:4, (April, 1968), 1084–91.

Ballard, Richard. *A New Dictionary of the French Revolution.* London: I.B. Tauris & Co., Ltd., 2011.

Beloc, Hilaire. *Danton: A Study.* New York: Charles Scribner's Sons, 1911.

Bemis, Samuel Flagg. "Washington's Farewell Address: A Foreign Policy of Independence." *The American Historical Review.* 39:2, (January 1934), 250–68.

"Benjamin Rush (1746–1813)." University of Pennsylvania Archives and Record Center, *Penn Biographies,* <http://www.archives. upenn.edu/people/1700s/rush_benj.html>, accessed 12 October, 2013.

Bennett, William J., ed. *Our Sacred Honor: Words of Advice from the Founders in Stories, Letters, Poems, and Speeches.* New York: Simon & Schuster, 1997.

Bergh, Albert, ed. *The Writings of Thomas Jefferson.* Monticello Edition. Vol. 8. Washington, DC: Thomas Jefferson Memorial Association, 1904.

————. *The Writings of Thomas Jefferson*, Definitive Edition, Vol. 9. Washington, DC: Thomas Jefferson Memorial Association, 1907.

————. *The Writings of Thomas Jefferson*, Library Edition, Vol. 9. Washington, DC: Thomas Jefferson Memorial Association, 1903.

————. *The Writings of Thomas Jefferson*, Vol. 10. Washington, DC: The Thomas Jefferson Memorial Association, 1905.

————. *The Writings of Thomas Jefferson.* Definitive Edition. Vol. 11. Washington, DC: Thomas Jefferson Memorial Association, 1907.

————. and Lipscomb, eds. *The Writings of Thomas Jefferson*, Library Edition, Vol. 12. Washington, DC: Thomas Jefferson Memorial Association, 1904.

————. *The Writings of Thomas Jefferson.* Definitive Edition. Vol. 13. Washington, DC: Thomas Jefferson Memorial Association, 1907.

————. *The Writings of Thomas Jefferson.* Library Edition. Vol. 16. Washington, DC: Thomas Jefferson Memorial Association, 1904.

Bernstein, R.B. *The Founding Fathers Reconsidered.* Oxford: Oxford University Press, 2009.

Beveridge, Albert Geremiah. *The Life of John Marshall*, Vol. 2. Boston: Houghton, Mifflin Company, 1916, 1919.

Biddle, Alexander, ed. *Old Family Letters copied From the Originals for Alexander Biddle.* Series A. Philadelphia: J.P. Lippincott Co., 1892.

Binger, Carl, M.D. *Revolutionary Doctor, Benjamin Rush, 1746–1813.* New York: W.W. Norton and Company, 1966.

Bishop, Joseph Bucklin. *Our Political Drama, Conventions, Campaigns, Candidates*. New York: Scott-Thaw, 1904.

Bourne, Henry E. "Improvising a Government in Paris in July, 1789." *American Historical Review*, 10:2, (January, 1905), 280–308.

Bower, George Spencer. "Camille Desmoulins." *The Westminster and Foreign Quarterly Review*, New Series; 62, (July and October 1882), 28–58.

Boyd, Julian P., ed. *The Papers of Thomas Jefferson, 1 April–4 August 1791*, Vol. 20. Princeton: Princeton University Press, 1982; National Archives: Founders Online. <http://founders.archives. gov/documents/Jefferson/01-20-02-0076-0003>, accessed 6 October, 2013.

Brewer, David J. ed. *World's Best Orations from the Earliest Period to the Present Time,* Official Edition, Vol. 1. St. Louis: Ferd. P. Kaiser, 1899.

Brighton, Ray. *The Checkered Career of Tobias Lear*. Portsmouth, NH: Portsmouth Marine Society, 1985.

Brodie, Fawn. *Thomas Jefferson: An Intimate History.* New York: W.W. Norton, 1974.

Brodsky, Alyn. *Benjamin Rush: Patriot and Physician.* New York: Truman Talley Books, 2004.

Brookhiser, Richard. *James Madison.* New York: Basic Books, 2011.

Burstein, Andrew. *Jefferson's Secrets: Death and Desire at Monticello.* New York: Basic Books, 2005.

Butterfield, L.H., ed. "The Dream of Benjamin Rush: The Reconciliation John Adams and Thomas Jefferson." *The Yale Review*, 40:2, (December, 1950), pp. 297–319.

———. *Letters of Benjamin Rush*, 2 Vols. Princeton: Princeton University Press for the American Philosophical Society, 1951.

Cappon, Lester J., ed. *The Adams-Jefferson Letters: The Complete Correspondence between Thomas Jefferson and Abigail and John Adams.* 2 Vols. Williamsburg, Virginia: University of North Carolina Press for the Institute of Early American History and Culture, 1959.

Carlyle, Thomas. *The French Revolution: A History,* Vol. 3., London: James Fraser, 1837.

Chambers, R., editor. *Book of Days: A Miscellany of Popular Antiquities*, London: W. & R. Chambers, 1864.

Charles Adams. Find a Grave. <(http://www.findagrave.com/cgi-bin/fg.cgi?page=gr&GRid=20772235>, accessed 12 October, 2013.

Chernow, Ron. *Alexander Hamilton*. New York: The Penguin Press, 2004.

Chinard, Gilbert. *Honest John Adams*. Gloucester, MA: Peter Smith, and Boston: Little, Brown and Company, 1933, 1964, 1976.

Claretie, Jules. *Camille Desmoulins and his Wife: Passages from the History of the Dantonists*. (Translated by Mrs. Cashel Hoey), London: Smith, Elder & Co., 1876.

Conlin, Michael F. "The American Mission of Citizen Pierre-August Adet: Revolutionary Chemistry and Diplomacy in the Early Republic," *The Pennsylvania Magazine of History and Biography*, 124:4, (Oct. 2000), 489–520.

Conway, Moncure Daniel, ed. Rights of Man: Being an Answer to Mr. Burke's Attack on the French Revolution, by Thomas Paine, New York: G.P. Putnam's Sons, 1894.

———. *The Life of Thomas Paine*, Vol. 2. New York: G.P. Putnam's Sons, 1892, 1908.

———. *The Writings of Thomas Paine*, Vol.3. New York: G.P. Putnam's Sons, 1895.

Coser, Lewis A. *Men of Ideas*. New York: Free Press Paperbacks, 1965, 1970, 1997.

Cox, Eric. "The Remarkable Dr. Benjamin Rush." *The Human Quest*, March/April, 1999, re-published in *Dickinson Magazine*, April 1, 2010, <http://www.dickinson.edu/news-and-events/publications/dickinson-magazine/2010-spring/The-Remarkable-Dr--Benjamin-Rush/>, accessed 13 October, 2013.

Crawford, Alan Pell. *Twilight at Monticello: The Final Years of Thomas Jefferson*. New York: Random House, 2008.

Crawford, Michael J., and Christine F. Hughes, "Historical Overview of the Federalist Navy, 1787–1801." *The Reestablishment of the Navy, 1787–1801, Historical Overview and Select Bibliography, Naval History Bibliographies, No. 4,* Department of The

Navy—Naval Historical Center, <http://www.history.navy.mil/biblio/biblio4/biblio4a.htm>, accessed 12 October, 2013.

Cunningham, Noble E. *In Pursuit of Reason: The Life of Thomas Jefferson*. Baton Rouge: Louisiana State University Press, 1987.

Cushing, Harry Alonzo, ed. *The Writings of Samuel Adams 1778–1802*, Vol. 4, Letter Press Edition. New York: G.P. Putnam's Sons, 1908.

Cusumano, Rudy. "About General Lafayette, The Man and His Times. From Valley Forge to Barren Hill and Back." American Friends of Lafayette. <http://www.friendsoflafayette.org/barren_hill.html>, accessed 6 October, 2013.

De Conde, Alexander. *The Quasi War.* New York: Charles Scribner's Sons, 1966.

De Tocqueville, Alexis, John, Bonner, trans. *The Old Regime and the Revolution.* New York: Harper & Brothers, 1856.

De Witt, Cornelius Henry. *Jefferson and The American Democracy.* London: Longman, 1862.

"Did You Know . . . Independence Day Should Actually Be July 2? And Other Little Known Facts About The Declaration Of Independence." National Archives, *Press Release,* June 1, 2005. <http://www.archives.gov/press/press-releases/2005/nr05-83.html>, accessed 12 October, 2013.

Doyle, William. *The French Revolution: A Very Short Introduction.* New York: Oxford University Press, 2001.

Elkins, Stanley, and Eric McKitrick. *The Age of Federalism: The Early American Republic, 1788-1800.* Oxford: Oxford University Press, 1993.

Ellery, Eloise, Ph.D. *Brissot de Warville: A Study in the History of the French Revolution.* Boston: Houghton Mifflin Company, 1915.

Ellis, Joseph J. *American Creation.* New York: Vintage, 2008.

———. *First Family-Abigail and John Adams.* New York: Vintage, 2010.

———. *Passionate Sage: The Character and Legacy of John Adams.* New York: Norton, 1993.

Etude Revolutionnaires, review of. *The Westminster Review*, American Edition, 55, (July 1851), 126–28.

Ferling, John E. *John Adams: A Life*. Oxford: Oxford University Press, 1992.

———. "'Oh That I Was a Soldier': John Adams and the Anguish of War." *American Quarterly*, 36:2, (Summer, 1984), 258–75.

Fleming, Thomas. *The Intimate Lives of the Founding Fathers*. New York: HarperCollins, 2009/2010.

Flexner, James Thomas. *George Washington: The Indispensable Man*. Boston: Little, Brown, and Co., 1969, 1973.

Foley, John P., ed. *The Jeffersonian Cyclopedia*. New York: Funk & Wagnalls, 1900.

Ford, Paul Leicester, ed. *The Works of Thomas Jefferson*. Federal Edition, Vol. 5. New York: G.P. Putnam's Sons, 1904.

———. *The Works of Thomas Jefferson*, Federal Edition, Vol. 6. New York: G.P. Putnam's Sons, 1904.

———. *The Works of Thomas Jefferson*, Federal Edition, Vol. 7. New York: G.P. Putnam's Sons, 1904.

———. *The Works of Thomas Jefferson*, Federal Edition, Vol. 8. New York: G.P. Putnam's Sons, 1904–05.

———. *The Works of Thomas Jefferson*, Federal Edition, Vol. 9. New York: G.P. Putnam's Sons, 1905.

———. *The Works of Thomas Jefferson*, Vol. 12. New York: G.P. Putnam's Sons, 1905.

———. *The Writings of Thomas Jefferson*, Letter Press Edition, Vol. 3. New York: G.P. Putnam's Sons, 1896.

———. *The Writings of Thomas Jefferson*, Letter Press Edition, Vol. 5. 1788–1792. New York: G.P. Putnam's Sons, 1895.

———. *The Writings of Thomas Jefferson*, Letter Press Edition, Vol. 8. New York: G.P. Putnam's Sons, 1897.

———. *The Writings of Thomas Jefferson*, Letter Press Edition, Vol. 9. New York: G.P. Putnam's Sons, 1898.

———. *The Writings of Thomas Jefferson*, Letter Press Edition, Vol. 10. New York: G.P. Putnam's Sons, 1899.

———. *The Writings of Thomas Jefferson*, Federal Edition, Vol. 10. New York: G.P. Putnam's Sons, 1905.

Ford, Worthington Chauncey. *Some Letters of Elbridge Gerry of Massachusetts, 1784–1804*. Brooklyn: Historical Printing Club, 1896.

———. "The Washington-Jefferson Letters." *The Nation,* 75:1936, (July 24, 1902), 112–13.

———. ed. *The Writings of George Washington*, Vol. 12. New York: Putnam-Knickerbocker Press, 1891.

———. "Jefferson and the Newspaper." *Records of the Columbia Historical Society,* Vol. 8. Washington, DC: Columbia Historical Society, 1905.

"*Founding of the University.*" Short History of U.Va. University of Virginia. <http://www.virginia.edu/uvatours/shorthistory/>, accessed 13 October, 2013.

Freeman, Douglas Southall; completed by John Alexander Carroll, and Mary Wells Ashworth. *George Washington, First in Peace*, Vol. 7. New York: Charles Scribner's Sons, 1957.

Furet, Francois, and Mona Ozouf. *A Critical Dictionary of the French Revolution.* Cambridge: Harvard University Press, 1989.

Gabler, James M. *Passions: The Wines and Travels of Thomas Jefferson.* Baltimore: Bacchus Press, 1995.

Gibbs, Philip. *Men and Women of the French Revolution.* London: Kegan Paul, Trench, Trubner & Co. Ltd., 1906.

Goodman, Nathan G. *Benjamin Rush, Physician and Citizen.* Philadelphia: University of Pennsylvania Press, 1934.

Gough, Hugh. *The Terror in the French Revolution.* Hampshire, UK and New York: Palgrave, 1998.

Greenstein, Fred I. "Presidential Difference in the Early Republic: The Highly Disparate Leadership Styles of Washington, Adams, and Jefferson." *Presidential Studies Quarterly* 36:3 (2006): 373–90.

Grimm, Kevin, Ph.D. *Thomas Paine, 1737–1809.* Mount Vernon Ladies' Association of the Union, Mount Vernon, Estate, Museum and Gardens. <http://www.mountvernon.org/educational-resources/encyclopedia/thomas-paine>, accessed 12 October, 2013.

Hayes, Kevin J. *The Road to Monticello: The Life and Mind of Thomas Jefferson.* Oxford: Oxford University Press, 2008.

Himmesoete, Marilyn, "Writing and Measuring Time: Nineteenth-Century French Teenagers' Diaries," Baggerman, Arianne, Dekker, Rudolf, Michael Mascuch, eds. *Controlling Time and Shaping the Self: Developments in Autobiographical Writing Since the Six-teenth Century.* Leiden, The Netherlands: Brill, 2011.

Hildreth, Richard. *The History of the United States;* John Adams and Thomas Jefferson, Vol. 2. New York: Harper & Brothers, 1863.

————. *History of the United States of America*, Vol. 5. New York: The Bradley Company, 1879.

"History." The Corporation for Jefferson's Poplar Forrest, <http://www.poplarforest.org/retreat/history>, accessed 12 October, 2013.

History of the APA. American Psychiatric Association. <http://www.psychiatry.org/about-apa--psychiatry/more-about-apa/history-of-the-apa>, accessed 13 October, 2013.

Hoffer, Eric. *The True Believer.* New York: HarperCollins, 1951, 2002.

Holly, H. Hobart, ed. *Quincy 350 Years.* Quincy, MA: Quincy Herit-age, Inc., 1974.

Holton, Woody. *Abigail Adams.* New York: Free Press, 2009.

Hunt, Gaillard, ed. *The Writings of James Madison, comprising his Public Papers and his Private Correspondence, including his numerous letters and documents now for the first time printed,* Vol. 6. New York: G.P. Putnam's Sons, 1900, <http://oll.libertyfund.org/title/1941/124440> accessed 11 October, 2013.

Hutchinson, James. *James Hutchinson Papers, 1771–1928.* Ameri-can Philosophical Society. <http://www.amphilsoc.org/mole/view?docId=ead/Mss.B.H97p-ead.xml>, accessed 13 October, 2013.

Hyland, William G., Jr. *In Defense of Thomas Jefferson: The Sally Hemings Sex Scandal.* New York: Thomas Dunne Books/St. Mar-tin's Press, 2009.

Irelan, John Robert. *The Republic; or A History of the United States of America in the Administrations, from the Monarchic Colonial Days to the Present Times,* Vol. 3. Chicago: Fairbanks and Palmer, 1886.

James, James A. "French Opinion as a Factor in Preventing War Between France and the United States, 1795–1800." *The American Historical Review,* 30:1, (Oct. 1924), 44–55.

Jarvis, William C., Esq. *The Republican; or, a Series of Essays on the Principles and Policy of Free States. Having a Particular Reference to the United States of America and the Individual States.* Pittsfield, MA: Phinehas Allen, 1820.

Jefferson, Thomas. "The 'Adam and Eve' Letter: Jefferson to William Short, January 3, 1793," in *The Atlantic Monthly* Magazine, October, 1996. <http://www.theatlantic.com/past/docs/issues/96oct/obrien/adam.htm>, accessed 11 October, 2013.

———. *First Inaugural Address,* March 4, 1801. Washington, DC. Yale University, Lillian Goldman Law Library, Avalon Project. <http://avalon.law.yale.edu/19th_century/jefinau1.asp>, accessed 12 October, 2013.

———. *Kentucky Resolution,* October 1798, Draft version, Yale Law School, Avalon Project. <http://avalon.law.yale.edu/18th_century/jeffken.asp>, 12 October, 2013.

———. *Notes on the State of Virginia.* London: John Stockdale, 1781–1782, 1787.

———. *Notes on the State of Virginia.* Boston: Lilly and Wait, 1781–1782, 1832.

———. *Second Inaugural Address,* March 4, 1805, Washington, DC. Yale University Law School, Avalon Project. <http://avalon.law.yale.edu/19th_century/jefinau2.asp>, accessed 12 October, 2013.

———. *Seventh Annual Message,* October 27, 1807, Washington, DC. *The American Presidency Project.* <http://www.presidency.ucsb.edu/ws/?pid=29449>, accessed 12 October, 2013.

———. "Tree of Liberty Letter: Jefferson to William Smith, November 13, 1787," in *The Atlantic Monthly* Magazine, October 1996. <http://www.theatlantic.com/past/docs/issues/96oct/obrien/blood.htm>, accessed 11 October, 2013.

———. to Dr. Benjamin Rush, April 21, 1803. Massachusetts Historical Society, *Proceedings.* 12, (1897–1899), 267.

———. to Maria Causeway, 12, October, 1786. Public Broadcasting Service. <http://www.pbs.org/jefferson/archives/documents/ih195811.htm>, accessed 12 October, 2013.

"Jonathan D. Sergeant (1746–1793)." *Penn Biographies.* University of Pennsylvania Archives & Records Center. <http://www.

archives.upenn.edu/people/1700s/sergeant_jd.html>, accessed 13 October, 2013.

Kennedy, John F. *A Nation of Immigrants.* New York: Harper Perennial, 1964, 2008.

Kirk, Russell. *The Conservative Mind, From Burke to Eliot.* Washington, DC: Regnery, 1953, 1960, 1972, 1985, 2001.

Kramer, Lloyd. *Lafayette in Two Worlds.* Chapel Hill: University of North Carolina Press, 1996.

Kurtz, Stephen G. *The Presidency of John Adams – The Collapse of Federalism, 1795–1800.* Philadelphia: University of Pennsylvania Press, 1957.

La Tour du Pain, La Marquise de (edited and translated by Walter Geer). "Recollections of the Revolution and the Empire," (From the French of the "Journal D'Une Femme De Cinquante Ans"). New York: Brentano's, 1920.

Laborers at Mount Vernon, "Mourning Washington." Mount Vernon Ladies' Association of the Union, Mount Vernon, Estate, Museum and Gardens. <http://www.mountvernon.org/educational-resources/encyclopedia/mourning-mountvernon>, accessed 12 October 21, 2013. <http://www.mountvernon.org/research-collections/digital-encyclopedia/article/mourning-washington-by-laborers-at-mount-vernon/>, re-accessed 7 October, 2014.

Lafayette to George Washington, March 17, 1790. National Archives; Founders Online, Source: Twohig, Dorothy, Mastromarino, Mark A., and Jack D. Warren, eds. *The Papers of George Washington*, Presidential Series, Vol. 5, *16 January 1790–30 June 1790*. Charlottesville: University Press of Virginia, 1996. <http://founders.archives.gov/documents/Washington/05-05-02-0159>, accessed 6 October, 2013.

Leary, Helen F. M. "Sally Hemings's Children: A Genealogical Analysis of the Evidence." *National Genealogical Society Quarterly*, 89 (September 2001), 165–207.

Leary, Helen F. M., CG (Emeritus), FASG, FNGS, *"Thomas Jefferson and Sally Hemings Research."* Lecture. National Genealogical Society, Internet, Produced by Kate Geis and Allen Moore; 2009, <http://www.youtube.com/watch?v=eO

f3VJYdW4k&feature=related>, accessed October 10, 2013. Also at National Genealogical Society website: <http://www. ngsgenealogy.org/cs/publications/videos/helen_leary/jefferson_ hemings_research>, accessed October 10, 2013.

Lefebvre, Georges. *The Coming of the French Revolution.* (Translated by R. R. Palmer), New Jersey: Princeton University Press, 1947, 1979.

Lint, Gregg L, and C. James Taylor, and Margaret A. Hogan. *The Adams Papers: Papers of John Adams*, Vol. 15. Cambridge: The Belknap Press of Harvard University Press, 2010.

Linton, Marisa. "Friends, Enemies, and the Role of the Individual." *A Companion of the French Revolution*, edited by Peter McPhee, West Sussex, UK: Wiley-Blackwell, 263–78, (2013).

Ludy, Robert B., M.D. *Historic Hotels: Past and Present.* Philadelphia: David McKay Company, 1927.

Lukens, Robert J. "Jared Ingersoll's Rejection of Appointment as One of the 'Midnight Judges' of 1801: Foolhardy or Farsighted." *Temple Law Review.* 70, (1997).

Lyman, Theodore. *The Diplomacy of the United States, Being an Account of the Foreign Relations of the Country, from the first treaty with France, in 1778, to the treaty of Ghent, in 1814, with Great Britain.* Boston: Wells and Lilly, 1826.

Lyon, E. Wilson. "The Directory and the United States," *American Historical Review*, 43:13, (April, 1938), 514–32.

Madelin, Louis. *Danton.* (Translated by Lady Mary Loyd), New York: Alfred A. Knopf, 1921.

Malone, Dumas, ed. *Correspondence Between Thomas Jefferson and Pierre Samuel Du Pont de Nemours, 1798–1817.* Boston: Houghton, Mifflin, 1930.

———. *Jefferson and His Time: Jefferson and the Rights of Man,* Vol. 2. Boston: Little, Brown, 1951.

———. *Jefferson and His Time: Jefferson and the Ordeal of Liberty.* Vol. 3. Boston: Little, Brown, 1962.

———. *Jefferson and His Time: Jefferson the President, Second Term,* Vol. 5. Boston: Little, Brown, 1974.

————. *Jefferson and His Time: The Sage of Monticello.* Vol. 6. Boston: Little, Brown and Company, 1970.

Marshall, John. "Letters of John Marshall When Envoy to France." *The American Historical Review*, 2:2, (January, 1897), 294–306.

Martin, Russell, L. "*Jefferson's Last Words.*" Thomas Jefferson Foundation. <http://www.monticello.org/site/research-and-collections/jeffersons-last-words>, accessed 13 October, 2013.

Mastromarino, Mark A., ed. *The Papers of George Washington*, Presidential Series, Vol. 9, *23 September 1791–29 February 1792.* Charlottesville: University Press of Virginia, 2000; National Archives; Founders Online, <http://founders.archives.gov/documents/Washington/05-09-02-0289>, accessed 6 October, 2013.

McCollough, David. *John Adams.* New York: Simon and Schuster, 2001.

McMillan, Joseph. "John Adams and John Quincy Adams, 2nd and 6th Presidents of the United States." *The American Herald,* 2, 2007, American Heraldry Society, <http://www.americanheraldry.org/pages/index.php?n=president.adams>, accessed 13 October, 2013.

————. "Thomas Jefferson, 3rd President of the United States, The Arms of Thomas Jefferson." *The American Herald,* 3, 2008, American Heraldry Society <http://www.americanheraldry.org/pages/index.php?n=president.jefferson>, accessed 13 October, 2013.

Meacham, Jon. *Thomas Jefferson: The Art of Power.* New York: Random House, 2012.

Methley, Violet. *Camille Desmoulins: A Biography.* London: Martin Secker, 1914.

Miller, Hunter, ed. *Convention of 1800, Treaties and Other International Acts of the United States of America*, Volume 2, Documents 1-40:1776–1818. Washington, DC: Government Printing Office, 1931; Yale Law School, Avalon Project. <http://avalon.law.yale.edu/19th_century/fr1800.asp>, accessed 12 October, 2013.

Miller, Mary Ashburn. *A Natural History of Revolution:Violence and Nature in the French Revolutionary Imagination, 1789–1794.* Ithaca: Cornell University, 2011.

Moorehead, Caroline. Dancing to the Precipice: The Life of Lucie De La Tour Du Pin, Eyewitness to an Era. Harper Perennial, 2010.

Morse, Jedidiah, D.D. *Annals of the American Revolution.* Hartford, 1824.

Nagel, Paul C. *Descent from Glory: Four Generations of the Adams Family.* Cambridge: Harvard University Press, 1983.

Nelson, Craig. *Thomas Paine, Enlightenment, Revolution, and the Birth of Modern Nations.* New York: Penguin Books, 2006.

Neuman, Gerald L., Hobson, Charles F. "John Marshall and the Enemy Alien: A Case Missing from the Canon." *Columbia Law School Report*, Winter, 2006. <http://www.law.columbia.edu/law_school/communications/reports/winter06/facforum2>, accessed 12 October, 2013.

Nicholson, Donald H. "Early French Policy Toward the United States." *Bulletin of the Chicago Historical Society*, 3:7, (January, 1926), 56–60.

North, Robert L., M.D. "Benjamin Rush, MD: Assassin or beloved healer?" *Proceedings,* Baylor University Medical Center, 13:1, (January, 2000), 45–49.

Oberg, Barbara, ed. "Thomas Jefferson's Letter to Philip Mazzei." *The Papers of Thomas Jefferson, 1 March 1796 to 31 December 1797, Vol. 29.* Princeton: Princeton University Press, 2002, 73–88; <http://jeffersonpapers.princeton.edu/selected-documents/jeffersons-letter-philip-mazzei>, accessed 13 October, 2013.

O'Brien, Conor Cruise. *The Long Affair: Thomas Jefferson and The French Revolution, 1785–1800*, Chicago: University of Chicago Press, 1996.

———. "Thomas Jefferson: Radical and Racist." *The Atlantic Monthly,* 278:4 (Oct. 1996): 53–74, <http://www.theatlantic.com/past/docs/issues/96oct/obrien/obrien.htm>, accessed 11 October, 2013.

Oliver, Bette W. *Surviving the French Revolution: A Bridge Across Time*. Plymouth, UK: Lexington Books, 2013.

Orieux, Jean. *Talleyrand: The Art of Survival.* Alfred A. Knopf, 1974.

Owsley, Frank. *King Cotton Diplomacy: Foreign Relations of the Confederate States of America.* Chicago: University of Chicago Press, 1931, 1959.

Paine, Thomas. *Rights of Man: Being an Answer to Mr. Burke's Attack on the French Revolution.* London: J.S. Jordan, 1791.

Paine, Thomas. *The Theological Works of Thomas Paine*. Chicago: Belfords, Clarke, & Co., 1879.

Palmer, R.R. *Twelve Who Ruled: The Year of the Terror in the French Revolution*, Bicentennial Edition, Princeton: Princeton University Press, 1941, 1989.

Parton, James. *The Life of Thomas Jefferson: Third President of the United States*. Boston: James R. Osgood, and Company, 1874.

———. "The Presidential Election of 1800." *The Atlantic Monthly*, July 1873.

Pasko, W. W. *Old New York: A journal relating to the history and antiquities of New York City.* New York: W.W. Pasko, 1890.

Personal Seal. Thomas Jefferson Foundation. <http://www.monticello.org/site/jefferson/personal-seal>, accessed 13 October, 2013.

Peterson, Merrill D. *The Portable Thomas Jefferson.* New York: Penguin, 1975.

Pickering, Timothy. *A review of the correspondence between the Hon. John Adams, and the late William Cunningham, ESQ., Beginning in 1803 and Ending in 1812,* Second edition. Salem, MA: Cushing and Appleton, 1824.

"President Jefferson signs the Embargo Act, putting a halt to all trading with any country in the entire world." Presidential Key Events, Thomas Jefferson; Miller Center. University of Virginia. <http://millercenter.org/president/jefferson/key-events>, accessed 11 October, 2013.

Priestley, Joseph, Dr., and Joseph Priestley. *Memoirs of Dr. Joseph Priestley to the Year 1795.* London: J. Johnson, 1807.

Quincy, Edmund. *Life of Josiah Quincy of Massachusetts.* Boston: Fields, Osgood, and Co., 1869.

Randall, Willard Sterne. *George Washington: A Life.* New York: Henry Holt and Company, 1997.

Randall, Henry Stephens. *The Life of Thomas Jefferson,* Vol. 2. New York: Derby and Jackson, 1858.

———. *The Life of Thomas Jefferson,* Vol. 3. New York: Derby and Jackson, 1858.

Randolph, Sarah N. *The Domestic Life of Thomas Jefferson.* New York: Harper & Brothers, 1871.

Randolph, Thomas Jefferson, ed. *Correspondence, and Private Papers of Thomas Jefferson.* Vol. 2. London: Colburn and Bentley, 1829.

———. *Correspondence, and Private Papers of Thomas Jefferson.* Vol. 4. Charlottesville: F. Carr and Co., 1829.

———. *Memoirs, Correspondence and Miscellanies from the Papers of Thomas Jefferson,* Vol. 3. Virginia: F. Carr, and Co., 1829.

———. *Memoirs, Correspondence, and Private Papers of Thomas Jefferson,* Vol. 3. London: Henry Colburn and Richard Bentley, 1829.

———. *Memoirs, Correspondence, and Private Papers of Thomas Jefferson,* Vol. 4. London: Henry Colburn and Richard Bentley, 1829.

Ray, Thomas M. "'Not One Cent for Tribute': The Public Addresses and American Popular Reaction to the XYZ Affair, 1798-1799." *Journal of the Early Republic,* 3:4 (Winter, 1983), 389–412.

Rayner, B. L. *Sketches of the Life, Writings, and Opinions of Thomas Jefferson.* New York: A. Francis and W. Boardman, 1832.

Reynolds, Siân. *Marriage and Revolution: Monsieur and Madame Roland* by Reynolds Oxford: Oxford University Press, 2012.

Richardson, James B. *A Compilation of the Messages and Papers of the Presidents, 1789–1902,* Vol.1. Washington, DC: Bureau of National Literature and Art, Inc., 1907.

Ripley, George, and George Dana, eds. "John Adams," *The New American Cyclopaedia,* Vol.1. New York: D. Appleton and Co., 1868.

Rothenberg, Gunther E. "The Origins, Causes, and Extension of the Wars of the French Revolution and Napoleon." *The Journal of Interdisciplinary History,* 18:4, (Spring, 1988), 771–93.

Rowlands, Walter. *Among the Great Masters of Oratory: Scenes in the Lives of Famous Orators,* Boston: Dana Estes & Co., 1901.

Rush, Benjamin. *Observations upon the origin of the malignant bilious, or yellow fever in Philadelphia, and upon the means of preventing it: Addressed to the citizens of Philadelphia.* Philadelphia: Budd and Bartram, for Thomas Dobson, 1799.

———. et al. *Old Family Letters Relating to the Yellow Fever,* Series B. Philadelphia: J. Lippincott, 1892.

————. and Louis Alexander Biddle. *A Memorial containing Travels Through Life or Sundry Incidents in the Life of Dr. Benjamin Rush written by Himself also Extracts from His Commonplace Book as well as A Short History of the Rush Family in Pennsylvania.* Philadelphia: Lanoraie, 1905.

Rutt, John Towill. *Life and Correspondence of Joseph Priestley, LLD, FRS, etc.*, Vol. 2. Hackney, London: George Smallfield, 1832.

Saint-Elme, Ida. *Memoirs of a Contemporary: Being Reminiscences of Ida Saint-Elme, Adventuress, of her Acquaintance with Certain Makers of French History, and of Her Opinions Concerning Them. From 1790 to 1815,* (translated by Lionel Strachey). New York: Doubleday, Page, and Co., 1902.

Samuelson, Richard. "The Midnight Appointments." *White House History*, 7 (2001).

Sawtelle, William Otis. "Talleyrand's Oath of Allegiance." *Sprague's Journal of Maine History,* 12:3, (July, August, September, 1924), 147–48.

Schama, Simon. *Citizens.* New York: Vintage, 1990.

Schom, Alan. *Napoleon Bonaparte.* New York: Harper Perennial, 1997.

Schutz, John A., Douglas Adair, eds. *The Spur of Fame: Dialogues of John Adams and Benjamin Rush*, 1805–1813. San Marino, CA: The Huntington Library, 1966.

Sedgwick, Ellery. *Thomas Paine.* Boston: Small, Maynard, & Company, 1899.

Sherwin, W.T. *The Life of Thomas Paine.* Glasgow: Muir, Gowans, and Co., 1833.

Shyrock, R.H. "The Medical Reputation Of Benjamin Rush: Contrasts Over Two Centuries." *Bulletin of Historical Medicine*, 45:6, (Nov–Dec 1971), 507–52.

Silverman, Sharon Hernes. "Joseph Priestley." ("Joseph Priestley: Catalyst of the Enlightenment." *Pennsylvania Heritage,* XXV: 3, (Summer, 1999). Pennsylvania Historical and Museum Commission. <http://www.portal.state.pa.us/portal/server.pt/community/people/4277/priestley,_joseph_(ph)/443569>, accessed 12 October, 2013.

Smith, Jean Edward. *John Marshall: Definer of a Nation*. New York: Henry Holt, 1996.

Smith, Page. *John Adams*, 2 Vols. New York: Doubleday & Co., 1962.

Smyth, William. *Lectures on History: The French Revolution*, Vol. 2. Cambridge: William Pickering, J. & J.J. Deighton, 1842.

Sparks, Jared. *The Writings of George Washington*. Vol. 1. Boston: American Stationers' Company, 1836.

————. *The Writings of George Washington*. Vol. 10. Boston: Russell, Shattuck and Williams, et al., 1836.

Spivak, Burton. *Jefferson's English Crisis: Commerce, Embargo, and the Republican Revolution*. Charlottesville: University Press of Virginia, 1979.

Stafford, Cornelius William. *Philadelphia Directory for 1797*. Philadelphia: William Woodward, 1797.

Stagg, J.C.A., ed. *The Papers of James Madison Digital Edition*. Charlottesville: University of Virginia Press, Rotunda, 2010. <http://rotunda.upress.virginia.edu/founders/JSMN-01-17-02-0167>, accessed 12 October, 2013.

Stanton, Lucia. *"Sally Hemings,"* Thomas Jefferson Foundation, 1989, 1994, 2012. <http://www.monticello.org/site/plantation-and-slavery/sally-hemings>, accessed 13 October, 2013.

State Papers and Publick Documents of the United States, 1797–1801, Vol. 3. Boston: T.B. Wait and Sons, 1815.

Stevens, Henry Morse. *A History of the French Revolution*, Vol. 1. New York: Charles Scribner's Sons, New York, 1905.

Stinchcombe, William. "A Neglected Memoir by Talleyrand on French-American Relations, 1793–1797." *Proceedings of the American Philosophical Society*, 121:3, (June 15, 1977), 195–208.

Stoll, Ira. *Samuel Adams: A Life*. New York: Free Press, 2008.

Swann-Wright, Dr. Dianne, et al., *Report of the Research Committee on Thomas Jefferson and Sally Hemings,* Thomas Jefferson Foundation. online <http://www.monticello.org/site/plantation-and-slavery/report-research-committee-thomas-jefferson-and-sally-hemings>, accessed 10 October, 2013.

Swearing-In Ceremony for President Thomas Jefferson, Fourth Inaugural Ceremonies, March 4, 1801. Joint Congressional Committee on Inaugural Ceremonies,. <http://www.inaugural.senate.gov/swearing-in/event/thomas-jefferson-1801>, accessed 12 October, 2013.

Tackett, Timothy. *The Coming of the Terror in the French Revolution.* Cambridge: Belknap Press of Harvard University Press, 2015.

Taylor, Alan. "John Adams" in Brinkley, Alan, and Davis Dyer, eds. *The Reader's Companion to the American Presidency.* Boston: Houghton Mifflin, 2000.

Taylor, C. James. *Diary of Charles Francis Adams, Vol. 1. Founding Families: Digital Editions of the Papers of the Winthrops and the Adamses.* Boston: Massachusetts Historical Society, 2007; online at <http://www.masshist.org/ff/>, accessed 11 October, 2013.

Temple Bar: A London Magazine for Town and Country Readers, 32, July, 1871; "Danton and Camille Desmoulins," London: Richard Bentley & Son, 1871, 475–90. (Note: No author cited. Likely George Henry Calvert.)

"Thomas Jefferson- First Secretary of State." US Department of State. <http://future.state.gov/when/timeline/1784_timeline/jefferson_first_secretary.html>, accessed October 11, 2013.

"Thomas Jefferson, 2nd Vice President (1797–1801)," United States Senate.   <http://www.senate.gov/artandhistory/history/common/generic/VP_Thomas_Jefferson.htm>, accessed 11 October, 2013.

"Thomas Jefferson Timeline: 1743–1827; The Early Republic, 1790–1799." The Thomas Jefferson Papers, Library of Congress. <http://memory.loc.gov/ammem/collections/jefferson_papers/mtjtime3b.html> accessed 11, October, 2013.

"Thomas Jefferson's Bible." Smithsonian Institution, National Museum of American History, Kenneth E. Behring Center. <http://americanhistory.si.edu/JeffersonBible/history/>,   accessed   13 October, 2013.

Thompson, C. Bradley. "John Adams and the Coming of the French Revolution." *Journal of the Early Republic*, 16:3, (Autumn, 1996), 361–87.

Trumbull, John. *Autobiography, Reminiscences and Letters of John Trumbull from 1756 to 1841.* New York: Wiley and Putnam, 1841.

Turner, Frederick Jackson, ed. "Correspondence of the French Ministers to the United States, 1791–1797." *Annual Report of the American Historical Association for the Year 1903*, Vol. 2. Washington: Government Printing Office, 1904.

Upham, Charles. *The Life of Timothy Pickering*, Vol. 4. Boston: Little, Brown, & Co., 1873.

Unger, Harlow Giles. *The Life and Times of Noah Webster: An American Patriot*. New York: John Wiley & Sons, 1998.

United States. "An Act to Suspend the Commercial Intercourse between the United States and France, and the Dependencies Thereof," *United States Statutes at Large, 1 U.S. Stat 565;* Yale University, Avalon Project. <http://avalon.law.yale.edu/18th_century/qw01.asp>, accessed 12 October, 2013.

———. *Joint Resolution of the House #175 of the 103rd Congress, 2nd Session*, "Designating October 1993 and October 1994 as 'Italian-American Heritage Month.'" US Government Printing Office, <http://www.gpo.gov/fdsys/granule/STATUTE-108/STATUTE-108-Pg1670/content-detail.html>, accessed 12 October, 2013.

———. "The Judiciary Act of 1801: 'An Act to provide for the more convenient organization of the Courts of the United States.'" 2 Stat. 89, February 13, 1801, in *History of the Federal Judiciary*, Landmark Judicial Legislation; at Federal Judicial Center online at <http://www.fjc.gov/history/home.nsf/page/landmark_03.html>, accessed 12 October, 2013.

———. *People v. Croswell*, The Founders' Constitution, Vol. 5. Amendment 1 (Speech and Press), Document 28, 3 Johns. Cas. 337 N.Y. 1804, The University of Chicago Press online at <http://press-pubs.uchicago.edu/founders/documents/amendI_speechs28.html>, accessed 12 October, 2013.

———. *The United States Statutes at Large, Fifth Congress, Session 2, 1798*. The Library of Congress: <http://memory.loc.gov/cgi-bin/ampage?collId=llsl&fileName=001/llsl001.db&recNum=689>, accessed 12 October, 2013.

Washburne, Elihu Benjamin. "Sketch of Edward Coles, Second Governor of Illinois, and the Slavery Struggle of 1823–1824." *Collections of the Illinois State Historical Library*, Vol. 15, Biographical Series 1. Danville, IL: Illinois Printing Company, 1882, 1920.

Washington, George. *The George Washington Papers at the Library of Congress*; Time Line: The Early Republic, <http://memory.loc. gov/ammem/gwhtml/gwtimeer.html>, accessed 11 October, 2013.

———. *Farewell Address,* September 19, 1796. US Government Printing Office. <http://www.gpo.gov/fdsys/pkg/GPO-CDOC-106sdoc21/pdf/GPO-CDOC-106sdoc21.pdf>, accessed 11 October, 2013; or Yale Law School, Avalon Project. <http://avalon.law. yale.edu/18th_century/washing.asp>, accessed 11 October, 2013.

Washington, H. A., ed. *The Works of Thomas Jefferson,* Vol. 4. New York: Derby & Jackson, 1859.

———. *The Works of Thomas Jefferson*, Vol. 7. New York: Townsend Mac Coun. 1884.

———. *The Writings of Thomas Jefferson*, Vol. 2. New York: Derby and Jackson, 1859.

———. *The Writings of Thomas Jefferson*, Vol. 3. New York: Derby and Jackson, 1861.

———. *The Writings of Thomas Jefferson*, Vol. 5. New York: Derby and Jackson, 1859.

Webb, Alfred. "Andrew Brown." *A Compendium of Irish Biography*. Dublin: M.H. Gill & Son, 1878. <http://www.libraryireland.com/ biography/AndrewBrown.php>, accessed 13 October, 2013.

Webster, Daniel. "A Discourse in Commemoration of the Lives and Services of John Adams and Thomas Jefferson." Faneuil Hall, Boston, Massachusetts. 2, August, 1826. *The Great Speeches and Orations of Daniel Webster.* Boston: Little, Brown, & Co., 1886.

Wheelan, Joseph. *Jefferson's War: America's First War on Terror 1801–1805.* New York: Carroll & Graf, 2003.

Wheeler, Daniel Edwin, ed. *Life and Writings of Thomas Paine*, Independence Edition. New York: Vincent Parke and Company, 1908.

Willard, Samuel, M.D., LL.D. *John Adams: A Character Sketch.* Milwaukee: HG Campbell, 1898, 1903.

"William Short," Thomas Jefferson Foundation. <http://www.monticello.org/site/research-and-collections/william-short>, accessed 11 October, 2013.

Wills, Garry. *James Madison*. New York: Time Books, 2002.

Winik, Jay. *The Great Upheaval: America and the Birth of the Modern World, 1788–1800*. New York: Harper, 2007.

Witcover, Jules. *Party of the People*: *A History of the Democrats*. New York: Random House, 2003.

Wood, Gordon S. *Empire of Liberty: A History of the Early Republic*. Oxford: Oxford University Press, 2009.

Wright, Louis B. "Jefferson, Man of Ideas." *The Yale Review*, 40:1, (September, 1950), 156–60.

Yorke, Henry Redhead. *Letters from France in 1802,* Vol. 2. London: H.D. Symonds, 1804.

Zacks, Richard. *The Pirate Coast: Thomas Jefferson, the First Marines, and the Secret Mission of 1805*. New York: Hyperion, 2005.

Index